A

W9-COV-709

13⁵

Ⓐ

THE GERMAN PUBLIC MIND
IN THE NINETEENTH CENTURY

By the same author

THE DEVELOPMENT OF THE GERMAN PUBLIC MIND, VOL. I
THE DEVELOPMENT OF THE GERMAN PUBLIC MIND, VOL. 2

THE GERMAN PUBLIC MIND
IN THE
NINETEENTH CENTURY
A Social History of German
Political Sentiments, Aspirations and Ideas

BY

FREDERICK HERTZ

EDITED BY FRANK EYCK

Professor of History, University of Calgary

TRANSLATION BY ERIC NORTHCOTT

ROWMAN AND LITTLEFIELD
TOTOWA, NEW JERSEY

First published in the United States 1975
by Rowman and Littlefield, Totowa, N.J.

This book is copyright under the Berne Convention. All
rights are reserved. Apart from any fair dealing for the
purpose of private study, research, criticism or review, as
permitted under the Copyright Act, 1956, no part of this
publication may be reproduced, stored in a retrieval system,
or transmitted, in any form or by any means, electronic,
electrical, chemical, mechanical, optical, photocopying,
recording or otherwise, without the prior permission of the
copyright owner. Inquiries should be addressed to the
publishers.

© George Allen & Unwin Ltd 1975

Library of Congress Cataloging in Publication Data

Hertz, Friedrich Otto, 1878-1964.
The German public mind in the nineteenth century.

Translated from an unpublished German manuscript, which
was to become v.3 of the author's The development of
the German public mind.
Bibliography: p.
1. Germany—Politics and government—19th century. 2.
Nationalism—Germany—History. 3. Germany—Intellectual life—History. 4. Austria—Politics and government—
1789-1900. 5. Public opinion—Germany—History.
I. Eyck, Frank, ed. II. Title
DD204.H47   1974   914.3′03′7   74-12071
ISBN 0-87471-580-6

Printed in Great Britain
in 10 point Plantin type
by T. & A. Constable Ltd, Edinburgh

FOREWORD

When Frederick Hertz died in London at the age of eighty-six in November 1964, the third volume of the culmination of his life's work, *The Development of the German Public Mind*, was not yet ready for publication. The author's widow, Dr Edith Hertz, whose busy life in London as a medical practitioner had not prevented her from taking an active interest in her husband's work, was rightly determined that a further volume should be made available to the public. She was supported in this by Dr G. P. Gooch,[1] an old friend, who recommended that I should be asked to help.

Posthumous publication offers considerable problems. Nobody can complete a book left by an author in exactly the way the writer would have wished. After consultation with the author's family it was decided not to add any further sections, but simply to edit the available material. There has been some shortening by eliminating detail which was not absolutely essential and by cutting out duplication. It is hoped that the reader's task will have thus been facilitated, without withholding important additional information from him.

The author was able to maintain his basic theme of what he called 'the German public mind' up to about the end of the Bismarck era. Particularly after 1890, however, the story in the manuscript he left was overshadowed by events of diplomatic history. The present volume therefore ends at about 1890, with Bismarck's dismissal. It may perhaps be possible, at a later date, to arrange for the publication of a further volume dealing with the years between 1890 and 1913. After the death of Dr Edith Hertz in April 1970, the son, Mr John Hurst, who had all along assisted his mother in London with the various matters concerning the current volume, took over as literary executor, supported by his sister, Mrs M. Levinson, who is living in the United States.

The manuscript Frederick Hertz left was in German. In view of my various academic commitments, Mr Eric Northcott, an experienced translator, was asked to prepare the English version.

Editorial work on the manuscript was begun while I was still living in England, and completed in Canada after I took up a professorship of history at the University of Calgary in 1968. Frequent visits to England allowed me to maintain the necessary contact with the author's family and with the translator. I was helped considerably in my editorial work

[1] Gooch wrote in *German Life and Letters*, Vol. 18, Oxford, 1964/5, p. 90: '. . . The closing years of a busy life were spent in preparing for the third and final volume of his *Magnum Opus*. . . . His readers in many lands will deeply regret the interruption of his fine enterprise and it is hoped that some younger scholar may be found to complete the long story. . . .'

by having had the privilege of meeting the author, who explained to me
what he was attempting to do in his book and showed me much kindness.

Frederick Hertz was a man of many parts and wide culture. Born in
Vienna in 1878 of a family of originally German descent, he studied
economics at the university not only in his native city but also in
Munich and London. After the First World War he served for a number
of years as a senior official of the Austrian government, before receiving
a call to the chair of economics and sociology at the German University
of Halle in 1930. By this time, Hertz already had an international
reputation as a writer on a whole variety of economic and sociological
topics. His interests centred mainly on questions of nationality and
race. Owing to the formation of the National Socialist regime, Hertz
had to leave Germany and eventually settled in London in 1938.
Though he had by then reached the age of sixty, he remained fresh
intellectually and full of vigour to the end of his life. He was able to
publish the first volume of his monumental *Development of the German
Public Mind* in 1957 and the second in 1962. Nobody who has read this
work will doubt that Hertz was a man of considerable learning in many
fields, one of the last shining products of an *Allgemeinbildung*, of a
universal education which has become so difficult to maintain in our
age of increasing specialisation.

Frank Eyck

Department of History
University of Calgary
Alberta
Canada

AUTHOR'S PREFACE

The term public mind is used here in the sense of the political and social feelings, opinions and aspirations of the various groups forming the German people, with special reference to those which have determined politics. In former times secular history dealt mainly with the political development of States, and since the principal criterion of States and politics is power, this led to the detailed presentation of struggles for power, which left not much space for public opinion, political ideals and ideologies. Attention was concentrated on the individuals engaged in these struggles, on rulers, statesmen and generals, though sometimes great thinkers, too, appeared in the background. In contrast to this approach other branches of historical research developed later; on the one hand the treatment of special fields such as law, arts, or economic life, and on the other hand schools embracing the general evolution of nations, with emphasis on civilisation, cultural achievements and social relations. It was increasingly believed that the course of events was not exclusively, or principally, determined by the State and power politics, and that there was also a collective psychology moulding the mind of the makers of politics. While the older type of political history emphasised the part played by great leaders, the new schools laid great stress on forces such as collective mentalities, tradition and the unfolding of the human intellect, conscience and sentiment, as well as their geographical background. The moving forces were sought in dominant ideas, the spirit of the ages, the evolution of the mind in successive phases, the character of nations, the Volksgeist, the ethos of élites or the interest of classes. Many of the attempts, however, were influenced by philosophical or psychological presuppositions leading to un-empirical conclusions. Political historians in the present age give much more attention to public opinion than in former times, especially in monographs on particular epochs, problems and personalities.

This book regards the public mind not as a uniform and persistent force such as the alleged national character, or the public opinion much invoked by politicians. A nation shows a multitude of characters; there are forces striving to integrate them in a unity, and others working for disintegration. As a rule there is not a single public opinion, but a variety of divergent trends. The idea that the policy of a government or the deeds of great men sufficiently expressed the spirit of their whole nation has often led to disastrous errors. The aim of this study is to show what the various sections of the Germans of every rank and class were thinking of the ruling men, how far they supported or opposed them, what were their wishes, hopes and fears, prejudices, ideals and standards of right and wrong. The influence of foreign thought, and parallels with the development of other nations, also require attention.

The study of the collective mind must largely be based on other sources than State documents which usually say little about the opinions of classes without a voice in politics. But a great deal about them can be found in religious and legal writings, works of literature, broadsheets, the verses of minstrels, folk-songs and later in newspapers. The analysis of the mentality of ruling personalities shows the inter-action between their individuality and the public mind.

In order to find space for the presentation of these facts it is necessary to cut down the recording of external events to the minimum needed to understand the function and movements of the public mind. But certain limits are set to this elimination by various considerations, among them being the fact that political theory and practical policy, even of the same party or nation, are often not in accord. This may be due to many reasons. The student of the public mind must follow both lines of development, the ideal and the practical. External events such as diplomatic manoeuvres or warlike actions require consideration when they imply questions of public psychology, but not if they are of a merely technical significance in the struggle for power.

The description of the public mind necessarily requires much space since the characterisation of its trends in general terms is not enough. It may even be misleading because these terms usually are very ambiguous. A particularly grave danger is involved in the application of modern concepts to conditions of former ages. This book further does not restrict itself to treating the affairs of the German Empire, as is usual in comprehensive surveys, but takes at least some account of the history of the principal territories. The reason is that important features of the German public mind can only be studied in territorial history. The multitude of German territories, however, renders it impossible to devote more than a few lines to the treatment of most of them. Many other issues, too, could only be dealt with in the barest outline because they were not of primary importance for our subject but could not be omitted altogether without causing serious gaps in surveying the course of events.

CONTENTS

I

THE AGE OF NAPOLEON

THE RISE OF NAPOLEON BONAPARTE

In 1792 the French Assembly began the war which, with brief interruptions, was to devastate Europe for two decades and opened to Napoleon the path to supreme power. The Girondins sought to retain control by using the glory won by French arms to foster patriotic feeling at home. The organisational genius of the army engineer and politician, Lazare Carnot, paved the way for Napoleon's triumphs. Carnot successfully raised many armies and founded a mighty war industry; the masses were called up, new tactics were introduced and ultimately general conscription was imposed. The armies opposing France, on the other hand, consisted partly of mercenaries and partly of conscripted nationals, many of whom were not particularly good soldiers; the long period of service, if nothing else, saw to that. Because of the risk of desertion, they were sent into action only in close order and their formations were not highly mobile, since their rations came from depots and transportation took time. The generals were elderly aristocrats: to hold a commission in the Prussian army was a privilege reserved for the nobility. Strategy, especially in the Austrian army, was cautiously defensive, since any aggressive conduct of a campaign would have cost a lot in blood and money. The French army still possessed many excellent institutions dating back to the days of the monarchy; both Carnot and Napoleon, as well as other outstanding leaders, were still to some extent rooted in the old tradition. However, the Revolution gave French soldiers a sense of national identity and a lively ambition; they could fight in open order, which offered great tactical advantages, but could also be committed *en masse*, since universal military service could easily make good heavy casualties. Their armies were mobile, for they lived off the land and where necessary commandeered food and money. Above all, there existed no aristocratic privilege to prevent talented soldiers from rising to the higher – or, in fact, the highest – posts.

Germany's defence against French attacks was sorely handicapped by political conditions. The particularism rife in the old Empire, and the deep gulf between Austria and Prussia, frustrated any effective fusion of their forces. Austria had far-off Belgium to defend and the Prussia of Frederick William II was more interested in Poland than the Rhine. French diplomats soon discovered that German princes could be won over by prospects of territorial aggrandisement at the expense of smaller neighbours. While Napoleon raised French national pride to its zenith by his victories and officially bestowed on France the title of 'la grande nation', German national sentiment, in so far as it existed at all, touched its nadir.

In a few years Napoleon climbed to a position of power such as the world had not witnessed since the days of the Caesars – indeed, to an even higher peak. The only continental power which constantly took up arms to defend herself and her empire was Austria, whereas Prussia very soon gave up the struggle against revolutionary France in order to swallow up Poland, and then stood idly by and watched Napoleon march from one victory to another. In 1806 he put an end to the Holy Roman Empire, reduced most of the German princes to vassals who had to supply him with cannon-fodder for further conquests, and shattered Prussia. Two years later he was at the height of his power. But he never ceased to cherish plans for subjugating Britain and her empire, either by force of arms or economic strangulation, and this later led to his campaign against Russia.

For a long time this vast concentration of power, which entailed harsh financial and economic exploitation and political oppression in the conquered countries, aroused in wide areas of Germany no national resistance, or at least only clandestine strivings towards it. The princes of the Confederation of the Rhine, whose 'protector' Napoleon was, for the most part sided willingly enough with him. Nothing could appear in print unless it served his policy, and when in 1806 a pamphlet entitled *Germany in the Depths of Degradation* appeared and its author could not be identified, Napoleon had the publisher, Palm, shot. The majority of those Germans who were politically-minded either admired the new Caesar or resigned themselves to their lot.

THE PRESS

Under such conditions the press could, of course, afford no insight into the thoughts and feelings of the various classes. The result of Napoleon's supremacy was that very many papers ceased to appear, some being suppressed while others closed down voluntarily; those which remained published only what they were instructed or allowed to. From 1807 to 1808 the philosopher Hegel, who was born in Stuttgart, was the editor of one of these, the *Bamberger Zeitung*, which appeared daily, printed in quarto on cheap paper and consisting of two sheets with a total of eight columns, and a paltry affair even to look at. The contents came mainly from the Paris *Moniteur* and other journals of a similar complexion. At the time Hegel was a warm admirer of Napoleon and his view of the state and of history was strongly influenced by the impression which Napoleon's triumphs made on him. In 1806 he had seen Napoleon ride through Jena and to him he appeared the 'Weltseele' – the personification of reason, the new popular idol. Although the French troops relieved Hegel of all his money, he could still none the less write in a letter that, like everyone else, he continued to wish the French army all good fortune, for they were intellectually far superior to their opponents. These good wishes were, in fact, realised, for Napoleon promptly proceeded to shatter the Prussian army.

The admiration which Hegel and many other German intellectuals felt for Napoleon stemmed from the fact that they considered him to be the man who was trying to translate into reality those sensible aims of the French Revolution: the rights of man, equality for all, modern laws and a kind of popular representation modelled on the constitutions decreed by Napoleon for France, Italy, Westphalia and elsewhere. In these constitutions there was no hint of what is today meant by political freedom; the 'representatives of the people' were in no sense freely elected by them but owed their office to the Emperor's favour. Although Hegel certainly took every care to avoid printing anything which might displease the powers that be, his paper was suddenly banned for unstated reasons.

Of much greater importance than this little paper were those put out by the Tübingen publisher, Johann Friedrich Cotta. He made his name by publishing the works of Schiller, Goethe and other great writers, but in many other fields he soon showed himself to be a successful progressive who commanded general esteem. In the nineties he managed, after some difficulty, to found a daily paper of unusual quality. He hoped to enlist Schiller as its editor, but the latter, deeply dejected by the course of political events, refused the post and devoted himself entirely to literature. Cotta then secured Ernst Ludwig Posselt, a first-class historian, as editor, but as there was a delay in founding the daily paper, Posselt first became editor of a monthly, *Europäische Annalen*, an influential review which appeared from 1795 to 1820. On 1 January 1798 a daily paper called *Neueste Weltkunde*, also edited by Posselt, appeared in Tübingen. Posselt lauded Napoleon to the skies, and when the French carried off priceless works of art from Italy, he wrote that the Italians were glad to sacrifice them in order to take the first step into the hallowed temple of liberty. He went on to attack Austria and Russia, who were waging war on Napoleon. The Austrian government first lodged a complaint with Württemberg and then put their grievance before the Imperial Court of Justice, which instructed the Duke of Württemberg to suppress the paper forthwith. Cotta, however, preferred to close the paper down himself and founded instead a new one in Stuttgart under the name of the *Allgemeine Zeitung*. The editor was Ludwig Ferdinand Huber, a former diplomat, who also reverenced revolutionary France. Posselt remained editor of the *Europäische Annalen*, and here, in his enthusiasm for Napoleon, he even went so far as to print the suggestion that one of the highest slopes in the Alps should be cleared and Napoleon's name inscribed on it in giant golden letters to shine out into the most distant corner of Germany.

In the skilful hands of Huber the *Allgemeine Zeitung* thrived, but it was banned in 1803, ostensibly because it had offended foreign governments but actually because, in a dispute between the Duke and the Estates of Württemberg, Cotta had sided with the latter. Cotta strove in vain to have the ban lifted and was already thinking of closing the paper down when he received invitations from no less than five German states to publish it on their territory. He chose Bavaria, where at the time censorship had been lifted. The paper first appeared in Ulm and then, from 1810, in Augsburg. After Huber's death, Karl Joseph Stegmann, an outstanding journalist, was for thirty-three years editor of the *Allgemeine Zeitung*, which became one of the leading German dailies. The rise of Napoleon forced the paper into a difficult position, since he strove to control it completely, finally succeeding.

AUSTRIA'S POLICY

In Austria the opposition to Napoleon was able to manifest itself earlier than anywhere else since she was repeatedly waging war on France. It was to Austria that German patriots now looked and many important writers entered her service and defended her policies, notably Friedrich Gentz, Karl Ludwig von Haller, Johannes von Müller and, later, Friedrich Schlegel and Adam Müller. Baron vom Stein and Ernst Moritz Arndt, in common with many of the Romanticists, pinned their hopes on Austria from time to time. In 1802 Hegel wrote that the Empire was no longer a state and that it could become one only if either Austria or Prussia took control. At the time Hegel preferred Austria because she had retained the assemblies of the Estates in her provinces, given her people rights and opened the way to the highest offices to everyone. Napoleon's propaganda was far superior to that of his German opponents, and managed to convince many German statesmen, philosophers, historians and writers that while his policy aimed at lasting world peace, England alone was repeatedly stirring up war and was thus draining the life-blood of the world in order to seize the trade of other nations. It is characteristic that even Johannes von Müller, who was considered the greatest German historian of the day, had an interview with Napoleon after leaving the service of Austria and was completely won over. Soon after, Napoleon made him a minister in the Kingdom of Westphalia under his brother, King Jerome.

Austria was the first power to attempt to stir up a national war against Napoleon, although her mixture of nationalities as well as the personality of Emperor Francis and the outlook of the court party which backed him made this difficult. The Emperor's brothers, the Archdukes Karl and Johann, and other members of the Imperial House were, however, accessible to libertarian ideas, which found a gifted champion in Count Philipp Stadion, who was Foreign Minister from 1806 to 1809. He and some influential circles were prepared to widen representation in the Estates. Stadion was in touch with Stein and shared his aims. Throughout broad areas of the Danubian Empire an unusual patriotic fervour prevailed, even among non-Germans, and masses of them joined the army as volunteers. The peasants of the Tyrol under Andreas Hofer struck the first blow and won considerable victories. Archduke Karl, the supreme commander, had long resisted this war, which he considered premature, but he finally agreed to it and declared in a proclamation to the army: 'The liberty of Europe has taken refuge beneath our banners; your victories will break its chains, and your German brothers, still in the ranks of the enemy, yearn for their release.' But this hope was dashed: the German princes in Napoleon's service supplied a substantial part of the army which was fighting Austria. Prussia, on the Tsar's advice, held off and Russia even joined Napoleon and sent an army into Galicia, though to be sure it hardly waged very serious warfare there.

Archduke Karl dealt Napoleon his first big defeat at Aspern in 1809. Napoleon later declared in conversation with a general that anyone who had not seen the Austrians at Aspern had not seen anything. But this success was not militarily exploited and it was Napoleon who emerged victorious from Wagram. Although Austria had not been brought to her knees, the Emperor thought it advisable to make peace.

Stadion had risked starting the war of 1809 without the help of allies because he knew that in large areas of Germany plans for revolt against Napoleon were being concerted and he hoped that Austrian victories would translate them into action which would compel the princes to rise against Napoleon in their turn. However, the course of the war did not favour these hopes; there was a series of uprisings, the leaders of which hoped to carry the people with them, but in vain. The most important venture of this kind was that of Major Schill, a Prussian officer, who on his own initiative set out with his regiment to whip up the people to revolt. The might of the French army crushed his forces, his head was cut from his corpse, many of his officers and men were shot and the other prisoners sent to the galleys in French ports.

The unhappy issue of the war of 1809 brought to the fore a statesman who was soon to exercise the greatest influence on the destinies of Austria, Germany and all Europe – Clemens Lothar, Count Metternich. He came from a Rhenish family whose members had distinguished themselves in the history of the ecclesiastical electorate of Mainz as well as in the imperial service. In his youth the spirit of the Enlightenment prevailed at the court in Mainz, prominent men there were Illuminati, and Clemens' father was a freemason. As a youth he was educated by a tutor who came from the circle of the philanthropes, idolised Rousseau and Basedow and regarded reason and humanity as the supreme ends. When Metternich went to the Universities of Strasbourg and Mainz, he had first-hand experience of the French Revolution and saw French troops march into the Rhineland. His father's position as Imperial Minister to the Austrian Netherlands, as well as a long stay in England, gave him a deep insight into political conditions. He next embarked on a diplomatic career and after the Peace of Pressburg (1805) was sent to Paris at Napoleon's request as Ambassador, but secretly he was working for the war which broke out in 1809. He then took over from Stadion, skilfully improved Austria's relations with France and even brought about a marriage between Napoleon and Emperor Franz's daughter, Maria Louise.

PRUSSIA'S REFORMS AND THE
MOVEMENT FOR NATIONAL INDEPENDENCE

After the defeats of 1806–7, Prussia was at Napoleon's feet, but he was unable to destroy the Hohenzollern monarchy, for he could not disregard the wishes of the Tsar, whose help he needed for his plans against England. The Peace of Tilsit reduced Prussia's territory and population to about half what it had been, and the continued French occupation as well as the burdens which Napoleon imposed on the country utterly exhausted her. The débâcle brought about the start of progressive reforms and the development of a movement to shake off the foreign yoke.

Prussia's collapse sprang from serious defects in her political, military and social organisation. Frederick II had been capable of keeping the highly complex machinery of state in motion, but his successors lacked this ability. Moreover, the French Revolution had shown what massive strength a national state possessed when absolute power was concentrated in the hands of a man like Napoleon. King Frederick William III was a right-minded ruler, peaceably disposed and well-meaning, but he possessed neither vision nor strength of will. He could never make up his mind and constantly vacillated between the alternative proposals of his advisers, though he never once relinquished the principle of personal rule. He was under the influence of a small circle of high officials from the middle class, who, well versed in administration, desired peace at almost any price in order to carry through reforms for the benefit of the people, particularly the abolition of feudal privileges. In 1799 a Prussian minister said to the French Ambassador: 'The wholesome revolution which you have carried through from below will take place in Prussia, by degrees, from above. In his way, the King is a democrat; he is constantly striving like a Joseph II to limit the privileges of the aristocracy, albeit slowly. In a few years there will no longer be a privileged class in Prussia.' This was an exaggeration, but it contained more than a grain of truth. In the following six years 50,000 peasants, as well as many agricultural workers, were settled as free men on the royal domains. The peasants received medium-sized holdings for their own exploitation. The King also wanted to free the serfs on the estates of the nobility, but this plan foundered on the latter's determined opposition.

Sharp differences between the King's advisers and the ministers also militated against reform. The ministers were for the most part from the old aristocracy and they disagreed both with the designs which the King's middle-class advisers had on the nobility and with their tendency to keep the peace with Napoleon at any price. The ministers, however, did not constitute a unified government nor was there any one minister responsible for general policy. According to the prevailing collective system, it was not the minister who decided what advice should be tendered to the King but the majority vote of the ministerial council. What is more, the King was also influenced by advisers who were not ministers. In such circumstances the Government could pursue no consistent course but often wavered between mutually contradictory policies.

The army similarly displayed serious defects in organisation, equipment and leadership. Unlike the French armed forces it lacked any national character, and consisted partly of conscripted serfs but mostly of foreign mercenaries, many of whom had taken service merely to escape the imprisonment which threatened them in their own country and who were only awaiting their chance to desert. They were miserably paid and had to eke out their pittance by doing other jobs, so that their quarters resembled workshops. The colonel of a regiment found it profitable to give his men leave, because while they were away he could keep their pay for himself. The officers were all noblemen, for the most part without any specifically military training, and they often treated the rank and file brutally. A large number of educated people looked upon war and things military as relics of barbarism.[1]

This policy of peace at any price was attacked by influential groups who smarted beneath the foreign tyranny and brooded on revolt. The landed nobility, particularly the officers and officials among them, felt grievously wounded in their patriotism as Prussians and longed for the restoration of their country's power and prestige. However, many prominent Prussian officers and officials, such as the two greatest statesmen of the day, Stein and Hardenberg, and the two most important military reformers, Scharnhorst and Gneisenau, were not Prussians by birth, and the same was also true of many leaders of the growing national movement, such as Fichte, Niebuhr and Arndt.

The most prominent of the reformers was Karl, Baron vom Stein. He was born in 1757 in Nassau and came from an old family of Imperial Knights, a class subject only to the Emperor and absolute rulers in their own little territories. Such origins helped to make Stein feel above all else a German and not the mere subordinate of a particular prince, although he was for a long time a Prussian statesman. He advocated the revival of many of the institutions of the old Empire, especially of the Imperial dignity, though suitably adapted to the changed times. As a student at Göttingen he heard Schlözer lecture and became a friend of Rehberg and Brandes, who came out in favour of a conservative liberalism on the English pattern. Throughout his life Stein remained a great admirer of England, where he spent nine months studying the political system. True, he realised that English institutions could not simply be taken over into Germany, where the social structure and traditions were fundamentally different. In particular, Germany lacked any politically controlling class like the English gentry. Stein was much exercised with how to make the German nobility more like the English and he pondered far-reaching reforms, such as restricting the inheritance of a title to the eldest son. As for the structure of the classes, he felt that property, not noble birth, should be the criterion. Germany did not possess a broad, urban middle class, prosperous and politically ambitious like the great English merchants and industrialists. Townsfolk in Germany were mostly small artisans and tradesmen who neither understood political matters nor wished

---

[1] Numerous voices were raised in Germany for the abolition of the standing armies. Cf. Max Lehmann, *Scharnhorst*, Vol. I, 1886, pp. 62, 68.

to have any part in discussing or deciding them. On the other hand, England had no peasantry comparable with that of Germany. In eastern Germany, which was backward, most peasants were still serfs. In the west serfdom had mostly vanished, although the peasants there were still often fettered with manifold feudal dues and restrictions.

For all his willingness to work for progressive measures, Stein none the less clung closely to the conditions obtaining in the old Empire. He wanted neither a centralised *Reich* nor a nation on the lines of revolutionary France; he was not in any way working to create a powerful militaristic state, but an empire able to defend itself. He cherished the now traditional particularism, even if he did detest the princes created by Napoleon. He saw in the landowners the backbone of the nation and in the landed gentry the class best suited to control national affairs. His opinion of Prussia and Austria fluctuated and the Germany closest to his heart was the territory outside both these great states, the western and southern parts of the Empire which were popularly called 'the *Reich*'.

Stein's work as an administrator was done mainly in the western areas of Prussia, where social development was more advanced than in the east. He had no special predilection for Prussia and certainly the spirit of Frederick the Great was not one which appealed to him. His aims were to abolish feudal privileges and serfdom, to set trade free from the fetters of the guild system and to introduce a substantial measure of self-government in the place of autocracy and bureaucracy. The Estates, which had assumed an important position in many German countries, were to be revived and supplemented by deputies from the urban middle class and the peasants. The parishes and districts were likewise to receive a considerable degree of autonomy. Above all, Stein considered it essential to sharpen decisiveness at the head of affairs by creating a responsible government.

These and other reforms aimed at the moral regeneration of a people oppressed by despotism and feudalism. The State was to receive a national character and thus be transformed into an organism animated by the spirit of a free people. In this way, he hoped, Prussia would grow strong enough to shake off the foreign yoke and make Germany independent. To Stein the power of the State did not appear as the supreme objective; on the contrary, the character of the nation was to be developed by self-government. Stein hated Napoleon and the French, whose supremacy stood between him and his goals, but he attacked the German princes and nobility no less vehemently than he did the foreigners. Most of his letters to his wife and other members of his family were written in French, and in other ways, too, he displayed many traits of the contemporary, cosmopolitan aristocrat. His political role was determined neither by personal appetite for power nor abstract idealism or romanticism but by his strong sense of justice. He prized liberty highly but hated radicalism as much as he did despotism. Furthermore, he had many prejudices and mistrusted anyone who was not rooted in the soil and tradition of his country.

Together with a circle of high officials and other public figures Stein worked for a fundamental reshaping of the State, and here Karl August, Baron von Hardenberg (1750–1822), who was later created Count and then Prince, played a leading part. The measures he and Stein introduced are usually called the Stein–Hardenberg Reforms. Hardenberg came from Hanover, where the nobility, although strongly influenced by French enlightenment and policy, regarded the English political pattern as its ideal. He was highly talented, adroit, unprejudiced and amiable and, in contrast to the puritanical Stein, a man of pleasure even in his old age. The reforms in East Prussia received enthusiastic support, especially from the aristocracy. Napoleon's embargo on trade with England hit the province hard, for its prosperity was based on its exports of wheat to England. In the capital, Königsberg, Kant had been lecturing up to a short time before and wielded an extraordinary influence. Kant's friend and colleague, Christian Jakob Kraus, who was Professor of Political Economy, was a prominent disciple of Adam Smith, whose doctrines he spread to great effect. These circumstances combined to make East Prussia the focus of Prussian liberalism.

The reform movement received further vigorous support from a circle of officers who considered it possible to free the country from foreign domination only with the help of an army raised on a national basis. The army was to become the concern of the whole people, not merely of the ruling house and the nobility. The leaders of this group were Scharnhorst and Gneisenau, Blücher's Chief of Staff at Waterloo. Scharnhorst had been trained in the military school of Count Wilhelm von Schaumburg-Lippe, who had not only distinguished himself as a general but who also ruled his small country as a true humanitarian. The Count loathed war and hoped to eliminate it by developing defensive strategy and to put it into effect by national conscription. His pupil Scharnhorst later served in the Hanoverian army and entered Prussian service in 1801. Scharnhorst set particular store by having officers who were drawn from all classes and thoroughly trained, and while he wanted to retain the regular army, he also wanted to reinforce it with a *Landwehr*, or militia. He also aimed at abolishing the degrading punishments to which the men were liable. The aristocratic officers sneered, saying that he looked more like a professor than a soldier, and he himself once wrote to his wife that he was not born to be a soldier and that he hated war. He and his helpers reorganised the army which was to bring down Napoleon.

Raising national aims, character and culture by increased personal independence also demanded reforms in education. Rousseau, Basedow and Pestalozzi had done pioneer work in this field; in the schools compulsion was to be replaced by freedom, and mechanical cramming by the natural, automatic unfolding of the youthful mind. Progressive educationists in Prussia greeted the theories of Pestalozzi with particular warmth and a large circle of his disciples was formed. The leading champion of this movement was Professor Süvern of Königsberg. In his addresses to the German nation Fichte emphasised the importance of Pestalozzi's teachings for the moral rebirth of Germany, and Stein and Gneisenau were deeply interested in the question. The reforms of Bell and Lancaster in England also aroused Stein's interest and approval. He was less concerned with higher education, although he himself possessed an uncommonly wide and deep fund of knowledge, particularly in political science and history, but he took the view that public life was a better form of schooling than academic instruction. He recommended putting Wilhelm von Humboldt in charge of the educational system, and this in fact was done.

Apart from the efforts of the government to transform education, there were many private organisations which pursued this aim. Thus, Jahn's movement to promote gymnastics and walking contributed to the spread of the idea of nationality and freedom. A *Tugenbund* (League of Virtue) was founded, although for a long time its importance was greatly overrated, whereas the masonic lodges, to which almost all the leading reformers belonged, exercised great influence, though they were not the creators of the new spirit, only its allies.

The introduction of the reforms began after the signing of the Treaty of Tilsit, by which Napoleon imposed extremely harsh peace conditions on Prussia. At Napoleon's insistence, Hardenberg was removed from his post as leading minister. Strangely enough, the Emperor recommended Stein to succeed him, but when a year later he discovered in an intercepted letter what Stein's true plans were, he banished him and confiscated his possessions. Stein was compelled to flee to Austria and later to Russia. During the period of his ministry, from the end of 1807 to the end of 1808, he put into effect by means of royal edicts a number of fundamental measures, notably the law of 9 October 1807, which abolished serfdom on the manorial estates, partly with immediate effect and partly after an interim period. The statute was already drafted when Stein joined the Government and he made some important changes in it. Land was freed from many encumbrances affecting conveyance, partition, inheritance and services.

The intention was to break down the insurmountable barriers between the nobility, the urban middle class and the peasants. Everyone was to be allowed to acquire land or carry on any trade he pleased. The abolition of the personal dependence of the peasants was even then supported by many progressive landowners, since they realised that a free man worked better and more intelligently. About this time A. Thaer introduced in Prussia up-to-date English methods of agriculture, which were essential to such collaboration between classes. Thaer energetically campaigned for the liberation of the peasants and was consulted when the measures were drafted. Serfdom had already become a completely untenable institution, since Napoleon had abolished it in the districts of Prussia he had annexed.

However, the suppression of some other feudal privileges met violent opposition from the landowners. For example, in minor cases they administered justice and possessed police powers; they had the right to demand services, and enjoyed freedom from taxation, hunting dues and so forth. On the other hand, it was their duty to support a tied peasant if he fell on hard times. The measure which has been mentioned did not settle these questions, but the worst thing was that it did not bestow on the liberated peasants that same unrestricted ownership of the land they cultivated which the peasants on the royal domains now enjoyed. Peasants on the estates of the nobility were merely tenant farmers, even though many of them had hereditary claims to the land. Apart from the opposition of the landowners, there was another circumstance which had a restrictive effect: many reformers believed in Adam Smith's axiom that as soon as labour and land were freely transferable, supply and demand would bring about the best of all possible conditions, and that where a peasant could not obtain land on favourable terms, he would as a free man move on somewhere else, if he could, or take up some other trade. In fact, this was not feasible for most peasants, and so four years later Hardenberg prompted the Edict of 14 September 1811, which was intended to solve these problems but which was soon after repealed. The final settlement dragged on and was far from satisfactory. Stein's intention had been to divide up the majority of the country into freehold estates of medium size. He wanted to retain the peasant's old protection against the confiscation of his land, but now the landowners frequently succeeded in acquiring peasants' holdings and in reducing the peasants themselves to mere labourers, besides retaining jurisdiction and police powers on their estates.

The transformation of Prussia into a national and liberal state demanded further great changes in the organisation of the government and administration. These were provided in two measures which were passed at the end of 1808, shortly before Stein's resignation. One of them gave the towns self-government, exercised through an elected town council, which appointed the mayor and other officers; the central government had the right of ratification. The leaders of the urban administration were for the most part unpaid. Opportunity of election to the town council was very extensive. Police duties were largely carried out by a civil militia. The autonomy thus granted to the towns was considerable and it was often difficult to find men equipped for these new tasks. In later years the basis of municipal government was repeatedly changed and the shadow of state bureaucracy fell across the town council. The other measure concerned the central administration. The King gave formal assent to the law but its effectiveness was delayed and impaired by Stein's fall. The law was intended to unify policy and created a new system of government, in which the King was exposed to strong influence from his ministers. Furthermore, the administration of justice was given to a separate department. The machinery of government was greatly improved, particularly by restricting bureaucratic interference in everyday life. In the preamble Stein declared that the nation must have a share in the administration, on the one hand through the Estates and on the other by co-operating with the civil service. At the same time he signed a memorandum drafted by one of his collaborators, Schön, and later called his political testament, in which he declared that other reforms were necessary, especially the setting up of a representative national assembly. But the time was not yet ripe for this; a considerable area of the country was still occupied by the enemy and the creation of a national parliament would by its nature have caused sharp partisan clashes which would have made a unified policy impossible.

A far-reaching military reform was carried through. It was the work of Scharnhorst and his associates and dragged on for a long time, since it ran into considerable opposition from the King and the big landowners which was not completely overcome until the war of liberation broke out in 1813. A decree of 6 August 1808 abolished the automatic right of the nobility to military commissions by declaring that anyone who possessed the requisite qualities could become an officer, and this was to be decided partly by examination. The army was not, as hitherto, to be formed by recruiting mercenaries but all Prussians fit to bear arms were to be liable for military service. This principle had first been established during the French Revolution, but Napoleon had introduced limitations by which a man liable to service could provide a substitute or buy himself out. This was not to be permitted in the new Prussian army. In the old army soldiers had often been beaten and barbarically punished for misdemeanours; this was now abolished.

Great importance was attached to trusting to the honour of both officers and men. Frederick the Great had once declared that only the nobility possessed a sense of honour and hence was alone qualified to provide officers; Scharnhorst, on the other hand, pointed to the French officers, who were drawn from all classes. Alongside the regular army he wanted to set up a national militia whose members should serve at their own expense and for a shorter period. Decrees issued by Napoleon made this impossible, but later the *Landwehr* sprang from Scharnhorst's original idea. The training of the troops aimed, as in the French army, at making it possible for them to fight in open order. All these reforms aroused the most violent resistance from the nobility, and, in fact, from some liberal statesmen too, who believed that making the educated classes liable to military service would have a detrimental effect on culture, while the King was persuaded that to arm the masses would be to court the danger of a revolution.

After Stein's fall an administration headed by Count Dohna and Baron von Altenstein was formed. The severity of the French occupation relaxed because Napoleon needed his troops for the war in Spain and the imminent struggle with Austria. The patriotic party urged the King to side with Austria but he could not make up his mind. The revolt of the Tyroleans and the Spanish stirred hopes of a rising by the Prussian people, but a few isolated ventures of this kind miscarried.

The greatest achievement of the Dohna–Altenstein administration was to set up the University of Berlin. Its founder was Wilhelm von Humboldt, who was advised by other eminent scholars. Some time before, the King had declared that the State must offset its losses in physical strength by reinforcing its intellectual resources. Humboldt himself had a first-class brain. He saw the University's purpose not as the mere imparting of knowledge for practical ends but as the development of the intellect on the ideal pattern of Greek civilisation. He combined neo-humanism with the ideas of Pestalozzi, and in this he was supported by Süvern.[1] His work for the free development of the personality was inspired by the same motives which animated the other reforms. Whereas elsewhere in Europe the universities in some cases served state policy exclusively and in others were under the tutelage of the Church, Humboldt posed the principle of the freedom to teach and to learn which contributed decisively to the extraordinary rise of the various branches of learning in nineteenth-century Germany.

In 1810 Hardenberg again became principal minister, this time with the title of State Chancellor. He now initiated a new epoch of reforms, opening with a programme of important fiscal measures. He planned to

[1] For a fuller account, see the excellent exposé in Franz Schnabel, *Deutsche Geschichte im neunzehnten Jahrhundert*, Vol. I, 1929, book 3, section 4.

introduce complete freedom of choice of trade, to make the nobility liable to land tax, to regulate the relationship between landlords and peasants, to give Jews equal rights and, finally, to set up a national assembly as the cornerstone for rebuilding the state. In 1811 a conference of notables from all provinces was held in Berlin to prepare public opinion, but these plans for reform stirred a large section of the nobility to fierce opposition, which Hardenberg sought in vain to break down by having two prominent aristocrats put under arrest pending enquiries. As a result of this opposition, many of the reforms planned were not carried through at all or only in an extremely diluted form. Hardenberg now entered on a course which diverged sharply from Stein's ideas on self-government, taking as his model Napoleonic measures to strengthen the power of the State.

In the ensuing period acute tension developed between Napoleon and Tsar Alexander, and the question of Prussia's attitude arose. Many patriots vehemently urged an attack on Napoleon but the King preferred to wait and see how Russia and Austria would act. Napoleon applied pressure and ultimately faced Prussia with the choice of either putting an auxiliary corps of 20,000 men at his disposal against Russia or being herself destroyed. Austria was in the same predicament and was forced to promise Napoleon an auxiliary corps 30,000 strong, though admittedly she secretly informed the Russian Government that these troops would only pretend to fight against Russia. The patriotic party was bitterly disappointed by the King's attitude, and many Prussian officers left the country to take service with Russia or England.

2

NATIONAL LIBERATION

IDEAS OF THE NATIONAL MOVEMENT FOR LIBERATION

Germany chafed more and more under Napoleon's rule. To be subject to an alien despotism and lose her national identity was bad enough; but it was still worse to have to furnish thousands of troops for France's further conquests and to make heavy financial and economic sacrifices. Liberation, however, had formidable obstacles in its path – Napoleon's genius and massive resources for one thing and, for another, the deep hostility between Austria and Prussia. Germany splintered into a host of small states, many of whose princes sided with Napoleon, partly as a result of his shrewd propaganda, which contrived to present England as the arch-enemy of peace. The champions of liberation were handicapped, for Napoleon had criss-crossed Germany with a network of spies and informers, Prussia was occupied by French troops and her king, together with influential circles, viewed the nationalist movement with misgivings, fearing that it might lead to a rising of the masses against their own rule.

Among the masses themselves there was scarcely any hatred of the French, apart from isolated instances where atrocities had outraged popular feeling. Germany had no fanaticism to show like that in Spain, for example, where the murder of individual Frenchmen was regarded as a meritorious act. Napoleon once remarked that not one of his soldiers had been murdered in Germany, although in 1809 there was an attempt on his own life. Friedrich Staps, the son of a clergyman and little more than a boy, tried to stab him but could not get close enough. A long knife was found on him, and when Napoleon asked him what he had intended to do with it, Staps calmly replied that he wanted to kill him because he was the bane of his native land. Napoleon considered Staps insane and wanted to pardon him, but the youth told the Emperor that he would nevertheless still try to kill him. Staps was shot. The whole incident made a deep impression on Napoleon.

Both particularism and cosmopolitanism were obstacles to the rise of any widespread nationalism. Many educated Germans admired Napoleon and considered the French soldier more efficient than his German counterpart. Hegel's remarks on this subject were typical of many. In the literature of the day, the French were often called the modern Romans; the Germans were to content themselves with the role which the Greeks had played in the Roman Empire, namely, distinguishing themselves by their intellectual accomplishments. It is characteristic that Fichte and other representatives of the national movement should see the problem of liberation as one of education. With this was soon linked the notion that it was the Germans' mission to guide all nations towards world citizenship and intellectual perfection. Many of the pioneers of liberation consulted the pages of Machiavelli or Rousseau to see how to awaken national feeling, but few of them omitted to stress that universal human values must take precedence over national considerations.

Ernst Moritz Arndt

Prominent among the literary pioneers of the movement towards liberation and nationhood was Ernst Moritz Arndt (1769–1860). He was born on the island of Rügen, which formed part of the Holy Roman Empire but which was under Swedish sovereignty. His family, originally serfs, had worked their way up to a position of freedom, prosperity and culture, and his origins had a great influence on his thought and activities. Among his early writings was a history of serfdom in his native Rügen (1803), and this played a part in inducing the Swedish Government to free the peasants in the German territories under its jurisdiction. At that time the peasants formed by far the largest section of the German people; Arndt more than once describes them as the most valuable part and, like Rousseau, idealises them. Like Herder, he was born at a place where one came into contact with many different peoples, and it was this which probably stimulated them both to investigate the nature, causes and worth of national character. If Herder and Rousseau had a strong influence on Arndt, it was the Bible, classical antiquity and Romanticism which fertilised his mind. Abstract philosophy, on the other hand, left him cold and he enjoyed poking fun at its aberrations. He studied theology at the Universities of Greifswald and Jena, but then abandoned it and travelled extensively, getting to know many different peoples at first hand, and he finally became a lecturer in history at Greifswald in 1800.

The French Revolution had produced a conflict in Arndt's mind. He fully admitted that a people had the right to overthrow a despotic régime by force and that the Revolution had unleashed some sublime

ideas, but its degeneration into the conquest and oppression of other
nations scandalised him. During his travels he had spent a considerable
time in France, and in his account of them, which appeared from 1801
to 1803, he passed very favourable judgement on the French. Soon,
however, he made their acquaintance as conquerors in Italy and on the
Rhine, and the gap between them and the Germans seemed unbridgeable. Napoleon's victorious progress filled him with bitterness, and the
fall of Prussia made him more conscious of being a German and less
of being a Swede. He began to work for the liberation and unification of
Germany, and all the while that Prussia was completely in Napoleon's
hands he stayed in Sweden. In 1809 he returned to Germany, and
when in 1812 the struggle for freedom drew near, he entered into close
relations with Baron vom Stein, becoming his secretary in Russia, and
encouraging the fighters for freedom with numerous pamphlets and
poems.

In the course of a long life Arndt wrote a vast number of works, most
of them filled with passion and poetic fire with Biblical echoes. He also
wrote songs, many of which were as rousing as the *Marseillaise,* while
others were sickening in their ferocity. His main theme was a call to
revolt against the arrogance of the French conquerors. His writings,
which aided war propaganda, also contain outbursts of national hatred
which are painful to read and scarcely in tune with his fundamental
views. Sometimes one has the impression that two currents are warring
within him. Like Fichte and Jahn, Arndt never surrendered the principle
that universal human values are the highest good. His most important
work is *Der Geist der Zeit* (The Spirit of the Age). The first volume
appeared in 1806, the second in 1809, the third in 1813 and the fourth
in 1818.

Like Herder, Arndt assumes that every nation has its own special
character and is distinguished primarily by its language (which,
incidentally, he believes should determine national frontiers). Arndt
describes the German spirit in the words: 'Industry, frugality, sobriety
of understanding, slowness without cowardice, honesty mixed with a
little climatic awkwardness, are the old, recognised national virtues.'
A glance at national fairy-tales, folk-songs and pictures makes him add:
'Simplicity, loyalty, love and truth – that is their character.' Even in
1844, when he was an old man, he writes: 'Simplicity, straightforward-
ness, honesty – that is what being German means,' and in his view
these qualities 'are, thank God, still to be found in the plain, un-
sophisticated and unspoilt German.' Elsewhere he lists, as features of
the past, strength, manliness, bravery, honesty, piety, integrity and
friendliness, and adds characteristically that even in his day they had
not completely died out. Arndt counted it a virtue in a section of the

people that they had not been corrupted by urban civilisation, and here there is an echo of Rousseau. It is also worthy of note that despite his leanings towards Romanticism, Arndt, like Fichte and Jahn, does not esteem in German history the deeds of the emperors and knights as highly as the raising of moral standards, especially that achieved by the Free Cities.

Arndt often described the national traits of the French, for the most part slightingly and quite often very unjustly, but in 1814, after the first War of Liberation, he wrote of the French Revolution:

'I should be very ungrateful and at the same time hypocritical if I did not openly acknowledge that we owe an infinite amount to this wild and crazy Revolution, that it has poured out a rich, fiery flood of inspiration from which every man who does not shun the light has been able to draw something, and that it has put into men's heads and hearts ideas which were utterly essential for founding the future, and which twenty or thirty years ago they still trembled to conceive. It has hastened that process of fermentation through which we have had to pass as through purgatory to reach the gates of the Paradise of our new condition . . .'

and more in the same vein.

Shortly before, in 1813, Arndt had written his essay on national hatred, in which he begins by admitting that every people has its virtues and its shortcomings, and that in general it is foolish to ask whether one people is better than another. Nevertheless, he rejects any interbreeding with other nations and demands that the Germans should hate the French, their hereditary enemies, for ever. Even if, he argues, belief in the superiority of one's own nation and xenophobia are prejudices, they do no harm and should become a 'sacred illusion', a kind of religion. But from here he goes on to say that for those who have scaled the heights of virtue, knowledge and art, national hatred must cease and the great community of nations must begin. 'Anyone who can then still hate is either a barbarian or an animal.' At the same time Arndt wrote a further series of propagandist works. At the end of 1813, when the Allies were about to invade France, four of Arndt's writings were submitted to the Prussian censor, who reported on them to Hardenberg, the Chancellor. Two of the pamphlets were passed for publication but the one about national hatred and another on Napoleon were banned. Hardenberg and the censor were of the opinion that they were incompatible with the spirit of moderation and future good relations with a highly civilised nation like France.

Arndt by no means glorified war for its own sake. In 1812 he wrote that any war which was not waged for the fatherland, justice and freedom was the greatest abomination. Christianity, he said, taught equality and justice, love and compassion for every living thing, and states and nations must heed this. Nevertheless, in his eyes wars were an inevitable, indeed a necessary, evil which contributed to human progress, and the Bible and history seemed to testify that God had so willed matters. However, he hoped that the nations would finally live at peace with one another within their linguistic communities. In 1819, after Napoleon's fall, Arndt published his *Stray Thoughts on Educating Mankind*, in which he said: 'It is a noble thing to love one's fatherland and to do all in one's power for it, but it is nobler, infinitely nobler, to be a human being and to hold everything human in higher esteem than that which pertains to one's fatherland.' An earlier work declared that man was always more important than the state and that it was the worst possible sign if the reverse became accepted. History, he said, could as yet afford no instance of an equitable state.

Arndt sought to explain national character largely in terms of environment and history, but he also assumed that a racial influence was present, although he did not enlarge on this.[1] At the time it was believed, even in France, that miscegenation gave rise to inconsistencies in national character. Tacitus had considered the Germans as an un-mixed race, a fact which Arndt accepted and held to be a great advantage. On the other hand, he stressed that the Germans in the north and east were largely Germanised Slavs. In his view, the real heart of Germany lay in the south and west, but he subsequently advances the view that it is precisely the Germans from these parts who are less characteristically Germanic than those from certain districts in the north. He later seems to have realised the brittleness of racial hypotheses.[2] In a work written in his old age, he stated that the Germans were a compound of Teuton, Celt and Slav and that the superiority of all Teutons was dubious and unprovable. He also pointed to the considerable Germanic elements among the French and disposed of the assumption that blue eyes were a Germanic characteristic by recalling that two great Germans, Goethe and Stein, had brown eyes.

[1] On occasion Arndt referred slightingly to the Jews, but when he was in Russia he gave his opinion that the Polish Jews were 'nobler, calmer and more balanced' than the German Jews and that the Russian Jews were better still. Cf. his *Erinnerungen aus dem äusseren Leben*, reprinted 1913, p. 134.

[2] In a letter written to a newspaper in 1848, he called the Poles racially inferior, but this was probably no more than a passing outburst. In his book *Versuch in vergleichender Völkergeschichte* (*Essay on Comparative History of the Nations*), 1843, p. 316 ff, he deals with the Poles in detail, pities them as a 'tragic people' but also calls them a 'big, wild boy' and a 'fool and good-for-nothing'; he goes on to say, however, that every effort must be made to restore Poland and that, if this succeeds, Prussia and Austria should cede the greater part of their Polish provinces to Poland (p. 326).

However this might be, Arndt certainly wanted to see all Germans united, regardless of their racial origins, and, indeed, a union of all the Germanic nations, in the broader sense of the term, which included the Scandinavians. Here his German-Swedish descent and his strong sympathy for Sweden were probably not without their influence. The essence of a nation seemed to him to reside above all in a common language, with which, according to a notion widely held at that time, an intellectual kinship was linked. But he extended the concept of a common tongue to closely related languages, such as the Low German spoken by the Dutch and Flemish. This, however, scarcely applied to the Scandinavians, for their languages are more remote from German than Dutch or Flemish. Arndt considered the Alsatians and the Swiss, as well as the Dutch, to be Germans. The Belgians, who spoke partly French and partly Flemish, he claims on one occasion for the French nation, on another for the German. He also considered natural frontiers and especially the possession of a coastline important for marking out the borders of a nation. Hence his intention of bringing the Dutch into the German community; the Netherlands, he declared, were indispensable to Germany by reason of their ports and he was thoroughly enthusiastic about a German fleet. He believed that the peoples related by language and tribal origins would gladly join the *Reich*, if only to safeguard themselves against fresh attacks by the French.

Politically Arndt advocated a 'democratic monarchy', in which the peasants were to play an important part. By 'democracy' he understood 'government for and by the people' and he was convinced that in the course of time all states would grow more democratic. Sovereign power and all that was great, he maintained, derived from the people. It is characteristic of the man that he was one of the first to recommend a spontaneous rising of the peoples subjugated by Napoleon, without their consulting their rulers. In 1811 he came out in favour of the choosing of the king, or the dynasty, by the people, whereas his ideas later turned to an election by the princes. The victory of particularism and legitimism at the Congress of Vienna forced him to adapt many of his ideas but he always supported a constitutional monarchy with powers limited by parliament. A strong monarchy seemed to him to be absolutely essential. Legislation was to be effected jointly by king and people, and the representative assembly was to consist of two chambers, an Upper House of the more important princes and high officials and a Lower House of elected representatives of the Estates. Apart from wage-earning workmen, everyone was to have the franchise. Since his original idea of a complete abolition of local sovereignty (*Landesfürstentum*), which he hated, proved impossible, he demanded for each *Land* a parliamentary assembly, which should send delegates

B

to the *Reichstag* (Imperial Diet). The army, with the King as commander-in-chief, was to consist mainly of the militia; regular soldiers
were to be responsible only for guarding the frontiers. Arndt also called
for ministerial responsibility, parliamentary immunity, jury courts,
freedom of the press and education, and autonomy for the towns.

Arndt wanted property and titles to pass only to the eldest son,
as in England. He advocated abolishing the minor nobility. Peasants
must receive their freedom and some land, and an international re-
settlement scheme on the grand scale would aim at increasing their
numbers and chances of making a living. Townsfolk, too, were to be
helped, but Arndt considered the development of Germany into an
industrial state neither possible nor desirable, lacking as she did colonies
and shipping. Industrialism, he believed, bred a proletariat, and free
enterprise aided speculation and moral decay, and so he wanted to
preserve the guilds and introduce social reforms, especially old-age
pensions for the workers.

Arndt saw the State's main function as 'the promotion of what is
intellectual in man and of reason and morality as being the sole and
supreme condition of liberty'. He had a vision of an agrarian state
with yeoman farmers as its backbone. The idea was to have as little
government as possible, but this, he admitted, was hard to achieve.
He was against meddling in world politics and the French offended him
deeply in 1840 by still considering war with Germany. The Germans,
he declared in 1812, were a moderate, peace-loving nation which should
preserve the peace of Europe. Two years later he wrote that the
Germans' feats of arms had bestowed on them the honour and good
fortune of once again figuring in world history as a powerful and
glorious nation. But in 1818 he warned the Germans to 'cherish a
silent, modest pride, as befits a great nation'. Towards the end of his
life he praised them as the greatest people in the world.

The course of the Congress of Vienna set Arndt against England,
who in his view had not taken German unity sufficiently into account
and was highly inimical to Germany as a maritime power. All the same,
he continued to regard England as a model and as Germany's natural
ally, and warned Germany against becoming estranged from her. If
England went under, he said, Europe's liberty would be lost. Even so,
there was still the danger of decadence among the English – once so
high-minded – because they judged everything by mercenary standards,
despised foreigners and indulged in excessive national pride.

Austria's courageous attitude towards France filled Arndt with
admiration. He hoped that Austria would unify the German nation but
later changed his views. For a long time the Prussia of Frederick II
appeared to Arndt, as to most of the Romanticists, a mere machine, a

despotic military state ruled by a monarchical aristocracy. 'The soul of this monarchy was alien to everything which bears the name German – and still is.' Nothing could be more ridiculous, he said, than to attribute patriotic German ideas to Frederick II: Frederick hated anything about a people which betrayed individuality because this conflicted with despotism. 'No, it is from the south and centre of Germany that German art and all higher culture have come. . . . Go to Swabia and the Rhine, and there the names of the loftier geniuses of Germany will ring in your ears.' Later Arndt felt it to be Prussia's task to unite Germany, and this was, in the event, accomplished by stages in the course of developments yet to be described. Arndt at first wanted the revived imperial dignity to go to Austria; then he advocated a system of dualism with Austria taking over the leadership of southern Germany and Prussia of the north, but in the end he preached the unification of Germany through Prussia. He demanded the right of national self-determination on the basis of nationality and linguistic kinship for other nations too, especially the Italians and the Poles. During the period of reaction Arndt was suspected of being a revolutionary and was prosecuted. This was admittedly unjustified, but retrospective suspicion could read into his utterances much which passed for criminal. Here, for example, is a sentence from his principal work, *Geist der Zeit* (Spirit of the Age): 'For despots and tyrants there are daggers and ropes, for such vermin should justly die only the common death at the executioner's hands.'

Friedrich Ludwig Jahn

Friedrich Ludwig Jahn (1778–1852) was the son of a Prussian clergyman in Prignitz, where the peasants were free and prosperous and there were none of the old manorial estates. Even as a boy he was distinguished for his wide knowledge of the Bible. From his youth he was a fervent patriot, and because he was born not far from where several frontiers met, he was able to see how the inhabitants of various German countries manifested towards one another a jealousy which at that time passed under the name of nationalism. Quite early on he began to travel extensively and gradually he covered wide areas of Germany and grew acquainted with the people, their dialects and customs. Out of these travels grew his yearning for German unity under the leadership of Prussia. At his grammar school his rugged, independent character often made life awkward for him. From 1796 to 1803 he attended the Universities of Halle, Jena and Greifswald, where he studied mainly history and the German language, but although he read widely, he was not the stuff of which scholars are made. Among the German students of his day conditions of incredible brutality prevailed; there were constant challenges to duels, brawls, drunkenness and immorality, and though Jahn was averse to duels he was often involved in brawls. He finally emerged as a champion of the moral reform of student life and from this the concept of the *Burschenschaft* (students' association) was later to develop. His main opponents were the *Landsmannschaften*, in which the students were grouped according to their geographical origins. During this period Jahn, who was poor, lived from hand to mouth; at times, indeed, his only shelter was a sort of cave he had made himself near a small allotment on which he grew potatoes.

When the French Revolution broke out, Jahn was fired with enthusiasm, his special hero being Danton. Later, like many other Germans, he was disillusioned by developments in France, and soon came to hate the French. He wrote pamphlets on how to promote Prussian patriotism and enrich the High German vocabulary. Disappointed in his hopes of an academic post, he had to earn a living as tutor to a landowner's family. When war broke out between Prussia and France, he tried to join the Prussian army but he was too late. The collapse of Prussia and the subjugation of all Germany to Napoleon moved him deeply and he now bent all his energies to the task of liberation. He first wrote a book on *German Nationhood* which contained his fundamental views.[1] After the Peace of Tilsit he completed his preparation for teaching at a training college and taught first at the Köllnisches Gymnasium in Berlin and then at the Plamann School, which was run on Pestalozzi's principles. Although Jahn was only a junior teacher with no title or rank, he had such an impressive personality that he established a reputation among wide circles. In particular, he was quick to win the admiration and affection of his own pupils and of young people generally, and this was especially apparent in the sphere of physical training, for which he coined the term *Turnen*. In 1811 the first gymnasium in Berlin was opened. The exercises themselves came from the curriculum of the schools of the Philanthropes where others had already been using them, but to Jahn must go the credit for developing them. He promoted not only apparatus work but also running, jumping, riding, swimming, fencing, competitions and games. Long walks were organised, which aimed not only at developing physical fitness but also at bringing together people from different parts of Germany and different social classes. Jahn demanded of his pupils frugality, comradeship and morality. The main aim was to prepare young people in mind and body for the struggle for liberation and to pave the way for German unity.

Just like Klopstock before him, Jahn was enthusiastic about the Germani as described by Tacitus. Like Rousseau he had a preference

[1] See p. 37. ff

for the lower classes, which in his opinion had preserved the traditional German virtues better than the *beau monde*, who had adopted the French language and French customs. This was why he rejected good manners and was rough and uncouth in his bearing. Gentlemen in those days were clean-shaven and wore their hair short after the French fashion, so it was only natural that Jahn and his disciples should let theirs grow down to their shoulders and sport a full beard, for this was felt to be Germanic. Incidentally, the French Romantics later adopted the same fashion, and in 1848 German democrats and socialists (and Karl Marx, too) were distinguished by long hair and beards, at which the English mocked. Jahn also devised a Germanic costume, made of cheap material and worn with an open neck and without a cravat; this also served as a kind of identifying mark. When at the Congress of Vienna the Prussian Chancellor, Prince Hardenberg, invited him to a diplomatic banquet, Jahn appeared in this costume and wearing dirty shoes to show that he was a man of the people. Since Jahn possessed both originality and humour, he made an impression even upon cultivated men – Ranke, for instance – though others found his personality repellent. Stein called him a grotesque fool, and insisted that, in any case, Jahn's ideas were not as Germanic as he believed, for he owed many of them to Rousseau and the French Revolution. When national movements arose among the Slav peoples, Jahn's methods of inflaming patriotism – gymnastics, public festivals, distinctive costumes and the like – were adopted.

In 1812, at the insistence of a colleague, Friedrich Friesen, Jahn proposed the foundation of a students' union to inculcate in the younger generation a true Germanism, to remove any friction among them and to induce them to devote their energies to the fatherland and the nation. They were to give up issuing the fashionable challenge to duels, but all the same they would be expected to defend their honour with weapons if the need arose. Fichte, as rector of the University of Berlin, vetoed Jahn's proposals. He declared that Jahn was confusing medieval ideas with Germanism: the manifestation of a chivalrous spirit and a standpoint of honour was, he said, completely un-German. Fichte compaigned energetically against the abuses of student life, particularly duelling. Germanism seemed to him inseparable from a moral task which could in no way be discharged by the sabre. He was, in fact, historically justified, for duelling was something which had grown up among the French nobility and become a kind of sport. Only later did it spread inside Germany.

In his book *Deutsches Volkstum*, which appeared in 1810, Jahn sums up his ideas. His native Prussia was still completely subject to Napoleon and Jahn could not write as freely as he wished, and whenever he criticised Napoleon or the French he did not name them specifically. The word *Volkstum* was coined by Jahn to denote both the amalgam of language, kinship, customs and traditions which makes a people into a distinct entity and fills it like one family with reciprocal love and a sense of solidarity, as well as the intellectual aims and forces which spring from such a community. In both French and German usage at that time it was customary to make a distinction between 'nation' (Nation) and 'people' (Volk). The nation denoted the educated and well-to-do classes; the people, the lower strata. *Volkstum*, therefore, was to form the democratic counterpart to the aristocratic 'nationality' as well as to express a natural organic individuality, whereas nationality in Western usage was more of an artificial legalistic concept. The Germans who were annexed by France acquired French nationality but not French *Volkstum*. Jahn held the conviction that the people were above the State just as the soul was above the body, and that the natural frontiers of a people did not necessarily coincide with the artificial ones.

Jahn also held that the individuality or the interests of a people did not constitute the highest values. Humanity was above nationality, and morality above interests: humanity could only be bodied forth by peoples; even Christianity could only develop on such soil and was shaped by the mind of the peoples. The Reformation, for example, arose in Germany because there the mind of the people had remained closer to that of early Christianity than elsewhere. The German character was marked by energy, loyalty, openness, piety and honesty. Every people serves humanity best by developing its own individuality, but it must not equate itself with humanity and attack other peoples or try to destroy their national character. The extinction of any *Volkstum* always impoverishes humanity. All peoples form one large family and are capable only in the aggregate of expressing the full nobility of human nature. Any intermingling of peoples should, however, be avoided.

The Germans, Jahn continued, like the ancient Greeks, are a people who cherish the spirit of humanity; they do not despise other peoples but are just in their dealings with them, perhaps too just, as Klopstock said in one of his odes. It redounds to their credit that they prefer the ploughshare to the sword. Jahn firmly rejects any policy which aims at the subjugation of others; political frontiers should follow those of the peoples, which on the whole coincide with the great natural frontiers. Germany's most natural western frontier was the one which preceded the conquests of Louis XIV. Jahn deplores the dismemberment of Germany and wishes for the *Reich* national unification under an emperor and a great, though not over-great, position in the councils of the leading European nations. In order to reach this goal, Germany will have to pass through a series of revolutions. The individual German states should not be suppressed. He obviously expects the unification of Germany to come from Prussia and wants Austria to give up several provinces, especially Bohemia – presumably to Prussia. Furthermore, Germany must make her Italian and Polish possessions independent states under Habsburg rulers, in order to expand in her turn east and south-east. Belgrade, not Vienna, should be the Austrian capital. The Habsburg Empire, said Jahn, would never be able to Germanise its numerous nationalities; it should rather recognise their national rights and form a great confederation as far as the Balkans but withdraw from Germany. The German confederation should include Switzerland, the Netherlands and Denmark and be given a capital to be founded on the Elbe under the name of Teutona.[1]

Germany was to receive a monarchical constitution, but with a central popular assembly and provincial diets. The franchise should be democratic – graduated according to the natural class structure – and no mere yes-men should be elected, nor should any one people be privileged. Titles should be bestowed only for special services and be non-hereditary. It was the State's task, he said, to promote the unity of the people, its education and the preservation of its traditions. There were to be common German civil rights and one common language (although the local dialects were not to be suppressed), as well as a code of common law, standard weights and measures, schools and so forth. The state should also work towards social unity and break down class barriers. At the time, Jahn argued, Germany was a pariah among nations because her social divisions approached the caste system of India. He went on to propose that the state should introduce insurance against all natural disasters and war damage, as well as pensions for officials and soldiers, welfare for the widows and orphans of former civil servants and for 'friends of the fatherland who were without means'.

Jahn's great love was education and he put forward a full programme of proposals on this subject which are not restricted to the young. The state appears to him primarily an institution for educating the whole people to be good citizens of the world, the fatherland and the national community as well as for stimulating all the creative powers of the people. First and foremost the mother-tongue must be fostered, and not a foreign language. Education for citizenship of the state was also highly important, and at every stage of education. The history of the fatherland claimed special attention. The British, who in the development of their popular institutions and traditions were far

---

[1] Parts of the Netherlands and Denmark later became members of the German confederation. Jahn was, of course, thinking of voluntary association.

ahead of all other peoples, also possessed the greatest historians, who far surpassed those of Germany. But Jahn condemned those historians who revelled in the representation of wars as 'sabre-rattlers' who had already been 'executed' by Schlözer. School-children must receive instruction in craftwork; physical training was likewise very important for building both the body and the character. Since the Peace of Westphalia what the Germans had lacked most was self-respect. Education was to make the people one large family which no enemy could possibly subjugate.

Any war not fought in defence of the fatherland appeared to Jahn unnatural, inhuman and foolish; he hated wars of conquest and the regular armies which served this end. Admittedly, he thought, small armies, as well as fortresses and the like, were necessary for warding off a sudden attack, but the brunt of the defence was to be borne by the people, who were to be concentrated in a militia and trained in the use of weapons. Every rifleman should own his weapon and some ammunition and, even when trained, take part in occasional target practice. Those without means would be given their weapons by the state. Officers up to the rank of colonel were to be chosen by the men and paid only while on active service. Corporal punishment was un-German and should be abolished.

Special emphasis was laid on the development of a national sentiment. The predilection for foreign customs, which had merely inculcated a servile spirit in the Germans, would have to go. In particular Jahn attacked slavish adherence to fashion – usually French – as wasteful, in bad taste and injurious to health. Besides, he said, fashion was responsible for the barriers which divided one class from another. Jahn hoped to see the introduction of a simple and cheap German costume, adapted to suit the sex, age and occupation of the wearer and one which only citizens should be entitled to wear. In certain legal proceedings this costume was to be obligatory. As further aids to promoting a sense of community, Jahn recommended festivals. entertainments, theatrical performances, writings and monuments. All these were to be aimed especially at celebrating great historical events and national heroes. Citizens who had performed acts of signal merit should, by popular consent, be honoured at special festivals.

To prefer a foreign language to one's own was particularly harmful to national consciousness. In every province the government and courts should use only the mother tongue and the ruler would have to be able to speak to every subject in his own language. Jahn deplores the fact that Joseph II wanted to replace the Magyar language in Hungary by German, and asserts that in Great Britain many risings would have been prevented if the King had spoken Irish or Gaelic. He regrets that

Frederick the Great was not allowed to marry an English princess, for in that case English liberty and civilisation would have prevented him from imitating French models. The mother tongue should also be purged of unnecessary foreign words[1] and German literature would have to produce works which could vie in popularity with those of Homer, Dante or Shakespeare. Hitherto Germany had possessed only the beginnings of such a literature. A German Plutarch should emerge and celebrate national heroes in epic verse. But in the whole history of Germany there were only two great feats: the freeing of the country from Roman domination by Arminius (Hermann) and Henry I's defence of Germany against the Hungarian cavalry in the tenth century and his supposed founding of cities as bulwarks against them. To Jahn, the campaigns of the medieval emperors, for all their romantic glamour, did not seem to be glorious pages in German history, but he did regard as praiseworthy great achievements for the benefit of humanity, such as the better treatment of women, the purer conception of Christianity, freedom of thought, tolerance, development towards world citizenship and the struggle against any power which strove for world domination, whether Romans, Huns, Mongols, Charles V or Louis XIV. For obvious reasons Napoleon was not mentioned in this context.

Jahn was convinced that the moral well-being of a people was closely linked with sound family life. The index of a people's humanity was the extent of its respect for women, and the Germans had done most to give them a fitting place, as Tacitus had already noted. Any lax divorce laws, loose living, the marriage of princes for purely political reasons and the like Jahn therefore found reprehensible. Although he was decidedly against preference for foreign languages and customs, he did not advocate isolationism and even saw in the Germans' penchant for travelling abroad an excellent quality which deserved encouragement. The state should make this possible for young people and thus widen their intellectual horizons. No one who had not travelled and seen the world should be eligible for election as member of a national assembly or as a mayor.

As long as Prussia was still occupied by Napoleon's troops, these national ideas could not be proclaimed openly, but they were fostered in secret societies, to which Jahn and his circle belonged. After Napoleon's defeat in Russia, Jahn and his friends launched into highly diversified activity. His gymnasts volunteered for service and he himself, who was in close contact with Hardenberg, the Chancellor,

---

[1] Jahn later tried to enrich the German language with new formations from German roots, and this makes many of his sentences almost unintelligible. He understood too little about Germanic philology to do this, as his mistaken derivation of the word *Bursche* from *Bur* (neighbour, companion) shows.

worked for the formation of volunteer corps. Jahn and Friesen were the first to join the Lützow Volunteers who, incidentally, did not prove a military success.

As already mentioned, Jahn's personality displayed some features which attracted and others which repelled. However, he knew how to handle and inspire young people; many, indeed, idolised him. Older, sober men of high intellectual standing were for the most part very critical of him. Many of the things he taught and did were in themselves sound and are today commonplaces in educational theory; but there was also much about him which aroused serious misgivings and his behaviour and mode of expression often appeared unpleasant or foolish. Jahn, who had an earthy sense of humour, delighted in disregarding conventional turns of phrase and tactful euphemisms and in calling things by the coarsest terms he could think of. This understandably delighted his younger followers. A grammar-school boy compiled an anthology of his sayings in a small volume entitled *Grains of Gold from the Lips of Father Jahn*. When in 1819 Jahn was suspected of revolutionary tendencies, the police found this book and put a criminal interpretation on many of the sayings in it. One of his ideas was that Germany should be separated from France by an artificially created wilderness, stocked with wild animals and other obstacles to intercourse between the two states, though this plan was certainly intended only as a joke.

Jahn gave such blunt and coarse expression to his Francophobia that after the wars of liberation he began to get on most people's nerves. Thus, for example, he delivered lectures in Berlin in the course of which he said that anyone who allowed his daughter to learn French was making it possible for her to become a whore. A Prussian captain in the audience, who was having his own daughter taught French, complained to Prince Hardenberg. The Chancellor disapproved of the remark and called on Jahn for an explanation. After this Jahn could no longer lecture in public but only in his own home. His book *Deutsches Volkstum* was translated into French in Lyons in 1825 by a doctor, P. Lortet, and another French doctor named Gilibert read a paper to the Académie in which he called Jahn 'the sage of Germany' and compared his system with that of Rousseau. Lortet repeatedly visited Jahn in Germany and formed a close friendship with him; indeed, he collected money for him when he fell on hard times. Finally they met in 1848, when they were both deputies.

In recent years Jahn has sometimes been represented as a forerunner of Hitler, although the ideas set out in his main work are utterly at variance with Hitler's. The idea that miscegenation should be avoided because it would damage the national character is admittedly non-sensical, but it is far from subscribing to the modern racial illusion, which did not exist at that time. Jews were not excluded from the ranks of Jahn's gymnasts. Wolfgang Menzel, one of Jahn's most thorough-going disciples, tells in his memoirs that on one of the gymnastic tours a Jew who was not over-strong fell out exhausted and earned a violent tirade from Jahn, who was very quick-tempered. Menzel thereupon spoke up for his friend, and after Jahn had cooled down he con-gratulated Menzel on his intervention.

Certainly modern German nationalism can be traced back in part to Jahn. Like Arndt and others, he attempted to square it with cosmopoli-tanism by declaring that humanity was above nationality. Both the gymnastic movement founded by Jahn and the student corps, which was influenced by him, made an unusually large contribution to the de-velopment of modern nationalism. It is obvious that its seeds were present in Jahn's activities, but history can show many examples of an ideology which has finished up in a form of which its authors never dreamt.

Johann Gottlieb Fichte

Unlike most German philosophers, Fichte did not come from the intellectual middle class but from the lower class. He was born in 1762 in a village in Saxony as the son of a poor weaver, and as a boy his job was to tend the geese. A philanthropic nobleman was so im-pressed by his intelligence and eloquence that he paid for his schooling, but after his patron's early death Fichte had a hard time of it. He had an impetuous and commanding nature which was ruled by an inflexible idealism. In personality he resembled a prophet yearning for the rebirth of his people and mankind. His intellectual development was determined by Kant and Rousseau, and even his early writings showed enthusiasm for the French Revolution and democracy. In 1794 he was summoned to Jena, where he soon wielded great influence among the students. He condemned the abuses in their way of life and won over the majority to his proposals for reform, but was soon in conflict with Protestant orthodoxy, which accused him of atheism, although he was a deist. In the end he had to leave Jena in 1799.

In his writings at this time, Fichte supported cosmopolitanism. When the French invaded Germany, he wished them total victory, hoping that the liberation of Germany would follow. The fact that they incorporated German territory into the French state did not at all offend his patriotism. He would even, he wrote, have gladly become a professor and a French citizen in French-occupied territory so as to work there for German liberty.

From Jena, Fichte went to Berlin, where he mixed with the Romanti-cists Friedrich Schlegel, Dorothea Mendelssohn-Veit (the friend, and later the wife, of Schlegel), Tieck and Schleiermacher, gave lectures and wrote books. Of his political works, *Der geschlossene Handelsstaat* (The Independent Mercantile State) deserves special mention; he considered it the best and most well-reasoned of his writings. He here describes his ideal state, which is one that ensures work and a livelihood for all its subjects and guarantees social equality. The nation is to be isolated from others in order to avoid commercial competition, in which Fichte saw the source of wars, social inequality and moral corruption. The end is to be achieved by a state monopoly of foreign trade, a separate currency, control of production and home trade as well as a ban on foreign travel except for cultural reasons. Fichte was influenced by the ideas of the socialist François Babeuf, who, along with his companion Darthé, was condemned to death and executed in France in 1797 for endangering private property.

After the turn of the century, Fichte's life and thought were influenced above all else by the fate of Prussia and the national movement against Napoleon's rule. Prussia's defeat in 1806 and 1807 shook him profoundly; he left Berlin, which was under temporary occupation by the French, but returned in 1807 and delivered his *Addresses to the German Nation*. He played a part in founding the University of Berlin, where in 1810 he became a professor and later its first elected rector. But he was soon at odds with most of the other prominent professors, who were more indulgent towards student excesses than he, and in 1812 he resigned the rectorship.[1] When the war of liberation broke out shortly afterwards, he tried to take part in it as a preacher at army headquarters but was refused permission. He died at the beginning of 1814, just when the allies had crossed the Rhine, of a fever which his wife had contracted while nursing the wounded.

Fichte's philosophy will be discussed here only in so far as it concerns our theme, i.e. without reference to his metaphysics, religious philosophy and one or two other points. In the political and social sphere, the

---

[1] One of the points at issue was the brutality shown by students towards one of their number who was Jewish. Fichte, rightly, wanted to punish this sternly. Cf. Max Lenz, *Geschichte der kgl. Friedrich-Wilhelm-Universität zu Berlin*, Vol. I, 1910, pp. 410 ff. This shows how unjustly Fichte was claimed by the anti-Semites as one of their number. In one of his early works he had sharply criticised the Jews, officers and aristocrats alike for having their own special prejudices and customs, but he added that Jews who could overcome these were heroes and that in any case all Jews were human beings and must therefore be treated with justice and humanity. A year later, he assured the Jewish philosopher Salomon Maimon of his highest esteem and friendship. In a letter to his wife dated 20 August 1799, Fichte further said that Dorothea Veit, a Jewess, had dispelled his belief that no good could come from the Jews and he praised them highly. Cf. J. Levy, *Fichte und die Juden* (undated).

similarity between Fichte's ideas and Rousseau's is marked, although there are some important differences. Both of them stress above all the sovereignty of the people. Rousseau was a man of the Enlightenment as well as a Romanticist, and this led to considerable contradictions. Fichte, too, was influenced by Romanticism, although less than Rousseau. At all events, his thoughts gradually moved away from reason towards feeling, from individualism towards collectivism, from the liberal idea of formal equality before the law towards the democratic, indeed socialistic, conception of social justice organised by the State, from exclusive cosmospolitanism towards an appreciation of the nation as the only way to the goal of revitalised humanity. At the outset the freedom of the individual appeared to him as something infinitely higher than the interests of the State, which was hardly more than a necessary evil. Later he realised that the State was more than a mere association, and that it approximated to an organism, even if he did not use precisely this term; he speaks only of an 'organised product of nature'. But Fichte did not adopt the idea of certain Romanticists, such as Schelling, that the State as a living entity was above single individualities. Shortly before his death he stressed that the State as such was an abstract idea and that only its citizens were real. He also doubted whether the true will of the people could ever be discovered by a majority vote.

So Fichte reached the conviction that the youth of the nation must be properly educated, and here the pedagogic ideas of Pestalozzi seemed to him the right way. He took the view that it was the duty of the State to educate the people intellectually and morally in such a manner that they could govern themselves, whereupon the State could then vanish. It is significant that Fichte wanted to vest power in a supreme council of teachers, a kind of professorial dictatorship. This was a renewal of Plato's dream of a state in which the philosophers should be kings and the kings philosophers. Furthermore, he proposed a league of nations, and even a world state. He also declared it to be out of the question that one free nation would attack another merely to rob it. The value of nationality was in his eyes exclusively determined by the striving for moral ends which all nations had in common. Thus, in 1804, he announced that the fatherland of every civilised European was Europe and, more specifically, that state which had made most progress in civilisation. Fichte spoke contemptuously of a patriotism bound up with the soil. Humanity, he said, was the supreme goal but we can serve humanity only in our own country. Thus it followed that patriotism strove first of all to attain the good within its own nation and then to impart it to all mankind and by this token to become cosmopolitanism. The State, he declared in his addresses, was not an end in

itself but merely the means for the higher purpose of developing
what was purely human in one's own nation.

Napoleon's power politics also stimulated Fichte's thinking.
Germany's position recalled that of sixteenth century Italy and
Machiavelli's yearning for liberation from the foreign yoke. His
writings were inspired by a strong nationalism and the remembered
greatness of the ancient Romans. In his view free nations could be led
by a predilection for power and expansion, and politics could not be
conducted according to the rules of private morality. Fichte studied the
writings of the great Florentine and they made a deep impression on
him. In 1806 he wrote an article expounding Machiavelli's views.
Like many authorities on the rise of the State, Machiavelli assumed
that he would put an end to the struggle of all against all. Granted,
there were conflicts of interests between states and hence no universally
valid system of justice. Each nation strove to spread as far as possible
its own good features and wherever practicable to incorporate the whole
of mankind within itself. Every great state was therefore forced to
remain constantly on guard to protect its strength and influence by all
available means, as well as to extend its power, if it wanted to escape
destruction. But this would not lead to constant wars; quite the contrary.
If all powers acted in this way they would hold each other in check.
A balance of power and a long peace would ensue. The youth of Europe
should devote its military abilities to the struggle with the barbarians,
who in any case were destined to be assimilated by our civilisation.
Peace would then prevail in the common European fatherland because
no one would dare to draw the sword. This article was written as a
counterblast to Prussian policy, which had long proceeded from the
assumption that somehow Prussia would be spared the effects of
Napoleon's power politics, even without taking counter-measures.
But how averse Fichte was to a warlike policy is shown by his earlier
remark that a policy based on a balance of power would lead to peace
and that the youth of Europe should fight only against the barbarians.

Fichte's famous *Addresses to the German Nation* were delivered in
the winter of 1807–8 in Berlin, which at the time was still occupied by
French troops. Just previously Napoleon had had the Nuremberg
publisher Palm shot for distributing a patriotic pamphlet. Fichte had
to reckon with a similar fate. He was not, however, arrested, although
his addresses gave offence to the French authorities. The reason for
his immunity was evidently that the addresses did not pursue an
immediately political aim. They were not a call to political action but a
programme for national education. The Napoleonic system was sharply
criticised, but neither the Emperor nor the French were mentioned
by name, and so the censor could not prevent publication. None the

less Fichte had great difficulties with the Prussian censorship. In earlier lectures he had described the moral decline of his day, the triumph of unbounded egoism and the blindness which had brought about Germany's political misfortunes. In his eyes the worst culprits were the upper ranks of society and the older generation, and he therefore pinned his hopes on the nation's youth and lower classes. The goal was to be attained – according to Pestalozzi's principles – by general education, which had as its central aim the creation of a pure, unselfish will and clear thinking. This would lead to the salvation not only of the German people but also of mankind as a whole, which would be lost without the intellectual help of the Germans.

In this task of the Germans – to bring about the moral and intellectual re-birth of all nations – Fichte was far from seeing something for which they were uniquely equipped by nature. He did not believe that racially they were better or more gifted than other nations but stressed that they were partly crossed with Slavs and partly related to the French and English. He did, however, ascribe a special virtue to the German language, because it alone had escaped dilution with Latin, which had played a great part in the development of other European languages. The Romanticists assumed that a language expressed the spirit of the people and from this tenet Fichte drew the conclusion that a people which loses its language loses its soul. The fact that the Germans had preserved their original language gave them an immeasurable intellectual pre-eminence. Their thought had preserved its dynamic nature, it had created the Reformation as well as a great literature and philosophy and would create a new, rational and republican state. In the other nations the corruption of their language had separated the upper classes from the people and thus lamed the creative faculty of thought. These other nations were not even capable of love for the people and had no true patriotism.

Fichte's conception of the unique merit of the German language is an extravagance which proves how dangerous the method of abstract deduction without practical verification can be in such matters. His assertion is so absurd that it needs no refutation; it is surprising that such a great thinker could overlook the countless obvious facts which contradict it.[1] His praise for the unparalleled creative power of the

[1] Fichte's inordinate praise of the German language was probably an unconscious reaction to the fact that in Germany French was still the language of the upper classes, who by using it had cut themselves off from the lower classes. In 1783 Frederick the Great had, through the Berlin Academy, which conducted its business in French, offered a prize for an essay on the reason for its widespread use. The prize was won by A. Rivarol, who argued that it excelled all other languages in clarity, logic and so forth, and for this the King conferred a high honour on him.

German intellect and for its future mastery of the world probably
filled numerous uncritical German readers with exaggerated pride. But
it would be mistaken to see in Fichte a forerunner of the later German
worshippers of national power. He condemned the foreign policy of
Frederick the Great (without mentioning him specifically by name)
as treacherous, disloyal and dishonourable, and he rejected his mechanistic despotism as un-German. Nor did the philosopher share the
illusions of the Romanticists about the Middle Ages. For him, the
only virtue in Germany's political past was the existence of the Free
Cities; the spirit of their citizens, pious, honest, modest, thrifty and yet
generous towards the community, seemed to him typical of the German
people. The German nation alone, he said, had shown by this example
that it could live under a republican constitution.

How little Fichte looked upon national power as a desirable end is
shown by his uncompromising rejection of a unified and centralised
state. He considered the multiplicity of German states to be a blessing
for civilisation and he advocated a league of German republics. In
writings which appeared at the same time as the *Addresses to the German
Nation*, Fichte passes scathing judgement on the German princes,
nobility and high officials. The regular army, he said, was also a source
of great evil and the realisation of his scheme for national education
would make it superfluous. He proposed to finance the plan by cutting
the military budget. Many influential writers of the day praised
Napoleon's empire, which was expected to bring about lasting peace.
Many Romanticists were likewise enthusiastic about a world state –
admittedly under the rule of the Pope. Fichte flatly rejected the idea
of world government and world politics and said that it was neither
in the interests of the Germans, nor was it their mission, to take part
in world conflicts which had as their aim conquest and spoil; they
should also be independent of world trade. Least of all should the
German mind let itself be dazzled by the illusions of Caesarism and a
world state with its centralisation and imposition of uniformity, which
could not but harm intellectual life. Nothing was more opposed to the
German mind than a world state which could only spring from rapacity,
barbaric harshness and ruthless egoism. In this way, he said, it was
possible to plunder and devastate the world but never to create a well-
ordered empire which would serve the common good. The habit of
admiring a great and powerful genius like Napoleon he thought un-
German. The German yardstick for greatness should be enthusiasm for
ideas which promote national well-being. Fichte believed, however,
that the French people had also had enough of the illusion of world
mastery. Before the wars of liberation Fichte neither glorified war nor
did he seek to inflame passions against the enemy. He brooded over the

problem of how political liberty and German unity could best be achieved. He hoped that the King of Prussia would unite Germany but that after his death a republic, a form of state without princes and nobility, would emerge. Prussia, the progressive state, would be peace-loving and content after winning back her territories. Fichte saw as the ultimate goal an age of universal justice which would conquer the spirit of war by the love of peace.

Fichte's conception of the nation was very different from Rousseau's. Although Rousseau was peace-loving and kind-hearted and condemned the striving for power and glory, he none the less praised national yearning for these things as a means towards unification. He admired the warlike patriotism of the Spartans and Romans, which set love for one's native country above all else and raised them high above the democratic Athenians. Every patriot, says Rousseau, is harsh towards foreigners; to him they are merely people, and hence nothing. This is inevitable but of small account. One's main duty is to be well disposed towards one's own people. Towards foreigners the Spartans were jealous, rapacious and unjust, but towards their fellow-citizens they were unselfish, just and peaceable. One could quote other passages from Rousseau's writings which defend nationalism of a highly dubious kind because it knits a people into a firm unity.[1] For Fichte the national community was only a means of moral education and the way to cosmopolitanism.

In spite of the attitude of Fichte which has just been described, German nationalists of recent years have praised him as one of their own number, and this is based on a complete misunderstanding of his ideas. Even scholars who have been in a position to understand him have sometimes fallen into such errors. Thus Bertrand Russell states that Fichte worked out a whole philosophy of 'nationalistic totalitarianism'.[2] The two leading French experts on Fichte's theories have reached quite different conclusions. Professor Victor Basch wrote that all the ideas of modern Pan-Germanism were alien to Fichte and that he had rejected and attacked all of them. Another French scholar, Xavier Léon, whose work on Fichte is today the standard exposition, declares that throughout his life Fichte was a disciple and fervent apostle of the ideals proclaimed by the French Revolution.

THE ROMANTICISTS

At the end of the eighteenth century and in the succeeding decades German Romanticism evolved, originally as a purely literary movement

---

[1] Cf. Franz Haymann's books on Rousseau and Fichte.
[2] *A History of Western Philosophy*, London, 1961, p. 690.

but one which subsequently invaded the sphere of ideology and politics. Later, among some intellectual circles in Germany, the opinion spread that Romanticism was the real German *Weltanschauung*, and of recent times it has been represented as a main source of German nationalism. A lot can be said in favour of these views but there are also solid arguments which one could advance to the contrary. A final verdict is made difficult by the fact that the most varied interpretations can be placed on the word 'Romanticism'. The usual view is that it was a reaction against the Enlightenment and saw feeling, as distinct from reason, as decisive. In reality, with people of any note, reason and feeling have always gone hand in hand, and to an especially marked degree in leading personalities. If the early Romanticists attacked the predominantly intellectual poetry of many versifiers they were certainly justified. Poetry is no mere technique which anyone can learn like a trade. Differences of opinion begin when a philosophy of life, ethics or politics are concerned.

Today German Romanticism is often taxed with having stood for a policy of feeling rather than reason, with having judged irrational strivings, old traditions and blind prejudices too favourably, and with putting the spirit of the people, national sentiment, the State, the classes and the Church above the judgement and interests of the individual. It is charged with having rejected cosmopolitanism, preached that morality is relative and denied freedom and equality. Finally, it is said, its intention was to replace progress by regression into the Middle Ages. To test the validity of such criticisms one would have to examine the whole history of literature and philosophy, which is not possible here. Fundamentally the Romanticists were poets, art critics, translators and philosophers who occupied themselves with all possible themes, and intellectual life interested them far more than politics. Feelings often change, especially among literary people, and a great proportion of the Romanticists considered it a precious privilege of their school to treat their own views with what has come to be called Romantic irony.

Many modern nationalists have gone back to poetic or other utterances of the old Romanticists and their contemporaries, very often, to be sure, without regard to their exact meaning or the circumstances of the time. Admittedly nationalism can be justified on the grounds of feeling more than reason, but the essence of modern nationalism is that the power of the national state is regarded as of supreme importance and the individual personality is degraded to the level of a small cog in a great machine. The question is how far the Romanticists held this view.

Any judgement on the German Romanticists must also take into account the fact that Romanticism, as its name implies, came to Germany from abroad, and the modern variety from England in particular. Important stimuli also came from Switzerland, where throughout the greater part of the eighteenth century writers constantly emerged who displayed many essentially Romantic characteristics – and, in fact, with republican tendencies. They turned against misleading abstract reason and the moral decline brought on by over-civilisation, as displayed in France, praised the unspoilt country folk and demanded of the rest a return to the healthy morals and customs of their ancestors. The character of the people, nationality, patriotism and liberty were the lode-stars of their thinking. The greatest of these Swiss writers was Rousseau, who also became the most powerful Romantic influence on Germany. Even before the emergence of those literary figures who are usually called the 'Romantic School', there were in Germany many important poets and thinkers who prepared the way for them and really belonged to the Romanticists, notably in their views on nationhood, the Fatherland, humanity and liberty: Klopstock and his disciples, the *Sturm und Drang*, Möser and the towering figure of Herder.

It has become customary to speak of an older and a younger Romantic movement. The former consisted principally of the poets Friedrich Leopold von Hardenberg, who called himself Novalis, Ludwig Tieck, and the Schlegel brothers, who studied, lectured and wrote on history, literature, Sanskrit and Indian philosophy. August Wilhelm Schlegel also produced translations from many languages, among them a masterly rendering of Shakespeare. This detailed absorption in the literature of many lands gave the Romanticists a markedly cosmopolitan character. The younger school grew up in Heidelberg. Clemens Maria Brentano and Ludwig Achim von Arnim published a collection of old folk-songs and other poems under the title of *Des Knaben Wunderhorn*. Heinrich von Kleist wrote, among much else, a drama which dealt with the struggle between the Romans and the Germans and contained lines full of burning hatred which were really aimed at the French conquerors. This circle of writers was in close contact with great scholars who were investigating German antiquity.

The main political enthusiasm of the Romanticists centred on the French Revolution; they nourished republican sentiments and revelled in dreams of cosmopolitanism. When the soldiers of the Revolution were transformed into conquerors, when Napoleon smashed the old German Empire and strove for world domination, the Romanticists were moved by patriotic emotions which they often sought to reconcile

[1] An Italian scholar, Professor Carlo Antoni, has brilliantly described these early Romanticists and given an uncommonly shrewd analysis of their thought. Cf. C. Antoni, *La Lotta contro la Ragione* (German translation under the title *Der Kampf wider die Vernunft*, 1951).

with their cosmopolitanism. The collapse of the *Reich* stimulated them to study and revive medieval culture as well as national poetry. Immersion in the past afforded them both comfort for the harsh realities of their own day and hope for the future. The fact that Austria again and again took up arms against Napoleon aroused in many Romanticists an enthusiasm to which they gave poetic expression. They hoped that Austria would restore the old Empire. On the other hand, the prestige of Frederick the Great, whose army, officers and tradition had failed so signally, sank in their eyes. His state appeared to them not as a national community but as a soulless machine. His Enlightenment, so warmly greeted by French intellectuals, his unscrupulous power politics and his thirst for military glory were felt to be un-German. Although foreign rule could be broken only by force, the Romanticists were far from desiring a unified German state with power, conquest and martial renown as its highest aims. Most of them were devoted to the small German states, although salvation could only come from great powers like Austria or Prussia. The conditions of the Middle Ages, which aroused their yearnings but gave them no practical goal to aim at, were quite unsuited to a big modern state. Justus Möser, who, if he did sometimes relapse into the world of ideas of the Enlightenment, was a Romanticist, loved the Middle Ages even for things which seem hard to justify. He did this only because the modern State had evoked in governments an arrogance of power which, he was convinced, grievously oppressed the liberty of the individual and the Estates. His ideal was a Germany made up of countless small republics. Möser's enthusiasm for England was largely focussed on those of her institutions which went back to the Middle Ages.

To many Romanticists the general decline of Germany seemed due above all to the conflict of religious belief. Luther's revolution appeared to them rationalistic extravagance, which must in the end lead to the collapse of all religion and morality and to political upheaval, and this view was even held by many Protestants. This led to admiration for the Catholic church and to some conversions. The Romanticists often enthused over the Papacy and Empire of the Middle Ages, though they forgot that the Popes had always had a deep mistrust of a strong state and had successfully worked against any emperor who seemed to be building up a position of strength. These considerations could not, it must be admitted, frighten off those thinkers who utterly rejected the power state, nor were these Romanticists offended by the fact that the Church saw in this national striving a new paganism, which threatened to swell into a pseudo-religion. A few leading Romanticists, like Friedrich Schlegel and Adam Müller, served Metternich, whose aversion from a powerful German national state was obvious. True, there were Romanitc poets like Rückert, who hymned Friedrich Barbarossa; one day the Emperor would awaken from his dream in the depths of a mountain and set Germany free. Rückert's reputation as a poet, incidentally, rested principally on his brilliant translations from Oriental languages, by which he hoped to advance cosmopolitan understanding. German historians had long been aware that it was precisely the policy of the Emperor Friedrich which had caused the loss of Germany's power and unity. Ernst Moritz Arndt, who was also an historian, remarked that, though the Germans complained about the dismal present, they were fond of boasting when they talked of the invincible power of their medieval ancestors – a power which had never existed.

One can derive from Romanticism any political principle one pleases except a sober, calculating policy which gives no scope for imagination or emotion. Rousseau's idealisation of the people and his praise of passion easily led to warlike nationalism. Herder developed the concept of a national spirit and arrived at a cosmopolitanism in harmony with the national sentiment of individual peoples. The German Romanticists were influenced not only by Rousseau and Herder but also by Edmund Burke. In his book which attacked the French Revolution, Burke made clear the significance of irrational feelings and traditions for the spirit of a state and championed the replacement of a mechanistic concept of the State by an organic one. Even though the State is neither a machine which can at any time be arbitrarily remodelled, nor an organism which is capable of change only slowly and within narrow limits, it does possess certain similarities with both a machine and an organism. The use of these concepts as an analogy is justified only if there are no better, more generally comprehensible ones. German Romanticism came to widely differing conclusions about the State and the people: Novalis, starting out with republican leanings, arrived at a poetic and mystical view of monarchy, while Adam Müller and Friedrich Schlegel saw in the aristocracy the true embodiment of the national spirit. Romanticism found the deeper reasons for historical development not in the actions of governments but in the working out of the national spirit. Many Romanticists, like Uhland, returned to Klopstock's and Herder's republican ideas.

Romanticism, like the Enlightenment, was not so much a precisely formulated philosophy as a mode of thinking which sprang from the spirit of the age and developed in many countries. The same mode of thought can be adopted by people with completely different ideals and can be combined with other philosophies. Thus it is that philosophers of the Enlightenment have considered the existence of God as something ascertainable by reason, or at least as something postulated by reason, but they have also denied it or interpreted it quite differently than the various religions have done. Some of the writers of the Enlightenment have represented monarchical absolutism as logical, while others make the same claim for the sovereignty of the people, liberalism or democracy. Many have defended planned economy, others free enterprise; many saw their ideal in capitalism or in freeholding, others in communism. What was common to men of the Enlightenment of all tendencies was the rejection of any authority except reason. But they held widely differing opinions on what reason had to say, and they did not always attack the same authorities. In any case these latter had ruled the past and the men of the Enlightenment had small regard for tradition. They expected everything of the present or the future.

The Romanticists were their counterpart, often more negatively than positively. They mistrusted the reason of individuals and esteemed instead that of collective personalities, above all that of the spirit of the people as expressed in its legends, customs and songs and also its common law. They saw in all this the wisdom of their ancestors, and for many of them this was also displayed in those institutions which had been highly esteemed in olden days, such as the Church and the old social order. This turning towards the past, too, earned their mode of thinking the title of 'traditionalism', which in many respects is preferable to the term 'Romanticism'. The turning away from the 'reason' of the protagonists of the Enlightenment is also shown in the exaggerated importance attached to feeling, imagination and the passions. But the Romanticists or traditionalists were just as divided over their ideals as the men of the Enlightenment. Many were enthusiastic about 'the people', and particularly the simple folk, unspoiled by modern civilisation, in whom human nature had been preserved in its pristine purity. Others preached a doctrine based on an ideal vision of the monarchy, nobility and clergy. In politics, too, their tendencies were widely diversified and ranged from feudalism, patriarchalism and hierarchism to democracy, anarchism and the cult of the superman, from humanitarianism to nationalism.

In poetry, music and the plastic arts Romanticism was a force of the greatest importance. It had an uncommonly stimulating effect on research in the humanities by directing interest into fields neglected or even despised by the Enlightenment. After all, to many of the writers of the Enlightenment the Middle Ages were the era of darkness, barbarism and superstition. In the life of the state the Romantic outlook opened up new vistas. To a man of the Enlightenment such as Joseph II of Austria, the fact that small nations clung to their language and traditions seemed irrational. National consciousness is admittedly something irrational but it is a factor with which we have to reckon and

Romanticism, even when in error, has sharpened our conception of
it.

The great Swiss historian Alfred Stern begins his monumental
history of Europe since the Congress of Vienna with a detailed appreciation of Romanticism, and sums up his findings in these words:

> It is impossible to measure what Romanticism has evoked by way of
> permanent creations in a wide field of knowledge and art. It has
> discovered new territory, full of the most magnificent fruits, and
> turned neglected wildernesses into lush meadows. But it has sown
> harmful seeds in many a field and robbed healthy growth of air and
> light by its luxuriant tendrils. Hence, for succeeding generations,
> who can measure its effects by the yardstick of time, it presents a
> Janus head.[1]

THE WAR OF LIBERATION

In 1812 Napoleon embarked on a war against Russia, which sprang first
and foremost from his policy of blockading the whole of Europe to
English goods, a policy which had met with Russia's opposition. But
the further plans of the Emperor aimed at world domination. He therefore assembled for the Russian campaign a huge army, estimated at
600,000 men and made up for the most part of troops from his vassal
states.[2] His aim was to dictate peace in Moscow and have himself proclaimed Emperor of Europe, Head of the European Confederation
and Defender of the Christian faith.[3] He then intended to march by
way of Tiflis to the Ganges, break the British rule in India and thus
overthrow the British Empire. This fantastic dream occupied him to
such an extent that urgent military dispositions were not made and the
warnings of his best generals went unheeded. The very size of the army
was disastrous, for in the conditions of that day it could not be supplied
in a country like Russia. The outcome of this adventure was the most
terrible catastrophe ever to befall an army, and of this whole gigantic
force only a few scant remnants returned home.

However, it was by no means certain that Napoleon's mastery over
other countries would also collapse. In Russian ruling circles opinions
on the policy to be adopted were divided. A strong group of Russian
statesmen and generals wanted to conclude peace with Napoleon on

[1] In various passages Stern gives a survey of Romanticism and its connection
with politics in the leading European states.

[2] The army consisted of 200,000 French, 147,000 Germans from the Confederation of the Rhine, 80,000 Italians, 60,000 Poles, 50,000 men from the
Austrian and Prussian forces, as well as southern Slavs, Swiss, Dutch, Spaniards
and Portuguese.

[3] Cf. Auguste Fournier, *Napoléon I*, Vol. III, Leipzig, 1889, p. 108.

condition that Russia should receive East Prussia, parts of Poland and areas on the Lower Danube, but this was irreconcilable with the interests of Austria and Prussia. On the other hand, some advisers, such as Stein, urged the Tsar to continue the war and free Europe from Napoleon's yoke. In 1812 Stein was summoned to Russia by Alexander I and appointed his principal adviser on German affairs. With the support of Ernst Moritz Arndt, he worked out plans for a German rising. The Tsar was favourably disposed towards Stein's proposals and now wanted to win over Austria and Prussia for a war against Napoleon. But in both these states there was a cleavage of opinion. The prestige and resources of Napoleon were still great, and a war against him hazardous: even if he were conquered, would not Russia then dominate Europe in his place? In conservative circles there were misgivings about mobilising the masses to conquer Napoleon. It was feared that a national war might easily degenerate into a revolution. French propaganda laid great stress on the argument that Napoleon had put an end to the French Revolution and saved the social order; Stein and the other Prussian leaders of the national movement were, it was hinted, dangerous Jacobins. This view had many supporters among the Prussian nobility; they hated Stein, Scharnhorst, Gneisenau and their followers as revolutionaries and looked on Napoleon as the protector of the existing social order.

Prussia's status was still that of an ally of Napoleon, if an unwilling one. Frederick William III wavered between peace and war. Towards the end of 1812, however, General von Yorck concluded on his own initiative a pact of neutrality with the Russian General Diebitsch. The King brusquely disowned this step, because otherwise there would have been an immediate break with Napoleon. Three weeks later the Estates of East Prussia and the neighbouring territories assembled in Königsberg and, on a motion submitted by Stein, agreed to a big call-up of volunteers. The movement for a national war gained more and more ground and might perhaps have assumed a revolutionary character had not the King acquiesced, even though he was doubtful of success. The feudalist anti-war group lost its influence. Scharnhorst was recalled and could now put his plans into operation. Volunteers from the middle classes, who had hitherto been exempt from military service, were called up, negotiations for an alliance were opened with Russia, conscription was introduced, mobilisation ordered and Yorck's attitude approved. Numerous volunteers came forward, particularly from among students and educated people. In those parts of Prussia which had suffered particularly under French rule, self-sacrificing patriotism prevailed among all classes. The negotiations with Russia led, on 28 February 1813, to the Treaty of Kalisch. Sweden associated herself with this and Britain promised financial support. Austria, under the leadership of Metternich, still remained neutral and at first tried to preserve peace by mediation. The Emperor Francis was very averse to war and Metternich feared that any significant growth of the power of Russia or Prussia might prove highly dangerous to Austrian interests. He therefore sought to induce Napoleon to make concessions where possible.

On 16 March Prussia broke off relations with France, and on the following day the King issued a proclamation to his people in which he stressed that the war was being waged for king and country, for freedom of conscience, honour and independence as well as the country's economic and intellectual interests and reminded the Prussians that they were also Germans. Soon after, Prince Kutusov, the Russian commander-in-chief, published another proclamation, which Stein had had a hand in drafting. The German princes were invited to join the common cause; if they did not they would be treated as traitors and destroyed by the force of public opinion and the just use of arms. The Confederation of the Rhine was declared dissolved and the hope was expressed that out of German national spirit a rejuvenated Germany would spring. In this proclamation Stein had wanted to call upon the German people to rise against their 'taskmasters' but this summons to revolution was suppressed by the allied monarchs and their advisers. In other ways, too, Stein's draft was so watered down that it lost much of its force. He was appointed head of a commission for the provisional administration of liberated or conquered territories. He hoped that most minor princes would disappear and their countries be united with bigger ones, thus furthering German unity. But the princes of the Confederation of the Rhine, far from deserting Napoleon, placed fresh troops at his disposal. The King of Prussia decreed that apart from the existing army a *Landwehr* and a *Landsturm* should be set up. The *Landwehr* was conceived as a people's army, that is, as a kind of militia. It was to serve in the field and be equipped by local representative bodies, which were also to appoint the officers. Later on, fresh officers were to be chosen by the existing ones. The role of the *Landsturm* was to wage guerrilla warfare and, where necessary, follow a scorched earth policy, but it was soon dissolved because the reactionaries feared that it might pursue revolutionary ends. The *Landwehr*, however, played a considerable part in the war and the liberals hoped it would become the strongest armed force and a bulwark of political liberty. In all, Prussia called up for active service more than 11% of the total male population; this was achieved partly through Scharnhorst's effective organisation and partly through the spirit of self-sacrifice which was so widespread.

In the meantime a huge new army was formed in France as well.

Napoleon was able to begin the war against Prussia and Russia with a considerable superiority and he won fresh victories. He then concluded an armistice in order to build up his strength even more. Metternich now made strong efforts to end the war by negotiation and he offered Napoleon unusually favourable conditions. His chief aim was the liberation of the German and Austrian territories on the right bank of the Rhine, with the large territories on the left bank left in French hands. Metternich said nothing about Holland, Belgium, Spain, Portugal or Italy, nor was the Tyrol mentioned, and special negotiations were to be conducted about Westphalia and a few other small areas. Napoleon, however, was not yet prepared to make concessions, since he feared a loss of prestige which might cost him his throne, and so Austria now declared war on him.

The struggle began afresh. The Allies gradually obtained a considerable superiority in manpower. The Battle of Leipzig was a terrible blow for Napoleon; his forces were largely annihilated, his German auxiliaries mostly went over to his opponents – usually even before the German princes deserted him – and his army was driven back across the Rhine. The German princes hastened to win favour with the Allies, and Metternich procured them favourable promises which at the peace negotiations formed a hindrance to a tighter unity of Germany. Only the King of Saxony made up his mind too late to leave the sinking ship. In Italy, Holland and Spain there were also risings against Napoleon's rule and further call-ups in France met with scant success.

The Allies were likewise war-weary. From their headquarters in Frankfurt they offered the Emperor peace and the return of most of the French colonies if he would content himself with France's 'natural frontiers'. This meant that the German Rhine provinces, Belgium and perhaps a part of Holland would remain his. Metternich wanted France to remain strong and well disposed towards the Austrian Empire in order to counterbalance Prussia later on. Napoleon played for time and continued negotiations, but simultaneously made the most strenuous efforts to squeeze new armies from his exhausted country. The Allies therefore came to the conclusion that negotiations were fruitless and decided to cross the Rhine. On 1 December 1813 they issued a manifesto to the French people in which they said that they were not waging war against France but against the rule which Napoleon had exercised for so long beyond the frontiers of his empire to the misfortune of Europe and France herself. They offered France a just and honourable peace and wished her to be great, strong and happy. The Allies had not yet made up their minds to overthrow the Emperor.

In the meantime the offer of the 'natural frontiers' had aroused displeasure in Britain, since it included Belgium and this threatened

British security. Consequently the Foreign Secretary, Castlereagh, wanted France to retain only her 'historic' frontiers, namely, those she had possessed in 1792. The other Allies agreed and demanded in addition that Napoleon should give up his protectorate over Italy, Switzerland and German territories. Considerable differences of opinion prevailed among them over Poland, Saxony and the future government of France. True, all the Allies were agreed that questions of the dynasty and constitution of France were to be decided by the French people alone, but after all they had to know with whom peace was to be concluded. There was still the chance of coming to terms either with Napoleon or with a Regency acting for his son, who was a child. Castlereagh was very much in favour of the old Bourbon dynasty, but he wanted neither to impose it on France nor to lower the Bourbons' prestige in their own eyes through their having received favours from the enemy. Austria and Prussia shared this view. The Tsar would have liked to bestow the crown of France on Bernadotte, the former Marshal who was Crown Prince of Sweden at the time, but this would have given Russia a predominant influence on the future government of France and the idea was rejected by the other Allies.

Napoleon found the proposals of the Allied powers deeply humiliating and utterly unacceptable. On 31 March 1814 Allied troops entered Paris. Prince Talleyrand, formerly Napoleon's intimate and minister, contrived to make the Senate and the Legislature depose the Emperor. The fallen dictator wanted to continue the struggle, but finally his marshals persuaded him to abdicate and accept the Allies' terms. He retained the title of Emperor and was given sovereignty over the small island of Elba, along with other concessions. Tsar Alexander was responsible for his being given Elba, although all the other statesmen had the greatest misgivings on this score.

3

THE RE-SHAPING OF EUROPE

THE FIRST PEACE OF PARIS

Even while the war was still in progress, the Allies emphasised that they were fighting against Napoleon as a conqueror and not against France or the French people, and flatly dismissed the idea that the nation bore a collective responsibility for the actions of its ruler. They went even further: the aim of the war, they said, was not to overthrow Napoleon but only to abolish his rule over other countries and his predominance in Europe. Until almost the last moment they were prepared to leave him master of France if he would give up her conquests since the Revolution. They attached great importance to leaving France completely free to choose her constitution and her dynasty. They realised – and rightly – that to humiliate so great and proud a nation was both foolish and dangerous; a defeated nation is always hypersensitive and must be treated with considerable tact. The idea of destroying or curtailing France's military strength or of limiting her industrial production was never even considered. Nor did the Allies contemplate occupying French territory or detaining prisoners of war to ensure that the peace terms were kept; the prisoners were to be released at once and the Allied armies to leave France without delay. At the Congress of Vienna France was soon treated as a power with equal rights. All this was the natural consequence of the principle that the Allies had been at war not with France but with Napoleon.

Only in one particular did they depart from their intention, and this could hardly be helped. They followed the principle of non-intervention in France's internal affairs and did not support the claims of the Bourbons; only when it became clear that peace with Napoleon was impossible did they allow the Bourbon pretender and his party to carry on political activity and in particular to take over the press. The installation of the new régime ensued by agreement with the Allies and in due legal form. The Senate, which Napoleon had once appointed,

voted for a new constitution and chose a king, Louis XVIII, on condition that he took an oath to respect it. The people seemed to confirm
this choice and greeted the King with enthusiasm. He showed an
understanding of the spirit of the age – a great disappointment to the
more die-hard monarchists.

The first Peace of Paris was concluded on 30 May 1814, a mere two
months after the end of the war and one month after the King had
returned from exile in England and formed a government. In the
negotiations the French diplomats asked for an enlargement of France's
historic territory by the inclusion of parts of Belgium and Germany,
maintaining that they had been promised fresh territories with a
million inhabitants. The Allies disputed this but granted France new
areas with 450,000 inhabitants; Britain, moreover, returned most of
the French colonies she had occupied.

France had no reparations or indemnities to pay, but had to promise
to settle debts owed to private individuals. The Prussian Government
estimated the amounts which Napoleon had levied in Prussia alone
between 1806 and 1812 at 1,228 million francs. Since contractual debts
were to be settled, Prussia demanded that France should pay her
169·8 million francs owing for goods supplied under commercial
agreements. But the French negotiators indignantly refused this demand, calling it humiliating.[1] The Tsar backed the French in this,
Prussia's demand was refused and a clause was inserted in the treaty
whereby all debts to a government arising from contracts, deliveries or
advances should be cancelled. The treaty similarly made no mention
of the many art treasures and antiques which Napoleon had carried off
from Italy, Belgium, Holland, Spain and Germany as spoils. At
Prussia's insistence a few minor objects were returned, but all the rest
remained in France's possession.

The French were convinced that the Rhine formed the natural
frontier of their country and that they therefore had a claim to the
German Rhine provinces, Belgium and a part of Holland. Sorel states
in his great work that the French had always striven to get the Rhine as a
frontier. Hence, he argues, the Great Powers would have acted more
wisely if they had taken account of this aspiration.[2] To this it could be
objected that from time immemorial the Rhine provinces had belonged
linguistically to the *Reich*. Numerous French historians have since

[1] The great French historian Albert Sorel comments that this Prussian
demand betrayed a mean and rapacious spirit! (Vide *L'Europe et la Révolution
Française*, Vol. VIII, 1904, p. 470.)

[2] Cf. Sorel, *op. cit.*, Vol. VIII, pp. 495, 504. It should be added that the
Allies were for a long time prepared to let Napoleon have the left bank of the
Rhine but, because of his attitude, they were forced to change their policy.

attempted to prove that the inhabitants had been very happy under French rule and would gladly have remained under it.

Historically, the relations between the Rhine provinces and France were of a varied pattern. Many princes and nobles kept on good terms with Paris, and quite a few of them were paid for doing so. Some French regiments drew their officers and men from the districts round the Rhine and were named after them. On the other hand, the Rhine provinces often suffered severely through French invasions. When the troops of the Revolutionary army marched in, they were often greeted with joy by youthful intellectuals, many of whom, however, were soon disillusioned. The great mass of the people cast a mistrustful eye on the 'liberators'. When they had to supply goods for paper money which rapidly became worthless and the Jacobin terror and the persecution of the Church set in, they grew very resentful. But Napoleon also brought the Rhinelanders great benefits. Formerly they had had to suffer much through the massive fragmentation of their country into small states but now a wide French market was opened to their industries and they were given a modern legal code, which provided notably for equality before the law. Great strategic roads were built which also facilitated trade. The abolition of feudal services was a benefit for the peasants, very many of whom had in any case obtained their freedom earlier. But there was a reverse to the medal: Napoleon's rule exacted heavy sacrifices in lives and money; only the well-to-do could buy exemption from military service; corruption was rife among the petty officials, who were miserably paid. There was no political freedom under Napoleon. The Estates, with powers to levy taxes, were abolished, along with local autonomy, and the press was rigidly controlled. The educational system was wretched; the Emperor took no interest in it. Some sections of the wealthy classes seem to have been not dissatisfied with Napoleon's régime. Although French was now the official language, educated Germans could in any case speak it as a matter of course. As far as freedom went, the French themselves were no better off. In any event, no opposition had emerged during French rule; this would have been very dangerous, for Napoleon's secret police had spies everywhere. Later, when the war of liberation was approaching, French agents and German officials reported much about the spread of anti-French and pro-German feeling. Furthermore, serious disorders arose over the conscription of recruits. When France's opponents marched in, they were often received with enthusiasm and numerous volunteers joined them.

The mood was not the same everywhere. Where territory had previously been under Prussian rule, its restoration was welcomed, but many occupied areas had been ecclesiastical lands and had a strict

Catholic population. The fact that they were now to be subject to a markedly Protestant state, whose traditions and system of government were alien to them, aroused much mistrust and hostility, which in the event were intensified by the measures of the Prussian Government. Thus it came about that in many places large numbers of people would have preferred French rule,[1] but one cannot conclude from this that the majority of the Rhinelanders would have desired it nor was there ever a movement which aimed at securing it, although French sympathies remained in many circles.

For Germany, Alsace played a similar role to that of the Rhine provinces for France. The leaders of the national movement and other influential personalities believed that the Alsatians, most of whom were German-speaking, would declare for Germany.[2] That this was a mistaken view was soon apparent. Many proposals were made for the future of Alsace, but the leading statesmen came to the conclusion that it should stay with France. The strict nationalists were indignant, while the liberals stressed that the Alsatians had been won for France by the French Revolution and would not turn to Germany again until she was a liberal state.

THE CONGRESS OF VIENNA

The main object of the negotiations was to create a lasting peace by the balance of power, i.e. to distribute disputed territory in such a way that no state had a preponderance of strength and to transfer important strategic points to those powers who could be counted on to prevent any breach of the peace. Britain and Austria were foremost in emphatically supporting this principle, while Russia and Prussia were primarily concerned with increasing their own power.

In the recent wars with France and her allies, Britain had expanded her colonial empire. The other powers, after a few adjustments, got back what they had lost. There was a general striving to preserve peace and the balance of power. For this reason, after the War of the Spanish Succession, Austria had kept Belgium and Lombardy. But in Thugut's phrase, Belgium had proved a millstone round Austria's neck, since

[1] Even Treitschke concedes this. Vide *Deutsche Geschichte im Neunzehnten Jahrhundert*, Vol. II, pp. 272 ff.

[2] Scarcely twenty years before many Jacobins had accused the Alsatians of feeling themselves to be Germans and had proposed that those who did not speak French should be deported and their property transferred to French nationals. Cf. passages from Jacobin speeches in my book *Nationalgeist und Politik*, pp. 155 ff. It seems that it was Napoleon who first won the Alsatians over to France.

she was very near France and very far from Austria. Some of the Belgians would gladly have returned to Austria's sheltering wing, but Vienna refused. Britain therefore arranged for Belgium and Holland to be united under one king from the house of Orange–Nassau; this appeared necessary for the protection of the nearby British coast and as a bulwark against France. By acquiring Lombardy and Venetia, Austria dominated Italy. In the north Castlereagh wanted to entrust the watch on the Rhine to Prussia, and across the Rhine a Germanic Confederation was to form a further bulwark against France. The permanent neutrality and independence of Switzerland were guaranteed by the Great Powers.

The Congress of Vienna entered a critical phase when the questions of Poland and Saxony came up for discussion. The Tsar wanted to unite the major part of Poland into a kingdom in its own right under his sceptre and give the country a liberal constitution. This plan appeared unacceptable to England and Austria because it would have increased Russia's power unduly. If the kingdom of Poland were formed, Prussia would have to contribute large areas which she had acquired in the second and third partitions of Poland but which had been recaptured by Napoleon. She claimed many Polish territories as essential for her own security and was prepared to cede the remainder only if she received the whole of Saxony in compensation. Prussian diplomacy further stressed that up to the very last the King of Saxony had not broken with Napoleon, although in the battle of Leipzig his troops went over to the Allies. He himself had been made prisoner and his country had been considered as conquered. He later joined the Allies. Austria opposed Prussia's claims, fearing that if they were granted she would become too strong, both militarily and politically. Many small German states, too, feared for their independence and the Saxons raised desperate protests about being handed over to Prussia. On the other hand, many champions of German unification considered a union between Saxony and Prussia advantageous, not least because in Saxony the Estates had always wielded influence. Dyed-in-the-wool monarchists were indignant that a king should be robbed of his country.

A long dispute over these questions broke out among the diplomats.[1] As for Poland, even the Prussian statesmen had considerable misgivings about the Tsar's intention to unite the greater part of the country under his rule. Stein, who was very close to Alexander, represented to him that his policy was against Europe's best interests, and he told the Prussian diplomats that the correct policy for their country was to

---

[1] Cf. the evidence in W. A. Schmidt, *Geschichte der deutschen Verfassungsfrage*, 1890, pp. 339, 342, 353, 361, 371. This work shows how false and tendentious Treitschke's history is in many places.

support loyally and unswervingly the defence of those interests. He suggested that they declared in favour of Polish independence. Wilhelm von Humboldt also talked on these lines. Frederick William III of Prussia, however, unconditionally supported the Tsar's policy. The question of how Prussia and Saxony were to be compensated was also highly controversial. Prussia proposed transferring some Italian or Rhenish territories to the crown of Saxony, but Austria and Britain refused. Britain wanted Prussia to receive the Rhine provinces and this, strangely enough, was backed by France's representative, Prince Talleyrand, although at first Prussia did not accept the offer.

Differences grew so sharp that Britain, Austria and France concluded a secret defensive alliance against Russia and Prussia. Metternich had already envisaged the formation of a Germanic Confederation without Prussia and the great majority of the German states sided completely with Austria against Prussia. In the end, however, a compromise was reached; Russia received the greater part of the available Polish territories, Prussia and Austria a smaller share and all three were placed under an obligation to grant their Polish subjects national rights and representation. Prussia was given a large area of Saxony and the greater part of the Rhine provinces together with some adjoining territories, and her position in Germany was greatly strengthened thereby. In all, her population was increased by a million.

By the Treaty of Vienna signed on 9 June 1815, navigation on all rivers which bounded or intersected two or more states – the Rhine being a notable example – was declared free. Shortly before the Congress ended, the German Confederation (or *Bund*) was founded by the German Federal Statute.[1] The general conditions governing the *Bund* were incorporated in the final treaty and placed under the protection of all the signatories.

THE SECOND PEACE OF PARIS

At the beginning of March 1815, while the Congress was still sitting, the representatives of the assembled powers received the news that Napoleon had left Elba and landed in France. The French troops confronting him on his march to Paris went over to him and he was greeted with enthusiasm on all sides. But not even the French army wanted fresh wars, still less the French people. Napoleon was well aware of this and so he constantly reiterated that he would now bend his energies solely towards securing peace and liberty, and did, in fact, promulgate a liberal constitution. A parliament was elected but only a small minority of its members were prepared to grant the Emperor unlimited powers.

[1] Vide, p. 73ff.

C

They were against a policy of conquest, although ready for any sacrifice to defend France. This attitude aroused the Emperor's anger, though of course he could not display this openly; he later confessed that if the outcome of the war had been favourable he would have abolished the Assembly. In order to impress the French people and his opponents, he assured them that he was peaceably disposed and he agreed to the peace treaty which had been concluded. In reality he considered war inevitable, but he hoped to gain time and divide the Allies. But the great powers were not hoodwinked; they issued a proclamation, drafted by Talleyrand, in which Napoleon was branded as a peace-breaker and they also renewed their alliance.

Not only Napoleon but also the Assembly stressed that France would continue the war solely to defend her frontiers, though the question of how far these extended was left open. That the Rhine was France's natural frontier was nothing short of a national dogma.

Napoleon's military prospects were not unpromising and so he took the offensive and hoped he would succeed in defeating his enemies singly before they could combine. But after a few successes his strategic venture failed at Waterloo, since at the last moment the British and Prussian forces managed to oppose him jointly. He was forced to flee, the Assembly demanded that he should abdicate, and this he did in favour of his son. The great powers had outlawed him as a breaker of world peace and the Prussian generals even wanted to have him shot as a war criminal, but Wellington demurred. Napoleon surrendered to the British Navy and, in accordance with a decision of the powers, he was taken to St Helena, where he died a few years later. Louis XVIII was now once more King of France.

On the one hand, the Allies felt it important to support the Bourbon dynasty, and feared that any unfavourable peace terms might lead to a revolution against the royal house. On the other, they considered a weakening of France's defensive capacity and a consequent strengthening of her neighbours as inevitable. By the second Peace of Paris France lost some strategically important fortresses and towns. Even so, her territory was still slightly bigger than before the Revolution. She was obliged to pay a war indemnity, part of which was to be used by her neighbours to build fortifications. The Allies left behind forces of occupation for whose upkeep France had to pay. The occupation was terminated after three years, since in the meantime confidence in France's pacific intentions had grown. When one includes other payments and reparations, France's total liability is said to have amounted to close on 2,000 million francs. The art treasures which had been removed to France had to be returned, which was felt by many Frenchmen to be particularly humiliating.

In the re-shaping of Europe there was one thing which all the powers had in common: a striving for peace after the apparently interminable sufferings and tribulations of a war lasting two decades. This hunger for peace was most strongly marked in Britain and Austria. Napoleon had looked upon Britain as his arch-enemy, but had never been able to gain a foothold on British soil and wage war there. Both at sea and on land Britain had won great victories, extended her overseas possessions and found herself in a situation which, provided the peace were kept, offered vast possibilities of increased prosperity. Castlereagh was strongly opposed to any policy of prestige or conquest, or any humiliation of France, an attitude in sharp contrast to British public opinion.

The Austrian statesmen looked on Prussia and Russia as the most dangerous opponents of their empire, but it was far from Metternich's thoughts to adopt a hostile attitude towards them on that account, although in the Polish–Saxon affair he had found himself obliged to conclude a secret defence pact with Britain and France against Russia and Prussia. But in general he believed that it was possible to live at peace with the other great powers; this was vital if he was to wage a successful struggle against revolutionary upheaval. Striving for national unity and power seemed to him one of the greatest threats to world peace and it was this consideration which determined his attitude towards the German national movement. Metternich has often been criticised for his hostility towards the Balkan peoples' aspirations for freedom and for not using his opportunities to extend Austria's power to the south-east, but it was clear to him that any expansionist policy in the Balkans would have meant war with Russia, and so he preferred to give up any idea of shifting the frontiers of the Habsburg Empire.

The second Peace of Paris was, it is true, less favourable to France than the first, but it avoided all unnecessary harshness. This helped to prevent any serious threat to European peace for a considerable time.

4

THE GERMAN *BUND*

MEMORANDA OF STEIN AND WILHELM VON HUMBOLDT

The aims of the national movement in the wars from 1812 to 1815 were independence, unity and freedom, but there were wide differences of opinion over what these aims implied in detail and how they were to be achieved. Later, in the field of politics and history, there arose a sharp controversy over whether the German people had taken up arms to ensure national independence, self-respect and strength through firm national unity or whether they had hoped to gain above all else political freedom; another question was whether they had risen of their own free will or on orders from above. But these questions took no account of the fact that, as a rule, mass movements have their origins in many interacting aspirations, that those concerned have for the most part only a hazy conception of their goals and that the strength of the various motives can hardly be assessed in isolation. The urge to be independent of foreigners was probably the most widespread. Backward nations have often fought a foreign conqueror with all their might, however great the hopes of progress his rule held out for them; and the more advanced the nation, the stronger the desire for independence.

The history of Germany shows clearly that her fragmentation into small states not only seriously threatened her external independence but often militated against her inner unity and freedom. The extraordinary multiplicity of princes and peoples and the consequent straitening of resources had fateful political and economic results, although they sometimes fostered culture. The lament over the inner disruption and atrophy of Germany's best powers had often been voiced in the days of the old *Reich*, and even more strongly during Napoleon's rule. The striving for national unity, certainly not unjustified, was, however, opposed not only by many princes and their governments but also by the peoples, with their deep-rooted attachment to their native land. Only a few felt themselves to be primarily Germans; most considered themselves first and last as Austrians, Prussians, Bavarians and so on, but even within these larger states there was still little sense of unity. Thus, for example, a subject of the King of Prussia was still above all else a Brandenburger, a Pomeranian or a Silesian. Things were even more complex in the Habsburg territories; for the Tyrolean, the Emperor was the Count of Tyrol, who, quite incidentally, ruled over several other peoples. This Tyrolean may perhaps have felt an affinity for other Austrians, while hating the Bavarians, who were his kin, and he looked upon other Germans as certainly no more than distant cousins, of whom the Protestants in particular were alien to him.

It must also be remembered that for a long time the national movement embraced only some sections of the people, particularly the intelligentsia and the younger generation, and that in many parts of Germany there was a strong opposition to it. Bavaria, Württemberg, Baden, Hesse–Darmstadt and other states had made substantial gains through the favour of Napoleon, since they were allowed to absorb many small pieces of territory. In time past the minor German states had formed the Kaiser's party, and their princes looked to him as their protector against their larger neighbours. The bigger states created by Napoleon, and on whose rulers he bestowed the titles of King or Grand Duke, looked on strong national unity as an impairment of their sovereignty and resisted it with all their might. Austria and Prussia, moreover, who were rivals, were not prepared to agree on who should lead a united Germany. Napoleon's rule, in many respects progressive, had reduced political freedom and had made the princes all-powerful *vis-à-vis* their subjects, while at the same time the urge for freedom had intensified.

The re-shaping of Germany was discussed in great detail even while the wars of liberation were being fought; a number of prominent statesmen had set out their ideas in the form of memoranda. First of all an understanding must be reached between the two great German powers, Prussia and Austria; Hanover was also called in because its connection with Britain gave it special importance. The lesser and the least of the German princes were to be consulted only when Austria and Prussia were in agreement. Stein opened the exchange of views with a memorandum dated 18 September 1812. His ideal was a Germany under a strong emperor but with some measure of decentralisation. He hated the German princes who had become vassals of Napoleon and would gladly have eliminated most of them or at least severely curtailed their power. By tradition he would have liked to see the Emperor of Austria at the head of a German state, but Prussia would never have agreed to this. He therefore first proposed giving Austria control in the south and Prussia in the north, with a firm alliance linking both powers. But this proposal at once ran into opposition from Count Münster, representing the Prince Regent of Hanover and Great Britain. These two states would have agreed to a restoration of the old *Reich* with a few modifications and would gladly have added to it Switzerland and the Netherlands, but they decisively rejected any subordination of Hanover to Prussia and would have preferred to enlarge Hanover at Prussia's expense. It could be expected that the other bigger states would also resist subordination to Austria or Prussia.

Stein therefore worked out a new plan, which was ready in August, 1813. He now proposed to separate both Austria and Prussia completely from Germany and to limit the latter's territory to the thirty-six medium and small states. The Emperor of Austria was to be the hereditary ruler of this German state. The small states abolished in 1803, which in the old *Reich* were on the side of the Emperor, were to be restored and the executive power was to be vested in the Emperor and an Imperial Diet. The princes would have sunk almost to Imperial civil servants, though admittedly their office would have been hereditary. Stein here gave expression to his hatred of the former vassals of Napoleon, calling them 'chieftains' (*Häuptlinge*) and accusing them of the grossest denial of justice and freedom, with fatal consequences for the character and national outlook of the Germans. To win over Prussia to this idea of vesting in the Austrian dynasty the dignity of ruler over this reduced Germany, Prussian territory was to be substantially increased. There would then have been three states, namely Austria and Prussia and a small Germany, who were to conclude a permanent alliance for joint defence.

This plan of Stein's was rejected by both Prussia and Austria. Metternich feared that if the princes' sovereign rights were too curtailed they would seek the protection of France and ally themselves with her. He was convinced that the Imperial dignity with no real power behind it would be unacceptable to Austria, but that to give the ruler power at the expense of the princes would be a revolutionary step. He hoped, rather, to win the support of the German princes by ensuring full sovereignty for them. Just at this time Austria joined the campaign against Napoleon and soon afterwards entered into the Treaty of Teplitz, by which complete independence was granted to the princes.

In December 1813 Wilhelm von Humboldt, at that time Prussian Ambassador to the Cabinet in Vienna, formulated the first of his great memoranda on the German question and sent it to Stein. He set out in masterly fashion that the future constitution of Germany must ensure for her people unity, freedom and strength in order to give them a sense of national identity, which was vital for their whole development. For a constitution to be effective and durable an appropriate national char-

acter was necessary. In Germany national consciousness had developed
only within the framework of the existing states and their multiplicity
had produced a great cultural diversity. Hence a unitary state was
neither possible nor desirable. The only thing to do was to create a
permanent confederation of independent states under sovereign princes,
and for this a firm friendship between Austria and Prussia, who would
jointly assume control, was indispensable. All princes should ensure
reciprocal defence by a formal alliance guaranteed by Russia and
England. The right to declare war in the event of aggression, as well as
to conclude peace, should be confined to Austria and Prussia. Germany
should keep completely free from entanglements in wars which did not
affect her immediate welfare. Humboldt went on to demand a common
supreme court of justice, the setting up in every state of diets which,
in the event of encroachments on their rights, could appeal to the
federal court, and, furthermore, improvements in the administration of
justice by the setting up of territorial supreme courts of appeal. On the
basis of the rulings of these courts a legislative council should gradually
fashion a code of German common law and the subject of any state
must have certain basic rights.

Soon after this memorandum of Humboldt's, Arndt, who was a close
collaborator of Stein's, also drafted a constitution for Germany. In it
he called above all for a supreme head of the *Reich* and an Imperial Diet
whose members should be elected by the Estates of the constituent
countries and include landowners, smallholders and members of the
middle class. The ministers were to be responsible to the Parliament.
Stein had cherished similar ideas in 1808, and had since discarded them,
but now as then he stood under the spell of the tradition of the old
Reich with its Habsburg Emperor and of the *Reichstag*, which was not
elected but made up of the Estates of the realm.

On 28 January 1814 the Allies laid down that Germany should
consist of a confederation (*Bund*) of independent princes. Stein thereupon proposed the founding of a German *Bund* with a directory and a
federal assembly. The administration of laws, foreign policy, command
of the army and decisions on war and peace should devolve on the
directory, to consist of Austria, Prussia, Bavaria and Hanover. Certain
rights of liberty should be granted to all subjects. The *Bund* would be
given powers of legislation which could override those of the individual
states which made it up.

Humboldt advocated the issue of a proclamation in which the Allies
should promise the German nation liberal reforms and, in the main, he
accepted Stein's latest proposals. He took a sceptical view of the
suggestion by the British Prince Regent that the Netherlands and
Switzerland should be invited to join the *Bund* but he recommended

the conclusion of defensive alliances. His advice that a liberal constitution for the *Bund* should be worked out forthwith was not taken.
The first Peace of Paris merely laid down that the German states
should be independent and form a *Bund*, but left the details to the
Congress of Vienna.

The Prussian Chancellor, Hardenberg, now drafted a plan on these
various proposals, and this was given to Stein to examine. The result
was a scheme for a federal constitution which ensured the rights of the
subject, left matters of general concern to the federal assembly and
particular questions to the individual diets. Stein returned to his idea
of excluding from the *Bund* most of Austria's and Prussia's German
territories. Hardenberg accepted this curious structure but insisted on
equal rights for Austria and Prussia in the control of the *Bund*. Stein
agreed but contrived that Austria should preside over all federal
assemblies. The plan further provided for the dividing up of Germany
into a series of districts (*Kreise*) under district administrators, which
closely resembled the constitution of the old *Reich*. At Britain's instance,
Switzerland and the Netherlands were to be invited to form a permanent
alliance with the *Bund*.

This plan was sent to Humboldt in Vienna so that he might win
Metternich's support for it, but he was against the exclusion of most of
the German territories held by Austria and Prussia and this point was
dropped in his negotiations with Metternich. As a result, however,
Austria and Prussia, both of whom also controlled territories outside
Germany, demanded exemption from the clause by which they might
wage war only with the agreement of the council of the major princes
and that by which the minimum rights to be granted to their provincial
diets would be dictated to them. Austria, Prussia and Hanover drew up
a new plan, which was to be laid before other German states. Stein
had misgivings about these deliberations, but suggested that the plan
should also be submitted to the great powers so that it might be discussed with the European balance of power in mind. On 14 October
1814 the new plan, called the 'Twelve Articles', was laid before a
committee of the Congress, on which, apart from Austria and Prussia,
Hanover, Bavaria and Württemberg also sat. Bavaria and Württemberg
raised strenuous objections to every article which restricted their full
sovereignty, although in earlier agreements such limitations had been
expressly provided for. It is notable that the energy shown by Metternich in supporting important articles which promoted national and
liberal development was by no means apparent in his subsequent
attitude. Stein sought to enlist the aid of the Tsar, the minor princes
and German public opinion against the objections of Bavaria and
Württemberg. In particular, he strongly advocated setting up provincial

diets with legislative powers. A manifesto by twenty-nine of the smaller princes supported this demand and called, moreover, for a restoration of the Empire.

The dispute over Saxony and Poland created an ugly situation. True, a war between Austria, Britain and France on the one hand and Russia and Prussia on the other was ultimately avoided, but a deep resentment remained between Austria and Prussia, which unfavourably affected further progress in the German constitutional question. Both states sought to win over as many of the medium and smaller princes as possible and therefore made them concessions which for the most part worked against national unity and freedom. None the less the negotiations made progress. In February and March 1815 Stein was agitating for a Habsburg Emperor with greater resources of power and he was supported by the Tsar: but this in turn met strong opposition, even from Emperor Francis. The stipulation that all states should have national diets also aroused tough opposition, because many princes felt this to be an infringement of their sovereignty. But some rulers agreed on their own initiative to the creation of diets, thus anticipating the constitution. After Napoleon's landing in France, many princes grew even more uncompromising and others withdrew from the negotiations. Austria, Prussia and Hanover, on the other hand, wanted to hasten a settlement and were therefore ready to make considerable concessions. Humboldt's stipulation about parliaments in all states was so altered as to be utterly ineffective. Freedom of the press, as well as various constitutional rights, met a similar fate. At Bavaria's instance the idea of a federal court of justice was dropped.

A FEDERATION OF STATES

The result was that Germany did not become one federal state but a federation of states in which national independence, unity and freedom were insufficiently marked or assured. This aroused great disappointment in many circles. It was cold comfort for the powers to declare that even incomplete provisions were better than none at all. Metternich stated that this was only a beginning, the outline of a constitution which the Federal Assembly (*Bundestag*) would itself have to fill in.

The memorandum of association, called the Act of Confederation, was later supplemented or altered in many respects. It set forth that the Federal Diet should at once draw up rules binding on all members for the freedom of the press and copyright as well as trade, commerce and navigation. The seat of the Diet was Frankfurt. Its members undertook to protect not only Germany but also each state individually against aggression, and in any war in which the *Bund* was engaged – the declaration of which needed a two-thirds majority – to conduct no unilateral negotiations with the enemy. They could enter into alliances but not against the *Bund* or its member states; in no circumstances could they engage in war with one another but had to submit any disputes to the Diet for settlement. In all countries of the *Bund* a constitution providing for assemblies of Estates was to be issued. Christians of all denominations were to have equal rights and the Diet was to discuss improving the civil rights of Jews.

The *Bund* was a permanent union of German states to preserve Germany's external and internal security and the independence and inviolability of the individual states. The number of founder members was 38 – 34 princes and 4 free cities. The former included the Emperor of Austria and the Kings of Prussia, Bavaria, Württemberg, Saxony, England, Denmark and the Netherlands. Five of these rulers were members of the *Bund* only in respect of their German territories. Many countries outside the *Bund* had a considerable German population. Austria presided over all the assemblies. The princes and Free Cities sent representatives to the federal assembly, which had an inner council with a total voting strength of 17 but which for all more important matters converted itself into a general assembly in which 69 votes could be cast. Here the greater princes had several votes but the minor rulers only one. When one consideres the size of the populations concerned, the distribution of votes appears absurd. The seven states of more than a million inhabitants numbered 26 millions in all and had 27 votes. The smaller states, with a total of a mere 4·2 millions, had 42 votes. Furthermore, in the general assembly a majority of two-thirds or unanimity, as the case might be, was necessary for a motion to be carried. Thus, in the most important matters some pygmy of a prince, or a group of such, could apply a veto in the face of those who ruled over the great majority of Germans!

The Diet had certain rights of legislation, jurisdiction and administration, but in practice their exercise was extremely limited. The stipulation of unanimity or a two-thirds majority on all important issues, as well as the great number of members of the *Bund*, put policy-making into the hands of thirty-eight states, which slowed up business considerably. The Diet was an assembly of diplomats whose members constantly had to refer back to their governments for instructions on how they should vote. Like the old *Reichstag*, it was not an assembly of elected national representatives and a parliamentary system could not develop, especially as in the general assembly there was absolutely no debate, merely a vote for or against the motions drawn up by the inner council. Moreover, from 1824 the assemblies were in effect held *in camera*.

In theory, the *Bund* had the full powers of a state *vis-à-vis* foreign countries; it could receive and accredit ambassadors, but it made no use of this power, and besides, the individual states of the *Bund* had the same rights of diplomatic representation. The *Bund* could conduct war and make peace. The princes of Germany who wore foreign crowns were supposed to rule their German and non-German territories separately, but in practice this was scarcely feasible. Thus Austria sent German troops to Italy and Britain Hanoverians to Portugal. The stipulation that princes who were not foreign monarchs might not conduct war independently had run into opposition from Bavaria and had consequently not been incorporated into the act of association, though in 1820 it was written into the final statute of Vienna.

The executive powers of the *Bund* could be exercised only by the organs of its members as the *Bund* possessed none of its own. The form of the civil rights guaranteed to the Germans was very unsatisfactory. In the old *Reich* the Peace of 1548 and the Peace of Westphalia of 1648 had given all subjects the right of free movement and trade in all states. In the Federal Statute this right was not guaranteed to them; it needed the approval of the government of the country concerned. The Federal Statute was incorporated in the Treaty of Vienna. This led to the contention that the *Bund* was thereby guaranteed by all the eight states which had signed the Treaty of Vienna, including Britain, France, Portugal, Spain, Russia and Sweden. Later Britain and France attempted to derive from this a right to intervene in German affairs, but the *Bund* rejected this. However, foreign powers, especially Russia, enjoyed considerable influence in Germany through family ties with German royal houses. Summing up, one can probably say that the *Bund* gave many Germans the feeling that Germany did not enjoy the same prestige as the other great powers.

It is quite understandable that the Federal Statute was not very well received by German public opinion. The press used what freedom it still had to voice sharp criticism and indulge in satire and cartoons. But one cannot help asking oneself how many Germans were really interested in constitutional questions or had any clear notions of them. Certainly there were many who were enthusiastic about unity and freedom but it was very difficult to make any concrete plans to achieve them. After the war, the broad masses had relapsed into political apathy and there was little tendency to keep alive the memory of German victories. Even Blücher, the most popular German general, did not live on in the memory of the masses. His picture was scarcely ever to be found in cottages or the parlours of country inns.

All this was principally due to widespread economic and mental exhaustion. The wars with France had lasted two decades and even those states who had bowed to Napoleon were hard hit. They had had to provide him with vast numbers of troops, and hundreds of thousands of German soldiers had fallen in battle both for and against him. True, his rule had brought some states advantages which should not be underestimated, but these were offset by the denial of all forms of freedom, such as assemblies of the Estates and free speech, by the grievous effects of the continental blockade, by oppressive war levies, high taxes and a paper economy with all its disrupting and demoralising consequences. After the war there were several bad harvests and a chronic economic crisis brought on by competition from Britain which simply could not be met. As happens after any long war, there were countless people who through wounds or sickness or the rigours of military life had been rendered unfit or unwilling to devote themselves to reconstruction. Small wonder that the great majority showed no interest in constitutional questions, and even the minority who were attracted by the ideals of liberty and unity persisted in the tradition of considering the State in which they had grown up as their fatherland. True, under Napoleon many small territories had been united with large neighbouring states, but the inhabitants of these areas showed strong resistance to such measures, even when they were in their own cultural and economic interest.

LIBERAL CRITICISM

Liberal tradition ascribes the shortcomings of the *Bund* to the narrow dynastic selfishness of the powers assembled at the Congress of Vienna. This is true, but it is not the whole truth. The strivings for reform by leading statesmen at the Congress were only frustrated by a small minority, headed by Bavaria and Württemberg, and by particular circumstances which forced acceptance of this minority's objections. It is in any case very doubtful whether an assembly in which the voice of the German peoples could have made itself heard would have created a stronger German unity.

The historian Gervinus saw a parallel to the origin of the *Bund* in the development which was proceeding at the same time in Switzerland. Here it was a question of giving the country a new constitution in place of the one dictated by Napoleon. In Switzerland there were no princes and it was a mixture of aristocratic and democratic elements – the urban patriciate, the guilds and the peasants – which had the say. The common people had more influence on politics than in any other state in Europe. However, the constitution which the Swiss secured for themselves was to a large extent an imitation of that of the *Bund*. The Swiss Federal Assembly, just like the German, was a congress of plenipotentiaries of sovereign states with very little legislative or executive power, There existed neither general civil rights nor common law, neither a standard currency nor freedom of movement, domicile or trade. Only diplomacy and the army were more unified than in Germany. Not until the revolutionary year 1848 did national unity make substantial strides in both Germany and Switzerland. Gervinus also observes that the delay in attaining national unity probably brought advantages as well. The fulfilment of Stein's dream – which many others shared – of giving the crown of Germany to the Emperor of Austria, would have linked Germany closely with the domains of the House of Austria. Would this have served the cause of German unity and freedom in the age of Metternich? On the other hand, as Gervinus also notes, the hatred which many German peoples felt for one another (particularly that directed against Prussia) would have reached a climax. He therefore argues that it was perhaps just as well that the mutually warring elements were not forced to combine but that time was gained in which internal divisions could be bridged. From this point of view, he says, the loose federation was perhaps an advantage, even a necessity.

A large section of German liberals was widely read in political matters and had also studied British and French politics. Many of them were aristocrats or state officials to whom the practice of diplomacy and administration was not familiar. Their main interest was the introduction of liberal reforms, such as the setting up of a popular representative body, freedom of the press, basic civil rights and an unfettered economy. As for German unity, this in no wise connoted for them a centralising constitution or the concentration of all resources for national power politics. The goal was co-operation between all German states and peoples to safeguard Germany against her enemies, to develop her economically and culturally and to win her a position of respect among the nations. The Federal Act was a disappointment inasmuch as it did not translate many hopes into reality. On the other hand, it did not debar the carrying out of its provisions, which were for the most part vaguely framed, in a progressive sense. Thus, for example, nothing stood in the way of a voluntary combination of the member states into a great economic unity. From the very outset there were, in fact, many well-informed Germans who hoped that the *Bund* would develop profitably. Professor August Crome, for instance, wrote a book devoted to the Federal Diet and set out a programme which he hoped it would implement. Crome was a highly respected scholar, whose books and memoirs show him to be a pronounced liberal. The main value of the *Bund*, he declared, lay in the preservation of peace, for of all evils war was the greatest. The large regular armies should be abolished and replaced by national militias, and this would put an end to wars of conquest. Crome came out in favour of improving international law, creating a common German legal code and a unified economic area, and establishing national education on Pestalozzi's principles. He also spoke out in favour of a free press, a very moderate censorship and the creation in every state of an assembly elected by all active citizens, and he recommended an hereditary emperor from the pacific House of Austria. However, he desired neither a centralised administration nor a joint national assembly. The Emperor's prime task appeared to him to be safeguarding the rule of law.

A remarkable book about the *Bund* was also written by the prominent historian, Professor Heeren. Under a highly centralised monarchy, he wrote, Germany might easily be tempted to aspire to predominance in Europe and this might become very dangerous for her own freedom. Therefore, he went on, the Peace of Westphalia had rightly established the principle of 'German freedom', i.e. that in practice the princes should be independent of the Emperor. The German *Bund* was, he said, strong enough for defence but too weak for attack. It was the bulwark of peace, order and justice in Europe.

THE FEDERAL STATUTE

The Federal Statute had laid down that the Federal Diet should begin work on 1 September 1815, but the date was postponed for more than fourteen months because all various territorial and other questions had first to be settled. Both Austria and Prussia offered Stein the post of their plenipotentiary at the Assembly and as the Austrian delegate he would have been President, but he declined Austria's repeated invitations and offered Prussia terms which her government found unacceptable. He was an embittered man and mistrusted Metternich and Hardenberg alike. The Assembly was finally opened on 5 November 1816. The Austrian delegate, Count Buol-Schauenstein, stressed in his inaugural address that the *Bund* was the outcome of national aspirations which were rooted in history. The German, he said, loved knowledge and scholarship, trade and industry, art and, in particular, religion. The German nation occupied a high place in all branches of civilisation, and this was mainly to be ascribed to the number and variety of its states and capital cities. But German nationality had always formed a unifying bond between them. He went on to say that the Emperor of Austria did not regard his position at their head as a means to engage in power politics but simply as one of management. He would always respect and act on the general will and abide by the principle that all members were equal and independent. This passage in the speech marked a contrast to Prussia's policy, which had repeatedly envisaged dividing up Germany between Austria and Prussia. The President further said that for historical reasons the *Bund* could not be either a federal state or a mere alliance but represented a federation of states which at the same time was to safeguard German nationality.

This definition of the nature of the *Bund* was criticised in those circles which cherished the ideal of a closely united Germany. The periodical *Nemesis* found the declaration of the President self-contradictory and argued that a federation of states could safeguard nationality only if it developed into one federal state. This was in fact the crux of the problem but hard to solve when so many states clung obstinately to their independence and individuality.

The Diet was largely composed of diplomats who leaned towards moderate progress in national and political matters. After all, such feelings were at the time widespread among educated people of all classes and even among senior public officials and heirs to thrones. At all events the Diet began work with the intention of nurturing the seeds of unity and freedom contained in the federal constitution. The assembly had received many complaints of alleged infringements of rights by individual governments, along with requests for help. Did the *Bund* have the right to intervene in the internal affairs of states to assist subjects against their own governments? There was general agreement that it was entitled to do so where there was any denial of justice, but it was often hard to prove that injustice had actually been done. Of especial importance were complaints from those subjects of the Elector of Hesse-Cassel who, under the former French régime, had bought portions of state domains. The new government declared the purchase invalid since the previous régime had been illegal. The question was knotty and occupied the Diet for many years.[1] The Elector of Hesse-Cassel made a sharp protest against the admission of the complaint by the Diet, but the president declared that such protests would not deter the *Bund* from helping oppressed subjects. Germany had been freed from foreign rule by the blood of her peoples and the rightful rulers had been restored to ensure that everywhere despotism should give way to the rule of law. The assembly unanimously adopted this declaration. So energetic a stand for the rights of the subject aroused the wrath of the Elector of Hesse-Cassel, and Metternich reproved the Austrian delegate Buol-Schauenstein for his bold speech. In a case like this, the *Bund* possessed no means of carrying out its decisions if the government concerned proved unco-operative. The public discussion, however, in which the most prominent jurists took

---

[1] Detailed exposés by prominent legal experts are those of Murhard in Rotteck and Welcker: *Staatslexikon,* 2nd ed. Vol. IV, pp. 99–130; and H. A. Zachariae in *Zeitschrift für Staatswissenschaften,* Vol. IX.

part, roused public feeling to such an extent that the Government of Cassel thought it prudent to make concessions. Later, negotiations were opened which led in many cases to satisfactory compromises.

The fact that the Diet had supported subjects against their ruler incensed the conservatives in a number of states. The delegates in Frankfurt were henceforth subjected to stricter control, and now had, in most cases, to refer back to their governments for instructions and these were often a long time in arriving. None the less, the majority of the delegates showed a certain liberal tendency for several more years.

The Diet further attempted in its early years to put into effect the somewhat indefinite promises in its constitution regarding civil rights and the safeguarding of the interests of the community. Thus, for example, leaving one state and settling down in another was made easier, although in some instances freedom of movement within federal territory was still subject to limitations. The constitution had held out prospects of laws governing the freedom of the press and copyright, and the assembly set about drafting a law for the press in a liberal spirit.

In 1816, poor harvests caused a steep rise in the prices of commodities, there was much suffering among the people and almost all states banned the export of foodstuffs. The Assembly sought to bring about an agreement whereby states with a surplus of corn and cattle should permit free export to other states, but this plan foundered on Bavaria's jealousy of Austria. Soon after, the questions of free trade within the *Bund* and protection against foreign competition were raised, the German manufacturers calling for measures against the strong competition from British industry, but even in this sphere no settlement was reached. On the other hand, the Diet did have more success in military matters. The principle that the *Bund* should confine itself solely to defence against aggression was established. In consequence, fortresses had to be built and in case of war every state was to make 0·5% of its revenue available for the federal army. The strength of the army amounted to 150,000 and the cost of maintaining it a little less than one million Rhenish florins. Building a fleet had not been considered, and when in 1817 German ships were attacked and plundered by pirates from Algiers and Tunis, the *Bund* was completely helpless.

The federal constitution had laid down that the legal position of the Jews was to be improved. This gave rise to long debates, especially with the Frankfurt Senate. The Diet, as well as Prussia and Austria, was favourably disposed to the claims of the Jews, while the city of Frankfurt wanted to continue to deny them civil rights. In the end a few concessions were secured, but the Jews felt justly disappointed.

The most important question which occupied the federal diet was the interpretation of article 13 concerning constitutions providing for the setting up of assemblies of Estates in all countries. Many delegates were of the opinion that the *Bund* had the right to compel states to allow these to be set up. Reactionary statesmen in the individual countries were naturally opposed to any intervention by the Diet in response to petitions demanding the restoration or introduction of state assemblies. The *Bundestag* adopted a resolution put forward by Austria and supported by Prussia, calling on all states of the federation which still had no assembly but wished to create one, to report progress to the *Bund* within a year.

Joseph Görres

Those spokesmen for a national movement who have already been discussed – Arndt, Fichte and Jahn – came from the Protestant North, as did also Adam Müller, who was later converted to Catholicism, and Friedrich Gentz. In South Germany the Confederation of the Rhine and Napoleon's régime had many convinced adherents. Hegel mocked at the movement for liberation, which he called 'North German patriotism'.

Joseph Görres (1776–1848) was a most unusual figure. He was a Rhinelander who had once greeted the French Revolution with rapturous enthusiasm; he had scarcely left school when he became a leading light in the movement to make his native country a republic under French protection. He would have liked best of all to convert the Rhineland, along with Belgium, Alsace and Switzerland, into a federation of republics between France and Germany, but since France insisted on incorporating the Rhenish provinces, Görres accepted this solution. Even as a young man he was a persuasive popular orator and writer, but closer acquaintance with French politicians and their venality sickened and sobered him so much that his attitude changed completely and he became a sharp critic of French despotism. Since he could not admit this openly he withdrew from public life and devoted himself to extensive scientific studies. In 1806 he settled in Heidelberg and joined the circle of the Romanticists there. Gradually his philosophy of life changed; in his youth he hated all churches and religions as enemies of freedom, and it was some considerable time before he turned to the Catholic church and finally emerged as a champion of the cultural and political aspirations of the German Catholics.

Early in 1814, when the war of liberation began and the Allies crossed the Rhine, Görres founded a periodical called *Der Rheinische Merkur*, which aroused attention throughout Europe. Napoleon himself is said to have remarked that now a fifth great power had declared war on him. The paper appeared four times a week and was written largely by

Görres himself. In addition, the Allies put him in charge of public education in the Rhine provinces, with the task of reorganising the schools. The *Rheinische Merkur* was so brilliantly written that Friedrich Gentz, one of the great publicists of his age and a declared opponent of Görres' policies, wrote that hardly any writer had ever surpassed Görres in his lofty, formidable, indeed diabolical vein. Görres was immensely knowledgeable and had a vivid imagination and a unique power of words. When the old *Reich* collapsed he had pronounced a satirical funeral oration over it which was a masterpiece. Now the fall of Napoleon moved him to publish an alleged proclamation by the Emperor to the peoples of Europe which was witheringly critical of the allied governments. It was generally accepted as genuine and widely published in the press. Even the French declared that it was the Emperor's testament and the best manifesto he had ever issued.

Görres himself now took up the cudgels for German unity and freedom, this time under a Habsburg Emperor who was to have effective power at his disposal. Görres' pronounced love of freedom and his independence soon brought him into sharp conflict with the German powers. In the states of the former Confederation of the Rhine, he was attacked by the newspapers which shortly before had been singing Napoleon's praises. In Bavaria, Baron von Aretin published the paper *Allemannia*, which vigorously attacked the ideas of the North German freedom movement. An anonymous article set about Görres with biting sarcasm and caused a stir. The most important daily paper in Germany, the *Hamburger Unparteiische Korrespondent*, was criticising Görres as early as 1814 because he wanted to outlaw the French people. The paper declared that this could only lead to their turning again to Napoleon for salvation and that Görres should be regarded as a Napoleonist in disguise. On 16 May 1815 the Prussian Chancellor Hardenberg finally issued a warning that the *Rheinische Merkur* was giving rise to serious complaints. War was being waged only against Napoleon, not against the French people, and Görres should stop whipping up passions, particularly by his agitation for a renewal of the German Imperial dignity. As Görres took no notice, his paper was suppressed on 3 January 1816, apparently at the instance of the Tsar.

Brockhaus's Deutsche Blätter

Another paper which is of interest is the *Deutsche Blätter*, founded in Leipzig in 1813 by the publisher F. A. Brockhaus and primarily intended to cater for the needs of readers in time of war. A peak circulation of 4,000 was reached, but this fell to 1,100 at the end of the war and, since the censorship continued to cause difficulties, Brockhaus closed the paper down. Most of those who wrote for it were scholars. As far as France was concerned, the paper shared Görres' views and made vigorous attacks not only on Napoleon but also on the French people, and demanded that France should cede all territories annexed from Germany. Even if the Alsatians were hostile to Germany, the paper argued, they did not wish to become French but merely to belong to a big state in the modern style. If Germany had nothing better to offer them than the conditions obtaining in a small German state, then one could not demand their incorporation. On the other hand, there was the possibility of annexing them and de-Frenchifying them and in three years they would feel themselves Germans. Furthermore, the fusion of the German states and the small contiguous states into one large federation was mooted. The attitude towards France was not, however, the same in all articles: in one[1] it was even said that the peace was not as bad as many people thought, and in any case it was better to endure injustice than to perpetrate it. If the return of the stolen territories had been insisted upon, then perhaps a fresh war would have broken out. Germany needed a period of calm for the constitutional struggles which faced her. The real enemies, the hyenas and those who fawned upon despots, were in Germany.

In home politics the paper was markedly liberal; Britain was its ideal. It called for a strong state under an emperor, who should be Austrian, but it was also well disposed towards Prussia, particularly because of her enlightenment and Protestantism. But Prussia lacked a national parliament; Austria could the more easily be forgiven this lack because of the backwardness of many of the nations within her ambit. The educated Jew who accepted baptism deserved civil rights, but not the orthodox Jew, who was a parasite.

Luden

A significant role was also played by the journal *Nemesis*, founded by a history professor at Jena, Heinrich Luden. True, he advocated a constitutional monarchy, but in reality he pursued republican aims. Luden was a friend of Jahn and shared many of his ideas. An article in *Nemesis* in 1814 dealt with the concept of *Deutschheit* (the distinctive attributes of the German), which exercised both Luden and Jahn very strongly. For Luden this was not so much the quintessence of specific qualities, like good faith, courage, liberalism and so forth – which other peoples also possessed – as mutual fraternal affection, pride in the German language and the rejection of alien things which did not promote what was good and noble in the people. If they chanced to do so

[1] Vol. III, p. 326.

none the less, then they should be used for Germany's own enrichment. *Deutschheit* was a matter of straightforward intentions and plain dealings.

In later articles Luden indulged in polemics with Arndt, in whose writings he found much to criticise. None the less, he praised Arndt for his noble enthusiasm for moral dignity, his great patriotism and his bold, liberal spirit. Luden condemned wars which aimed at destroying other nations' independence. After the war, Germany should receive her linguistic frontiers, which, in his opinion, coincided almost everywhere with the natural frontiers necessary for the mutual security of both sides. Since Luden included Low German as part of the German language, he regarded Belgium and Holland as falling within the German sphere, as well as Switzerland and Alsace. But if these peoples preferred to remain under foreign rule, then this merely demonstrated that Germany was in great need of improvement by internal reforms. Luden believed that the German-speaking population of France would gladly join an independent Germany, and so would Switzerland, Belgium and Holland.

When Napoleon returned from Elba and was jubilantly acclaimed by some sections of the French people, this gave rise to a discussion in *Nemesis* about whether the French people should not be held responsible for the war and whether it would not be justifiable to reduce France's power to the greatest possible extent. Many who took part in the debate in the pages of *Nemesis* inclined to this view, but one article, probably by Luden himself, took the other view: the majority of the French, it ran, could not be made responsible for the lack of principles of a minority, and the partition or enslavement of France would not only be cruel and inhuman but also inexpedient. If German unity became a fact, then one would have nothing to fear from the French.

In many articles Luden directed sharp criticism at the constitution of the *Bund*. It was not a federation of peoples but of princes, he said. The hope that the constitution would later be improved was ill-founded; it would, rather, grow worse. Luden protested especially at the fact that the Federal Statute declared the princes to be sovereign.

On the whole, Luden's experience of the results gained shortly before by diplomacy filled him with bitterness. The peace treaty, he said, was not based on justice towards either the Germans or the French. In contrast to these gloomy views there appeared an article signed 'O', probably from the pen of Professor Lorenz Oken. In his view freedom was everywhere on the march. The great powers had, in noble concord, concluded in Paris a very wise peace which excluded blind vengefulness and foolish expansionism and was based on justice and moderation.

Oken

Oken, too, published a weekly paper – *Isis, Enzyklopädische Zeitung* (1817–8). He was a distinguished personality, humane, devoted to his ideals and marked by a bluntness which involved him in many controversies. His subjects were science and natural philosophy and he sought to develop Schelling's doctrines in these fields. Soon after his paper was launched, Oken published an article in which the new constitution of the Grand Duchy of Weimar, in which he lived, was described as an utter failure. This constitution, because it was one of the first to be granted, was made much of by the liberals. Oken criticised it for giving intellectuals the franchise only if they were property-owners and for not establishing basic civil rights. Soon after, the paper printed a memorandum by Baron von Wangenheim, who wrote that political liberty was striding irresistibly forward and could not be suppressed. There were two extreme tendencies which must both be rejected – despotism and Jacobinism. He criticised the King of Prussia and the Montgelas régime in Bavaria for wavering between the two extremes, adding that this might lead to the danger of a general revolution in Germany. In political matters Oken's style was often very intemperate, and in 1818 he was sentenced to six weeks' confinement in a fortress for libelling the prince and the authorities of his own and other countries, but he was acquitted on appeal. Goethe, as a minister in Weimar, was for suppressing *Isis* but the Grand Duke was against this idea. Finally Oken was removed from his chair, but in 1827 he received another in Munich, from which he was dismissed in 1832, and he ultimately took up a professorship in Zürich.

The Kieler Blätter

The press enjoyed freedom in the Duchies of Schleswig and Holstein and this favoured the founding in 1815 of a bi-monthly, the *Kieler Blätter*, published by the professors Dahlmann, Welcker, Falck and Twesten. This paper was soon one of the leading organs of liberalism; Dahlmann became the most outstanding liberal leader in North Germany and Welcker in the South. The paper was widely read not only in academic circles but also by aristocratic landowners and Protestant clergy. The *Kieler Blätter* championed all liberal demands, most notably for assemblies, both in the individual states and Germany as a whole. The Estates, the paper claimed, had been illegally suppressed, and at the same time it called for their reform and for a wider franchise which should be extended to smallholders and those in the liberal professions, who at the time were excluded in England and many other countries if they were not property-owners. The suffrage was to be used for direct representation. Count Baudissin advocated the abolition of all aristocratic privileges. As in England, only the eldest son should inherit the title and property. More political activity on the part of the nobility was desirable; they could act as a moderating influence and the guardians of tradition. The editors were well versed in English history and politics and considered the political experience they had gained in England useful for Germany's future. The paper published the letter of an anonymous Englishman who had come to Germany to study conditions there. The writer had wanted to verify in particular whether the prevailing opinion in England that German literature was immoral was well founded. He found that it was, adducing as proof Goethe's *Werther*, Schiller's *Räuber* and works by Wieland and Kotzebue. He found the reason for this in the fact that the Germans esteemed form at the expense of moral content and utility, not only in literature but also in science, education and military matters.

The *Kieler Blätter* held that it was important for every people to preserve its national characteristics and evolve a public mind. Welcker took the view that the Germans, by their disposition and humaneness, left the way open to far too many unfavourable influences. Nationality was necessary in order to give to the people within a state an inner unity, to counteract class distinctions and to promote the formation of public opinion. A Councillor of State, von Berger, declared that the Germans, by reason of their isolated situation, the infertility of their soil and so forth, had been spared Roman rule and hence had enjoyed a more peaceful, if slower, development. He condemned the preaching of hatred towards the French, saying that only in a semi-barbaric stage of civilisation did national differences lead to war. The ultimate aim was to unite all peoples in a federation of states. Man's true fatherland was the realm of the mind and it was the Germans' greatest glory that they tended towards cosmopolitanism.

Naturally enough, the *Kieler Blätter* gave considerable attention to the relations between Germans and Danes in Schleswig-Holstein.[1]

DIFFICULTIES FACING THE PRESS

The periodicals which have been described above were founded and published to represent liberal and national views. With few exceptions the publication of newspapers was scarcely profitable and journalism offered no financial attractions as a profession. The press suffered under the régime of Napoleon and the long period of economic exhaustion. In consequence, even in larger towns newspapers had a small circulation and their very format looked wretched. At the end of 1815 the Prussian Government collected circulation figures for the

[1] Vide infra, p. 233ff.

Rhine provinces, an area which was economically the most advanced. The leading paper was the *Kölnische Zeitung*, which printed between 1,500 and 2,000 copies. After this came others with sales of 1,600, 1,400 and 1,200, but of all the remainder not one printed more than a few hundred copies.

The launching of new papers was made extremely difficult by the fact that those already in existence enjoyed great privileges. In earlier times one needed permission from the Government to start a newspaper, and for this a considerable sum had to be paid, which in its turn protected the papers against new competitors. Sometimes a Government might own a paper which it handed over to a contractor to run in return for an annual payment. There were also cases in which a Government granted a newspaper a monopoly in order to help its publication. In Prussia Frederick William I had decreed in 1727 that *Intelligenzblätter* should be founded in all the larger towns; their task was to publish Government decrees and to print news which might be of technical use to farmers, craftsmen and so on. The Government granted them the monopoly of publishing advertisements, for which they were paid; they were, of course, completely at the beck and call of the Government and avoided any political utterance which was not officially inspired. In consequence publishers or writers who wanted to found a new paper to further their political ideals often met stiff resistance from the older papers, which invoked their privileges. If, however, newcomers did succeed in founding a paper, then there usually began for them a long struggle with the censor, who often found the most petty fault with the articles which were to appear and punished any lapses with temporary or permanent prohibition. Consequently many newly-founded papers closed down, sometimes on instructions from the Government but often because the publisher himself had grown tired of the unending pinpricks.

In these circumstances the formation of public opinion was an extraordinarily difficult matter, but gradually, in spite of all obstacles, some newspapers of a higher journalistic calibre, with editors for the most part liberal in outlook, established themselves. But it required great skill, discretion and luck to avoid fatal conflicts with the censor. An adroit journalist could convey a great deal by allusions or by adducing historical parallels, but this presupposed a highly literate readership and was suitable neither for the less educated classes nor for the young and ardent. Many liberals were, moreover, very doctrinaire. They waxed enthusiastic over Montesquieu and Rousseau, Kant and Fichte, they were well read in the history of revolutions in England and France and believed that there they would find all the lessons necessary for Germany. Unfortunately they often knew little of what the lower classes in their own country thought and needed, and they were just as unfamiliar with the upper strata of society. They were frequently incapable of rousing the interest of the lower classes, whereas the land-owning aristocracy and officials who had dealings with the broad masses of the people were much better informed and therefore played a large part in the liberal movement.

A prominent position in the German press was occupied by Cotta's *Allgemeine Zeitung*,[1] which was now appearing in Augsburg and had 2,719 subscribers in 1815. This dealt tactfully and succinctly with German politics and was not in sympathy with the national movement. On the other hand, it devoted great attention to French politics and always retained a number of sound Paris correspondents who kept the editorial desk well primed with news. The detailed reports of debates in the French Chamber which appeared in the *Allgemeine Zeitung* strengthened in many liberals the hope that in Germany, too, a constitutional way of life would emerge. This was the only German paper which also circulated widely in Austria. Cotta had close links with the Austrian Government, and this restricted his freedom to discuss Austrian affairs critically. Prussia was dealt with even more cursorily in his columns. The *Allgemeine Zeitung* could scarcely be called a liberal paper, although the publisher, editor-in-chief and many who wrote for it were friends of progress and liberty and sometimes wrote articles in a liberal vein. The paper thus made some contribution to the spread of liberal views.

Johann Friedrich Cotta, created a baron in 1817, played a great part in the establishment of a liberal constitution in Württemberg and was for a long time vice-president of the Diet. In 1829 his diplomatic skill succeeded in getting Bavaria and Württemberg admitted to the German Customs Union. Not only was he the leading German publisher of books and newspapers, but he also founded other large concerns, acquired extensive property, improved agricultural technique and promoted many cultural aims. Kings and leading statesmen entrusted him with important missions and confided their secrets to him. For all this, Cotta was always at pains to help young and talented radical writers like Boerne and Heine, Wirth and Gutzkow. He gave them good posts on his papers and enabled them to make a name for themselves. Nor were his aims in this by any means predominantly commercial, for the *Allgemeine Zeitung* and other undertakings were not running at a profit and when Cotta died it was found that his liabilities exceeded his assets. However, his son, who succeeded him, soon settled his debts and continued to run the firm in the old traditions.

[1] Vide supra, p. 15f.

5

NATIONALISM, LIBERALISM AND RADICALISM

ARGUMENTS OVER WAR AIMS

The war was barely over when the progressives and reactionaries clashed. Theodor Schmalz, a Prussian administrator, professor, judge, and brother-in-law of General von Scharnhorst, wrote a pamphlet in which he accused the Prussian patriots who had fought in the wars of liberation of revolutionary aims in the re-organisation of Germany and called them latter-day Jacobins. Their plans for German unity, he said, did not accord with the spirit of the German people; harmony could not be achieved by agitation for civil war. Schmalz dismissed the argument that the people had made heroic sacrifices in order to win political freedom; they had simply obeyed the King's orders out of a sense of duty. The supposed patriots, he said, were organised into secret societies which plotted revolution.

This pamphlet caused lively controversy. Niebuhr rejected Schmalz's assertion as false, and said that despite all rumours no secret societies existed. In any free and vigorous country political parties were a necessity, and those suppressing them were playing into the hands of despotism. The Prussians were not of a revolutionary cast of mind and knew that without the King the state would break into pieces. The people had risen against foreign rule not merely out of obedience but out of positive conviction.

Ludwig Wieland, son of the celebrated writer and editor of the Weimar liberal paper *Der Patriot*, wrote that Schmalz asserted always having opposed the ideas of the French Revolution. This was quite correct, he continued: Schmalz and a few other obscurantists had been the only German writers to do so. All the others, including the very greatest, had seen in the Revolution the dawn of a brighter future.

STUDENT MOVEMENTS

Professors and students have always played an important part in shaping political opinion in Germany. In England it was principally the landed nobility, the gentry and the business world which took the lead, and in France the cultured aristocracy, lawyers and journalists were to the fore. Germany's trade and industry and general prosperity were far less developed, but on the other hand her division into numerous states had produced an extremely large number of universities, officials and intellectuals who were also prominent in politics. The organisation of German universities differed from that in other Western states. The English universities were independent of the government and had more ties with the Church than with the State, and the preservation of the medieval collegiate system in England helped to maintain discipline. In France, Napoleon had made the universities completely dependent on the Government. In Germany, too, the universities were dependent on the state but they possessed a considerable measure of self-government. The principal income of the professors came from the fees paid by the students. The professors and students were exempt from state jurisdiction except in serious cases. Most civil and criminal cases were heard by university courts, which usually winked an eye if a student did not pay his creditors or came to fisticuffs with the police. If a student had committed a serious crime, his friends often protected him by threatening to leave the university *en masse* if the charge against him were not dropped, for they could easily find another university not too far away where they would be readily admitted. Hence the mere fact that the universities were numerous impaired discipline.

For a long time the behaviour of students had given rise to serious complaints. They often lived a wild life, drank immoderately, fought many duels and were always ready to break the peace on the slightest pretext. Students from different parts of Germany were organised into *Landsmannschaften* (regional corps) according to their place of origin, and these corps were constantly brawling with one another, which, to use the term current at the time, was put down to their 'nationalism'. In the old empire, the *Reichstag* and many governments had tried in vain to stamp out the worst excesses of student life.

The wars of liberation had an extraordinary effect on the students. Even earlier, Fichte had tried hard to lead them away from their dissolute life and improve their morals. In doing so, he himself had to suffer from the coarseness which was customary in their circles, but he did succeed in gathering round him a large and enthusiastic following. Later, when he joined in the movement for liberation, he wanted to assign a great historic mission to the younger generation. They were not only to bring political freedom to the German nation but to refine its spirit and thus set an example to all nations. Arndt, Jahn and other prophets also addressed themselves to the young. The war gave them an opportunity to fight for the removal of foreign domination and thus open up the path to freedom. Words like these, of course, gave the rising generation an extraordinary sense of its own worth.

Such sections of German youth as were exposed to influences like this underwent a significant inner change. They were filled with a sincere urge for moral, social and political progress. Their aims were to efface the evil effects of the fragmentation of Germany, to bridge social divisions and to translate the idea of freedom into reality. Even during the war organisations were founded to preserve patriotic spirit, further national aspirations and serve Germany's moral re-birth. From the Romanticists emerged the concept of a Christian-German character which the students should foster. Many evinced religious enthusiasm and praised Luther as a champion of freedom. But the Christian-German ideal was often linked with hostility towards the Jews, some of whom had made considerable profits on army contracts in the Napoleonic period and who were, for the most part, among those who supported Napoleon as their liberator. The national movement also tended to oppose the German upper classes' taste for the French language and French customs, and to look instead to the Teutons of old as their pattern. Tacitus had praised their frugality, chastity and good faith and the student movement was all for emulating them in acquiring these virtues. Many student leaders also aired at length disparaging views on the French character.

The first important student organisation to back the national movement was founded in 1815 at the University of Jena and, at Jahn's suggestion, was called a *Burschenschaft*. Jahn took the word *Bursche*, which meant, among other things, a student, to be a word of Germanic origin which suggested his ideal of the German character, though it was actually derived from the Latin *bursarius*. The aims of the *Burschenschaft* were expressed in the phrase: 'Honour, Liberty and Fatherland' and its constitution was democratic. All its members addressed one another with the fraternal pronoun 'du'. Their colours were black, red and gold. It was also expected that the *Burschen* should wear the German costume devised by Jahn; hitherto students had dressed either in fantastic clothes or with a deliberate sloppiness. Duelling was to be permitted only as a last resort when the efforts of a court of honour to settle the dispute had failed. Many duels were, in fact, prevented and other bad habits among the students were curbed. The *Burschenschaft* was by no means revolutionary; Grand Duke Karl August of Weimar, who directly controlled the University of Jena and had the reputation of being one of the most liberal princes in Germany, was very satisfied with its spirit. It was supported by a number of professors, notably Heinrich Luden, Lorenz Oken and Jakob Friedrich Fries. The movement spread rapidly and *Burschenschaften* were formed at many other universities.

On 18 October 1817 a great festival of students from all parts of Germany was held at the Wartburg in Saxe-Weimar, where Luther had spent some memorable years. Their purpose was to celebrate the tercentenary of the Reformation and the fourth anniversary of the Battle of Leipzig. The tone of the speeches was temperate and solemn, but after the close of the proceedings a group of radical students from Jahn's circle demonstrated their hatred of the ruling powers. They gathered round a bonfire and threw into it various objects symbolic of political reaction. Among these were bundles of papers with the names of writers considered reactionary and anti-German. One of these was August von Kotzebue, a successful dramatist, whom the students blacklisted because of his History of Germany, in which, among other things, he had characterised Charlemagne as a despot and conqueror. In fact, Kotzebue had been one of the first writers to turn against Napoleon and in 1811 the French censor had banned the book because Napoleon looked on Charlemagne as his spiritual ancestor.

The festival and its sequel aroused violent controversy. Some press reports gave an exaggerated picture of what happened, conservative circles waxed indignant over the new 'Jacobins', the Governments of Prussia and Austria considered taking severe measures, while the liberals defended the students' behaviour. Luden sought to appease those who were hostile by drafting a political manifesto which proposed a democracy in the form of a monarchy. He laid this before a general assembly of students, who rejected it. Many speakers declared that it was not radical enough, while others stated that the movement should pursue only moral ends and keep out of politics. The Governments were so uneasy that the Prussian Chancellor Hardenberg and the Austrian Ambassador Count Zichy went to Weimar in person to gather information about the alleged revolutionary movement. They asked Kotzebue, among others, for his opinion, and he told them that it was only a handful of malcontents who had attempted to sway the feelings of the rest.

However, these events soon had very serious consequences. One of Kotzebue's assignments was to send the Tsar regular reports on the latest publications in Germany. One of these reports happened to fall into Luden's hands and he published it. The liberal press burst out into violent attacks against this 'Russian spy', although Kotzebue had not deserved this description. His reports merely contained extracts from new books along with his comments. The affair led to long and bitter altercations and a series of court cases. In 1818 there were student disorders in Göttingen, Tübingen and Heidelberg which, although they had no political significance, gravely disturbed conservative circles. The Empress of Russia visited the Grand Duchy of Weimar, and in her honour an arch was erected in Jena for her to drive under, but it was pulled down by students. The Tsar commissioned one of his councillors named Stourdza to write a confidential report on the situation in Germany, and by some indiscretion this became public and a fresh storm blew up. The report painted the student movement in the German universities in very gloomy colours and recommended drastic intervention. The students were now convinced that it was Russia's influence on the German princes which was preventing them from meeting liberal demands. Some of the German reigning houses – those of Württemberg and Weimar, for instance – *were* related to the Tsar and were accustomed to ask him for advice on purely German questions. The students' indignation was heightened by an article of Kotzebue's which defended Stourdza's report and cast scorn on their aims. Kotzebue also attacked so-called academic freedom, which, he said, was a mere pretext for licence. He dismissed as nonsense the argument that this freedom was necessary to allow the development of great talent; after all, students at English universities were subject to strict discipline and there was no lack of talent there. Stourdza had very sensibly raised the question of abolishing academic jurisdiction: students should be treated like any other citizens. Two members of a *Burschenschaft*, both of them counts, challenged Stourdza to a duel but he declined to meet them.

The Gymnastic Association held similar views to those of the *Burschenschaft* and had a more extensive membership. About this time, an eminent historian, Karl Adolf Menzel of Breslau, launched a sharp attack on the Gymnasts, whom he accused in a pamphlet of pursuing, with their idea of an all-powerful state, a cult which was heathen and hostile to Christianity; of preaching hatred towards the French; of glorifying the Germans as the chosen people; and of being Jacobins. All this, he said, was utterly un-German. This pamphlet stirred up a long and heated discussion. Kotzebue joined in, reminded the 'Teutomaniacs' that they had once mocked the French for styling themselves 'the great nation', but, he asked, was the nationalistic boasting of Jahn's followers any better?

A year after the Wartburg festival representatives of fourteen universities met in Jena and formed a union. This *Deutsche Burschenschaft* now claimed the sole right of student representation, and was highly intolerant of any other bodies. Although it proposed to go on supporting German unity and freedom, it declined to meddle in politics or to draw up any more precise political programme, but it was soon evident that this intention was far from being observed everywhere.

REVOLUTIONARY ASPIRATIONS

At the University of Jena, the prime aims of the majority were to purge student life of abuses and, in general, to support national and liberal principles. At Giessen, on the other hand, a movement had been evolving since 1814 which was patently charged with political radicalism. The leading spirit was Karl Follen, or Follenius, a young man of unusual gifts. Possessing great intelligence and a will of iron, he was a brilliant speaker and writer, besides distinguishing himself in fencing and gymnastics. Along with all this he held strong religious and moral convictions and was an ardent republican. His personality exercised an almost magical influence on his friends. His circle of the Giessen 'Blacks', who consisted of students and workers, included a theological student and an apostle of equality named Weidig, who later emerged as a communist. As early as 1816 a Christian-German *Burschenschaft* was founded in Giessen under Follen's leadership (Jews were excluded). Follen demanded of his followers high moral standards and self-sacrifice. They kept away from women because their life was to be devoted solely to their ideals. Their leader strove, not altogether successfully, to suppress duelling. Follen merely smiled at the students' routine fanaticism for 'Germanhood' and was soon entering into clandestine relations with French radicals, in order to secure their help in unleashing revolution.

In 1818, Follen, who was then twenty-two, became a lecturer in law. He was also active in various popular movements and incurred the suspicion of the authorities, so he transferred his activities to Jena, where he lectured with great success on Roman law. Many of his disciples followed him to Jena and the 'Blacks' obtained by some manoeuvre or other a majority on the committee of the *Burschenschaft*, but in Jena Follen never had the same influence over the students as in Giessen; he seems to have made only three close friends there, one of whom was a Jew.

The 'Blacks' deployed a vigorous political propaganda; for example, they submitted a petition to the Federal Diet for the introduction of parliaments throughout Germany and canvassed support up and down the *Bund*. Their real purpose in this was, however, to form connections for revolutionary ends. Follen toyed with the idea of rallying thousands of students on the battlefield of Leipzig on the pretext of celebrating the victory, but in reality to proclaim the republic and its constitution. It was, however, very doubtful whether the time was ripe for so bold a step or whether the people would support the students. Opinions were divided and so Follen decided for the time being to continue influencing the students with his ideas and to build up for himself a praetorian guard on whom he could rely implicitly, however great the danger.

The 'Blacks' were convinced that everyone was bound to act in the manner dictated by his personal code, formed after careful reflection, without reference to the law or traditional morality; any means was justified to achieve a great ideal. Follen defended his new moral principles in the discussions which Professor Fries organised for students, and to his youthful admirers his arguments were far more cogent than those of the timid old professor. On such assumptions it was easy to reach the conclusion that the assassination of tyrannical princes and their helpers was a moral duty.

Follen also wrote spectacular poems which he or one of his brothers set to music. In his *Grosses Lied*, regicide was hymned as a solemn sacrifice of blood. Anyone who gave up his life for humanity had moral standards as lofty as those of Christ.

Follen worked out a detailed plan for the assassination of Alexander I during a visit to Weimar, though it came to nothing because the Tsar changed his plans. It is possible that this was a device of Follen's to find out which of his intimates would not shrink from obeying orders, however extreme. Anyone who demurred was regarded as unfitted for important tasks and was no longer invited to secret deliberations. The 'fully committed' (*Unbedingten*) were ready for any acts of violence which did not conflict with honour, and the 'razor-keen' (*Haarscharfen*) would even commit, for political ends, crimes generally regarded as dishonourable: perjury, fraud, treason, theft, seduction, and so on.

On 23 March 1819 Kotzebue was murdered by Karl Sand, a Protestant theological student. This was one of the most sensational crimes of the day and had dire consequences for German liberalism. Kotzebue had no political influence nor was he a dangerous enemy of the national movement. He had once been enthusiastic about democracy but had later tended to the Right, although even then his articles supported some liberal demands. True, he criticised the youthful hotheads and tried to make them look ridiculous, but he hardly ever broke the rules of fair political debate. Moreover, he was on the point of leaving Germany in order to live on his estate in Russia's Baltic provinces. His murderer had been active in the student movement and was one of Follen's intimates. Of Kotzebue's many writings he knew only one article which mocked the conduct of the radical students, but conversations he had heard between other students had convinced him that Kotzebue was the incarnation of infamy and a Russian spy. The idea of murdering him had probably originated in the Follen entourage; it was Follen himself who had given Sand his fare to Mannheim, where Kotzebue lived. The main object of the crime was to observe how public opinion in the broadest sense would react. The choice of victim fell on Kotzebue because he was readily accessible.

Sand's intention was doubtless known to other students. When the news of the murder reached Jena – so the historian H. Leo reports in his memoirs – the students were so excited that one could easily have found another three or four score of them prepared to do the same. Radical propaganda had created a mood in which such acts were inevitable. After killing Kotzebue, Sand had gravely wounded himself in an attempt at suicide. The judicial investigation revealed no accomplices. In order to protect Follen, Sand falsely alleged that one of his best friends had given him his fare. Follen and his cronies toyed with the idea of starting fires in several places in Mannheim, where Sand was under arrest, in order to make it possible for him to escape. After a year, the doctors declared that Sand had recovered sufficiently to be executed, and the sentence was then carried out. Investigations by the Baden Government showed that in ordinary life Sand was a placid, respectable, conscientious and deeply religious man with mystical leanings. He was convinced that everyone should do what mature reflection showed him to be right, regardless of the law. Politically, he declared, he aimed at a humane and free state. When asked what he understood by freedom, he replied: 'Nothing more or less than what can be read every day in the newspapers or the works of great authors: ending complaints of intolerable taxes, for example, and abolishing the censorship.' He regarded it as the duty of the State to educate everyone into a high-minded, free human being who was conscious of his God-given dignity. Sand was far from advocating senseless violence or anarchy. When questioned about recent political events, he seemed to know very little, if anything, about them. In his eyes the arch-enemies of the German nation were first the Roman Catholics, then the monks and the soldiers, that is, the regular armies, which he regarded as tools of despotism. He belonged to the Gymnasts and was an active member of the *Burschenschaft*.

In Germany there was widespread sympathy for Sand. His motives often won understanding, even approval, not only from students but also from reputable men in responsible positions. In liberal newspapers he was described as a martyr, a hero or a saint, guilty of nothing more than an error. A professor of theology, de Wette, in a letter to Sand's mother, expressed admiration for his character, though not approval of his action. For many years a cult was dedicated to his memory and his victim was unjustly portrayed as a contemptible and worthless being.

Soon after the murder of Kotzebue an attempt was made on the life of the leading official of the Nassau Government, Karl von Ibell. The man responsible was a young chemist named Löning, a member of the 'Blacks' and acted in collusion with Karl Follen's brother August. The President was only slightly injured but suffered such a shock that he had to retire from public service. He was a German official of the best type; he had carried through many beneficial reforms and through him Nassau had received a very liberal constitution earlier than other states. Löning committed suicide in prison.

The hopes of the 'Blacks' were particularly dashed by the indifference of the masses towards revolutionary acts of violence. What possible meaning could the death of an author like Kotzebue have for the peasants who had never even heard of him? The choice of victim had, of course, caused the 'Blacks' quite a few difficulties. Metternich was too well guarded, none of the German princes at the time was especially hated and many of them were even popular. The masses were utterly un-interested in politics. In the summer of 1819 there were widespread outrages against the Jews, not only in Germany but in other countries too. The people had for years suffered under fluctuations in food prices for which the Jews were blamed. In many places students took part in the disorders, although in Heidelberg, under the leadership of Professor Thibaut, they defended the Jews. The Governments regarded these excesses as further proof of the underground agitation of a revolutionary party.

Many prominent liberals also condemned the attitude of the *Burschenschaft* and the radical leaders, especially that of Jahn.

REACTIONARY MEASURES

In many German governments leading statesmen had long been con-vinced that a very dangerous revolutionary movement was at work and must be energetically suppressed. Alexander I of Russia had great influence on the policies of the various courts. His initially progressive views received a rude shock when he discovered that the revolutionary spirit had gained ground even among the aristocratic officers of his own guards regiments. Napoleon and the French Revolu-tion had sown the seeds of nationalism and liberalism throughout Europe and caused a revolutionary ferment. As a result, conservative politicians in many countries proceeded to ruthless repression. Even in England the Tory Government followed this policy in the im-mediate post-war years.

In Germany the danger of revolution was probably far less than in

D

many other countries. As yet there was no great industrial proletariat, since manufacturing was only in its infancy. Although distress was acute in many areas, there existed no mass movement as there did in the industrial areas of England or among the Irish peasants. Germany had no capital city comparable with Paris, where an uprising could carry the whole country with it. Moreover, the contrast between rich and poor was less marked in Germany than in those Western states where capitalistic development had set in earlier. Where revolutionary tendencies did exist they were confined to youthful intellectuals. In influential circles, liberals and a number of moderate conservatives disapproved of a purely repressive policy and considered reforms necessary to take the wind out of the radicals' sails. In particular, many conservative politicians proposed reviving the historical Estates, while the liberals aspired to popular assemblies where the peasants should also have seats and votes but the decisive power should be vested in the educated classes and the landowners.

Between 1818–20, the governments of six of the larger German states introduced new constitutions. The development of a parliamentary system admittedly ran into many difficulties, most of them due to lack of experience. The reactionaries used these teething troubles to represent the whole policy of concessions as mistaken. Metternich sought to interpret the thirteenth article of the Federal Act as referring solely to the old diets of the Estates with their preponderance of the privileged classes, and not to assemblies representing broad sections of the people. Furthermore, he maintained, the diets should be given only an advisory role, even though the old Estates in many countries had had – to take but one example – a decisive voice in approving taxation. In Austria Metternich's view prevailed; the Estates remained in being and possessed certain rights to authorise taxes, but had no real power. True, they clung to the old ceremonial forms, which made them appear to be the pillars of the State, but in reality they degenerated into willing tools of the Government.

Of crucial importance was how the King of Prussia would carry out his repeated promises to grant a new constitution. His Chancellor, Hardenberg, had for a long time envisaged a liberal constitution with Estates in every province and over them a joint Prussian parliament. But among the Prussian nobility there was a conservatism which placed unremitting pressure on the King to thwart Hardenberg's plans. This faction was secretly supported by Metternich, for he saw in the introduction of a Prussian popular assembly not only a decisive step towards the total victory of liberalism in Prussia and all Germany, but also the danger that Prussia would gain the support of all German liberals and win predominance in Germany. He was therefore at pains to frustrate

Hardenberg's intentions, and advised the King of Prussia to approve only provincial diets with very limited powers.

It was a great help to the reactionaries that Hardenberg was old and hard of hearing and that, as a result of his lax private life, his influence had waned. In the end, it was the radical movement among the students and Gymnasts that gave the ultra-conservatives a glorious opportunity to frighten the King with the bogy of imminent revolution and to implant in him the ineradicable conviction that a popular assembly for the whole of Prussia would lead to catastrophe. As early as January 1819, the King decreed that a programme of stern measures against revolutionary tendencies should be drawn up. Hardenberg promptly reprimanded Arndt for something he had published and forbade Jahn to go on teaching gymnastics. At the same time a prominent civil servant, Hagemeister, was commissioned to draft a press law, although he was known to be opposed to any form of censorship. In addition, Wilhelm von Humboldt was taken into the Government, and the liberals regarded this as a good omen.

After Kotzebue's murder the Prussian Government took particularly sharp measures not only against the radicals but also against moderates with liberal and national aspirations. Many suspects were detained, among them Arndt and Jahn, while Görres escaped arrest by fleeing to France. The police searched houses, confiscated documents and opened letters. Numerous periodicals were banned and lectures and sermons were attended by informers. An official gazette announced that the Government had convincing proofs of the existence of a great conspiracy to set up a republic on the American pattern. Some universities protested against the Government's measures and there were magistrates who tried to prevent arbitrary acts by the police by demanding a judicial enquiry to investigate accusations impartially. Arndt was persecuted for years and forbidden to lecture; he had to wait twenty years before he was reinstated, and that was when a new king came to the throne. Jahn suffered particularly harsh treatment; after a long investigation he was accused of various grave crimes and it took five years for the court to acquit him of high treason and incitement to murder. All the same, he was condemned to two years' imprisonment for disrespectful and impudent attacks on the existing constitution. After a further year had passed he was completely cleared on appeal although he was still kept under police surveillance and forbidden to reside in any town where there was a university or secondary school. Like Arndt, he had to wait twenty years in all before he recovered his full freedom.

The measures to stamp out the revolutionary spirit in Prussia and other German states were aimed above all else at the universities and the press. Metternich and Gentz were convinced that the professors were the major offenders. Later Gentz wrote in a memorandum that there did not exist in Germany at that time one single privately-owned periodical which right-minded people could look on as *their* paper. This had never happened before, not even in the days of bloodshed and anarchy in France. The initial plan was to give the Federal Diet the task of suppressing the revolutionary movement, but this would have run into opposition from a group of liberal members as well as from the particularists. The stipulation that important decisions required a two-thirds majority or unanimity was an obstacle, and so Metternich intended to attain his ends by reaching agreements with Prussia and the larger states and subsequently using the Diet to enact these agreements in the form of a federal law. He met the King of Prussia, who had been deeply shocked by the alleged discovery of a revolutionary plot, at the Austrian spa of Teplitz, and made a secret treaty with him by which Austria and Prussia would act in concert. Prussia promised to shelve the question of a constitution for some time. Governments of those states of the *Bund* which already had representative parliaments were to be supported in revising their constitutions. Stern measures against suspect journals and their editors, as well as against liberal professors and students, were agreed upon.

Metternich arranged a conference of ministers in Carlsbad to which governments considered unreliable were not invited. First of all, emergency decrees for the next five years were settled on, and these were to be introduced in the individual states. Every printed work had to be submitted to the censor before publication except for books of more than twenty sheets, that is, 320 octavo pages. It was assumed that books of such length were mostly of an academic nature and would not be read by the masses. Furthermore, the *Bundestag* was empowered to ban publications for specific reasons. Editors, professors and teachers could be dismissed or suspended and the universities were subjected to special supervision. The *Burschenschaft* and similar organisations were banned and ex-members were barred from the civil service. A central committee of investigation was set up in Mainz to direct the campaign against the forces of revolution. The Federal Diet was vested with executive powers and could call on military aid from member states.

The Carlsbad decrees were placed before the Diet and unanimously adopted as a federal law after the two major German powers had manipulated the rules of procedure in order to force a quick decision.

Public opinion viewed these events with a consternation which could not be voiced in the press. There were various public protests. Austria and Prussia applied the new law with severity. True, Metternich had never tolerated a liberal movement in Austria and there was little need of further repression, but in Prussia liberal ideas had strong backing among high officials and other influential circles, who tried to mitigate these Draconic measures. All the same, the persecution of the 'demagogues' assumed some very ugly forms.

Austria and Prussia kept a strict watch on the smaller states and when necessary exerted pressure on them. Many states, in fact, used their powers to limit the freedom of the press even more than had been prescribed; but there were also states in the *Bund* where progressive members of the Government offered resistance and applied the censorship and other measures only mildly. Bavaria promulgated the federal law under reserve and Württemberg insisted on proclaiming a new constitution, although this was in clear contrast to the spirit of the Carlsbad Decrees.

The manner in which the Decrees became federal law was considered on many sides as a grave violation of the main principle of the *Bund* – the independence and equality of all its member states. The loose federation of sovereign states seemed to have been transformed into a federal state over which the two strongest members exercised joint control. This development disturbed the particularists but their fears were unfounded. True, Metternich had put through his anti-liberal measures by means which were hardly compatible with the spirit of the federal constitution, but he did not for a moment intend promoting the forces working for German unification. The Federal Act had laid down only the outlines of a constitution and left it to the Diet to work out a basic structure. However, in all major matters this task was now taken out of its hands and transferred to a conference in Vienna of federal states under Metternich's management. The conference lasted six months and worked out a law with sixty-five articles, known as the Final Act (*Schlussakte*) of Vienna. The Diet ratified it on 8 June 1820, as a basic law with the same force and validity as the Federal Act (*Bundesakte*) itself.

At the conference of Vienna there were many arguments between strict particularists and the partisans of moderate unity, ultra-conservatives and moderate liberals. On the one hand, particularism won the day, because even the liberals now saw in it a defence against reaction. On the other, there was a rapprochement over the constitutional issue: it was agreed that monarchical power should be limited by the Estates only in certain respects. Metternich dropped his plan to revise existing constitutions in a reactionary sense and it was agreed that any changes should be made only by constitutional means. The Diet was to work towards the introduction of the promised constitutions everywhere, to guarantee them if asked and to intervene if there were an uprising. Various attempts to limit the rights of the Estates were defeated.

A result of both conferences was that the Diet lost much prestige. Metternich succeeded in excluding from it those delegates who opposed his policy and in having them replaced by reliable anti-liberals. Important debates in the Diet were no longer reported, and, since no one was interested in the others, publication of the Diet's proceedings ceased completely.

EFFECT ON PUBLIC OPINION

The liberal and national movement was nowhere so systematically and ruthlessly persecuted as in Prussia. In Bavaria, Hesse-Darmstadt and Holstein no drastic measures were taken at first, while in other states, such as Saxony and Baden, they were applied only mildly. In Austria, Metternich had already prevented any spread of impermissible ideas among young people. Many liberals now detested Prussia more than Austria, which at least had not betrayed the cause of freedom. Prussia's militaristic and bureaucratic traditions and the influence of the Junker class made her highly unpopular in the rest of Germany, especially in the south and west. Whereas the liberals had earlier advocated a strong central power and unified federal institutions, they now preferred particularism. After all, in Carlsbad and Vienna it was the opponents of strong national unity, like Bavaria and Württemberg, who had resisted the plans of the enemies of liberty. Hence, in liberal eyes, the fullest possible independence of the federal states seemed the only protection against the might of reaction.

This mood was also expressed in the revival of the idea of a 'Third Germany' or 'Trias'. Many of the smaller states had always watched the dominance of Austria and Prussia with misgivings and jealousy, and had sometimes sought the protection of foreign powers, especially France, as for example in the Confederation of the Rhine under Napoleon. Now the idea spread that Austria and Prussia were not at all genuinely German powers, since their most important interests lay outside Germany. Why should the German people expose itself to danger in the cause of Austrian sovereignty over northern Italy, or become entangled in war over Prussia's Polish possessions? The German people, they argued, wanted peace and liberty; both Austria and Prussia were militaristic powers hostile to liberty. Even their populations were largely non-German. In Austria the Germans formed only a minority, and of the Prussians many were Slavs or of Slav origin. Pure Germanism lay in the south and west, the birthplace of most of the great cultural achievements which were the pride of the Germans. The supporters of the trias plan wanted a group of smaller states to be formed within the *Bund* under the leadership of Bavaria and Württemberg, to counterbalance the influence of the two great powers which were only half German.

A prominent statesman of this persuasion was Karl August, Baron Wangenheim, at the time the delegate for Württemberg and leader of the liberal faction in the Diet. He advocated the formation of a bloc of the smaller states and applied the trias idea to the military, economic and other questions which occupied the Diet. He was an intelligent man, fertile in ideas and progressive in his views.

But there was also an extreme form of trialism which aimed at dissolving the existing *Bund* and forming a new federation, that of the true Germany. It should be recalled that in the preliminary discussions on the German constitution both Stein and Hardenberg at first wanted to restrict the federation completely or predominantly to the 'Third Germany'. In 1820 a book was published in London with the title *Manuscript from Southern Germany* and bearing the name of George Erichson as publisher, not author. The book first described the complete collapse of the old *Reich*, whose dissolution by Napoleon, along with the foundation of the Confederation of the Rhine and the Continental blockade aimed at Britain's trade monopoly, the writer termed a benefit. The Napoleonic system, he argued, had not simply been imposed on the states of the Confederation of the Rhine and its peoples; the best Germans had felt that they were serving a great cause when they allied themselves with the French, who had won immortal victories. They had been proud of the distinction of the Légion d'Honneur which Napoleon had conferred on them, and still celebrated the glorious days of the triumph over feudal darkness and the dawn of a new life. The book poured scorn on the 'popular fanaticism' of the anti-French movement and on Görres' 'notorious' *Rheinischer Merkur*. The *Bund* and the conferences of Carlsbad and Vienna had been the outcome of a selfish and despotic tutelage imposed by Austria and Prussia on the true, pure Germany, for whom Bavaria and Württemberg spoke. The policy of the two great German powers was sharply criticised. The diplomats who assembled in Carlsbad were trying in vain to eliminate the democratic principle from the constitutions. The fear which the mere rustling of a liberal paper inspired was proof enough of how great the power of the liberal spirit was.

The book considered the *Bund* as indefensible because a number of the states in it were primarily European powers and therefore had other interests than Germany. The Hanseatic cities, too, were in reality British colonies and their trade was thriving at the expense of Germany's. The national character and economic interests of the North Germans differed from those of the South Germans. Germany proper comprised about ten million inhabitants and the other states about eighteen millions; a separation of the two parts was desirable in the interests of both Germany and Europe. Bavaria and Württemberg were competent to head the German states. The natural ally of the true Germany against the ambitions of Austria and Prussia was France.

The book aroused a storm of controversy. It became known that its author was a radical journalist named Lindner, who was often employed by the King of Württemberg as a literary agent. The Prime Minister of Württemberg, Count Wintzingerode, asked the King for permission to sue Lindner because his book was a provocation to the great powers and threatened the security of the country. To his surprise the King replied that he himself had given Lindner the essential ideas and that the latter had merely expanded them.

German particularism had for centuries regarded the King of France as the protector of 'German liberty', that is, of their independence from the Emperor. In later times many liberals admired the French Revolution and Napoleon and felt themselves to be the heirs of 1789. This feeling now revived and hopes of liberation from despotism and feudalism through co-operation between the Germans and the French ran high. In France the Napoleonic legend represented Bonaparte as a friend of the people who, after a conclusive victory, desired to establish lasting peace on the basis of liberty, and this legend won much credence in many parts of Germany. The tightening of the censorship by the Carlsbad Decrees prevented the German press from writing much about domestic conditions and so the newspapers reported all the more about France. The liberals eagerly read French and English papers in the reading rooms which had sprung up in many German towns and which were open to all who could afford the price of admission. Many governments sought to restrict these facilities, but they could not prevent foreign news from being followed with the greatest interest by many people or freedom movements from being hailed with enthusiasm. There were some writers who by their literary skill eluded the severity of the censorship and in some places censorship was not over-strict.

PERSISTENCE OF STUDENT MOVEMENTS

The radical student movement, which had given Metternich his opportunity to begin persecuting the demagogues, did not collapse but went underground. The *Burschenschaft* was dissolved but it soon revived in other guises. Conferences took place at which delegates of the

Burschenschaften of various universities took part, and as early as 1820 one was held in Dresden at which nine universities were represented. The university authorities probably winked an eye, and after a few years it was scarcely necessary to keep the student movement secret any longer. The original *Burschenschaft* had declared itself non-political and in any case a section of the students was always opposed to any political activity, but control lay in the hands of small groups with strong political convictions. During the twenties, revolution broke out in the countries of southern Europe which aroused great sympathy among German students and many went to Italy, Greece or Spain in order to fight for freedom there. Many of their leaders, persecuted in their own country, fled to Switzerland and organised revolutionary propaganda in Germany from there.

Karl Follen's propaganda was known to the police in 1820 and he would have been arrested if his friends had not got him away to France. There he made contact with prominent leaders of the Left, but soon had to leave the country, for otherwise the Government would have extradited him to Germany. He went to Switzerland and became a lecturer at Basle University. His main aim was to build up a secret organisation in Germany, a League of Youth and an association for adults, in order to prepare for a major revolution. The association for adults remained only an idea on paper, but the League of Youth quickly grew, had branches at many universities and possessed energetic leaders, who, it must be said, were often at loggerheads with each other. It is characteristic that a number of Prussian officers should also have supported the plan for a revolution, among them the commandant of an important fortress, Major von Fehrentheil, who was prepared to hand it over with its stocks of ammunition to the insurgents. The plan was to assemble a large number of students on the pretext of an expedition to Greece to fight against the Turks, but in reality they were to start the revolution within Germany. The plot foundered on the disunity of its leaders, who gradually discovered that the common people were not ready to support a revolution. Many of the conspirators were caught and severely punished; Fehrentheil was sentenced to life imprisonment but made good his escape to America. The German powers demanded Follen's extradition from Switzerland and although this was refused he was none the less deported. He emigrated to America, became a lecturer at Harvard and later devoted himself to the Unitarian Church and the movement for the abolition of the slave trade. He died in 1840 in a shipwreck.

The political ardour of the Germans was notably reanimated after the July Revolution in France, as can be seen from the appearance of the literary movement known as *Junges Deutschland*. The changing spirit of the times was evident in the new attitude of the students to the Jews and the French. The original *Burschenschaft* had admitted Jews but excluded *Wälsche* (a term embracing Italians and southern peoples) and Frenchmen as 'eternal enemies of the German race'. In 1820 it was laid down that Jews were not to be admitted, because they had no native land and no interest in that of the Germans, though they were not to be prevented from becoming as closely assimilated to Germans as possible, nor from developing intellectually in every respect. Moreover, they could be admitted if it should appear that they were prepared to accept the 'Christian-German' spirit for the good of the people. As liberalism spread, the attitude towards the Jews changed. Even before this they were accepted if they underwent baptism; Heinrich Heine, indeed, was admitted before baptism. The Bamberg student assembly of 1827 deleted the word 'Christian' and thus made the unrestricted admission of Jews possible for some decades. Relations with the French likewise changed. The German democrats hoped for joint action with them in carrying through a German revolution. After the Polish uprising, there was great enthusiasm for Poland and the *Burschenschaft* was on excellent terms with Polish student associations.

The change in the political mood was fairly rapidly accomplished. Wolfgang Menzel, who had fled to Switzerland when the prosecutions began, returned to Germany in 1824 and found to his astonishment that the patriotic German movement had vanished and been replaced by a liberalism of French hue. He saw this as a success for Metternich's policy and the anti-national tendency of Hegel which prevailed in Berlin. But a contributory factor was certainly the fact that in the South German states, where there were popular assemblies on liberal principles, a political life had developed which, despite many limitations and defects, impressed wide circles and awoke an urge for full political freedom. Finally, too, the prosecution of students regarded as subversive, who in Prussia in particular received long prison sentences, gave rise to much bitterness.

The French July Revolution of 1830 gave the partisans of the freedom movement in Germany the signal for vigorous action. There were numerous demonstrations, disorders and risings which in many states led to the setting up of popular assemblies. This was particularly the case in North Germany, where constitutional development lagged behind and for the most part took the outdated form of diets of the Estates. In southern German states, too, numerous democratic and republican newspapers and associations had sprung up, so in 1832 Metternich submitted proposals to the Federal Diet, which were adopted as the Six Acts and forthwith led to a ban on all periodicals, societies and assemblies regarded as revolutionary.

ASSAULT ON THE FRANKFURT GUARD HOUSE

In 1831 a student convention was held in Frankfurt at which numerous universities were represented. A motion pledging the students to join in the expected uprising was passed and confirmed at a similar gathering in Stuttgart in 1832. Outside the student body, a conspiracy was hatched involving links with republican circles in France and Switzerland. Pamphlets urging revolt were printed, guns were bought and ammunition prepared, and it was believed that armed irregulars from abroad would assist. The revolution was to begin in Frankfurt, where it was planned to seize the building in which the Diet met. It was hoped that there and in the banking house of Rothschild ample funds would be found for waging war on the princes. A start was made at Easter, 1833, when sixty conspirators, including at least forty students, attacked the main guard post and a police station in Frankfurt, seized rifles and drove out the occupants. The tocsin was sounded to tell the people that the revolution had come, and the conspirators hoped that vast masses would come streaming along and take up arms, but the expected reinforcements never materialised, and very soon troops appeared and after a short struggle restored order. Many students were captured, while others fled.

This coup caused the measures for the suppression of revolutionary acts to be revived. The Central Commission of Investigation instituted in 1820 was set up again in a somewhat changed form and was given wide powers. In 1834 conferences were held in Vienna in which ministers of the states of the *Bund* took part and passed numerous resolutions, which were then in the main adopted by the *Bund* as well. A large number of people were then charged with working for the overthrow of the existing order. Arrangements were also made for the surveillance of suspects, the tightening-up of the censorship and so on. Among those arrested and interrogated were many former members of the *Burschenschaft* and the mere fact of their having once belonged to it was punished as a crime. The Prussian Supreme Court alone found 204 accused persons guilty and sentenced 39 of them to death; the King, however, commuted the sentences of four of them to life imprisonment and of the rest to thirty years' imprisonment. His successor, Frederick William IV, released them all. To quote but one instance, Fritz Reuter, who subsequently gained fame as a writer, was imprisoned for seven years and he later wrote a deeply moving description of this experience. The real conspirators had for the most part escaped abroad.

6

AUSTRIA

THE AGE OF METTERNICH

Austria, although the biggest state in the *Bund*, belonged to it only by virtue of her western provinces, where the German language predominated, and even here there were non-German minorities. Almost 80% of the inhabitants of the Austrian Empire, to which all the lands of the House of Austria belonged and which was named after it,[1] were non-Germans. In 1846 the Empire comprised 40·7% Slavs, 21·6% Italians and Rumanians, 21% Germans and 16·7% Magyars. But both the Slavs and the Romanic peoples were divided into different nationalities and there were about a dozen distinct peoples in all. Thus, no one people had an absolute majority or even the possibility of joining with a closely related nationality to obtain one. Many of them were economically and culturally backward; some, indeed, had not fully developed their language and these were for the most part in countries where the Germans were paramount. The situation of these various nationalities will be dealt with later in more detail; suffice it to say at this point that in the period under review national consciousness developed in nearly all of them. The conduct of foreign policy lay in the hands of Metternich until the revolution of 1848, while in internal affairs his rival Count Kolowrat gradually acquired decisive influence, and, in matters touching the police and censorship, Count Sedlnitzky. Their policy aimed at keeping the peace, fighting revolutionary movements everywhere in concert with the great powers and suppressing liberalism in the *Bund* as far as possible, but after the Congress of Vienna revolutionary movements sprang up in all the countries of southern Europe.

Austria felt the impact of these events. For a long time the Serbs hoped for liberation at Austria's hands and were prepared to unite

---

[1] It is distinguished from Austria proper by the designation 'Imperial State' (*Kaiserstaat*).

with her, though there was also a pro-Russian movement among them. The unification of all the southern Slavs was the subject of propaganda in Austria by Croatian writers. For a time Napoleon had united large southern Slav areas under his rule and Austria later allowed them to continue for a while as the Kingdom of Illyria. Metternich, however, did not promote this policy, as it would have set Austria at odds with Russia and the Magyars and was probably more than she could cope with.

By the constitution of the *Bund*, Austria was its president and there she exercised a certain influence on the other member states, who feared her less than they did the traditionally expansionist Prussia. Metternich succeeded, moreover, in winning over the King of Prussia completely to his way of thinking, with the result that the representatives of national and liberal principles could not assert themselves in Prussia. Later ,it must be said, this policy of Metternich's led to a pro-Prussian reaction. A criticism levelled at Austria was that she had to make too many allowances for the non-Germans who formed the great majority of her population. When at the Congress of Vienna Austria withdrew from the Rhine, she relinquished responsibility for the defence of Germany against France, and this passed to Prussia. In other ways, too, the external interests of Germany and Austria diverged. Austria's lay in the east and south, Germany's in the west and north.

Metternich's policy had its strongest supporter in Emperor Francis I, who was even more hostile than he to any liberal or national concessions to the spirit of the age. In his youth, Metternich was attracted by the spirit of the Enlightenment and in many respects always remained true to it, even though the French Revolution had filled him with deep mistrust of its demands for freedom. Napoleon was also an heir of the Enlightenment and the Revolution, and Metternich found much in him to approve of, except for his policy of aggression and expansion. Metternich's main concern was to preserve the peace of Europe; this was of the greatest importance for Austria, for the *Bund's* military resources were at best suited to a defensive role. In many points Metternich agreed with the demands of liberalism, except for those touching a popular assembly, freedom of speech and freedom of the press. There were occasions at the Congress of Vienna when he supported important national and liberal demands with a vigour[1] of which in later years no one would ever have believed him capable. Even in the years immediately following the Congress there were a number of signs in Austria that the government wished to follow a liberal policy.[2] Indeed, Metternich even proposed to the Emperor the formation of an

---

[1] Vide W. A. Schmidt, *Geschichte der deutschen Verfassungsfrage*, p. 233.

[2] G. G. Gervinus, *Geschichte des 19. Jahrhunderts*, vol. I, 1855, p. 233,

Imperial Council of the countries ruled by Austria, but reforms foundered on the positively morbid aversion of Francis I to any innovation.

Liberal historians have justly held the Emperor and Metternich largely responsible for the blows which fate subsequently dealt to Austria and Germany. In any case, the general conditions prevailing in Austria had become so critical through the long Napoleonic wars that perhaps even the very greatest and most liberal-minded statesmen could have achieved no better results. The state of the economy was so catastrophic that in 1811 state bankruptcy had to be declared. Only after long exertions by the Government could solid foundations for trade, industry and finance be restored. Public discussion of the financial situation would certainly have proved beneficial but there were also important reasons against holding it. Austria was utterly exhausted, inflation was having its inevitable effects, capital and credit for the development of the economy were lacking. Outside a small circle of senior officials there were hardly any experts, and inflation had made Vienna a centre for unscrupulous speculators. The Diets of the Estates were little suited for discussion or applying sweeping reforms; on the contrary, they were an obstacle, forming as they did a bulwark of privilege and tradition against the common weal. Consultation with the middle classes, which would have been a possibility under Leopold II, had now become much more difficult; besides, they were much more entangled in the toils of outworn traditions than large sections of the upper classes.

Added to all this was the problem of nationalities. True, nationalism as we understand it was still in its infancy, but none the less there were not infrequently sharp contrasts between one country and another which were sometimes more social and religious than national. In such a political climate one could often expect popular assemblies to do no more than underline existing differences rather than set to work on beneficial reforms.

The liberals' answer to such misgivings was that the people could be politically educated only if it were given adequate rights. If it abused them, then these were but teething troubles which simply had to be accepted. The liberals further declared that it was the duty of the educated and well-to-do classes to represent the people. The strict conservatives who preponderated in Austria were utterly opposed to such experiments for the French Revolution had inspired in them the fear that any concession to liberal demands, especially granting freedom to the press, would inevitably have unforeseen consequences.

Although Austria was an absolute monarchy whose power was centralised, this did not ensure that national policy was formed quickly, durably or coherently. The machinery of government was very complicated – just like the structure of the State itself. There was no Prime Minister, since such an office would run counter to the idea that the monarch alone determined the course of policy. In the ministries and other important offices, the senior officials formed a council in which all questions were discussed and decided by a majority vote. This system was meant to ensure full consultation, impartiality and continuity; in fact, it made the conduct of affairs slow, protracted and expensive, and diluted responsibility.

The lack of real self-government and parliamentary control had unfortunate consequences. The diets of the provincial Estates were brought back or set up afresh, but they had no influence on economic policy or legislation. Military expenditure continued to run at a high level. Within the country, keeping a close watch in all quarters in order to forestall activities dangerous to the state required a vast police machinery which had its informers everywhere, so that every day the Emperor received detailed political reports, even on the most trivial matters. The censorship kept an eye on the theatre and all forms of literary activity in a way which even Metternich and the Emperor on occasion described as ridiculous. Authors who feared a ban on their works usually got them published in Leipzig, Hamburg or other German towns. The police allowed booksellers to import virtually any book from abroad, though dangerous or suspect books could not be displayed or advertised, to avoid inflaming the masses. Besides this, anyone regarded as politically reliable could easily get permission to order banned foreign books and newspapers, and in coffee houses and reading rooms the *Times*, and the *Augsburger Allgemeine Zeitung* and similar papers were available. The educated well-to-do made good use of these opportunities. The police supervised all societies and lectures; quite harmless ones were often banned.

Of the reforms introduced by Joseph II, the supremacy of the State over the Church had been fully maintained. Francis, though a much stricter churchman than Metternich, saw to it that this situation continued. While the religious toleration introduced by Joseph's edict continued to be a legal fact, the limiting provisions were interpreted and applied much more narrowmindedly than before. Besides this, the Estates in many provinces claimed special historical rights, with the result that Protestants and Jews in one province might receive very different treatment from those in another, and sometimes suffered considerable oppression. Thus, for example, the Tyrolean Estates maintained that the Edict of Toleration did not apply to their province, and in the face of stout opposition from the Government they managed to secure the Emperor's approval for expelling a few hundred subjects who had become Protestants. After Joseph's death his agrarian reforms had been partially repealed, and serfdom and other feudal services continued in some places, notably the Slav provinces. Legal reforms, introduced by Joseph, progressed in a number of directions. The 1811 code of common law was a masterpiece, and even the penal code of 1803, for all its defects, reflected the views of enlightened justice held at the time. In Rotteck-Welcker's *Staatslexikon*, the Bible of the older liberalism, a prominent jurist described these laws as simple and clear and observing the principles of humanity, equality before the law and the independence of the judicature. Although the death penalty, abolished by Joseph, was reintroduced, it was only for a very few crimes of signal gravity. It must be admitted, however, that there were neither juries nor oral proceedings in public.

A valuable legacy of the age of Joseph was the fact that his spirit was still very much alive among civil servants. The influence of the aristocracy had grown, but talented officials from the middle classes rose to the highest posts and received titles, and their influence largely counteracted any shortcomings at the head of affairs. The aristocracy, too, still numbered many humane men who were proof that Joseph's spirit was not dead. There was, for instance, one of the leading liberal poets, known to the world as Anastasius Grün, but whose real name was Count Anton Alexander von Auersperg, a member of the old nobility. His works were published abroad but were also read with enthusiasm by liberals throughout Austria.

In education the institutions of Maria Theresa and Joseph were preserved and developed, if not always along the lines they had intended. All children between six and twelve had to attend school, and the older children refresher courses on Sundays. Primary education was largely free. Of children of school age 60% went to school; the remainder lived mainly in very mountainous or undeveloped districts. Many Galician landowners were opposed to their peasants' being taught anything, and whereas in the German and Bohemian provinces nearly all the children went to school, in Galicia just under one-seventh attended; in Venetia the proportion was about a quarter. In the thirty years from 1810 to 1840, the number of primary schools doubled. For a long time teachers were poorly paid and ill-trained, but this situation gradually improved. The clergy had much more influence on the schools than they had enjoyed under Joseph. In higher education the government strove not so much to promote scholarship as to train officials and experts along the lines of the existing system for the benefit of the public. Thus a great deal was done to produce good doctors and efficient engineers, and the natural sciences, statistics and other branches of practical knowledge received special attention.

The Danubian empire was so vast in extent and so varied in natural resources that its economic possibilities seemed limitless. But there was a reverse to the medal, often overlooked, which made their translation into fact very difficult: the main provinces were a long way from the sea and hence from world markets; few rivers flowed in a convenient direction; developing communications in the mountains was not easy; there were few towns; and important raw materials, coal in particular, were not available. Over and above this there were interminable wars, the fetters of feudalism, the lack of a numerically strong and prosperous middle class and shortage of capital for economic development. In earlier times forests, hydraulic power and rural outwork were major elements in industry and Austria was rich in them, but when steam power, coal and the concentration of factory workers in towns became decisive factors, Austria fell behind.[1]

Since the seventeenth century, successive Austrian governments had striven to overcome these drawbacks and had made significant progress. Francis I's government continued in essence the industrial and commercial policy of Joseph II. Meanwhile, the steam engine and other inventions had appeared and competition from the great industry which had grown up in Britain contributed much to the depression prevailing from 1816 to 1830. The Government entrusted first-class officials with the task of smoothing the path for industry. They set about it with great vision and energy. Despite the protests of the guilds, many restrictive practices were lifted, the patent laws tidied up, first-rate technical schools founded, machinery from England introduced and industrial exhibitions held. Excellent roads and ship canals were constructed, a start was made on building railways and maritime and river navigation was opened up. The population of Austria and Hungary, without the Italian provinces, rose by 39% during 1800–40.

THE SLAVS

The Slavs, who made up about 40% of the population of the Empire, were split up into seven peoples, between whom differences of language, religion and social progress had created significant contrasts. Although some of these people spoke closely related languages, there was for the most part no sense of community between them, rather the opposite.

---

[1] I have described the historical difficulties in detail in my books *Die Produktionsgrundlagen der österreichischen Industrie*, 1918, and *Nationalgeist und Politik*, 1937, pp. 61 ff. It is there demonstrated statistically that in many respects Austria was formerly industrially superior to Germany or Prussia, but was then overtaken, largely because Prussia produced much more coal. In the 1840s, the value of Austrian mining and steel production was double that of Prussia, but in 1910 the latter's was five times that of Austria.

In many countries Slav peoples were sharply divided from non-Slavs, who were dominant economically, politically and culturally. In the Bohemian provinces the Germans were the leaders; in the Hungarian, the Magyars; and in the Illyrian the Italians. Widely diverse, too, was the attitude of the Slavs to their Habsburg rulers. The Polish aristocracy hated them as foreigners, whereas their Polish and Ruthenian serfs looked on the Emperor very much as their protector against their Polish masters. The Croats, Slovenes and Czechs were likewise faithful subjects, whereas among the Serbs a leaning towards Russia, based on a shared religion, was sometimes manifest.

The Czechs occupied a particularly important position. The Bohemian nobles, in order to escape enslavement by the Turks, had once chosen the Habsburgs as their kings, but had later to a large extent risen against them, only to be subdued. But in the course of time the Habsburgs had succeeded in once more winning over the Czechs. Many of the rebels had been Protestants who subsequently emigrated, and the Bohemian and Moravian nobility, which was still powerful, consisted for the most part of Czechs who had not forgotten their origins. Many of the leading statesmen and generals of the Habsburgs were of Czech extraction, as for example Lobkowitz and Kaunitz, Wallenstein and Radetzky. Even under Francis I, two statesmen from the Czech nobility – Count Kolowrat and Count Sedlnitzky – exercised the strongest influence on home policy, far greater than Metternich's.

The Habsburgs, as German emperors and princes of many German lands, were naturally Germans too, but of very supra-national hue. Under Leopold I, the language used at court was Italian; under Charles VI, it was in part Spanish; and under Francis I, French. The Austrian aristocracy, too, had a very international complexion. In earlier times the nobles in the individual countries had exercised great influence in administration and legislation. Later, centralisation proved essential to resist attacks from without and to create a modern state. The absolutist welfare state came into ever closer touch with the common people, and the administrators had to know both the language of the people as well as a common official language which they used in dealings with the Central Government and with each other. German was the only possible official language, one reason being that the other languages were in the main far too underdeveloped to meet the demands which would be made upon them. Besides this, many of the Emperor's best officials came from German territories, and, in large areas of the *Reich*, German was the language of higher culture and international trade, with only one serious rival – Italian, in the south. Joseph II wanted to make German the general language throughout the state.

His attempt failed, but it did help to kindle and spread a vigorous effort in Hungary and Bohemia to develop the native tongues into national languages. In Bohemia the German language had thrust Czech far into the background. This was not primarily the doing of the Government but arose from the fact that in the Sudeten provinces Germans were both economically and culturally to the fore. Anyone who hoped for higher education or who wanted to prosper had to understand German. There were no scientific or literary textbooks written in Czech, nor could one run any business which catered for more than the narrowest local needs without using German. Only the peasants and the lower classes spoke Czech exclusively; the educated classes spoke German. If the Czech language was preserved, the credit must largely go to the Government in Vienna, which granted it an increasing place in the elementary schools, the courts and the administration, as well as in higher education later on.

This process was a gradual one and did not spring from a conscious policy. All children who were able to attend the elementary schools were, to begin with, taught in their own tongue, but if they wanted to go on to higher education they had to learn German. Then gradually intermediate and senior schools for the other languages were founded. This had already been done earlier on in the academies so that officials and officers might learn German. Even after Joseph, in government and law German was, at least in principle, the official language; in one or two places Latin or Italian was used. The parties involved could use other languages and their statements were then translated into the official language, for which purpose sworn interpreters were available. But the Government soon found itself obliged to issue instruction after instruction that officials who came in contact with the people must understand their language. An authority of the forties reports: 'Up to 1808, the urban and judicial authorities in Czech towns drew up all judgements, together with the reasons for their verdicts, in the Czech language only, which even now is still the official language used there. A Court Decree of 1808, however, enjoined Courts of Appeal and the Supreme Court of Justice to attach a German translation to each written judgement with the supporting grounds for it.'

The general increase in the use of Slav languages in the courts and the administration, as well as their teaching in schools, is linked with the rise of nationalist movements among the various Slav tribes. Isolated champions appeared early on, but only at the end of the eighteenth century did anything like a movement begin to develop. The German Romanticists played a part in this, notably Herder, who described the Slav character in warm and idealistic terms. The German professor Schlözer also devoted much attention to the Slavs, their languages and their history, and was favourably disposed towards them. Among the Czechs pioneer work was done by Joseph Dobrovski, who, along with Schlözer, can be regarded as the father of comparative Slavonic philology.

At the end of the eighteenth century, and for some time afterwards, Czech and other Slav languages were so backward and undeveloped that even some of the leaders of the nationalist movement doubted whether they would survive and themselves wrote mainly or solely in German. When in 1832 the Czech historian Palacky and others sent out a circular in German appealing for contributions to set up a fund to promote national literature, they mentioned the possibility that both the Czech language and nation might disappear. In consequence, much work was devoted to developing the language, extending its vocabulary and codifying its grammar. As with all movements of this kind, a comprehensive cultural and political ideology also developed. The nationalist writers complained that Slav peoples everywhere, with the exception of the Russians, were dependent on other nations politically, culturally and economically. This they found all the more surprising as the Slavonic tongues were closely related; indeed, in the opinion of many scholars, they really formed one single language which was spoken by more inhabitants than any other in Europe. Many of their scholars therefore devoted themselves to a study not only of their own people but also of Slavs in general.

In this way there arose a cultural and political Pan-Slavism which preached the union of Slavs everywhere with the greatest and most powerful of all the Slav nations – Russia. Many even wanted to bring the individual languages closer to Russian or by fusion to create a uniform Slav tongue. The wide distribution of the Slav languages aroused great pride and lively hopes; there was talk of a great Slav mission in the world. The oppressors of the Slavs, above all the Germans and the Magyars, came in for considerable hostility and history was so portrayed that all blame attached to the enemies of the Slavs. It was also argued that, long before the Germans, the Slavs had developed a high degree of civilisation.

The nobles of Czech origin supported these aims, although many of them scarcely spoke a word of Czech. The Austrian minister Kolowrat and Sedlnitzky were thoroughly in sympathy with the nationalist movement, and the Emperor and his Government also supported them in principle – as long as they were not too Russophile. A large section of the nationalists was by no means hostile to Austria or her dynasty and this was also true of the other Slav countries with like aspirations. In an article written in 1838, Metternich declared that complete respect for every nationality was one of the happiest principles of Austrian public administration. This grandiose and liberal view, he wrote, had brilliantly solved the difficult task of welding into a whole the most heterogeneous elements, something which no other state with a centralised system had been able to achieve.

In the Bohemian provinces the relations between the Germans and the Czechs were far from hostile. A whole series of German–Bohemian writers of a liberal turn of mind displayed in their works a lively sympathy for Czech nationhood and there were also Czechs who responded to these sentiments. Among the German nobility, too, this attitude was widespread and many of them stressed that they were neither Germans nor Czechs but Bohemians; one of the best known of these was Count Leo Thun, who later, as Minister for Education, did much towards meeting Czech wishes. Among Czech and German peasants it was the custom to exchange children for a time so that they could learn both languages. In consequence these children had close ties with families of both nationalities and were accustomed to address the heads of both families as their parents.

HUNGARY

Francis I was an absolute ruler in most of his provinces but he had to govern Hungary as a constitutional monarch. After the state bankruptcy of 1811 he did try to rule without the Hungarian Diet, but in 1825 he had to abandon the attempt. It was still only the nobility who, according to Hungarian constitutional law, made up the nation; it was uncommonly numerous and enjoyed privileges. The Diet was markedly feudal in character.

Hungary, without Transylvania but including Croatia, had at this time some twelve million inhabitants, but of these only five millions were Magyars; the rest were Slavs, Wallachians and Germans. In social terms, the ruling nobility was mainly Magyar, and the townsfolk German, while the Slavs and Wallachians were mostly serfs and agricultural workers. The Magyars fell into two groups: the wealthy magnates and the minor nobility. The former were mainly Catholic and pro-Habsburg, and had long been cosmopolitan in outlook; many of them spoke German and French but little or no Magyar. The latter, Calvinistic and mostly impecunious, were traditionally anti-Habsburg and nationalistic. National differences were, however, not much in evidence, because the language of the Diet, the courts and the civil service was Latin. Joseph II had tried to make German the official language, but this, among other measures, had aroused massive opposition which assumed revolutionary forms. Joseph and his successor Leopold had therefore repealed the most controversial decrees. Between

1830 and 1840 Magyar was declared to be the national tongue, and attempts were now made to impose it on the other nationalities – who in any case formed the majority – and this led to further tensions.

ITALY

After Napoleon's fall Austria obtained a key position in Italy. Lombardy and Venetia were united into a kingdom under Austrian rule; in the duchies of Tuscany, Modena and Parma collateral branches of the Austrian dynasty ruled, Metternich had concluded treaties with the kings of the Two Sicilies and Sardinia, and the Pope was also strongly under his influence. At the outset Austrian rule was not unpopular among the broad masses of the people in many areas. The conservatives and particularists were averse to nationalist schemes, which were often linked with political radicalism, and nationalism meant little to the ordinary folk, especially the country dwellers. But Austria had many enemies, above all among the army officers, officials and other adherents of the earlier, Napoleonic governments and among the rapidly expanding liberal circles, to which many aristocrats, writers and students belonged. The national movement reflected the spirit of the age; it rooted deep in history and had powerful motive forces. This had not escaped Metternich's notice and he was therefore at pains not to wound Italian national sentiment; he believed that by showing consideration for it in some degree, and by granting autonomy and good government, he could compensate for the lack of complete independence.

The Kingdom of Lombardo–Venetia enjoyed better government than the other Italian states, but here Austria's policy of intervention in Italy did much to exacerbate feeling. A few years after the new order in Europe (1820), a great surge of revolution swept through southern Europe. It began in Spain and the Spanish colonies, ran through Portugal, spread to Naples, Sicily and Piedmont and then set the Balkans ablaze. The European powers held several congresses to discuss counter-measures. In 1821, with the agreement of the powers, Austrian troops marched to put down revolutions in Naples and Piedmont. Lombardy and Venetia remained calm, although leaders of the nationalist movement had made preparations for a revolution. A number of them had to pay for it with long prison sentences in Austrian fortresses. After the July Revolution of 1830 there were some risings in Italy, as the nationalists hoped for French support, but these outbreaks were put down by Austrian troops. However, the nationalist movement took on a radical complexion through the emergence of Mazzini.

7

PRUSSIA

Most of the Prussian provinces, with a population totalling 7·9 millions, were admitted to the *Bund* in 1818. The principal exceptions were East and West Prussia and Posen. Greater compactness had been achieved in 1815 by treaty exchanges of territory with other states, though Prussia was still geographically divided by Hanover and the Electorate of Hesse. Some enclaves and exclaves remained, and the length of Prussia's frontiers was 340 German miles longer than France's, although in area the country was only half as big. On the whole, the Congress of Vienna left Prussia dissatisfied. This sprang partly from her ambition and her conviction that she had contributed most to ending foreign rule. The re-drawing of frontiers exposed her to fresh dangers without giving her a corresponding increase in military strength. The exclusion from the *Bund* of East and West Prussia and Posen, that is, of the areas bordering on Russia, awakened doubts whether in the event of war Prussia could count on the support of the *Bund*. An attempt by the King to gain admission foundered on the jealousy of the other member states. By acquiring the Rhine provinces, Prussia was exposed to the hostility of France, whereas in the eighteenth century both powers had united against the Habsburg Empire.

Prussia had also to reckon with enemies inside Germany. The truncated kingdom of Saxony hoped for Prussia's speedy downfall, and the fact that the Poles in her eastern provinces were not patriotic Prussians could hardly be held against them. The Catholic Rhinelanders, and the particularists in the many small pieces of territory which Prussia had received from the legacy of the old *Reich*, thought largely along the same lines and the South Germans were for the most part very anti-Prussian. In this situation Prussian liberals were well aware that enmity with Russia and the Austria of Metternich – those arch-enemies of political freedom – might well prove fatal for their country.

Prussian tradition granted the army pride of place. Frederick William III was, however, so peace-loving, frugal and humane that in the years preceding the clash with Napoleon he had allowed the army to fall into neglect and he subsequently let himself be talked into the war of liberation only with the greatest difficulty and almost under compulsion. When the war broke out, the statesmen and generals who supported the idea of national freedom had introduced conscription and a militia called the *Landwehr*, measures intended to fill the whole people with patriotism of the sort to which the French had owed their successes. The King and the section of the nobility hostile to reform had stubbornly resisted these innovations in the belief that they would lead to a revolution against their own position of power; this was by no means the opinion of Stein, Hardenberg or Scharnhorst. But many liberals saw in the *Landwehr* a popular counterpart to the King's professional army, and in many ways the *Landwehr's* organisation justified this conception, not least because the officers were mostly drawn from the middle classes and were not regular soldiers. For a long time liberal policy aimed at replacing the regular army to a very large extent by the *Landwehr*, so that if a conflict broke out the people's cause would have support against King and nobility. Many wanted to abolish the regular army completely, or so reduce its effectiveness that in an emergency it would be forced to call in the *Landwehr*.

The reactionary court party, on the other hand, would have preferred to abolish conscription and the *Landwehr*, or at least to subordinate the latter completely to the troops of the line under predominantly aristocratic officers. Despite the opposition of the War Minister, Hermann von Boyen, the *Landwehr* was brought into close association with the regulars, and so in 1819 he resigned. This marked a reactionary swing in Prussian politics, to which the other liberal ministers soon fell victim. The complete abolition of the *Landwehr* and conscription was prevented by the influence which the progressive Adjutant-General, von Witzleben, brought to bear on the King. The prevailing austerity and the antiquated strategy and tactics of the reactionary generals also considerably lowered the standards of equipment and training.

The main aim of the national movement was, for Germany and for each of its states, to secure constitutions which guaranteed popular representation and the basic rights of the subject. In those individual states which had acquired many new subjects and territories, it was hoped in this way to awaken a consciousness of unity and to increase the sense of responsibility among the citizens. The attitude of the King of Prussia wavered: at times he was disposed to grant a constitution, at others he let the reactionary faction change his mind. Even among those who wanted a constitution there were widely differing views. The progressives demanded national Estates with some powers, elected by the people, by which they meant the middle classes. The partisans of the old order would concede only provincial diets, with the main influence in the hands of the landowning aristocracy, and powers limited to advising the Government. Even Hardenberg for a long time envisaged a purely consultative assembly.

A provisional 'national representation' in line with conservative views existed from 1811 to 1815; it was made up partly of elected members and partly of members appointed by the King, among whom the nobility was in the majority. The assembly demanded an extension of its powers and a definitive constitution. Hardenberg did in fact have a draft measure worked out, the King promised the individual provinces a constitution and repeated this promise in a decree of 22 May 1815. A commission of officials and representatives of the provinces was set up to work out the constitution. In the meantime Metternich brought his influence to bear on the King for some years to prevent the creation of a genuinely popular representative body. At the very most, he urged, provincial diets based on the old Estates could be allowed but only after careful scrutiny to preclude any danger of a revolution. Hardenberg finally submitted to the King a draft constitution covering the self-government of the rural areas, towns, districts and provinces, laid down an electoral procedure and placed at the head a general diet to which the elected members of the provincial diets should themselves elect deputies. Many of the provisions of this draft were progressive, but on the other hand the legislative powers of the representative bodies were very limited. The plan was stillborn. Influenced by revolutions abroad and the radical movement among the students at home, the King lost confidence in Hardenberg and went over completely to the reactionary party. In 1819, differences of opinion between Hardenberg and Humboldt led to the latter's resignation; the other liberal ministers left with him. The law of 17 January 1820 governing the national debt contained the solemn assurance that the existing debt would not be increased without the consent of the *Reichsstände*, i.e., of the assembly for all Prussia; and yet, in the absence of the Chancellor through sickness, a new committee on the constitution recommended that for the time being all idea of a central assembly should be shelved and only provincial diets set up. Despite Hardenberg's counter-arguments, the King accepted the recommendation. Hardenberg died in November 1822.

Feudal reaction had carried the day. A law of 5 June 1823 created

provincial diets in which the aristocratic landowners predominated.
The diets were merely permitted to examine general matters referred
to them by the Crown. Later, district decrees (*Kreisordnungen*) were
issued, which gave the owners of estates in the east a privileged position.
Nothing more was heard of the reorganisation of the rural communities. Some of Stein's reforms, in the sphere of both urban organisation and agrarian legislation, were repealed.

On the positive side Hardenberg did succeed in modernising the
machinery of administration. In 1817, a Council of State was set up to
which new laws were submitted for examination. Leading officials
belonged to this council, which was looked on as a kind of 'officials'
Parliament' and a substitute for a popular assembly. In addition, the
national finances, which had been badly dislocated by the war, were
restored to some sort of order. Despite complaints from the guilds,
unlimited freedom of trade was preserved. Last but not least, the
development of industry was greatly furthered by the setting up of a
big, unified Prussian customs area.

The transformation of the old Prussia into a closely-knit economic
unit brought excellent results, politically as well as economically. The
particularism which was rife in many districts gradually gave way to a
sense of community of interests. The tariff did not follow the old
mercantile principle of rigid exclusion but laid down very low rates on
weight, which amounted to between 5-10% of the value of industrial
goods and 20% on colonial produce. The customs tariff unintentionally
gave the impetus for the formation of the German Customs Union
(*Zollverein*) which was also being propagated by South Germans like
Friedrich List and Karl Nebenius, though these latter thought that it
might be realised through the *Bund* – an utter impossibility. Gradually
a number of states – at first the smaller ones – joined the Prussian
Customs Area. Although the Customs Union was not political in origin,
it aroused great anger against Prussia in many states; Metternich sought
to check its growth, Britain and Hanover worked towards the same end,
and several customs unions were founded or planned which were
intended to prejudice the Prussian one. All the same, the conviction
spread that joining the Prussian *Zollverein* would offer the greatest
economic advantages and Prussia made some skilful moves to widen the
association. In the thirties she took the initiative in forming the German
Zollverein, which finally embraced nearly all Germany, with the exception
of Austria. Metternich's attempts to thwart this growth of Prussian
power had no success.

Prussian customs policy and the German *Zollverein* contributed
decisively to the economic rise of Germany. In 1838 a well-drafted
railway act was passed and at the same time the first stretch of railway in

Prussia, linking Berlin and Potsdam, was opened. Railway construction was at first left to private enterprise because the state could not raise the necessary loans in the absence of a Prussian parliament, and besides this many high officials had their doubts about railways. But alongside unprogressive ministers and officials there were also men to be found in the Prussian bureaucracy who possessed great technical knowledge and public spirit, allied with humanity and vision. One of these was von Altenstein, whom Hardenberg had appointed Minister of Education. During the many years that he held this post, Prussian universities became world-famous. The work of the Privy Councillor (*Geheimrat*) Johannes Schulze was also highly fruitful; he was imbued with Humboldt's spirit and supervised secondary education most efficiently. Primary education was re-cast in the Pestalozzi mould and Adolf Diesterweg wrought wonders in the training of teachers. At this time the Prussian educational system was unrivalled by that of any other German state.

The conflicting currents in the policy of Prussia caused the public's attitude towards her in the other states of the *Bund* to fluctuate. The creation of a common German economic area as well as the attention paid to scholarship and national education won her many friends; on the other hand, her government's political measures evoked widespread distaste. When in 1831 Poland rose against Russia in a serious insurrection, a considerable part of the German people felt the warmest sympathy and admiration for the Poles, whereas the Prussian court sided with Tsar Nicholas, who was Frederick William's son-in-law. The heroism of the Poles inspired many German poets, notably Platen, Uhland, Lenau and Freiligrath, to write poems which are outstanding and moving even today. When the rebellion was quelled, hordes of refugees passing through Germany to seek asylum in France and Switzerland were fêted and helped on their way by members of all social classes. Hitherto, the Prussian Government had observed the rulings of the Congress of Vienna in respect of the nationality of their Polish subjects in Posen. Polish was used for official business and taught in the schools and Poles received important posts in the administration, but all this now changed and a policy of gradual Germanisation was adopted.

In the sphere of religion a union of the Lutheran and Reformed (Calvinistic) faiths had taken place as early as 1817. Although a section of the orthodox Lutherans broke away, a great step had none the less been taken towards breaking down religious differences. Relations between the Prussian Government and the Catholic Church turned out less happily. Violent disputes over the denomination and education of children of mixed marriages arose with the ultramontane wing of the

church, and during the controversy the Government imprisoned the
archbishops of Cologne and Posen.

In the main, however, significant economic and intellectual progress
was achieved in Prussia, above all because the peace was not disturbed.
Prosperity and education spread and laid the foundations of a strong
desire for freedom.

8

CONSTITUTION AND POLITICS IN THE SMALLER STATES

GENERAL SITUATION

Austria and Prussia were large states with a European role to play; in consequence, they were far less inclined than the smaller states of the *Bund* to allow popular representatives any hand in making important decisions. These smaller states had no foreign policy worth mentioning to conduct and no large armies, and were thus unimpeded by the main obstacles which Austria and Prussia faced over giving a parliament any decisive voice in foreign affairs. Nor could a foreign policy which consisted primarily in combating freedom movements in Europe and involved costly military intervention command popularity or acceptance among representative assemblies. The great influence of the military on the State in Austria and Prussia scarcely accorded with constitutionalism. The Prussian army aristocracy stood in a special relationship to the King, the 'supreme war-lord'. In Austria any constitutional system was rendered even more difficult by the multiplicity of nationalities.

Hence it was easier for the smaller states of the *Bund* to approach the concept of a representative assembly by the founding of diets, though the timing and extent of the implementation of this liberal demand depended on many local circumstances. The great obstacle was economic and social conditions. The broad masses of the people had other things to worry about than politics. Twenty years of wars which had spread over most of Europe had left the German countries utterly exhausted. Countless people had lost their lives, their health or their resources; many were reduced to beggary. In addition the first few years of peace brought bad harvests and terrible famines. Both in industry and agriculture there were crises lasting for years; unemployment was widespread; national finances and the credit situation were in a wretched state and the burden of taxation was oppressive. All this affected the interest taken in politics by large sections of the community. The liberal historian Gervinus, who lived through this period, writes that

the lively youth of the day were in despair over the political apathy
of the middle classes; the average German citizen, none too well off and
tied to his home and business, had hitherto had neither time nor
inclination for public affairs; he would have preferred to avoid all civic
responsibility and in return would gladly have waived all civic rights.
He had, Gervinus concludes, left all concern for the State to the aristocracy and the officials, much as he resented them; besides, the old diets
had by no means always championed the common good, and in consequence new assemblies had appeared to the average citizen expensive
institutions of dubious utility.

The greater part of Germany's intelligentsia, both conservative and
liberal, looked with admiration at political life in England. But in that
country there was a rich upper class and a prosperous middle class,
which had for centuries taken an active part in politics and grown
practised in the art. In Germany the number of prosperous middle-class
people with an interest in politics was much smaller. There scarcely
existed a political press and there were no political parties at all.

Soon after the Congress of Vienna some of the states of the *Bund*
were given constitutions which more or less met liberal demands,
while others had longer to wait. After the July Revolution of 1830 in
France, a spasm of constitutional yearning agitated Germany; there were
disorders – even riots – in many places, and a number of constitutions
were re-cast in a progressive form.

Many of them took the shape of a contract between prince and people,
so that they could not be altered unilaterally, and this, incidentally,
was also forbidden under article fifty-six of the Vienna Statute of 1820.
Many were negotiated by both parties; others were first promulgated
by the ruler and then assumed the character of a treaty which the
prince solemnly swore to observe, whereupon the representatives
of the people did homage to him. Provisions concerning the rights of
parliament and citizens varied from one constitution to the next.
Usually there were two chambers, who had to agree on measures,
which then needed the assent of the monarch. In many countries the
rights of the deputies were very limited, in others they were more
extensive, and sometimes the lower chamber could overrule the upper
if there was disagreement.

Although the franchise was governed by provisions which excluded
the lower classes and made stipulations about the property to be held,
most of the deputies came from less well-to-do classes than in England
or France, many of them being simple country folk who were politically far from mature and interested only in immediate questions.
Very often when elections were held, the voters supported candidates
who were state officials. These possessed the necessary knowledge and

could live without financial support from the voters, since they were drawing a salary and, as deputies, allowances, and usually lived in the capital where the parliament sat. This tendency was not confined to Germany, but it was a great disadvantage that some governments refused opposition members from the civil service the necessary leave of absence. Furthermore, many electoral systems sought as far as possible to exclude lawyers, authors and journalists because of their predominantly liberal outlook.

To prevent the spread of progressive views, strict censorship regulations were often imposed at the instigation of the *Bund*, books were confiscated, newspapers were forbidden to be sent by post and assemblies and clubs were banned. But those concerned frequently found ways of circumventing such measures: there were always places where censorship was less stringent and particularly radical writings were smuggled in from abroad.

Bavaria before 1830

The state of Bavaria had, in the re-distribution after the break-up of the old *Reich*, increased its population by more than 60%. There were sharp contrasts between old and new. The original Bavarians were in the main strict Catholic and conservative farmers, who for the most part still lived under a system of patriarchal agriculture and observed up to 200 holidays, whereas the new Bavarians were predominantly Protestant; they included the population of historic cities like Nuremberg, Augsburg, Würzburg and Bamberg and had reached a higher economic and cultural level. The constitution of 1818 was intended to fuse these elements and, despite its many defects, was hailed as very progressive. Although in many respects reminiscent of the French constitution of 1814, the franchise in Bavaria was much less linked to wealth than in France. In the upper chamber the aristocracy predominated. The peasants elected half of the second chamber, the towns a quarter, and the landowners, clergy and universities the rest. Many of the deputies were simple country folk, often village mayors, millers or publicans. The majority of the Catholic clergy among the deputies were of rural stock. The liberals were returned mostly by the towns and universities and were usually landowners, civil servants or professional men. Prominent among them were the Mayor of Bamberg, F. L. von Hornthal, a former lawyer of Jewish origin, and Professor Wilhelm Joseph Behr.

In the assemblies (*Landtage*), which met every three years, the liberals sought above all else to eliminate defects in the constitution. They also demanded that the army take an oath of allegiance to the constitution and that the military budget should be cut and this frequently brought them into conflict with the Government. The country folk showed little understanding of constitutional issues, particularly as they were suffering under a serious agricultural crisis. When the second election was held many liberals, including Hornthal, lost their seats. The Government refused leave of absence to Professor Behr, who had meanwhile become Mayor of Würzburg, on the grounds that the municipal administration also had state tasks to fulfil and that in consequence government consent was needed; the deputies endorsed this decision by 83 votes to 25. Joseph Ludwig, Count Armansperg, now became the principal spokesman for the liberal opposition.

Maximilian I died in 1825 and was succeeded by his son Ludwig. The liberals placed great hopes in him, for he had long been enthusiastic over liberal and national aspirations and had made statements which horrified Metternich. In one of his poems he declared that it was magnificent to rule over a free people; but he was strongly influenced by Romantic ideas and believed it possible to combine far-reaching royal privileges with political freedom. He was above all else a patron of the arts. In Italy he had mingled as an equal with painters; it was his dearest wish to make Munich a city of art and learning, an aim which he realised handsomely. Military matters held no interest for him; he cut the budget and severely weakened the national defences. For a time he was just the king the liberals wanted. He dismissed the conservative minister, Count Rechberg, and brought Count Armansperg, the liberal leader, to power and prominence by appointing him Minister of the Interior and Finance Minister. But the King was also accessible to quite varied advisers. In the elections of 1827 the liberals, who were split in various groups, gained a majority. The Government introduced twenty-five bills of a progressive nature, which were sharply opposed by the upper chamber because they curtailed the rights of the nobility. To break this resistance Ludwig appointed a number of liberals to the upper chamber. In this way, to take one example, an important measure was put through whereby the districts (*Kreise*) were given local government. But the liberals were disunited and the aristocratic party succeeded by skilful tactics in forming in the lower chamber an opposition which many liberals also joined. Several progressive bills were thrown out and the radicals mocked that the Government was more liberal than the chamber. In 1818 the Catholic poet Eduard von Schenk became Minister of the Interior, while Armansperg continued to direct the Ministry of Finance and also became Foreign Minister.

The better treatment shown to the press by Ludwig after his accession had favoured the founding of political newspapers and an active interest in public affairs. A Catholic conservative circle published the periodical *Eos* on which the leading spirit was Joseph Görres. Originally a republican and freethinker, he had now become an adherent of Catholicism and mysticism, wielding a powerful pen and supported by other prominent scholars and writers like Baader, Döllinger and Friedrich Schlegel. They fought against the liberal spirit of the age and its optimistic belief in the power of reason and advocated, just as Lamennais was doing in France at this time, an alliance of Catholicism with democracy. The King, it is true, was sincerely religious but disapproved of the activities of clerical circles and even warned his Minister of the Interior, Schenk, against any kind of Jesuitism. Liberal newspapers circulated widely and had great influence. The publisher Cotta and the author Coremans, a Belgian by birth, both founded journals.

Gottfried Eisenmann, a doctor, began, in agreement with a group of professors in Würzburg, to publish the *Bayerische Volkszeitung*. All these papers started by being moderately liberal; they wished to improve the constitution and were not carrying on opposition for opposition's sake, but some of them did veer to the left. Behr and Hornthal criticised the all-too-moderate liberals; the radicals preferred French liberalism to the aristocratic English variety, were sharply anti-clerical and were really working towards a republic. But even Coremans at that time held up Bavaria as a paradise of constitutionalism.

Württemberg

Although the kingdom of Württemberg was Bavaria's nearest neighbour, its historical development had made it utterly unlike Bavaria. For centuries it had possessed a parliament which Charles James Fox had compared with the one at Westminster, and which consisted of representatives of the Church, citizens and peasants but not the nobility. The people were strict Lutherans up to the time when Napoleon had reorganised the country. When its territory and population were doubled, many Catholics and some nobles – a rarity until then – were added, though even in 1841 only 2% of the productive land, mostly forests, belonged to the nobility. Nine-tenths of all families owned agricultural land and many of them also carried on a trade. The first king of the reconstituted Württemberg, Frederick I, proceeded with dictatorial ruthlessness to fuse all the new territories into one administrative unit. The Estates and local self-government were abolished. This aroused great discontent. The King tried to win over the people by laying a new constitution before his chosen representatives and putting it into effect forthwith. This constitution suited the changed circumstances and was in many respects more liberal than the old one, but it was almost unanimously rejected by the assembly, which declared that a new constitution could only be created by agreement between

E

king and people. Until then, they said, they were determined to cling
to *das gute, alte Recht* (the traditional phrase in Württemberg for its
time-honoured code of laws), which must be the basis of any new
constitution. This principle was widely and firmly held by public
opinion. The King yielded and agreed to negotiations. The spokesman
for the people was the fiery Count George von Waldeck. In October
1816, before agreement could be reached, Frederick I died. He was
succeeded by his son William, who had the reputation of being liberal.
The opposition was divided and for a long time the mass of the people
sided with the intransigents. William issued eleven decrees which
introduced highly beneficial reforms and were well received. In order
to forestall restrictive measures by the *Bund* after the murder of
Kotzebue, there was now a strong desire in Württemberg to settle on a
constitution quickly. This was done on 24 September 1819 amid
general rejoicing. The new constitution contained some very liberal
provisions and was, above all, the result of an agreement freely negotiated between king and people. To be sure, only a few days later
Württemberg once more had to withdraw complete freedom from the
press, since the *Bund* decreed the introduction of censorship, but this
was exercised only mildly in Württemberg. The activity of the subsequent assemblies, however, disappointed the hopes of realising liberal
or national ideals. This was due not only to the reactionary *Bund* policy
inaugurated by Metternich along with the Prussian and other governments, but also to the fact that the new constitution linked the franchise
with the payment of land or trade taxes. Owners of capital, lawyers,
doctors, teachers, writers and officials did not possess the franchise
by virtue of the taxes they paid but only if they happened to possess
fairly substantial holdings in land. Besides this, only members of a
Christian faith were eligible for election. The majority of the deputies
consisted of well-to-do farmers, provincial tradesmen and such officials
as enjoyed the favour of these circles and the Government.[1] They had
only professional and local interests and German unity meant little to
them; for them, it was enough to be Württembergers. They supported
guild privileges and low taxation and had no love for the educated
classes, jurists, or those of other faiths, especially Jews. On the other
hand, they had sympathy for the class known as 'clerks' (*Schreiber*), a
unique social feature of Württemberg, who were a very numerous
guild of local government officials with a voice in many matters and
distinguished by scanty education and venality. Whereas the civil

---

[1] The second chamber consisted of 13 deputies from the landowning aristocracy, 6 Protestant and 3 Catholic clergymen, the Chancellor of the University,
7 deputies from the larger towns and 63 deputies from the larger districts
(*Oberamtsbezirke*), most of which were rural areas.

service consisted mainly of graduates in law, the 'clerks' had no academic qualifications. But the peasants and townsfolk were of the opinion that an ounce of practice was worth a ton of theory whether in administration or farming or following a trade. They liked it when the Finance Minister got up in the chamber and assured them in broad Swabian that he himself had started in a very small way.[1]

When the *Landtag* met in 1820, there was no sign of an opposition, but towards the end of the year Friedrich List was elected; he drew up a plan of radical reform, which, without regard for persons or traditions, demanded a complete reorganisation of the administration. For this the Government prosecuted him for libel and proposed his expulsion from the chamber and, although a few deputies stoutly defended him, the motion was carried by 56 votes to 30. The Government was under strong pressure from the *Bund* to allow no opposition to emerge. In 1823, Austria, Prussia and Russia recalled their ambassadors from Stuttgart. The *Bundestag* complained that in Württemberg the Carlsbad Decrees were in some cases competely ignored and had in others been applied in a highly unsatisfactory manner. Radical papers appeared in Stuttgart attacking Metternich's régime. Although King William hated and despised Metternich he had to give way, and it was a long time before the great powers declared themselves satisfied.

In the first decade of its existence, the *Landtag* passed many useful laws, taxes were considerably reduced and the national finances put into impeccable order. The size of the army and the period of service were reduced. The electors soon showed an increasing tendency to return to parliament civil servants who were experts in particular fields and who would on occasion criticise government bills. On many issues, such as the franchise, admission to trades and the civil rights of the Jews, many deputies showed themselves less liberal than the officials who had drafted the measures. Over constitutional matters the deputies were very reserved. The out and out liberals were sadly disillusioned and many of them relinquished their mandate. The upper chamber was for the most part without a quorum, because the powerful aristocrats stayed away and by the constitution the decision was then left to the lower chamber.

Baden

The Grand Duchy of Baden was Napoleon's creation. Previously it had been a small margravate with a population of 200,000. The new duchy included a number of territories with a strong tradition of independence, such as the Breisgau, formerly Austrian, with its famous University of

[1] Cf. R. v. Mohl, *Lebenserinnerungen*, 1902. Vol. I, p. 15, and Vol. II, p. 21.

Freiburg, Heidelberg and the big industrial town of Mannheim. The state bordered on Switzerland and France and maintained close relations with these countries. When all liberal movements in Germany were persecuted, many of their champions fled to Switzerland or Strasbourg, and from there smuggled revolutionary pamphlets into Baden for use in promoting agitation throughout Germany.

When the Grand Duke gave his country a constitution in 1818, its liberal lines were intended to win over the various sections of the community which had hitherto been estranged and to make them conscious of being citizens of Baden. Anyone who enjoyed civic rights in a municipality was entitled to vote, though having such a right usually implied house or land ownership. Whenever the two chambers could not agree, they held a joint session at which the people's deputies could outvote the nobles of the upper house. The first of the liberals to come to the fore were, in the lower chamber, Professor Karl von Rotteck[1], the member for Freiburg University, and, in the upper, Ludwig, Baron von Liebenstein. Liebenstein, who came of an old aristocratic family, had been a keen student of English and French politics. He and his followers put down many motions which aimed at liberalising the constitution and legislation. Of the sixty-three deputies, thirty-seven were state or municipal officials, among them Liebenstein and another liberal leader, Ludwig Winter. It is noteworthy that members who held public office hardly ever let this fact deter them from criticising government measures. In the lower chamber, Rotteck, one of the most prominent theoreticians of liberalism, frequently spoke in the same sense as Liebenstein in the upper, and often far more radically.

Differences soon developed between the two chambers as well as between the upper chamber and the Government, for the latter contained reactionary as well as liberal elements, and this led to fluctuations in policy. So it came about that the Government sometimes refused Liebenstein and other officials the necessary leave of absence to attend to their parliamentary duties, and would then relent. Liebenstein entered the service of the ministry and prevailed upon the Government to make some far-reaching concessions to liberal demands. In the next session he appeared mainly as the Government spokesman, while the leadership of the liberals was assumed by Johann Adam von Itzstein, who usually voiced more radical views than Liebenstein. It also happened that Liebenstein and the Government were sometimes more liberal than the majority of the country deputies, as for example in granting Jews full civic rights. Compromises were reached over some questions. When the lower house wanted to cut the military appropria-

[1] Vide infra, p. 201 ff.

tions, this led to a conflict with the Government, of which the liberal Ludwig Winter was now a prominent figure. Liebenstein tried to persuade the chamber to agree to concessions but Itzstein emphasised that a matter of principle was involved and the chamber supported him by 30 votes to 29. The session was suspended and the Government refused to sanction the measures agreed on. Soon after this, in 1824, Liebenstein died.

The last session had marked a considerable recession of liberalism in the chamber. Fresh elections took place in 1825, the Government exerted strong pressure on the voters and the great majority of the new deputies were now on the Government's side, a state of affairs which lasted until the end of the twenties.

North Germany

In constitutional development North Germany lagged behind the South, and this was principally the fault of the landowning nobility. This Junkerdom was strongest in Mecklenburg, where it successfully defied all attempts by the Grandduke to abolish medieval conditions. But even in the Kingdom of Saxony, which had made unusual progress in industry, finance and culture, feudal institutions and outlook died hard. The old Estates continued in being but were completely dominated by the nobility, who went so far as to try and exclude the bourgeoisie and newly-ennobled landowners by more stringent stipulations in the matter of pedigree. The town members were appointed by the patrician town councils and the peasantry was not represented at all. The Estates could impose taxes, but had only an advisory role in legislation. In trade the strict guild principle prevailed. The old king, Frederick Augustus, and his head of Government, Count Einsiedel, were opposed to any innovations. The people's concern for their daily bread at first left them little leisure for politics, but as the country gradually recovered liberal demands were raised, both in the Estates and by the printed word.

In Saxe-Weimar, the Grand Duke Karl Augustus agreed with the Estates on a new constitution. The chamber, which consisted mainly of deputies from the nobility, townsfolk and peasants, had to submit the budget and any legislation to the Government for approval.

The Kingdom of Hanover had a personal link with Great Britain. The King resided in London, where Hanoverian affairs were dealt with by the 'German Chancellery' under Count Münster, while a Governor-General was appointed in Hanover. The nobility had got back its privileges, which had been abolished by the French. In every province there were Estates divided into 'curias', whose agreement was necessary for any decision reached. These provincial Estates were a stronghold of aristocratic power. By a royal decree of 1814 a general assembly of the Estates was set up and this was divided into two chambers in 1819. The nobility wielded the main influence. The towns elected state officials for the most part in order to save the added expense of deputies' salaries. The peasants were only sparsely represented; they came mainly from East Frisia, where free peasants had always formed part of the Estates.

The royal power lay in the hands of Count Münster, who had gained at the Congress of Vienna the reputation of being a champion of liberalism, but as things turned out he did not fulfil this promise. In Hanover the ministers were drawn from the nobility, although the influential statesman Privy Councillor Rehberg was a bourgeois. However, in 1821 the nobility brought about his fall. Karl Bertram Stüve, a lawyer and mayor, who became a deputy in 1824, vigorously campaigned for the removal of the tax privileges enjoyed by the nobility and the manifold feudal services still incumbent on the peasants.

The Duchy of Brunswick had in time past enjoyed a succession of good rulers. Under Napoleon it had formed part of the Kingdom of Westphalia; feudal privileges were abolished and modern laws introduced. After Napoleon's fall, the nobility strove, with only partial success, to regain their privileges and revive the old Estates system. The constitution granted in 1820, however, in no way met the needs of the age. Until 1823 the hereditary prince, Karl, was under the guardianship of a committee of the privy council with the King of England – represented by Count Münster – at its head. When Karl came of age he soon showed how little suited he was to his office. Devoid of any sense of his obligations, he was rapacious, brutal and surrounded by vicious toadies. He refused to recognise the constitution and other decisions of the Minority Council and prosecuted some worthy state officials. The Federal Assembly redressed some injustices and ordered the repeal of one or two of his measures, and the Estates protested against his rejection of the constitution.

The Grand Duchy of Hesse (Hesse-Darmstadt) was ruled by Ludwig I, a very clever and capable prince, who in the days of the Confederation of the Rhine had dismissed his disorganised and demoralised Estates and subsequently introduced many important reforms, including, in 1820, a new constitution and a law governing the responsibility of ministers and leading state officials. In the Electorate of Hesse (Hesse-Cassel), William I sought to restore the old constitution based on the Estates, but after lengthy conflicts he ruled without them. So did his successor, William II, who, by reason of this and of his dependence on a mistress, stirred up widespread discontent among his subjects.

LIBERALISATION AFTER 1830

The first decade and a half of peace had, it must be said, seen great progress, not least in commerce and the arts, but the high hopes with which so many, when peace was signed, had looked forward to the future had given place to deep disillusion. A large section of the intellectuals, and especially the students, had believed that national unity and political freedom would soon be a fact, but the founding of the *Bund* showed how remote these ideals were. Both radicalism, to which a part of the students had gone over, and the demagogue-hunt which began with the Carlsbad Decrees, opened up an unbridgeable gap between opposition and Government. The stringent censorship which prevailed in many countries, the shackles on the press and the harsh suppression of liberal aspirations had a thoroughly depressing effect. Although a section of the nobility advocated reforms, or looked favourably on them, the feudal aristocratic party was still paramount. In many places the peasants suffered under the heavy burden of aristocratic prerogative. In the towns, government was to a considerable extent in the hands of privileged families and trades were fettered by the selfish practices of the guilds. The lower classes were victims of superannuated privileges and rising industrialism. Religious antagonisms flared up again and led to open conflict. In the diets it was too often apparent that many country and townsfolk were interested only in the narrow concerns of their own callings, and governments had a knack of debarring officials and other educated people from any political activity towards liberal goals.

All the same, towards the end of the twenties there were many indications that the urge for greater freedom was still very much alive. In July 1830 a revolution broke out in France which had repercussions throughout Europe. As a result Charles X fled, Louis Philippe of Orleans, the 'bourgeois king', backed by the prosperous liberal middle class, came to the throne. The new French Government sought to steer a middle course in its policy, equally far removed from the extremes of right or left. Soon afterwards a revolution against Dutch rule broke out in Belgium, and in Poland there was a serious rising against the Russian overlords. Shortly before this, the Greeks had won their freedom and the Rumanians and Serbs had drawn nearer independence. Soon after the July Revolution, riots broke out in Italy, and even in Switzerland the rule of the oligarchy was overthrown in many places by democratic movements. In 1831-2 the Reform Bill, which considerably extended the franchise, was passed in England.

This mighty wave of liberalism also reinforced German exertions towards freedom. Just at this time, the masses there were in an ugly mood through the rise in food prices brought on by poor harvests. At first popular feeling was directed against those rulers who had made themselves personally disliked. The young Duke Karl of Brunswick happened to be in Paris when the Revolution broke out and at once hurried home, where he met a very hostile reception. A vast crowd assembled outside his castle, whereupon he lost his nerve and fled abroad, leaving the castle in flames. His fate was richly deserved. The Diet of the *Bund* requested his brother, Duke William, to take over the government and he was later recognised as ruler. In Brunswick, after exhaustive negotiations between the Estates and the Government, a new constitution was agreed on in 1832 which gave the towns and the peasants stronger representation and extended the franchise. In addition, all the peasants' feudal services were abolished and autonomy granted to the towns.

In Hesse-Cassel, the Elector William II was very unpopular. In the autumn of 1830 there were serious disorders, the citizens were armed and William was forced to summon the Estates, which had not met since 1816. These worked out a new constitution which came into force at the beginning of 1831. The form it took was largely the work of the Marburg professor, Sylvester Jordan, the son of a poor Tyrolean workman and a pupil of Rotteck, whose doctrines he enthusiastically supported. A single chamber was formed which possessed uncommonly wide powers, and equality before the law and other important rights were guaranteed to all subjects. The constitution was based on a contract between the Elector and his people. He, as well as his ministers and officials and even army officers and NCOs, had to take an oath to respect it. Infringements were made actionable, feudal services and dues were abolished and guild restrictions done away with. The militia remained in being. This constitution was considered the most liberal in Germany.

Public opinion was gravely affronted by the Elector's shabby treatment of his wife, the sister of the King of Prussia; William was completely under the influence of his mistress, a commoner on whom he had bestowed the title of Countess Reichenbach. Since her presence in Cassel was not tolerated, the Elector lived with her in castles remote from the capital, where consultation with ministers, which the constitution demanded, was impossibly inconvenient. The Diet therefore gave him the choice of either breaking with the Countess and moving to Cassel or abdicating. In effect he chose the latter alternative, by agreeing with the Diet on a measure which made the hereditary prince Frederick William a co-regent and sole ruler all the while the Elector was absent. He then lived permanently outside Cassel, mostly abroad. The new ruler soon proved to be a stubborn reactionary.

Frederick William soon afterwards appointed the *Obergerichtsrat* Ludwig Hassenpflug as his Prime Minister. Hassenpflug was an exceedingly capable official who had become a sharp opponent of the parliamentary system, though this was not at first evident. Government and Parliament worked together and passed numerous important laws. But then differences arose between them. Hassenpflug used every means to defeat the liberal majority and then destroy it – by refusing leave of absence to officials, for example, and by frequently dissolving the chamber. The liberals used all constitutional means to counteract these measures, notably by proceedings against the minister in the High Court, but in vain. It was now clear that the provisions of a constitution alone were not sufficient if a government and the competent officials were determined and able to circumvent the law. These events coincided with the rise of radicalism, which emerged in many German states and gave the Diet of the *Bund* the chance to take reactionary counter-measures.

Hassenpflug's differences with the Regent caused his resignation in 1837. He took service with other German states and finally with Prussia. Although his successor was able to moderate the constitutional struggle, Sylvester Jordan, who had drafted the new constitution, was arrested in 1839 on the totally unfounded suspicion of revolutionary activities. In 1843 he was sentenced to five years' imprisonment but was completely cleared by the Supreme Court in 1845, having spent six years in prison before his innocence was established. It is not surprising that strong radicalism developed in Hesse.

In the Grand Duchy of Hesse (Hesse-Darmstadt) Ludwig I, who was remembered with affection, died in 1830. But even in this state serious disorders broke out, though their causes were less political than social. Relations between Government and Parliament were better here than in the Electorate, though on occasion there was no lack of contentious issues. The two chambers contained many distinguished parliamentarians and a large number of progressive measures went through. In the thirties there was a strong radical movement, in which Georg Büchner took part. This talented writer not only demanded political revolution but also social upheaval. Threatened with imminent arrest, he contrived to escape to Zürich, where he became a lecturer at the University, but he died young in 1837. Among his close friends was a clergyman, Weidig, who played a leading role in a secret organisation. Weidig was arrested and so maltreated by the investigating magistrate that he committed suicide; the case caused a sensation and vehement protests against the police. Numerous people were interrogated on suspicion of high treason and disseminating seditious writings and many were sentenced to long terms of penal servitude, though the Grand

Duke pardoned most of them. One, Karl Zeuner, showed no remorse but declared that he would do the same again if he had the chance. He was pardoned none the less, but on condition that he emigrated to North America.

A notable phenomenon in the political life of Hesse was the von Gagern family. They were Knights of the Empire and Hans von Gagern, a diplomat, politician and writer, represented the Netherlands at the Congress of Vienna. His ideas were a happy compound of conservative and liberal, national and cosmopolitan elements. His sons Friedrich, Heinrich and Max were imbued with the same spirit and likewise played an important part in the politics of their own day. Hans von Gagern was a member of the first chamber of the Grand Duchy of Hesse and his son Heinrich of the second, where he gained the superb parliamentary experience which he was to display as one of the leading statesmen in the Frankfurt National Assembly of 1848–9.

Hanover

In Hanover the peculiar circumstances which had found expression in the constitution of 1819 persisted. The privileged classes – the nobility, a municipal oligarchy and the officials – still predominated, while the mass of the people had no representation. But with the rise of liberalism this system aroused great discontent, especially among the intellectual classes. The July Revolution touched off disturbances in a number of towns and rural communities; in some parts of the country people even refused to pay taxes. This caused concern among the ruling classes and a barrister, von dem Knesebeck, published a pamphlet in which he called for open warfare with the revolutionary elements, indeed for abrogation of the constitution. He headed the work with a saying of Napoleon's: 'When the rabble has the upper hand, it is no longer called the rabble, but the nation'. The pamphlet caused great indignation. In the Harz town of Osterode two lawyers published radical articles, the second of which called upon the people to use its strength. The municipal authorities thereupon decided to form a local militia, the Government sent troops and both agitators were carted off in handcuffs to Hanover. The Government also wanted to arrest three lecutrers at Göttingen University on suspicion of holding revolutionary views, but in this they did not succeed, as disorders broke out in the town. A crowd of students and townsfolk, led by two lawyers named Eggeling and Seidensticker, occupied the town hall, passed a resolution to form a civic guard and petitioned the king for a completely free constitution. The authorities dared not offer resistance. The civic guard was placed under the command of a university lecturer, Dr von Rauschenplatt, and the movement seemed to be spreading right across the country. A pamphlet was distributed which made the most monstrous accusations against Count Münster, who directed the Hanoverian Chancellery in London, and compared him with Attila and Nero. The Göttingen radicals now split up. One faction wanted to build barricades and take up arms while the other called for negotiations. Soon the whole revolutionary party was in disintegration. Government troops met with no opposition and the ringleaders took to their heels to avoid arrest. Some of them were brought to trial in Hanover.

The reactionary elements in the Government at first called for stern measures, but these were prevented by the reasonable attitude of the Duke of Cambridge, who represented his elder brother, William IV of England, in Hanover. Count Münster was dismissed and William declared himself ready to accept constitutional reform. In the subsequent elections, many towns returned independent representatives of a liberal complexion instead of officials. Professor Dahlmann of Göttingen was given the task of drafting a basic state law which was then made the basis of the deliberations of the Government and the towns. There were some strenuous struggles with the privileged classes before the constitution was achieved; it came into force on 26 September 1833. In the first chamber, apart from a few princes, nobles and church representatives, as well as four notables appointed by the king, there sat 35 deputies from the knights. The second chamber consisted of a few deputies representing the Church and the universities, 37 deputies from the towns and 38 representing smaller communities and the peasants. A more active constitutional life now developed, but it soon died down again, as the increase in radicalism in South Germany caused the reactionary great powers to take new and stern measures against all liberal movements. A good index of the participation of the classes in politics is given by the results of the second election, held at the end of 1833: 34 state officials, 18 municipal officials, 5 lawyers, 5 merchants and manufacturers, 4 clergymen and 18 landed proprietors were elected to the second chamber. The well-to-do middle class was thus very weakly represented, the minor nobility more strongly and the officials most strongly of all. There was not a single farmer among the deputies, although in Hanover some were very well-to-do. These elected either an official or a larger landowner.

In 1837 William IV died and was succeeded by his niece Victoria, but as women were excluded from the throne of Hanover, William's brother, Ernest August, Duke of Cumberland, became King. The new ruler brought with him a gigantic burden of debt which he had incurred by his dissolute life, and he tried to appropriate the profits of the domains which by the constitution of 1833 had become state property. When he arrived in Hanover he appointed the leader of the reactionary nobles, Geheimrat Georg von Schele, his Prime Minister, and the latter advised him to abolish the constitution. This provided, in article 13, that homage should be paid only when the king had sworn to respect the constitution and royal power was thus made expressly dependent on the king's recognition of the constitution. Ernest August evaded this obligation, declared the 1833 constitution null and void and that of 1819 as valid, and released officials from the oath they had taken to the former. This brutal breach of the constitution aroused consternation and rising indignation throughout Germany. Even out-and-out reactionaries disagreed with the course Ernest August had taken and would have preferred any change to be made in due legal form, even though this would have meant strong pressure on and intimidation of public opinion. Metternich shared this view. In England the ultra-conservative *Times* criticised the king's action.

At this moment seven of the most prominent professors at Göttingen registered a solemn protest. They declared that they considered themselves bound by their oath to the 1833 constitution and would act accordingly. The seven in question were the jurist Albrecht, the historian Dahlmann, the two Germanists Jakob and Wilhelm Grimm, the Orientalist Ewald, the physicist Wilhelm Weber and the literary historian Georg Gervinus. A section of the faculty and the great majority of the students sided with them, though there were some professors who disapproved of the step they had taken. The King proceeded to use force against the seven, arbitrarily dismissing them and ordering Dahlmann, Jakob Grimm and Gervinus to leave the country within three days. As a result of the general indignation which was felt throughout Germany, contributions for the support of the seven men of Göttingen were collected. Many universities, municipalities and prominent people raised protests. Numerous parliaments requested their governments to call upon the Diet of the *Bund* to condemn this breach of the constitution.

When the Hanoverian Parliament had assembled in the form prescribed by the king, the second chamber protested against the breach of the constitution, but the Government succeeded, by dissolving the chamber and exercising pressure, in forming an assembly of deputies which decided on a new constitution in accordance with the King's wishes. Many of the liberal provisions of the earlier constitution had disappeared from it.

The town of Osnabrück, which formed part of the Kingdom of Hanover, asked the faculties of law at the Universities of Heidelberg, Jena and Tübingen for an expert opinion on the King's action. All three reached the conclusion that it was a breach of the constitution and Tübingen went on to declare that in consequence the King had no right to rule, that officials should not obey him and that all citizens were entitled to offer active and passive resistance. The Government of Hanover now called upon the Diet of the *Bund* to intervene against this proclamation of revolutionary principles. The Diet agreed that the declaration was revolutionary, forbade its further dissemination and expressed the expectation that the King of Württemberg would proceed against the professors involved, particularly in respect of the affront they had offered to the King of Hanover. But Württemberg did no such thing; in fact, her king was the first to appoint one of the seven professors to a chair at Tübingen.

Finally Bavaria and Baden moved, on the basis of article 56, that proceedings should be taken against Hanover, but for formal reasons the Diet of the *Bund* rejected this motion by 10 votes to 6. Those for intervention in Hanover were Bavaria, Saxony, Württemberg, Baden, the Saxon duchies and the free Cities; those against were principally Austria, Prussia, Hesse-Darmstadt and Hesse-Cassel and a few smaller north German states.

Saxony

In the Kingdom of Saxony there was much discontent over grievances, real and imagined. King Antony was well-meaning but very old; the Prime Minister, Count Einsiedel, averse to innovations; the Estates and the municipal administration – which enjoyed a large degree of autonomy – corrupt, and the economy crippled by a slump which caused great hardship among the working class. Hence disturbances arose shortly before the July Revolution. Many of the middle class aimed at reforming the administration of the municipalities, which was in the hands of a small oligarchy. The masses complained of the police in the towns, the high cost of food and the technical progress which, they said, was taking the bread out of their mouths. In Leipzig the big publisher Brockhaus could only save his steam presses from destruction by putting them out of commission. The private carriers saw a serious competitor in the Royal Post, with its faster coaches, and tried to destroy them. In Leipzig the police threw in their hands, so a civic militia was formed which admittedly restored order, but remained under arms and demanded communal reforms. Next, serious disorders broke out in Dresden, the capital; the town hall and police headquarters were stormed, records burned and interior fittings smashed. Here, too, the townsfolk were called up and given weapons from the arsenal. They demanded a reform of local government, the summoning of the Estates and the entrusting of the running of the state to the very popular Prince Frederick Augustus. The aged King agreed to all these demands, Frederick Augustus became co-regent, Count Einsiedel was dismissed and Baron Bernhard von Lindenau became head of the Government.

Lindenau, a member of an old aristocratic family, was not only a very experienced and successful official, but also a scholar who enjoyed international fame as an astronomer. He was a philanthropist who gave the greater part of his considerable income to charity. Politically he was a liberal, but he had to tread warily with the reactionary great powers, who regarded him with considerable suspicion and were prepared to go to any lengths to stop far-reaching reforms. The new Regent, who on the death of King Antony a few years later became King Frederick Augustus II, was a thoroughly well-meaning, cultivated and amiable man, with a sound scientific education, especially in botany. His brother John, an experienced statesman, supported him in his policy and was, incidentally, a brilliant scholar, famed for his annotated translation of Dante.

The disorders spread to many other towns and villages. A large number of rural communities demanded representation in the Estates and the abolition of feudal rights. The guilds wanted protection for craftsmen and small traders against non-guild elements, such as settlers, foreigners, Jews, women and pedlars, as well as against capitalistic concerns. Unemployed workers took part in threatening demonstrations. The Government first satisfied demands for municipal reform by a provisional measure. An attempt was made to organise an effective militia to preserve order, but this ran into great difficulties since many citizens soon grew disinclined to perform guard duties at night. In Dresden there arose a citizens' society which was at first animated by a mixture of narrow-minded and radical guild outlook, but then veered to the left, published the draft of a democratic constitution and threatened revolt if it did not become law. In 1831 in both Dresden and Leipzig there were uprisings in which part of the militia went over to the insurgents, but the riots were bloodily suppressed by the military.

Meanwhile the Lindenau administration was working out a draft constitution, which was submitted to the Estates. It was a compromise between monarchical and parliamentary principles and was consequently sharply attacked by both the left and the right. A system of municipal administration was also laid before the Estates. Furthermore, the King was prepared to make over his domains, castles and collections to the state in return for a very modest civil list. The bills were discussed in great detail for six months and the Government accepted many amendments. The 1831 constitution, as in most states, provided for two chambers. The first consisted of members of the ruling house and the nobility, the clergy, university members, the mayors of the big cities and notables appointed by the King. Prince John was a member for twenty years and made many important speeches. The big landowners, who were not always nobles, elected 20 deputies to the second chamber. The towns returned 25 deputies, commerce and industry 5 and the peasants 25. The franchise was linked with a modest tax qualification. Officials needed leave of absence from the government, but this could be refused only for important professional reasons, not political ones. Parliament had extensive powers. The system of municipal government, which was introduced at the same time on the Prussian and Bavarian model, afforded a large measure of autonomy, and the vote in local elections was liberally bestowed. Even residents without municipal citizenship had the franchise; what is more, they were in a majority. The feudal services of the peasants were to be removed, in some cases gratuitously and in others with compensation, and a special bank granted favourable credit terms for this purpose. Later, too, local government was granted to the rural communities. For all this, it did not prove possible to eliminate the municipal guild privileges or the patrimonial and city courts. The right to vote for a candidate for the Diet was given to members of the liberal professions only if they were resident in the constituency or owned a house or land there.

A serious defect was the absence of real freedom of the press. In 1833 Richter, who edited *Die Biene* (The Bee), published a petition for the abolition of feudal dues without compensation. The majority of the second chamber was highly indignant at this and refused Richter – who was incidentally a deputy – a hearing. He was sentenced to six months' imprisonment, but released on condition that he left the country. This case demonstrated the power of the landowners. The lifting of the censorship was often mooted, but all Lindenau could say in reply was that Saxony was bound by the decisions of the Diet of the *Bund*. In 1832 and 1834 the latter imposed very reactionary regulations for all member states, which Saxony accepted, with the proviso that the rights of her *Landtag* should be safeguarded.

The Lindenau administration held office for thirteen years and brought in a wealth of beneficial laws and institutions which contributed to Saxony's prosperity. In the *Landtag* there was neither a government party nor an opposition party – indeed, the very term 'party' was taboo. The most important representative of the liberals was Dr Christian Eisenstuck, a lawyer from Dresden, who proposed the abolition of the death penalty as early as 1833, though without success. Measures were passed which marked significant progress in the legal code.

The thirties and forties brought a rapid economic upswing. Saxony joined the German *Zollverein* and in railway construction and industrial progress outstripped all the other German states. The national finances showed considerable surpluses, taxes were repeatedly reduced and national loans repaid. The rate of interest on government loans was reduced by voluntary conversion to 3%. Taxation was radically reformed and the removal of the feudal services made rapid strides. This encouraged the peasants to join forces with the landowners and form an agrarian bloc in the *Landtag* which more than held its own with the urban deputies. Both the town and country members often followed a narrow policy of self-interest. For a long time civil equality was denied to the Jews. At the end of the thirties, a group of radical liberals came together to demand the abolition of the first chamber, electoral reform, freedom of the press and similar reforms; their number included two lawyers, Julius von Dieskau and Karl Braun from Plauen, and a landowner, Otto von Watzdorf. The Leipzig publisher Heinrich Brockhaus voted with them on many issues. He founded the first big independent paper, the *Leipziger* (later *Deutsche*) *Allgemeine Zeitung*.

For some time Saxony had a mild censorship but with increasing pressure from the two great reactionary powers and their supporters it became stricter. All the same, it was not as rigorously applied as in many other countries, especially where books were concerned. Leipzig was the centre of the book trade and the censorship of books was in the hands of university professors, who usually thought along liberal lines. As a result of this comparatively mild censorship, many liberal and democratic writers from all parts of Germany settled in Leipzig or Dresden. Ruge, for example, who published the most important radical periodical – the *Hallischen Jahrbücher*, later called the *Deutschen Jahrbücher* – transferred it to Dresden in 1841 so as to escape Prussian censorship. He immediately opened a vigorous campaign against the Prussian system and the Government in Berlin managed to get Saxony to ban the paper.

Antagonism between the right and the left grew steadily more acute and made Lindenau's policy increasingly difficult, and in 1843 he relinquished office. His successor, Julius von Könneritz, introduced a very strict censorship and took other measures against liberal politicians in order to placate Prussia. In 1842 and 1843 the draft of a new legal procedure was laid before the chamber. The opposition demanded oral proceedings in open court but the Government refused this amendment. After a long and brilliant debate, the chamber rejected the Government bill almost unanimously and called for another to be drafted on the lines indicated by the Opposition. This was a great victory for the liberals in a chamber where they were in the minority.

Saxony was also a focus of religious controversy and was one of the main centres of German Catholicism and of the so-called *Lichtfreunde* (Friends of Light). These movements had political overtones. The Government was accused of encouraging religious intolerance to support political reaction. Robert Blum, the most outstanding leader of the German democrats in 1848, was one of the founders of German Catholicism.

Tension between Opposition and Government was greatly heightened by an event which occurred in 1845. At a mass demonstration against Prince John the troops opened fire and killed a number of demonstrators, thus kindling an almost revolutionary frenzy. But the social distress which spread in the wake of the industrial revolution and was aggravated by the appallingly bad harvests of 1842–3 and 1846–7, also had political effects. The conservative régime was compelled to make many concessions to liberal demands in order to pacify the people. Könneritz left his post as minister of justice in 1846, although he remained President of the Cabinet, and his successor was Albert von Carlowitz, who had first suggested a liberal constitution in his memorandum to the King seventeen years earlier.

Bavaria

The July Revolution also had a considerable influence on Bavaria. It was hailed by the liberal press, who hoped that the King would have the constitution altered along the lines they proposed. Ludwig himself lived in constant dread of a revolution and Grandaur, the head of his secretariat, played on these fears, whereas his ministers, including Schenk, sought to reassure him. The liberals held the clerical party – especially Schenk, whom they strongly attacked – responsible for the change in the king. Radical movements developed, notably in newly-acquired provinces like Franconia and the Palatinate, where discontent with Bavarian rule and the influence of their neighbour France were particularly strong. The leaders of the democrats were a civil servant, Philipp Siebenpfeiffer, who was a disciple of Rotteck, a lawyer and writer named Johann August Wirth, Hoffmann, who was a judge, and a curate named Hochdörfer. In 1830 Siebenpfeiffer and Hoffmann brought out a periodical, *Rheinbayern*, in which they called for a dilution of the power of the monarchy – though not its abolition – by the introduction of republican institutions. The government promptly decided to transfer Siebenpfeiffer to another post where he would have been unable to continue his agitation, but a strong protest came in from the district where he worked; eighty mayors demanded that the order, which in any case was ignored by Siebenpfeiffer, should be rescinded. The authorities thereupon stopped his salary, but he took the matter to court and won the case, so they had to leave him in the Palatinate and continue to pay him. At this time it was not uncommon for the courts to acquit persons charged with political offences on the grounds that existing legal provisions did not apply to the case.

In January 1831 elections took place at which the liberals won a great victory. Fifty-four officials had been elected; five of them were refused leave of absence, but one, Baron von Closen, gave up his official post and kept his seat in the chamber.

Immediately after this, a decree was published by which even articles concerning internal politics – hitherto subject to no restrictions – were liable to be censored. This measure, which the King had himself enacted, unleashed a storm of anger. Several towns asked the King to withdraw the decree, there was talk of refusing to pay taxes or of impeaching the ministers, who themselves advised the King to repeal the decree and complained openly that irresponsible persons were influencing him over their heads. They also advised him to negotiate with the opposition leaders, which he was prepared to do, though only on condition that the other side should also make concessions. Negotiations were opened, but the Opposition's stubborn resistance made them difficult. In his speech from the throne, Ludwig declared that the constitution would be scrupulously respected. At this time Metternich was trying to persuade the Diet of the *Bund* to declare the new constitution of the Electorate of Hesse invalid because it had been extorted from the ruler, but Bavaria objected vigorously. Ignatz von Rudhart now undertook to mediate between the King and the liberal opposition. Rudhart wanted to combine all moderates against the extremists, whether of the left or the right, and to unite the King and the chamber of deputies against the first chamber, which was dominated by the aristocracy. A powerful speech by Rudhart on the freedom of the press was a major cause of von Schenk's resignation. Soon after, the Government repealed the censorship decree and introduced a measure by which the press was to have full freedom of comment on all domestic issues, but, where foreign policy was concerned, only on those countries where the press was also free. This was intended to prevent the radical press from making sharp attacks on Austria and Prussia and thus incurring their hostility towards Bavaria. If a newspaper broke the law, it would have to answer for it before a jury.

Meanwhile the finance committee of the chamber of deputies had begun to debate the budget, and some items came in for sharp criticism. The Government had exceeded the estimates for building and were seeking retrospective approval. The opposition was particularly incensed over the expenditure on art collections and the embellishment of Munich, and it was claimed that the provinces were being neglected for the capital. Various items were negatived, including the cost of the great art gallery, the Pinakothek, which is today Munich's greatest treasure and attracts countless visitors from abroad. The peasant and provincial deputies failed to see the need for a picture gallery; in their view the provision of some new prisons was far more urgent. In addition, the cost of the royal secretariat, whose head, Grandaur, exercised a reactionary influence on the king, was not approved because the constitution made no provision for it. The civil list was cut. All these decisions taken in committee were endorsed by large majorities in the chamber. Furthermore, they refused to pass the press bill because it did not grant complete freedom, one of the Opposition leaders declaring that their standpoint was all or nothing.

King Ludwig was greatly angered by the chamber's attitude, especially since it frustrated his plans to make Munich an outstanding artistic centre such as Florence had once been. With the end of 1831 came the resignation of the liberal ministers. Prince Oettingen-Wallerstein became the head of the Government. He was a highly cultivated magnate of moderately liberal views. Later, at the time of the 1848 revolution, he joined the left, but at the present juncture he tried to steer a course between left and right. However, as he later complained, this course was constantly made impossible by the intrigues of Grandauer, who increasingly set the King against progress. On 1 March 1832 the censorship was reimposed, the formation of political associations forbidden and a persecution of the left began. Bavaria drew closer to Austria and Prussia and supported their reactionary policies.

The King's attitude caused the democrats to intensify their propaganda and turn towards republican ideas. Their attacks on the monarchy became bold and sharp. In Franconia the leaders who have already been mentioned set the tone, but the radicals of Rhenish Bavaria were even more outspoken. When Siebenpfeiffer's periodical was suppressed, he at once founded a new one with the title *Deutschland*, in which he took up the cudgels for German freedom and unity. Hochdörfer, too, brought out a new paper but it soon ceased publication. Among the Franconian democrats, Dr Wirth now grew ever more prominent. He first published a journal, *Kosmopolit*, which appeared in Bayreuth, was then for a short time editor of the liberal daily *Inland* and in 1831 founded the *Deutsche Tribüne*, which at first appeared in Munich and later in the Palatinate. A constitutional monarch, he wrote, was now a man of straw, utterly useless and not worth wasting money on. In another article he wrote that a king cannot be a friend of mankind, because the serpent of flattery poisons him and the ice of selfishness so freezes him that no love for his fellow-men can enter his wicked heart.

Radicalism reached a climax at the Hambach festival of 27 May 1832. It was Siebenpfeiffer who proposed that a mass meeting should be held on the hill in the Palatinate where the ruins of the ancient castle of Hambach stood. The extensive preparations alarmed the police, and at first they banned the rally. Many towns and villages objected to the ban, and so great was the wave of protest that the Government felt obliged to lift it. When the day came, many thousands climbed the hill from all sides, while the bells rang and cannon boomed. Estimates of the number present varied from 15,000 to 30,000. Many of them came from other German countries or from abroad, some even from Paris. Impassioned speeches were made, kings were accused of enslaving and exploiting their peoples, though there was no suggestion that words should be followed by action. Wirth ended his address by calling for three cheers for a union of German republics fraternally linked with a republican federation of Europe. In point of fact, only a few could hear what the speakers were saying, for the majority were enjoying themselves with wine and song. The organisers had forgotten to appoint a chairman to keep order, nor had they prepared any motions as a basis for adopting a resolution. Youthful hotheads were expecting the distribution of arms for a revolution. There were rumours that a government was to be announced for the German republic which was to be set up, but this was empty talk. To crown it all, a violent dispute broke out among the organisers. Wirth had said that many patriots pinned their hopes completely on France, but, he went on, the ruling classes there were the rich who wanted peace at any price and would not altruistically support a German revolution. Even if France did intervene militarily, the price for such assistance would be the Rhineland, and this was unacceptable. These remarks were taken in very bad part by others present and they accused Wirth of preaching hatred against France.

The hope that France would support a German revolution was actually widespread among the radicals. Shortly before this, Siebenpfeiffer and Schüler, the chairman of the committee which had been set up, had been in Paris to size up the prospects. Now the ruling classes in France were in fact the rich; the franchise was much more restricted there than in Bavaria, and neither these circles nor the King wanted a war, least of all a war for the establishment of democracy in Germany. The hope of a swing to the radicals, who had warlike leaders, was illusory, since the radicals formed only a small fraction of the French people.

The Hambach Festival and one or two other radical moves had a fateful influence on the course of German politics: they gave Metternich and those in the other German states who shared his views a golden opportunity to organise a ruthless campaign to stamp out the freedom movement. Many of its doughtiest champions fell victim to this campaign and had to spend the best years of their life in prison if they did not succeed in escaping abroad. In Bavaria many judges who were well known as liberals were dismissed or transferred to posts where they had nothing to do with political cases. The organisers of the Hambach

Festival were charged with incitement to rebellion, and although most of the jury were state officials, the accused were all acquitted. The Government thereupon arraigned them before a police court on other charges and they received heavy prison sentences. Fearing riots in the Palatinate, the Government despatched Old Bavarian troops there and they treated the population brutally.

In Franconia, too, the democrats had demonstrated vigorously against the reactionary tendencies of the King and the court party. Just as in the Palatinate, so here the antagonism between the liberals and the Old Bavarians played a part. There were several radical groups, the most important of which collected round Professor Behr and a doctor named Eisenmann, and they were also backed by many professors and students of Würzburg University. Behr lost his post and his seat in the Diet by falling foul of the Government, but he remained Mayor of Würzburg and enjoyed an uncommon popularity. For thirty years he had written many weighty books on political science as well as numerous treatises and pamphlets on contemporary politics. His book on the needs and aspirations of the Bavarians, which appeared in 1830, subjected the existing constitution to penetrating criticism and contained the draft of a new one. He was a zealous disciple of Kant, on whose doctrines he founded his system. His leading principle was the sovereignty of the people. A king, he argued, might well offer advantages as head of the executive, but if Behr's draft constitution had been adopted the king would have been no more than the hereditary president of a republic. Behr demanded universal suffrage for men and women over twenty-one, but on condition that they were versed in the rights and duties of every citizen and were economically independent either by owning property or being able to earn their own living. The upper house was to be abolished and wide powers were to be vested in the commons. The army was to take an oath to respect the constitution and ultimately be transformed into a militia. The economy, education and the law were to be reformed on libertarian principles. Finally, Behr advocated a league of nations, an international court of justice and a world republic.

Although Behr was more democratic than most of the liberals of his day, he was not in favour of armed revolution, though if it should break out, then according to his theories the people would in any case be in the right, since after all they were sovereign. Many influential professors, officials and writers shared Behr's views or were attracted by his personality and general attitude. Even the King was for a long time considered to be a friend of his and, so it was believed, listened to his advice. Radical youth raved about him and the majority of the citizens of Würzburg were proud of their mayor, though he had many enemies who were awaiting their chance to bring about his downfall. But radical as Behr was, he never employed the methods of the demagogue. There were other Franconian writers who showed far less moderation, as, for instance, Baron von Dalberg, who in his journal *Der Scharfschütze* popularised Behr's doctrines but later became estranged from him, and Gottfried Widmann, who in his *Volkstribüne* represented a republicanism with a strong admixture of socialism and imposed no restraints at all on his language.

In 1832, at the time of the Hambach Festival, a mass meeting took place at Gaibach near Schweinfurt at which the leaders of the Franconian radicals made speeches. On this occasion Behr condemned the constitution and demanded in its place a contract between people and king. The young people applauded Behr and bore him shoulder-high; there were shouts of 'Long live the republic!' and, with reference to Behr, 'Long live our Duke of Franconia!'. Eyewitnesses declared that he was, in fact, almost proclaimed Duke of Franconia. Behr's enemies felt that their opportunity had now come. They first succeeded, by arguing that the King's disfavour would harm Würzburg, in inducing the town council to depose their mayor. They also inflamed the guilds against him, quoting things he had said against guild privileges. In the end he was accused of high treason and lèse-majesté and was brought before a court, though not the competent one. His words were grossly distorted to support the charge, and it was not until four years had passed, in 1836, that he was sentenced to recant before a picture of the King and then to be imprisoned indefinitely. After three years' detention, he was allowed to live in a specified town and placed under strict police surveillance. He was not released until 1847, and a year later was elected to the National Assembly at Frankfurt. Dr Eisenmann and Widmann received a similar punishment. Eisenmann, who refused to recant in front of a picture of the King, remained in prison until 1848 and then, like Behr, was elected to the Frankfurt National Assembly. Siebenpfeiffer, Wirth and Coremans escaped abroad. The universities were subjected to a minute investigation and democratic professors dismissed. At Würzburg alone seven professors were suspended, including the pathologist Johann Lukas Schönlein, who immediately resigned. He first went to Zürich, then to Berlin and became world-famous. Frederick William IV appointed him his personal physician, but he remained a sincere democrat and declined ennoblement and the title of 'Excellency'.

In the years immediately following 1832, many liberals reached the conclusion that the motto 'All or nothing' was a mistake. At the *Landtag* of 1834 the great majority supported the Government and passed a permanent civil list, which greatly pleased the King. The liberals'

Trade Act of 1825 was altered in a reactionary guild sense. It was a great step forward when, in 1833, Bavaria joined the *Zollverein* and in 1835 opened the first steam railway in Germany. The King now wanted to govern in person and occupied himself with every detail, but all the same he was for strictly observing the constitution. When in 1837 the King of Hanover arbitrarily revoked his country's constitution, the King of Bavaria was one of the rulers who asked the Diet of the *Bund* to reverse this decision. In 1837, with the rise of the ultramontane Catholics, Karl von Abel became Minister of the Interior, and censorship once more grew very strict.

While the second chamber seldom opposed the Government, the upper house now frequently displayed a critical attitude towards autocratic and clerical tendencies, and an Opposition came into being which was often more progressive than that in the second chamber. Even the Crown Prince sometimes voted for Opposition motions. For a few years attempts were made to force Protestants in the army to bow the kneee if a priest raised the monstrance in their presence, but in 1842 the decision went in their favour. Another great step forward was the reform of civil and criminal law, in which the principle of public oral proceedings, which the King had always wanted, was conceded.

Württemberg
In Württemberg the July Revolution had only minor consequences, apart from the fact that the King and many hitherto liberal circles now leaned more to the right because they feared the spread of radicalism. In connection with the coup directed against the *Bundestag* in Frankfurt in 1833, a conspiracy engineered by an army lieutenant was discovered in Württemberg, but there were no further disorders. The middle-class farmers and townsfolk, who controlled the *Landtag* in Württemberg, were for the most part satisfied with the constitutional position, mistrusted any radical innovations and were indifferent to political demands which seemed to have no immediate practical purpose. Nor was the issue of German unity of any interest to the majority of the deputies, although just at this time a Württemberger, Paul Pfizer, published a pamphlet entitled *Correspondence between two Germans* which caused a sensation throughout Germany. Pfizer criticised the anti-Prussian and pro-Austrian feeling prevailing in South Germany and advocated a Prussian hegemony in Germany. This attitude roused the indignation of the King and those wide circles for whom Württemberg alone was their native land.

At the same time, the liberal movement made considerable progress at first and a number of political journals written in a popular vein sprang up. Political parties with numerous local groups were also formed. Most important of all, a number of capable liberal leaders emerged, men like Ludwig Uhland and Albert Schott, who had already gained distinction, Friedrich Römer, Paul Pfizer and others. But the liberal agitation put the King into a bad humour, especially when at the end of 1831 the so-called 'Party of Movement' (*Bewegungspartei*) gained great successes. He thereupon banned political associations and meetings, a measure which aroused great bitterness. Soon after this, the Diet of the *Bund* also decided on restrictions of political freedom and many papers were suppressed. The King appointed Johannes Schlayer as his Prime Minister. Schlayer was a talented man of humble origin who for sixteen years had a decisive say in Württemberg's domestic policy; he had previously been a liberal deputy for Tübingen and when he was in office represented a moderate tendency which, though liberal, was against extending the powers of the parliament.

In the *Landtag* which met at the beginning of 1833, out of the 93 members of the second chamber only 32 were Government supporters, 39 were opposition liberals and 22 were uncommitted. The liberals advocated very strongly a free press and extension of the franchise. In a masterly speech Pfizer denied the validity in Württemberg of the decrees of the Diet of the *Bund* and went on to attack the 'monarchical principle' underlined by the federal measures. The speech stung the King into demanding that the chamber should reject Pfizer's 'impudent' motion. This interference with the freedom of debate made feelings run high in the *Landtag*. Uhland drafted an energetic address in the sense of Pfizer's motion which at the same time administered a sharp rebuff to the King's presumption. The address was adopted by 53 votes to 31, and the King thereupon dissolved the *Landtag*. Fresh elections were held amid strong government pressure and were influenced by the news of the assault on the Frankfurt Main Guard, but the Opposition was returned only slightly weakened in numbers. When the Government refused to grant leave of absence to those liberal leaders who were state officials, they resigned their posts in order to remain deputies. The Opposition continued to wage a vigorous struggle and brilliant speeches were made but very little achieved. Even bills which were in the popular interest were resisted by the Opposition because they did not go far enough. When joining the *Zollverein* was being debated, the liberals were split. Most of their leaders voted against joining because they loathed reactionary Prussia.

The Schlayer Government contrived to win over popular feeling by introducing bills of great practical importance. Among these were measures for educational reform, the abolition or redemption of feudal services by substantial government subsidies and tax cuts. When the breach of the constitution occurred in Hanover, the Württemberg chamber raised the sharpest protest and the Government requested the Diet of the *Bund* to intervene on behalf of the rightful constitution.

The opposition lost the support of considerable sections of the people by concentrating on constitutional issues. The Government pointed out that the Opposition had voted against most of the bills aimed at improving the public lot, even against the proposals to abolish feudal services. Before the 1838 elections, the liberal leaders withdrew from politics and announced that they would not be standing. The number of liberal deputies was considerably reduced. The Government supported the election of men from the clerical class (*Schreiberklasse*), which consisted mainly of minor officials from the rural communities. Thus the new *Landtag* was mainly made up of members of mediocre ability with no grasp of wider issues. However, the forties saw a revival of the liberal party, and in the elections of 1844 some of their leading figures were returned to the *Landtag*. The censorship continued to be very strict and the Opposition repeatedly demanded its removal or relaxation. Although the king was disinclined to do this, he was after all finally compelled to move in the *Bundestag* for a change in the censorship regulations. The Opposition continued their agitation and by this means succeeded in getting public opinion in many places to support their policy.

Baden

The arrival of 1830 saw the accession of Grand Duke Leopold, who had a genuinely constitutional cast of mind, to which he gave expression in various measures which he introduced. The July Revolution led to an upsurge of liberalism in Baden. At the 1831 elections, the Government refrained from exercising any pressure and the liberals won a great victory. Rotteck was elected in five constituencies and other liberal leaders, too, gained majorities in several districts. The professor and publicist Karl Theodor Welcker became a deputy for the first time. The conservative cabinet resigned and the liberal Ludwig Winter now became the leading Minister. The new *Landtag* passed numerous laws which realised liberal demands; of 44 bills introduced by the new Government, 38 were passed. Welcker sponsored a resolution calling for a parliament for all Germany but the Government feared the consequences and the issue was not debated.

However, the growth of radicalism stirred the forces of reaction to take energetic steps to suppress it and to use the Diet of the *Bund* for this purpose. The Government of Baden thus found itself compelled to introduce censorship, although the chamber protested and declared it unconstitutional. When in 1835 the entry of Baden into the *Zollverein* was on the agenda, the whole chamber conceded that this step promised the greatest advantages, but all the same most of the convinced liberals voted against it, because to them any link with reactionary Prussia seemed to threaten the liberty of Baden. Rotteck declared that he preferred freedom without German unity to unity without freedom.

The Vienna Conference of 1834 loosed a flood of reaction. In Baden, Baron von Blittersdorf was a fervent adherent of Metternich's policy and in 1839 he succeeded in gaining control of the Government, which thereupon removed the freedom of the press, influenced the elections and exercised pressure on the state officials in the chamber. The speeches of liberal leaders vanished from the press, whereas those of the ministers had to be printed. These tactics had their effect on public opinion and the number of thorough-going liberals in the chamber decreased. But their leaders did not follow the example of those in other assemblies who had withdrawn from political life; Rotteck, Itzstein and others remained deputies, and even in the darkest days kept the liberal flag flying by directing withering criticism against the forces of reaction. Quite often they succeeded in persuading a majority of members to vote with them.

In 1841 Blittersdorf began to intensify his policy by refusing leave of absence to two deputies who were judges – a step the Government had never before ventured to take and one which caused a considerable stir in the country. In the *Landtag* the strongest group was the centre, whose leader, Bekk, was a judge of the high court. The right and the left were roughly equal in strength. Bekk moved the annulment of the refusal to grant leave and this was passed unanimously. Since the Government was not prepared to make any concessions, the chamber resolved – almost unanimously – to introduce a vote of censure on the infringement of the constitution but in the end this was not supported by the first chamber. Itzstein and Welcker proposed the refusal to pay taxes, but this was defeated. Welcker was thereupon removed from his university post. When the Grand Duke, at Blittersdorf's instigation, issued a declaration along the lines of his minister's policy, the chamber confirmed their earlier decision by 31 votes to 26. On this, the Government dissolved the chamber. At the elections of 1842 there was a keen struggle in which the masses also took a vigorous part. The Government exercised considerable pressure, particularly through the big newspapers, which they controlled almost completely, but the Opposition members were returned in greater numbers than before and among the new deputies were Karl Mathy, Friedrich Daniel Bassermann and Friedrich Hecker, who were later to come into prominence. The left numbered between 26–8 members, the centre between 8–10 and the right 23. There was now a sharp contrast between right and left although even the right called itself liberal. The centre was led by Bekk, who was unanimously chosen as President.

A long tactical struggle ensued, in which the out-and-out liberals under the leadership of Itzstein showed themselves as energetic as they were adroit. Blittersdorf was forced to resign. He had considerably underestimated the spread of liberal ideas, particularly among state officials. The liberals had constantly been working towards an extension of the rights of the *Landtag* by their interpretation of the constitution and they insisted particularly that a minister should possess the confidence of the people. In their speeches they stressed the concepts of the sovereignty of the people and of democracy. In this way the political interest of the public was stimulated, the spectators' galleries of the *Landtag* were always well filled and the deputies made tours of the country, in the course of which they were applauded and fêted by the people. Several new papers with liberal and radical ideas were founded and revolutionary ideas were expressed in pamphlets which came from German refugees across the Rhine.

Succeeding governments consisted of both liberal and conservative officials and policy fluctuated between right and left. Freedom of the press and of assembly remained limited, while many laws of a markedly liberal character were passed or promised for the near future. In 1846 there was another election at which the liberals made greater gains. Bekk became head of the Government.

The constitutional struggles also led to the growth of radical movements, headed by two lawyers from Mannheim – Gustav von Struve and Friedrich Hecker. Both of them were well versed in the law and expert agitators, who had taken over many of the ideas of French democrats and socialists. Struve led vigorous attacks on the bourgeois liberals who aimed at securing freedom only for the rich. He also said that one lion was better than sixty-three hares. The people's chamber had sixty-three members and this remark was taken to mean that Struve was the lion who would set up his dictatorship. But soon Hecker had displaced him as the idol of radical youth.

9

THE LAST DECADE BEFORE THE REVOLUTION

PRUSSIA

In the twenties and thirties neither the progressives nor the reactionaries won a decisive victory. The successes of the enemies of liberal reforms were transitory and deceptive, for by their brutality and contempt for justice they swelled the ranks of the progressives and spurred them on to renewed efforts. But the progressives in their turn suffered severely from the splintering off of radical movements, the operations of which ultimately benefited reaction. In any case, the political struggles within the small states could achieve nothing decisive, for everything depended on how things turned out in the two large states, Austria and Prussia, who lagged far behind in evolving modern forms of constitution. Besides this, of course, what happened in other great states, especially England and France, had an effect on the development of Germany, and to this one must add the influence which changes in economic, cultural and social conditions exercised on politics. This latter gave a powerful impetus to liberal and national movements.

Both in Austria and Prussia the death of the rulers who had hitherto blocked constitutional progress was of immediate importance. Frederick William III of Prussia died in 1840 and in his political testament he warned his successor against exposing the power of the monarchy to any constitutional changes which might weaken it. The provincial Estates, local government and other institutions allowed the subject only a very limited say in policy. The King had not created any *Reich* Estates – that is, a parliament for all Prussia – as he had once promised.

He was followed by Frederick William IV, whose accession at first inspired great hopes. His was a complicated character; he possessed brains and imagination, was a brilliant speaker and a friend of science and the arts. As a rule he was amiable and kindly, but he often lapsed into fits of sudden and violent anger. What he lacked most was a realistic outlook and decisiveness. His mood often fluctuated between extremes, he was a mass of contradictions and saw things in the light of a rigid ideology. In his old age he was mentally unbalanced; he had probably always had a tendency to be so. He has often been described, and rightly, as a Romanticist, not only because of the excess of feeling and imagination in his nature but also because he took over the ideas, elaborated by many Romanticists, of a Christian-German state with a revived medieval spirit and patriarchal rule, and used them to resist liberal demands. He was a devotee of the political theories of the Bernese patrician, Karl Ludwig von Haller, and possessed a strong religious sentiment with a leaning towards Catholicism, like many of the Romanticists. He had no taste for power politics or martial glory; just as little did he wish to procure for Prussia the leadership in Germany. He would gladly have left the imperial power to Austria and restricted Prussia to control of military matters in the *Bund*.

Frederick William was confirmed in these views by a few intimate friends who were all men of note and culture. The leading lights were the Protestants Leopold and Ludwig von Gerlach, who for religious reasons were averse to any form of nationalism; the spirited Catholic general, Josef Maria von Radowitz and the scholar Christian von Bunsen. Of the ministers appointed by the King, many were of a conservative and pietistic persuasion, while others tended more towards liberalism. The King, however, did not want to give any one of them too much power but to rule for himself. He also wanted to show from the moment he came to the throne that he was above party. A general amnesty for political offenders was proclaimed, the persecution of demagogues stopped and Jahn and Arndt were freed of the restrictions laid on them. Dahlmann, the leader of the seven Göttingen professors, was given a chair and so too was Friedrich Julius Stahl, a conservative jurist of Jewish origin, who gained great influence in right-wing circles. The philosopher Schelling was summoned to Berlin as a counterblast to the Hegelian school. The great naturalist, Alexander von Humboldt, a declared progressive, became a member of the State Council but an equally committed reactionary like Ludwig Hassenpflug also received a public post.

One important development occurred when the King ended the conflict with the Catholic church – a struggle which he had inherited from his father – by acceding to the demands of the ultramontanes and making other concessions as well. A political Catholicism began to take shape which later reached its climax in Bismarck's day in the struggle between the Church and the State known as the *Kulturkampf*. The spread of intransigent ultramontanism led to the rise of a movement which called itself *Deutschkatholizismus*. In many other ways, too, there were signs that religious faith and antagonisims between the confessions were very much alive among wide sections of the public and these also had political effects.

Frederick William's accession coincided with a crisis between the great powers which threatened war. In a dispute between Turkey and Egypt, Palmerston was pursuing a policy which aroused hostility in France and provoked a warlike mood. The liberal minister Thiers, who as an historian sang the praises of Napoleon, took certain preparatory measures which were directed at Germany as well. French newspapers demanded the tearing up of the peace treaties of 1815 and the conquest of the Rhineland, and to this the German press reacted violently. But neither the King of France nor the King of Prussia wanted war and Thiers was dismissed by Louis Philippe, who was eyed very sourly by the Chauvinists for thus keeping the peace.[1]

Frederick William took many other political steps which revealed an inner conflict. The censorship was considerably relaxed; pictures, drawings and books were completely freed from control. A supreme court of censorship was created with the aim of eliminating the arbitrariness of many individual censors. But one consequence of the increased freedom of the press was that the Government and the King himself were criticised and ridiculed in the most unbridled manner and the regulations were soon tightened up again. A disciplinary measure aimed at state officials held a threat to the independence of the judiciary. Policy towards Polish subjects in Posen was changed in a progressive sense: the Germanisation which had been going on for ten years was given up and the Poles were once more allowed to develop their own culture.

The King wanted to rule personally, but lacked the ability to survey the whole field of policy or to conduct it coherently and his ministers did not always start out from the same principles as he. The really important question was that of the constitution. His father had repeatedly held out prospects that one would be granted, and this obviously implied a popular Assembly for all Prussia, but all he had done was to permit provincial diets with very limited powers to be set up. The great majority of politically-minded people were, however, not satisfied with this. The desire for a truly popular Assembly had spread in recent decades and this was seen as a prerequisite for a constitutional state and national liberty. It was felt to be a disgrace

---

[1] Even today an outstanding French historian takes the view that the King's policy represented an exaggerated pacificism (*pacificisme à l'outrance*) which harmed national prestige Cf. F. Ponteil, *L'éveil des nationalités*, etc., 1960, p. 410.

that Prussia had lagged so far behind many smaller countries in this respect. It must be admitted that certain circles among the nobility, the army and the officials shared the King's disinclination for a National Assembly for the whole country with considerable limitations on the King's power, but it was plain from the attitude of several provincial diets that the progressive trend was in the ascendant; it even had supporters among senior officials. The King vacillated for a long time. First he decreed that the provincial Estates should form standing committees and in 1842 these were summoned to Berlin as 'United Committees', to some extent filling the role of a Central Assembly. The King subsequently toyed with the idea of a union of the Estates of all eight provinces, which, however, would meet only rarely. The United Diet was to have the right to act on petitions and complaints. The Assembly was divided into two chambers; the aristocracy formed an upper house and the knights, burghers and peasants a lower house. On questions concerning the approval of loans and taxes, the houses were to sit jointly and take decisions; in all other matters they were to sit separately.

Public opinion did not react favourably to these measures. The United Diet was opened on 11 April 1847, and the King delivered a speech from the throne which was a brilliant exposé of his ideas. In the course of it he said that only an assembly like this suited the German character and that he would never agree to the relationship between the country and its ruler being changed by a written constitution as in some other countries. The majority of the deputies listened to this speech with great displeasure, for they inferred from it that the Crown wished to reserve full powers for itself. The speech from the throne was answered, on the English pattern, by an address which led to a controversy between King and assembly. The Opposition voiced its criticism and put forward several motions which greatly displeased the King, even though he was prepared to make further concessions. He caused his displeasure to be conveyed to the Assembly. The Diet refused to give its agreement to the raising of a loan to build the Eastern Railway and to a guaranteed rate of interest from the national annuity banks. The Assembly based its refusal on the grounds that the right of agreement was vested in Reich Estates; they could not put themselves on an equal footing with Reich Estates because corresponding powers had not been bestowed on them. The King later decided to allow the United Diet to meet every four years, but he insisted that its rights derived solely from the Crown. All these events caused a considerable stir throughout Prussia. They were discussed in many pamphlets, and the formation of political parties began. Certain personalities began to catch the public eye, some as champions of conservative views, others of liberal, and a year later these were the obvious protagonists when the revolution broke out. Bismarck himself first became generally known as the representative of a markedly monarchical and conservative viewpoint.

Public opinion in this last decade before the revolution is brilliantly described in Varnhagen's diaries. He noted down almost from one day to the next what he had heard from people in all walks of life and his own views on events. It is a picture of great intellectual ferment, of bold attacks by young authors and poets who set about the enemies of freedom with vigour, not even sparing the King himself, and who were in consequence ruthlessly persecuted by the Government, though it was not unusual for the courts to acquit those brought before them. Not infrequently public sympathy was manifestly on their side. In 1844 a former mayor named Tschech made an attempt (unsuccessful) on the life of the King; the act obviously sprang from political motives. It was a sign of the times that even highly placed personages did not regard him as a criminal, and much as they disapproved of what he had done, they showed great esteem and sympathy to him personally. Many of them were outraged when the King did not pardon him and he was executed.

But it was not only the struggle for political freedom which unleashed a far-reaching movement. There were also numerous signs of social ferment at work within the great masses both in town and country and threatening to lead to outbreaks of violence. In 1847 and 1848 crop failures caused frightful famines, but the desperate plight of the lower classes sprang above all from social developments which had not been foreseen and for which no remedies were known. There was also an agitation for communism but it was still-born. As early as 1842 Varnhagen confided to his diary that the ferment in Germany must inevitably lead to a major revolution.

AUSTRIA

The Emperor Francis died in 1835 and was succeeded by Ferdinand I, who was good-natured but ailing and indecisive. The conduct of political affairs was in the hands of a Conference of State consisting of two archdukes, Metternich and Kolowrat. The rivalry between the two ministers was not without a disruptive effect on government policy. Metternich was mainly concerned with foreign policy and Kolowrat with home affairs.

The Polish question was important both for the internal and external policy of Austria. After the collapse of the Polish uprising against Russia, the revolutionary wing of the Polish nobility sought to bring about another uprising in 1846, this time in Galicia, but the peasants there, who were largely Ruthenians, regarded their Polish masters as their enemies and Austria as their protector. Their reply to the Polish call to revolt was to rise against the Polish landowners, many of whom they killed, to burn down their castles and commit other atrocities. Since the Austrian authorities, lacking resources, at first did nothing, they were accused by the Poles of having incited the peasants. The Government in Vienna finally made Count Franz Stadion Governor of Galicia; he took firm measures and restored order. He also sought to help the peasants who were so sorely oppressed by the nobility. As a consequence of these events Austria, with the agreement of Prussia and Russia, annexed the republic of Cracow, one of the main bases of the conspirators. England and France protested against this infringement of the Treaty of Vienna.

Political events in Hungary had a great effect on conditions in Austria. As early as the thirties a great national and liberal movement had arisen in Hungary which aimed at bringing the outmoded constitutional position up-to-date and introducing thorough-going cultural and economic reforms. The greatest of its leaders was Count Stephan Szechenyi, whose passionate idealism went hand in hand with practical realism and self-sacrificing devotion. In addition to his name there began to emerge others which in succeeding decades were to determine the history of Hungary and the whole Danubian Empire – Ludwig Kossuth, Franz von Pulszky and Franz von Déak. Right from the outset the Hungarian national movement tended to weld all the inhabitants of the country into a united people and to give the smallest possible play to national peculiarities. There were some Hungarian statesmen far-sighted enough to desire a just settlement of the problem of nationalities, but most of them strove to Magyarise the national minorities. Even then the national intolerance of the Magyars caused concern in Austria, for although the Germans wielded the decisive influence in Austrian economic, cultural and political affairs, prudent statesmen among them were always at pains to allow self-expression to the other nations.

At the same time as the Hungarians were striving for reform, the provincial Estates in Austria were also beginning, under the leadership of the nobility, to assert themselves and to demand a progressive revision of the constitution. The nobility played a large part in restoring the Czech language to general use and fostering its literary development. It was the nobility, too, in most countries who wished to compound the peasants' feudal services for money, though this ran into difficulties of credit. A book entitled *Austria and her Future* appeared anonymously in Hamburg in two parts (1841 and 1847). It was sharply critical of the

F

prevailing system and demanded numerous reforms, above all an up-to-date revival of the provincial Estates by the admission of the townsfolk and peasants, as well as an Imperial Diet, control over taxation, freedom of the press, public legal proceedings and a radical re-shaping of the nobility on the English pattern. It later transpired that the author was Victor, Baron von Andrian-Werburg, a Tyrolean nobleman who occupied a high public office. Although the Government sought to prevent the spread of the book by buying up as many copies as possible and placing Andrian under police surveillance, the work none the less exercised a great influence.

IO

ECONOMIC DEVELOPMENT

At the beginning of the period here discussed, economic conditions in Germany were much worse than those in Western Europe as a whole. While many governments had striven hard in the eighteenth century to improve their economy, their predominantly mercantilistic methods had not achieved the desired end and long wars prevented any healthy growth, particularly the accumulation of capital. Nor had the efforts of enlightened rulers succeeded in either abolishing or vitiating the medieval privileges enjoyed by many classes. But it was German particularism which proved the greatest single obstacle to a modern economy, which calls for big markets, cheap transport and mobility of capital and labour. Napoleon's interventions had, it is true, reduced the number of small states but only partially. Between one state and the next there often existed considerable difficulties of transport. With the founding of the *Zollverein* and the construction of roads and railways, the situation improved, but there still remained many anomalies, some legal and others which impaired economic development. At the beginning of the nineteenth century and even later, the country folk lived on food they had themselves produced and they also made most of the industrial goods they needed. As consumers, therefore, they offered no great market for trade and industry. Except in the territories bordered by big rivers, transport was so expensive that the farmer could sell his products only in the immediate neighbourhood. Thus it could happen that in one area famine was rife, while not far away there was a surplus of food. Even the town-dwellers produced a considerable part of their own food. Many of them owned land and cattle, so that they bought little from the farmer. The urban craftsman worked to order for customers who were known to him and not for middlemen who acted as distributors.

It struck English travellers that there were no shops in German towns as there were in London and Paris. The separation of town from country in Prussia was especially marked. Up to 1818 the towns were isolated from the surrounding district by customs boundaries; there were forty-seven different tariffs and traffic between town and country met constant obstacles. These had been even greater before the Stein–Hardenberg laws, which were the first measures to remove many restrictions on the dividing-up or sale of land. In addition, the roads in Prussia were particularly bad, because Frederick II saw in this a safe-guard against invasion. While the separation of town and country was mainly determined by fiscal policy, political considerations also played their part. It was feared that the removal of industries to the country would loosen the feudal ties of the peasants to the soil and their sub-servience to the nobility.

Freedom of movement for peasants and their dependants, indispens-able for any large-scale industrial development, had already been made possible in Prussia by the Stein–Hardenberg laws. In the other German countries feudal privileges were removed partly before and partly after the setting-up of the *Bund*, although traces remained right up to the Revolution of 1848, and, indeed, later still. But it was not only the nobility who possessed privileges; in many German countries the guild system prevailed for a long time, offering master-craftsmen protection against strong competition by making it difficult or impossible for their apprentices to attain independence. Besides this, the guild system stood in the way of efforts to improve trade by the introduction of machines and modern methods. True, by edicts of 1806, 1808 and 1810 Prussia had introduced freedom to practise a trade, but this was subject to manifold restrictions. In 1845, a certificate of proficiency, which required an examination by master-craftsmen, was made compulsory for many trades, while the pursuit of others depended on police approval. In most of the other states, many trades remained more or less restricted by the influence of the guilds even in those places where freedom to trade was acknowledged in principle. Nor was the number of artisans at all rapidly reduced by the rise of industry or replaced by a proletariat of revolutionary outlook, as Marx imagined would be the case. Statistics from the early decades of industrialisation show that the number of artisans increased considerably and that master-craftsmen greatly outnumbered journeymen. These lived with their masters and there was no class distinction. Both worked with their hands, and many masters worked without apprentices. Even if artisans often took part in riots against the Government, there was none the less a conservative, patriarchal element in the craft system. Moreover, the guilds frequently carried on a sort of social welfare. The number of independent workers also increased enormously through the growth of trade in consequence of the market economy which was taking shape.

German intellectual circles were overwhelmingly in favour of economic freedom and hence considered the guilds to be pernicious. This view predominated even among most of the senior civil servants. At the universities the doctrines of Adam Smith were in fashion, and were expounded by a number of first-rate professors. It is true that reactionary circles also existed which looked to medieval institutions for their model, but the guilds had long since relinquished the important political and social role which they played in the Middle Ages and it was impossible to put the clock back. All the same there was a movement to protect the artisans which had some success, but it could not prevent the rise of industry and commerce.

Other economic groups had formerly possessed privileges which reserved to them in some places the exclusive exercise of their profession. Thus, for example, on the big rivers the citizens of certain towns had staple-rights and boatmen had the privilege of plying over certain stretches of water. Many trades were tied to the ownership of a particular house. The Church and the nobility were particularly favoured institutions. One can label all these special rights social particularism, which ranged itself alongside territorial particularism. These privileges were an obstacle to building up a unified nation. Moreover, they engendered a narrow, petty outlook which found its expression in many squabbles between the classes. Thus there were countless bickerings over any departure from tradition – about who, for example, had the right to produce a new article. This outlook sprang from the territorial and social isolation which was worse in Germany than in many other countries. In England and France travel was helped by the very nature of the country, access to the sea and the absence of particularism. In these respects Germany lagged far behind. Kant never left the province of East Prussia, where he was born. Goethe never saw Vienna, or, indeed, most of the big cities of Germany, let alone Paris or London. To be sure, German apprentices had to move about a lot in order to become masters of their craft, and apart from them there were many Germans who travelled, but in general ties with the soil, class, trade and tradition were uncommonly strong in Germany. If, later on, progressive writers like the Young Germans made bitter references to German Philistinism, then this can probably be traced back to the circumstances just mentioned. In the *Bund* many of these restrictions had already been removed, but all the same the outlook which had taken shape over the centuries persisted for a long time yet.

The wars which had been waged for decades in numerous European countries had caused Germany great losses in men, since German troops had had to fight for Napoleon not only in Germany and Austria but also in Spain, Russia and elsewhere. Napoleon's troops were fed from local resources by means of levies and requisitions and this weakened the economy of the occupied countries, including Germany. The territories incorporated with France gained access to a large new market for their goods; the others were protected by the continental blockade from British competition but, as against this, lost other markets. The fall of Napoleon in many cases led to the collapse of the industries fostered by his policies. There now followed a huge influx of English industrial goods which were produced much more cheaply than in Germany. Agriculture was likewise hard hit. Prussia had formerly exported considerable quantities of corn to England and other western states. This had ceased under Napoleon, and the former importing countries had increased their own production of corn behind high tariff walls. These tariffs were now retained and in consequence Prussian agriculture was in distress for many years. Most of the big landowners had to sell their estates.

What the German national economy lacked was freedom of movement, both territorial and social, a knowledge of new techniques and marketing, and a widely spread, well-to-do and enterprising middle class with sufficient capital and cheap credit at its disposal. In addition there was no big internal economic area; the roads were all too often very bad; there was no unified currency and, in Austria, there was a massive national debt.

EMIGRATION

The population of the German states expanded considerably in the first few decades following the war. On many sides it was feared that Germany was over-populated and lacked enough fertile soil to feed the extra mouths. At that time the theory of Malthus, that population tended to increase much more quickly than the necessary food production, made a great impression. As yet little was known of the extent to which industrial development and improvements in the crop yields could provide for the needs of a growing population. In Germany there were large areas of arable land which had scarcely been cultivated, and a lot of forests, pastureland and fen which could be turned into fertile soil. In many countries, of course, such as Württemberg, land was in fact very scarce in relation to population and had for years been divided and re-divided between heirs, so that in the end many holdings were so small that a family could not live from them. The manufacturing industry was as yet underdeveloped in Germany. In a number of states at that time measures were passed to deal with the supposed danger of over-population. Thus, for example, marriage needed government permission and this was only forthcoming if the ability to support a family could be proved, whether by private means or an assured income from a trade or profession. Such laws hit the poorer classes hard; they led to an increase in irregular sexual relationships and ran counter to the idea of the rights of man.

A number of circumstances created conditions which encouraged emigration. In many German states, land holdings could not be divided up between heirs but went to the eldest son, while the younger members of the family received a trifling sum in compensation and could earn their living only as servants or farm labourers. The guild system made it hard to attain independence. Many municipalities, in order to save the expense of increased poor relief, sought to make it impossible for the unpropertied to settle. In general the persistence of the feudal guild spirit and particularism helped to swell the numbers of emigrants and in the course of time many hundreds of thousands sought a new home outside Germany. Distaste for military service, the denial of full civic rights and religious considerations also played a part. Emigration was greatest from the thinly-populated agricultural areas, and was much less from the more densely-populated industrial areas, even though there was much unemployment in many of the latter. The factory workers often owned a piece of ground which afforded them food when they had no other earnings.[1]

By far the greatest emigration was to North America, where there was still unlimited free land, and where in many parts there was such a big German population that a German state seemed likely to arise within the framework of the United States. Emigration and settlement were organised by foreign companies with numerous agents in Germany. These tried to attract as many emigrants as possible by offering them their passage and some land, but at the same time often misled them in an utterly unscrupulous manner, so that many fell upon very hard times. A number of German governments therefore restricted emigration, while others watched over the interests of emigrants and issued regulations designed to protect them. In addition, non-profit-making organisations were formed to pursue this aim and in 1847 a national association for German emigrants was founded. Many thousands went to Australia, Russia and South America. While the majority succeeded in making a new life for themselves, some were grossly exploited and found themselves second-class citizens. This caused many German writers to urge the founding of German colonies and the development of German shipping.

[1] Cf. statistics and many details given in the periodical *Die Gegenwart*, Vol. XI, 1855; Dr Gaebler in *Jahrbuch für Volkswirtschaft und Statistik*, 1852.

THE DEVELOPMENT OF INDUSTRY, TRADE AND COMMUNICATIONS

When the German *Bund* was founded, it was hoped that agreements between its members would lead to a common customs area and other institutions beneficial to the economy. This hope was not realised, but Prussia soon took the initiative. She began, in 1818, by introducing a customs tariff which enclosed her own territories in one economic area and as early as the twenties some other states joined in. By the end of 1837 the union embraced the greater part of the German people and was thenceforth called the German Customs and Commercial Union (der Deutsche Zoll- und Handelsverein). Only a few states in the north-west which were situated on or near the coast, as well as German Austria, remained outside. The founding of a great internal market and a unified trade policy with the outside world was the basis of an extraordinary boom which other circumstances also helped to promote. Above all, Germany enjoyed a long period of unbroken peace which aided both the stabilisation of national finances and the creation of the capital necessary for economic development. More than this, an extraordinary improvement in communications was achieved. In many states a start was made on replacing obsolete roads by modern ones with firm foundations which were negotiable even in bad weather. In 1816 Prussia had only 522 miles of modern roads, most of which had been built in the Rhine provinces under Napoleon. In 1834 they had increased almost threefold to 1,546 miles, and in the next two decades this figure was almost doubled. But the greatest revolution in communications and production was brought about by the introduction of steam power. Steamers began to ply on the Rhine in 1827. The Congress of Vienna had declared navigation on the Rhine to be free, but not until 1831, after 514 sessions, had the negotiations between the riparian states to implement this principle been crowned with success, since Holland in particular had done her best to secure a monopoly of Rhine navigation.[1] Bavaria opened the first steam railway in 1835. The first railway concession in Austria was granted in 1836 to the House of Rothschild. Now more and more industrialists appeared and invested large sums, and even governments participated.

The Customs Union helped to promote uniform systems of measurement and coinage. The 1818 tariff gave industry only a very small customs protection, but in the thirties and forties, at the instance of industry, many protective duties were substantially increased. The Customs Union also improved export conditions for industry by

[1] Cf. *Staatslexikon*, Vol. XI, article on 'Rheinoctroi' by Mathy, and 'Rheinschiffahrt' by G. F. Kolb; *Staatswörterbuch*, Vol. IX, *Schiffahrtsverträge*, Vol. II. *Flussschiffahrt* by Kaltenborn.

concluding commercial treaties with preferential clauses. The development of German shipping was for a long time checked by the measures of other states which imposed very high duties on imports carried in German ships.

German industrial production was also helped by numerous factors unconnected with the Customs Union. State banks were set up, mercantile law was brought up to date, particularly by regulations governing joint-stock companies, and professional training was furthered. The plight of the industrial workers and the artisans led to a demand for state intervention on their behalf, and a few measures were in fact introduced, though these at first helped only special cases of need, notably children employed in factories. On the other hand, scientific research at the universities made great strides, especially in the fields of chemistry, physics and agriculture. In 1833, two professors, Gauss and Weber, invented the electric telegraph but in its practical application they were anticipated by Morse in America. In the forties telegraph lines were put up all over Europe and soon afterwards submarine cables were laid. Justus Liebig did some outstanding pioneer work in chemistry. Steam engines, locomotives and other technical devices were at first imported from England, but technology soon developed in Germany. In 1840 the British Government sent Dr John Bowring to Germany to report on industrial development there. In his report he emphasised that the art of pattern making, the lighter metal industry and the production of chemical preparations were more highly developed than in England. He attributed this to the widespread education among the people; many countries in Europe regarded the German educational system at that time as a model.

After the Congress of Vienna the population of Germany increased considerably. In 1816, for the purposes of the German *Bund*, to which territories with non-German populations also belonged, a general census was held, which yielded a population figure of 29,189,800. By the end of 1843, that is to say within twenty-seven years, the figure had risen to 41,054,702. The growing customs receipts, the great majority of which were on luxury goods, show that the larger population enjoyed, on an average, a better standard of living than the smaller. Production likewise rose sharply, as can be seen from the increased imports of raw materials. In the thirty years following the founding of the *Bund*, agricultural production on the same area of land was at least doubled. The number of factory workers in Prussia was 186,612 in 1816, and thirty years later 631,939. The crafts had far more labour at their disposal than industry, and the master-craftsmen outnumbered the apprentices. In Saxony, factories employed 135,328 workers and the crafts 228,326. The growing importance of industry was also apparent from the significant increase in iron and coal production.

A large number of the factories developed from the cottage industries, the handwork being replaced by mechanical production. The extensive linen weaving, which was done on hand looms, suffered heavily from the superior competition of English machine weaving until mechanisation had developed in Germany. The factories, moreover, were at the outset much smaller than those in England, France and Belgium.

In 1833 the British government carried out a survey of the social position of workers in various countries, and the findings were laid before Parliament.[1] It turned out that wages in England were several times higher than in Germany and that the difference in the standard of living was very great. Rent and bread were twice as dear in England as in Prussia. The Prussian worker consumed half the amount of meat an Englishman did. Cotton goods averaged 6 lb per head in England as against 2 lb in Germany. The number of poor people and beggars was much greater in England. As already mentioned, many factory-workers in Germany also possessed a smallholding which they or their family cultivated to supplement the family budget. Thus a completely accurate statistical comparison is not possible. The largely rural nature of Germany where the crafts predominated made many writers hostile to industrialisation and desirous of preserving the semi-feudal conditions of an agrarian Germany with her handicraft industries.

The survey further revealed that in Britain taxes per head of the population amounted to some 12 thalers, compared to only 4 thalers in Prussia, where a large army and a civil service had to be maintained. The 1838–40 budget showed an expenditure of 52·7 million thalers, of which 23·4 millions went to the army. It may seem surprising that Prussia, and other states as well, were run on substantially less money than Britain, despite the fact that Prussia had far more officials. This was partly due to the practice, which was still widespread, of living on home-grown produce, to low prices, plain living and low taxable capacity. In the years of the *Bund*, however, the German states, with the exception of Prussia and Austria, had no expensive policies to pursue on the scale of the great powers; they neither possessed fleets nor waged wars. Their liabilities were for the most part inconsiderable and were chiefly incurred for building railways and other profitable undertakings. Many states also possessed large domains. Their military budget was moderate, for they left their protection to Prussia and Austria.

Besides, in many matters the governments pursued a very thrifty

[1] Cf. G. R. Porter, *The Progress of the Nation*, 1847, pp. 99–106, 193–200, 424, 464.

policy, in order to give the national diets and the voters little cause to form an opposition. In Saxony the finances were so healthy that in 1840 1841, 1843 and 1845 half the trade and personal tax could be remitted, and in 1845 a part of the land tax as well. The rate of interest on the national debt was reduced in 1834 from 4% to 3%. In Bavaria between 1819 and 1845 direct taxation was reduced from 8·8 million gulden to 6·4 millions. As a result of increased consumption indirect taxation rose from 9 to 12·5 million gulden. Thus taxes went up in all by more than a million. The rate of interest dropped to $3\frac{1}{2}$%. The same happened in Württemberg, where the finances were similarly healthy. In many states the national debt was reduced; these included Prussia, Bavaria, Württemberg, Hesse-Darmstadt and Hesse-Cassel.

FRIEDRICH LIST

In the years following the Congress of Vienna few Germans were as concerned over the future of their country as the political economist Friedrich List. He was born in 1789 in the free and imperial city of Reutlingen, a small Swabian town which in days gone by had enjoyed an almost republican autonomy and even at this time had a great measure of independence, until in 1803 it was incorporated into Württemberg. When List considered the proud traditions of Reutlingen's past, he felt an utter abhorrence of the petty, corrupt and brutal bureaucracy which was particularly marked in the Württemberg civil service. Although Württemberg possessed not only a superior, ducal corps of civil servants but also influential Estates, the *Schreiber* formed a powerful, caste-like group of minor and not-so-minor officials who were a fearful plague to broad sections of the people. As a young man, List was himself destined to become a *Schreiber* and had received the necessary training, but he was filled with the deepest distaste for the whole institution. He made the acquaintance of the minister von Wangenheim, who fully shared his views and established a chair of political science at Tübingen in order to break the influence of the *Schreiber* system. List was appointed as first professor but he did not retain his post for long, as his support for a liberal constitution and self-government earned him the hatred of the bureaucrats. At that time the struggle for the 'Old Rights' (of Württemberg) was raging and on this issue Wangenheim was brought down. List also founded and became general secretary of an association of manufacturers and merchants, which called for the abolition of all customs duties inside Germany and the creation of a German Customs Union. His enemies in the bureaucracy declared that this was inadmissible and List voluntarily relinquished his chair.

In 1821, as a deputy, he laid before the Württemberg Diet a sweeping programme of reform which was accompanied by biting criticism of the whole administration of the country. For this the Government preferred a criminal charge against him, he was expelled from the chamber and sentenced to imprisonment in a fortress. When he then looked for another position, he found nothing but difficulties in his way. He finally emigrated to America and there made a fortune by opening up coal mines and building railways. The American Government wanted to appoint him their consul in Hamburg, but the Hamburg Senate refused to acknowledge this 'demagogue' as a diplomatic representative. In 1830 he went to France, where he advocated the building of railways, which at that time still met the utmost scepticism or even flat refusal in all European countries. When in 1832 he proposed the setting up of a big German railway network, he found no backing.

List had long cherished the idea of bringing out an encyclopaedia of political science, and in 1833 he proposed to Professor Rotteck and Professor Welcker that they jointly compile one. After great difficulties, the *Staatslexikon* was founded, the first edition appearing in 1843. List wrote numerous contributions, but was not one of the editors.[1]

In 1834 List became American consul in Leipzig, although the Saxon Government too raised some objections because of the Württemberg affair. List now applied himself with great zeal to the development of a railway network in Germany. He succeeded in overcoming the prejudices against the scheme and winning over the organs of public opinion, but he was not in a position to profit personally from railway construction. His personal finances were severely hit by a big economic crisis in America and there were fears that all his money was lost.

At last he could no longer stomach working in Germany, and so in 1837 he went to Brussels and on to Paris. Both in Belgium and France he was received with every mark of esteem by the leading statesmen. He now devoted himself for three years to an intensive study of history and political economy and this culminated in his principal work, *Das Nationale System der Politischen Ökonomie*. At this time, too, he resumed his former connection with Cotta's *Allgemeine Zeitung* and published in its columns numerous articles which he later incorporated into his book, which first appeared in 1841.

This work, which contained a vigorous attack on Adam Smith's theory of free trade, caused a great sensation and was soon sold out. List went to his native Württemberg and was given a warm and respectful welcome. The King and the Government were also well disposed towards him now. Cotta was prepared to give considerable backing to his literary projects, and the first fruits were the appearance of a weekly

[1] On the subject of the *Staatslexikon*, cf. p. 202 ff.

Zollvereinsblatt in which List could set out his ideas in detail. They met with a hostile reception in most German newspapers, since the free trade party was in the ascendant, but all the same they made a considerable impact and List's following grew rapidly. All the parliaments in Southern Germany and some of the Prussian provincial diets came out in his favour. The industrialists, who were interested in increased duties, supported his efforts. But he was not, as his opponents claimed, in the pay of German industrialists; contributions from industry were only on a very modest scale. List, now living in Augsburg, would have much liked an official position in the administration of the railways.

In 1843 he got in touch with Metternich and Kübeck, the leading statesmen in Austria, and in the following year he went to Austria and Hungary, where he made a close study of economic conditions and worked out great new plans. In Hungary he met with special acclaim; prominent Hungarian politicians were very interested in his ideas.

Not until the middle of 1845 did List return home and resume his editorship of the *Zollvereinsblatt*. He now had a large following but was also the target for sharp attacks. The Prussian Government's retention of low customs rates threatened to demolish the *Zollverein*; in South Germany, there was serious talk of breaking with Prussia and forging trade links with Austria instead. List set his face firmly against this, and stressed that Austria, because some of her peoples were still very backward, could only be 'the faithful ally of a united Germany'. The spirit, the interests and the hopes of Germany, he maintained, did not fit into the framework of the Austrian Empire. List also came out decidedly in favour of a German parliament which was to grow out of the *Zollverein*. The attacks on his views cut him to the quick. In a letter to Robert von Mohl he expressed his bitterness at conditions in Germany and wrote that only a revolution would lead to unity.

When in 1846 the British Prime Minister, Sir Robert Peel, went over to free trade and repealed the Corn Laws, List spent some time in London studying events. He attended important parliamentary sessions and met Cobden and other politicians. Although convinced that free trade was not for Germany, List was politically the greatest admirer of England. At that time he recommended an alliance between Germany and Britain, but without success.

This failure was largely responsible for robbing List of all hope. For a long time he had been sick in body and mind; his nerves were in pieces, his energy sapped and he was a prey to utter despair. He undertook one more journey south to recuperate, but was held up by bad weather at Kufstein on the Tyrolean border, where, at the end of 1846, he committed suicide.

List's main importance does not lie in the field of theoretical political economy but in that of its practical application. He was pre-eminently a passionate fighter and an indefatigable journalist who founded a dozen periodicals. His whole life was a struggle to achieve one single, free and powerful German nation, which, he was convinced, could be built up only on the foundation of a strong industry and with the help of an economic policy harking back in many respects to mercantilism. He saw that the fundamental originality of his doctrine lay in the fact that he opposed to Adam Smith's cosmopolitan theory a national one. Smith's theory, he said, taught how the whole human race could achieve prosperity but in the prevailing circumstances served British interests only. His own system of national economy, on the other hand, was intended to demonstrate how one particular nation could, in the existing world situation, attain prosperity, civilisation and power. List recognises that Smith's aim of a far-reaching division of labour among the nations of the world would bring great advantages in the long term, but raises the objection that this would hold good only if all the nations capable of doing so had already developed their resources to the full. This would call for moderate protective tariffs (List called them *Erziehungszölle*, i.e. corrective tariffs), which could later be removed. He sought to prove that even Britain owed her huge prosperity not to free trade but to a very pronounced system of protection of her national output.

But there were other reasons, List explains, which in some circumstances justified protective duties. International free trade could function properly only if peace and justice between nations were assured. While this was not the case, a nation needed a measure of self-sufficiency to enable it to weather a war without being dependent on its overseas trade. Furthermore, a national economic policy must not merely aim at increasing the wealth of the individual but also at increasing the productive capacity of the nation, by which List means not only its industrial and commercial institutions but also its political institutions, its cultural heritage and its national spirit. List finally reaches the conclusion that it is above all the development of industry which rouses the full powers of a nation and should therefore be aimed at even if it can only be realised at the expense of agriculture. List attempted to justify his principles by making an all-out attack on Adam Smith. Some of his arguments can be rejected, but many of them contain a seminal idea, as, for example, his theory of productive resources, which rightly emphasises that economic progress does not spring exclusively from the pursuit of profit by individuals but from the combined political, social and cultural powers of a nation. List has finally carried the day against Adam Smith in so far as all nations, even Britain, have given up the principle of undiluted free trade and practise protection to a greater or lesser extent. One may regret this, but it has been largely brought about by exigencies which were hardly imaginable in Adam Smith's day, such as the frequent danger of a world war unleashed by the spread of nationalism.

Today we live in an age in which even small and backward nations strive their utmost to promote an industry because they see in this something demanded by their prestige, their power or their very existence. List would certainly not have approved of this; indeed, it contradicts his principles. The fact remains that, in common with his American and French teachers, List stimulated lines of thought which have a direct bearing on our modern problems, although he himself could scarcely have foreseen this. His thinking is dominated by the concept of the nation as the supreme value. He considers it impossible to oppose its natural development, and he assumes that all nations capable of such development pass through essentially the same process of evolution and will finally unite into a universal society, a league of nations, as soon as they have attained equal maturity and independence economically and intellectually. It must be said that List reaches the conclusion that only few peoples possess the prerequisites for achieving full nationhood – namely, a broad territory richly blessed with natural resources and a large population, without which intellectual growth, economic prosperity and political power are not possible. Dwarf nations would, in List's view, be forced to join the larger ones. Thus he believes that Holland, Denmark and Switzerland would be incorporated by treaties into Germany. List's attitude to Britain is remarkable, fluctuating as it does between admiration and hostility. In one place he writes: 'The progress of the world has not been hindered but infinitely helped by Britain. She has become a model and pattern for all nations. Who knows how backward the world would still be if no Britain had existed? And if she ceased to be, who can measure how far humanity would be set back?' Yet in his eyes her superiority seemed a danger to all other nations, and he therefore called for a permanent alliance of all continental European nations, under Germany's leadership against the dominance of British trade and the British fleet. Only such an alliance, he said, could ensure equal rights for all nations and a long peace. The continental powers should then act in concert to secure large markets overseas and force Britain by commercial pressure to open up her own colonies to other nations. Sparsely populated countries, like Australia and New Zealand, should be divided up among them. Further, the European powers should, on the pattern of the British rule in India, take over and administer all Asiatic nationalities, thus including Turkey, Persia, China and Japan. List wanted to reserve the South American markets for Germany.

Of these demands it must be said above all that they were impracticable and that no government would have been prepared to back them. Such an alliance as List suggested was as unattainable as it was unworkable. The *Zollverein* at that time did not even possess any ports which could have served as a base for a maritime and colonial policy.[1] Besides, trade and industry in Germany were still very far from being sufficiently developed to make her an economic world power. Indeed, where trade was concerned, a German colonial policy was superfluous, for the liberals in England, who were on their way to power were in any case calling for an open door for all the nations of the British Empire and were convinced that the colonies would in the end obtain independence. In the course of the century misgivings arose in Parliament over any extension of Britain's colonial possessions. Also history has shown that Germany was able to become a world economic power even without colonies.

But List's ideas on these questions were important all the same, because they paved the way for the subsequent efforts of a nationalistic Germany to acquire a large colonial empire and a powerful fleet, which led to rivalry between Germany and Britain and contributed so much to the outbreak of the First World War. List himself was by no means a supporter of power politics and this distinguishes him from the Pan-Germans of more recent history. But even in his day there were some German writers, principally poets, who had enthusiastic visions of their country exalted to the rank of a world power with a large fleet – Georg Herwegh, for example, who soon after became an active revolutionary and roundly condemned Prussian militarism. List himself probably realised that his dream of a continental coalition against Britain's maritime and colonial supremacy was an impossible one. The swing to free trade in England induced him to change his attitude completely. He now proposed an Anglo-German alliance and discussed this idea in detail in memoranda written in the summer of 1846.

After surveying the world situation, List argued that the task had now fallen to Britain of bringing order out of the existing chaos and pursuing a policy which would ensure international leadership for her and freedom and civilisation, peace and prosperity for all nations. There were three nations, he wrote, who strove to dispute world hegemony with Britain: France, Russia and America. First came the French, who, brave and talented though they were, were not by their nature equipped in matters of commerce, shipping or the art of government to assume the leadership. Their inordinate love of martial glory

---

[1] The *Zollverein* was at that time cut off from the North Sea and important Baltic harbours because Hanover, Oldenburg, Bremen, Hamburg, Lübeck, Schleswig-Holstein and Mecklenburg had not yet joined.

dominated all else and they would never cease to demand the Rhine as a frontier. Russia, as a barbarian state, had become great only by virtue of successive conquests, and war, the biggest scourge of civilised nations, was the one element in which she could live. France and Russia were inclined towards an alliance directed against England and Germany. List ascribed this to the supposed fact that the Latin and Slav races were not as capable as the Teutonic of civilising barbarous countries and educating them for self-government. Thus there existed, he argued, a defensive community of interest between Germany and Britain against Russian and French expansionism. List envisages Britain's ruling Asia Minor and Egypt commercially and Germany the European provinces of Turkey, which was in a state of dissolution. In this way an assured land and sea link between Britain and India would come into being and both Britain on the one hand and Germany and Austria on the other would have the chance of absorbing large and extremely fertile territories. But British policy should not continue to try and thwart the development of the *Zollverein* or of German industry. Even what had happened so far had shown that since the founding of the *Zollverein* British exports to Germany had risen far more rapidly than to other countries and Britain therefore had no reason at all to fear the economic unification of Germany. But out of this economic unification a political one would also spring. An uprising for political unification was imminent. Public opinion in Germany had been roused by recent events, especially the aggressive demonstrations of Thiers in 1840; the power of the middle class had grown, and even the nobility were beginning to realise that Germany's existence depended on her unity.

Thus List wanted above all else to extend the *Zollverein* to the whole of Germany and in all likelihood to Austria too, and to make the Balkans a German sphere of interest, probably by economic treaties. The political and economic control of overseas countries should be left to Britain; indeed, List wanted her to expand as widely as possible overseas so that she would need Germany, with her military strength, as an ally. The Anglo-German alliance should also form a common front against the growing power of the United States, which might well threaten Canada and other British colonies. List's plans were doomed to founder on two hard facts of European politics: Britain's independent position and the collaboration of the Eastern powers.

The later champions of Germany's bid to become a world power, who came to the fore only after Bismarck's fall, made most use in their propaganda of those utterances of List's which were directed against England and stressed Germany's goal of power. His other views were passed over in silence. Now List differed considerably from later

nationalists. Granted, he stood for national power, but he did not see
in this the highest aim to which all else was to be sacrificed. His motto
was: 'Et la patrie et l'humanité' (For fatherland as well as for mankind).
Much as he esteemed and loved the German people, he did not see
it as a higher race called to world domination. If he sometimes talks
of races, a concept then coming into fashion, this is not to be linked
with the ideology of a later day. He was against a policy of Germanisation and disclaimed any right to supremacy for the Germans. As
immigrants in North America and Hungary, he writes, they should
attach no undue importance to preserving their own language but should
adopt the language of the majority and become assimilated. He often
discusses the advantages of miscegenation, even between white and
coloured people, and considers the British, not the Germans, as the
representatives of the Germanic race with a special talent for spreading
civilisation and the art of politics. He also doubted the value of German
colonialism and said it would never occur to the Germans to strive for
world domination. Even if he did finally envisage a great British world
empire incorporating a German sphere of interest, this seemed to him
the best way to spread prosperity, freedom and civilisation.

II

RELIGION AND POLITICS

THE LEGACY OF THE PAST

The religious struggles of the past had a profound effect on German history and helped to bring about the extraordinary territorial and social fragmentation of the Empire. Whereas, after the Reformation, a single religion rose to dominance in both England and France, Catholicism and Protestantism were about equally strong in Germany, and as a result neither could dictate terms to the other. The Peace of Westphalia (1648) had even laid down that no religious questions could be decided by a majority vote in the *Reichstag* but that an amicable settlement must be reached by the representatives of the two great faiths.

The Reformation had increased the power of the rulers by making each the head of the Church in his own dominions. Supervision was admittedly exercised by special authorities, the consistories, which sometimes enjoyed considerable independence, especially where the ruler of a Protestant country had gone over to Catholicism, but even so the Church was largely subject to the State. In the Age of Enlightenment in many Catholic countries the rights of the State in church affairs were extensive; the Austria of Maria Theresa and Joseph II is one example. At the same time, a certain religious tolerance and equality of rights were for the most part achieved. A feature of the old German Empire had been the numerous ecclesiastical states, ruled by a bishop or abbot elected by the canons. Even these states were gradually permeated by the spirit of the Enlightenment and were incorporated into secular principalities shortly before the end of the *Reich*.

The Age of Enlightenment often saw a watering-down of orthodox doctrines, and, indeed, religious faith was sometimes supplanted by philosophical views. Even in the early years of the *Bund*, political prejudices rooted in the diversity of religions had by no means vanished. Orthodoxy was still alive in the hearts of many people of all classes, and even the 'enlightened' not infrequently showed themselves spiteful towards those of a different faith. Many Protestants in Prussia viewed Catholicism as an enemy of culture, freedom and the national movement, and not a few Catholics nursed considerable prejudices against the Protestants. On the one hand leading political theorists saw in Protestantism the mainspring of the libertarian movement; on the other, there were even some Protestant writers who taxed their religion with having split Germany or spreading pernicious rationalism.

CATHOLICISM AND POLITICS

The struggles which led to the dissolution of the old *Reich* hit the Catholic Church especially hard. The annexation of German territory on the left bank of the Rhine as well as the arrangements made in the 'final recess' of 1803 (*Reichsdeputationshauptschluss*) marked the end of the ecclesiastical states. West of the Rhine they were incorporated into France, and to the East sovereignty and possession passed to German princes, who, in consequence of this and of other annexations of German territories, became vassals of Napoleon. The Church in France had long since trodden the path to establishment and Napoleon completely subordinated it to the State. He also abolished the pontifical state and held two successive popes prisoner. His German vassals in many instances followed his example. Moreover, even before the French Revolution there had been a movement in the German church towards a sort of national church. It was fostered by the archbishops and their demands were laid down in 1786 in the 'Punctation of Ems' but were not implemented. Soon after, the Vicar-General, Heinrich Ignatz von Wessenberg, began to make similar efforts, with an equal lack of success. After the fall of Napoleon the Catholics faced the task of rebuilding the Church in Germany and strengthening religious spirit.[1]

On religious matters, the Federal Statute of 1815 laid down in article 16 merely that the existence of differing Christian faiths in the countries of the *Bund* could not justify any discrimination in granting civil or political rights. Of the larger states, only Austria and Bavaria were predominantly Catholic. The annexations of the German territories mentioned above, the two treaties of Paris and the provisions of the Congress of Vienna had created a number of German states of mixed religion. Thus it happened that Prussia, Hesse, Württemberg and Baden had strong Catholic minorities and Bavaria a large Protestant one. As time went on this had important political consequences. Many states concluded with the Pope concordats which laid down for which

[1] Vide Franz Schnabel, *Deutsche Geschichte im 19. Jahrhundert*, Vol. IV. His brilliant account of the subsequent development of the churches is also indispensable reading.

church affairs the state was the competent authority and for which the Pope. These arrangements conceded very far-reaching rights to the state, particularly in education and the appointment of bishops. In addition, the boundaries of bishoprics were re-drawn to match the changed circumstances.

Among the Romanticists there was a strong leaning towards Catholicism, which led to the conversion of Protestants such as Friedrich Schlegel. Politically, Görres was prominent in pointing the way to new aims. In his youth he had been a vigorous enemy of all religions and churches and it was some time before he went over completely to Catholicism. However, when he did he placed his extensive knowledge and extraordinary talents as a writer completely at the service of the church.

Clerical writers at this time often spoke out in favour of the union of 'throne and altar' and praised religion as the surest bulwark against the onset of the revolutionary spirit.

In the South German parliaments, groups sprang up which pursued a conservative policy from a Christian standpoint and often worked together with representatives of Protestantism. In 1831 the *Berliner Politische Wochenblatt* appeared, on which prominent men from both camps worked side by side. In 1838 a Catholic organ was founded in Munich, the *Historisch–Politischen Blätter für das katholische Deutschland*, edited by Görres, which soon supplanted the *Wochenblatt*. Munich became the great focus of cultural and political Catholicism, and Ludwig I gave its aspirations energetic support. Prominent Catholic scholars were called to the university there, and Munich proved to be the Catholic counterpart of Protestant Berlin.

In Prussia, as in other German states, attempts were made to win over the Catholic Church for a close working alliance against the revolutionary spirit. There had meanwhile been a reaction among the intellectual leaders of the Catholics. True, the forces of revolution, which assailed religion and the Church with any means to hand, were also enemies of theirs, but they realised that monarchical absolutism with its bureaucracy and police was positively inviting revolution. Much as the Catholic publicists disapproved of liberalism and enlightenment, they also rejected the militaristic and bureaucratic power state. Liberalism did, however, have a significant influence on a part of the Catholic Church. After the July Revolution, Lamennais, Lacordaire and Montalembert promoted a liberal Catholicism and a party of this persuasion was formed. In Belgium the independence movement owed its success to an alliance of clericals and liberals. In Germany, too, there were Catholic publicists who paid homage to the new ideas, while others took their stand on the conservative principles of legitimacy, the historic Estates and ecclesiastical privileges. German Catholicism has always had both a conservative and a liberal wing. Among the first prominent liberal Catholics were the brothers August and Peter Reichensperger from the Rhineland; through the Church struggle of 1837 they had joined forces with the political wing of liberal Catholicism and they were later co-founders of the Centre Party. Catholic politicians early recognised the importance of having a social policy. In their eyes handicrafts and agriculture were often more important than trade and industry. Priests like Ketteler and Kolping campaigned above all for the journeymen apprentices. In the forties Kolping began to form journeymen's associations which promoted social welfare and spread over all Germany. Ketteler espoused the cause of the workers on the land, while others did much for the relief of the poor and sick.

PROTESTANTISM

German Protestantism was split up, wherever the State did not intervene to prevent it, by the formation of sects, and the Enlightenment undermined religion far more in Protestant countries than in Catholic. Broadly speaking, the division in Germany was into Lutherans and Calvinists (Reformed Church). At the Protestant universities a Bible criticism developed which in the end led to a rejection of Christianity. The extraordinary preoccupation with philosophical speculation was a result of the decline in religion and the search for a substitute. Pietism continued to operate and often strove to overcome the antagonisms between the faiths and to mitigate social evils by good works. Schleiermacher came from the Herrnhuter (Moravian) movement; he put forward that religion should be a completely emotional experience – an entirely new conception.

In the wars of liberation propagandists like Arndt enlisted Protestantism in the struggle against the foreign conqueror, and to the Gymnasts and the *Burschenschaften* it was the expression of true Germanhood. The Prussian reformers sought to replace the provincial churches by an established church subordinated completely to the State. The State was to bear a markedly Protestant character. Stein and Schleiermacher wished to give the Church autonomy with lay participation but did not put this measure through. In 1817, on the occasion of the tercentenary of the Reformation, Frederick William III made a plea that the two Protestant churches should unite, and in this he was supported by Schleiermacher, but attempts to standardise doctrine, liturgy and constitution aroused violent opposition from the Lutheran orthodoxy and were scarcely more welcome to many members of the Reformed Church. The Prussian Union brought with it a centralised, established church over which the Government had full control, but this led to no real unification. The Protestants continued to split up into numerous sects, which were often bitterly at odds. Orthodoxy, pietism and rationalism all had a large following. A liberal Protestantism also developed, which aimed at combining the Christian ethos with the classical ideal of humanism and full freedom for science. Among the Protestants no predominant political tendency arose as it had among the Catholics. In Prussia the Catholics formed the minority in a state which positively professed Protestantism and this fact alone produced in them an opposition not only in religious matters but also in political, economic and social questions. The majority of the Protestants adopted Luther's attitude to the State and politics, and this led partly to conservatism and partly to the avoidance of political commitment. The liberal Protestants indulged in fierce opposition to the Church of Rome and hailed Luther as a national and liberal hero, which is historically quite untenable. A large number of the liberals became estranged from religion and thereby lost their hold on wide sections of the people who clung fast to the Church. Like the Catholics, the Protestants pursued extensive charitable activities and came to grips in earnest with social distress, though scarcely by political means.

THE JEWS

Since the late Middle Ages, the Jews in all the Christian states of Europe had been grievously persecuted. In England, France and Spain they had all been driven out. In the old German *Reich* they had been almost completely expelled from all the Free Cities, but they managed to maintain a footing in many German countries, where they were protected by the princes. The prosperous upper classes as well as many temporal and spiritual rulers were not hostile to them, while the lesser nobility, the clergy, artisans and peasants often hated them, probably, in the main, because they were money-lenders. These classes forbade them to carry on a trade. Later, in many states, Jews were admitted to certain trades for economic reasons. With the development of the modern state, which was built up on finance, Jews proved to be indispensable money-raisers, suppliers and financial advisers to the princes. From time to time in most German states the 'Court Jews' played a considerable part and occupied a favoured position. But almost everywhere the great mass of ordinary Jews were kept in economic servitude by the governments.

In Prussia, Frederick the Great had no love for the Jews, though he made use of them in founding his industries, and his decree of 1750 was highly repressive. However, the wars he waged enabled many

Jews to make money as army contractors, and some, by running new industries, succeeded in making fortunes. Frederick's successor, Frederick William II, and his principal minister Wöllner were well disposed towards them and tried to help them, but their attempts were frustrated by the attitude of a section of the civil service. In Austria, Joseph II freed the Jews from many humiliating restrictions on their personal rights and even bestowed titles on some of them, but after his death a reaction set in and things grew worse again.

In the second half of the eighteenth century a movement arose to free the Jews from the numerous legal degradations to which they were subject. Moses Mendelssohn, Lessing and Dohm were their champions in Germany. Soon after the Revolution, Jews were once again recognized in France and their status considerably improved. In 1808 two conflicting decrees were issued simultaneously, one favourable to the Jews, the other unfavourable. In 1818, after Napoleon's fall, the prejudicial measures were repealed. As conquerors the French everywhere granted Jews freedom and equality, even in the extensive German territories which were subject to France. In some of the states of the Confederation of the Rhine considerable progress was made.

In Germany, meanwhile, a climate favourable to emancipation prevailed among influential circles. The movement which had begun with Mendelssohn had greatly promoted among educated and well-to-do Jews assimilation to their environment, the cultivation of the German language and culture and the laying aside of Jewish characteristics. The Age of Enlightenment had seen the spread of both tolerance and religious indifference. This all helped to shrink the gap between Jews and Christians. In Berlin and Vienna there were rich Jewish bankers whose salons were frequented by the cultural élite, leading statesmen and the nobility. Hardenberg and Metternich, as well as Wilhelm von Humboldt and many other national and social leaders, were favourably disposed towards the Jews. But this group was relatively small; the majority of the circles which wielded influence in the state shared the attitude of the masses, who wanted as little change in the situation as possible. In 1812 Hardenberg succeeded none the less in putting through Humboldt's measure granting the Jews equality of status. The only thing from which they were still debarred was public office, although Humboldt had wished to remove this disability too.

In the wars of liberation, numerous Jewish volunteers had joined the forces fighting against Napoleon and a considerable number received decorations. At the Congress of Vienna the draft constitution for the *Bund*, worked out by Humboldt, proposed the grant of full civil rights to the Jews, but this clause could not be put through in the face of the opposition of the other German states. Finally, in paragraph

16, the Jews were guaranteed no more than the retention of their existing rights in the individual states of the *Bund*.

Luther's attitude strongly coloured the Protestant tradition. The great reformer, originally friendly towards the Jews, attacked them immoderately in later writings and condemned them, causing protests in the *Reichstag* from the Catholic party. Quite apart from this, the Jews had for centuries been painted in the darkest colours, and an image of them had arisen among all classes which could not be effaced overnight by means of pamphlets and speeches.

Out-and-out nationalists, students in particular, maintained that the Jews did not belong to the German nation but were a nation apart, as their language and customs proved. For centuries, of course, the Jews themselves had maintained this very thing and cherished the belief that the Messiah would lead them back into their own land. The orthodox majority among them still believed this and resisted any assimilation to German customs and habits. It was demanded more than once that the granting of civil rights should be made conditional on the Jews' giving up foreign customs.

Opposition to the emancipation of the Jews was mainly on economic grounds. They were accused of exploiting people by usury, fraud, price-rigging and an utterly unsavoury commercial morality. Generally such charges could neither be proved nor refuted. At all events it is understandable that the centuries-old persecution of the Jews and their restriction to those occupations which were despised, wretchedly paid or dangerous was scarcely conducive to the growth of sound commercial morality among them. A further criticism was that they shirked manual work, but the guilds had for a long time forbidden them to practise a craft and the feudal system had shut them off from work on the land. There was also a fear that they would carry on trade and commerce not in the traditional manner but as capitalists. In the textile industry many Jews had started by supplying hand weavers and had then gone over to the running of factories. In other professions, too, Jewish competition was feared.

The clause in the German Federal Statute resulted in many areas in a considerable worsening of the legal position of the Jews, especially where they had been given equality under French rule. In many states they ceased to be full citizens and became 'Schutzjuden' once more – that is, people merely tolerated and of inferior legal standing, although they were not again subjected to the worst repressions they had known as late as the eighteenth century. In Prussia the legal position they had attained in 1812 was considerably eroded. They were barred from a whole host of occupations, especially those which in one way or another depended on the State; they could not become, for example, surveyors, pharmacists, medical referees or, indeed, even executioners. In the army they could not now rise above non-commissioned rank, whereas in the wars of liberation many had been commissioned on the battlefield. Later they could not even become corporals. In 1828 and 1836 Jews were forbidden to assume Christian first names. Frederick William III went so far as to forbid the Jews to say their prayers in German, whereas other German states laid down that they should. These pinpricks were apparently aimed at forcing the Jews into baptism. In 1822 a 'Society for the Conversion of the Jews' was founded in Berlin with strong support from the King. Many of them underwent baptism, and in this way received full equality. These conversions were for the most part motivated by an honest ambition to be absorbed into German life. They attempted to assimilate themselves to the Christians in their business life. Prussian statistics showed an unusually great increase in the number of Jewish artisans.

In 1819 there were disorders in several parts of Germany with an element of Jew-baiting. In Bavaria numerous petitions against granting equal status to the Jews were addressed to the Estates and in 1822 the Government declared that the time for such a measure was not yet ripe, the force of prejudice still being all too strong. Gradually considerable progress was made in Baden. In central and northern Germany, the situation of the Jews was particularly onerous, notably in Saxony, which was known as 'Protestant Spain'; in Hanover, the ruling nobility deprived the Jews of the liberties they had enjoyed under French rule. They were better treated in the Electorate of Hesse but not in the Grand Duchy. In many small states there were philanthropic rulers who gave them almost complete freedom, even though their Estates protested. In Saxe–Weimar considerable burdens were imposed on them and even Goethe, who was a minister, mistrusted them. The free cities took a hard line. In 1814 the Hamburg senate introduced a motion to give Jews civil rights on certain conditions. It praised their conduct and saw in their admission great benefits for the city. But, just like the townsfolk of the other free cities of Frankfurt, Lübeck and Bremen, the Hamburg tradespeople and craftsmen were concerned about Jewish competition, and so the motion, which was supported by the wealthier merchants, was defeated and very repressive conditions were imposed. Austria and Prussia sought to change this attitude on the part of the Free Cities. In the days of the Confederation of the Rhine, the Jews of Frankfurt had been able to buy their emancipation for considerable sums of money, but after the founding of the *Bund* the city authorities withdrew many of their rights and proposed to lower their status. The Jews protested, and received the support of Metternich and Hardenberg, as well as of Britain and Russia. Metternich in particular told Frankfurt bluntly that its decree infringed the law. Thereupon the Frankfurt council waged a battle for years before the Federal Assembly, and at last, in 1824, accepted a ruling of the *Bund* and enacted a fresh law. This mitigated the earlier measure but still contained many very repressive provisions. Later on further relaxations were made.

The question of the legal position of the Jews was also discussed in many pamphlets and articles and the upshot was that the attitude of wide sections of the public swung round in the Jews' favour. In this better atmosphere they were no longer so much a race apart from the Christians. They extended the use of German to their religious services and schools and their children began to attend state schools. Many left their traditional professions and became manual workers or devoted themselves to the liberal professions, scholarship and literature. Soon the Germans were spellbound by the words of Heine and the music of Mendelssohn and Meyerbeer. Boerne was the leading light of the Young German movement, and scholars of Jewish descent like Stahl, Gans and Neander were in the forefront of their particular fields of enquiry.

In a number of German states, the July Revolution brought about national movements which led to liberal constitutions, and this was a further help to the Jews. In 1833 in the Electorate of Hesse they received full equality, except for money-lenders; in Hesse–Darmstadt they had to wait until 1845, and even then public posts were still closed to them. In Brunswick their rights were similarly adjusted, though marriages between Jews and Christians remained illegal. In Saxony, on the other hand, their lot was only slightly bettered. The petty bourgeoisie, which had great influence in the Saxon parliament, feared their competition and was hostile to them, whereas the cultivated Prince John, who later became King, was in favour of granting them equal rights. The Grand Duke Frederick Francis of Mecklenburg–Schwerin also worked indefatigably in their interest, but met strong opposition in the Estates from the nobility.

As long as Frederick William III ruled in Prussia, no radical improvement could be expected. All the same, the Jews of Posen, valuable as a counterweight to the Poles, secured reforms. In a few places the more blatant injustices were removed. Frederick William IV's attitude to the Jews was not one of quite such strong disapproval as his father's. His romantic, medieval views and his ideal of a 'Christian state', however, precluded any reasonable reform. When he proposed lifting the Jews' liability to military service, they protested so emphatically that the idea was dropped. By now public opinion in Prussia was predominantly favourable to them. As late as 1822 all eight provincial parliaments had come out unequivocally against legislation in favour of the Jews.

Between 1843 and 1845, the parliaments of the five provinces in which seven-eighths of the Prussian Jews lived took a decidedly pro-Jewish stand. In the United Diet of 1847, the 'curia' of the landowners, cities and rural communities supported almost complete equality for the Jews, whereas the 'curia' of the old nobility adopted the attitude of the government, which was far less positive.

In Bavaria the chambers repeatedly demanded equal rights for Jews, but the Government's attitude was disapproving and the guilds refused to admit the Jews to trades. In Württemberg they were admitted to most professions in 1828, and in 1847 both chambers proposed complete emancipation; the Government agreed in principle and held out prospects of a measure to this effect. The situation in Baden was similar.

While in Austria the reforms under Joseph II had not been completely swept away, they had been modified by new regulations. In matters of domicile, freedom of movement, marriage, property ownership and choice of profession, the Jews were subject to extraordinary restrictions, taxes and duties which varied from province to province.[1] The financial straits of the country and economic conditions had, however, led to the emergence of some highly successful Jewish firms enjoying wide privileges. Many Jews tried to settle in Vienna, where there were better salaries to be earned than in other parts of the monarchy. The number of officially-domiciled Jews in Vienna was far less than the actual total of those who lived there permanently. Their official status was that of visitors in transit, who were supposed to move on after a few days. The Government winked an eye at this evasion of the law whenever the Jews concerned were serving the economic interests of the community.

There is on record an excellent description of this pre-1848 situation by a writer, Sigmund Mayer, who lived through the period and knew conditions at first hand.[2] He testifies to the fact that Jews could move freely in Vienna, live where they liked, carry on business and were everywhere treated without prejudice. Their main activities were in the textile trade and the marketing of agricultural produce, which they bought from the aristocratic landowners. They could not practise a trade as the guilds would not permit this. They often began on a very modest scale, but some of them, by dint of thrift and hard work, worked their way up to become wholesale dealers, some even millionaires. A surprisingly large number were given titles by the Government. Many spent their wealth on big charitable foundations and for cultural purposes. The majority remained loyal to their origins, though

[1] The best historical account is to be found in the *Österreichisches Staatswörterbuch*, Vol. II, p. 946.

[2] Cf. Sigmund Mayer, *Die Wiener Juden* (1700–1900), 1917.

some went over to the Christian faith and turned their backs on Jewry.

It was above all the Jewish merchants in Vienna who undertook the exchange of many products between the countries of the vast Danubian Empire. Many of them had immigrated from Bohemia and the East; they knew the local conditions and languages, and now, in Vienna, they learned how to run wholesale businesses and carry on international trade. In addition, they found here credit facilities which were not available in their home regions. Thus there arose in Vienna a class of Jewish merchants, industrialists and bankers which became of great importance for the economic development and opening-up of vast areas of Austria-Hungary.

12

POLITICS AND THE ARTS

PHILOSOPHY AND POLITICS

In the period with which we are concerned, Germany distinguished herself by producing a great number of eminent philosophers. This was a source of pride for many Germans, who were inclined to exalt it into a national virtue; but there were many others, such as Ernst Moritz Arndt, who criticised the highly speculative and metaphysical line the philosophers took, on the grounds that such rarefied thinking diverted Germans from the most urgent national tasks and from sound common-sense. But the extraordinary growth of philosophical speculation in Germany was widely regarded as highly significant. Schelling attributed it to the fact that only among the Germans was there a deep religious rift, which had caused them to strive for spiritual unity on the philo-sophical plane. Pfizer likewise saw in it an attempt to bridge the national cleavage by the development of a common philosophy of life and to regain for the Germans a fitting place among the nations by scaling the intellectual heights.[1]

Of the thinkers who developed a comprehensive philosophy of life, Kant, Fichte and Hegel were paramount in their influence on the forma-tion of the political mind. Kant laid the philosophical foundations for freedom of thought, the constitutional state and a system of international peace. It was due above all to his personality and teachings that for a long time Königsberg was the stronghold of Prussian liberalism. Fichte's outlook had republican, democratic, indeed even socialist elements. He championed the cause of liberation from foreign rule but was opposed to the ambitious nationalism which delights in conquest.

Georg Wilhelm Friedrich Hegel (1770–1831), a Württemberger, was in his youth an enthusiastic supporter of the French Revolution and

---

[1] Cf. Schelling, *Münchner Vorlesungen zur Geschichte der neueren Philosophie.* Collected works, Vol. X, p. 194; Pfizer, *Briefwechsel zweier Deutscher*, 1831, p. 153.

later a great admirer of Napoleon. When the war of liberation broke out, he was completely on the side of the French and sought to dissuade young men from flocking to the colours against the Emperor. His greatest hour came in 1818, when he was appointed to the University of Berlin. Leaders of the state and society thronged to his lectures, although he was hard to follow and no great speaker either. He had great influence on the Government, his philosophy was looked on as 'Prussian state philosophy' and he was a power in the intellectual life of Germany, and indeed, far beyond her frontiers. He died of cholera in 1831.

In many respects Hegel had affinities with Kant, Fichte and Schelling, but Spinoza, Montesquieu, Rousseau, Gibbon and Ferguson also influenced him strongly. He used his extraordinary knowledge in many fields and his powerful acumen to erect a system of imposing compactness. The idea of a personal God was replaced by that of the 'world mind' or 'world reason', which, in the course of the ages, was inevitably to prevail and rise to heights of ever clearer self-awareness. According to Hegel this would come about in three stages of a dialectical process culminating in a higher synthesis. In this victorious march of reason, however, irrational powers would also play a part, and these Hegel called the 'cunning of reason'. Above all, he held that great heroes like Napoleon, driven on by their passions, act as unconscious helpers of world reason and in doing so carry out the real will of their peoples. During their ascendancy their nation appears as the most advanced representative of reason and thus takes precedence over all other nations. But once its mission is accomplished, it falls back and another nation takes its place. Every people has its own individual mind, a product of climate, soil, race, religion, political and social organisation.

Hegel's idea of the state corresponds to his view of history. He simultaneously rejects Haller's reactionary theory of the patrimonial state, the liberal idea of natural law and the social contract and the Romantic enthusiasm for the Middle Ages. The true State appears to him an intellectual organism, produced by world reason and therefore vested with the highest authority. It is not tied to the rules of everyday morality and exists to realise true morality, intellectual freedom and the real popular will. To be sure, many states do not fit this conception; they suppress freedom and the welfare of the people and are therefore doomed to perish. Hegel's celebrated (or notorious) dictum that what is actual is rational does not refer to defective and transitory institutions. Mere outward strength alone is not in the long run sufficient to preserve a state; the State must also reflect the true will of the people, which is not necessarily expressed by voting that, after all, might be wrongly influenced by demagogues. Hegel's conception of a popular representation is obviously greatly influenced by Napoleonic institutions. Such a body should consist of especially well-qualified representatives of organised social classes who should combine to evolve the national will by public discussion and criticism. The identification and formulation of the general will is to be undertaken principally by a civil service with its leadership entrusted to an élite of highly educated experts who possess practical experience and the greatest conscientiousness. (One is reminded of Plato's ideal of government by wise men). The unity of the will of the state is to be embodied in the monarch as a decorative head.

This system of government by highly qualified officials with a monarchical façade and a semi-parliamentary advisory council seemed to Hegel better fitted to serve the public weal than British parliamentarianism. Shortly before his death he wrote a criticism of the Reform Bill which was under debate in England at the time and which seemed to him to contain the danger of democratisation. Hegel feared above all else any form of revolution, in which reason must inevitably succumb to mass passions. He was convinced that reason would in the end prevail without violence.

Hegel saw no possibility of controlling the relations between states by an international code of law. Great conflicts could be resolved only by war. He also held that wars were necessary to prevent the public mind from growing slack through a long peace and to inspire patriotism, an argument which he adopted from Gibbon and Ferguson. But he was by no means obsessed with martial glory and conquest. By patriotism he did not mean heroism but the discharge of the daily round of civic duties, and he remarked ironically that people for the most part found it easier to boast of their readiness to act the hero than to meet their obligations to the state by conscientious activity. True, he recognised that war could also help the state to survive, but he showed no enthusiasm for war or power politics for their own sake.

Hegel's doctrines lent themselves to some extent to misuse by nationalism, but his philosophy did not view this movement with favour. He did not esteem a nation for its power or prestige but for the degree of reason which its civilisation manifested. He rejected the German national movement and was regarded as an enemy by its leaders. The mission of the Germans in the world seemed to him to lie in their achievements in the field of philosophy.

Hegel's philosophical system captivated his disciples, although they could not agree on its interpretation and, moreover, in many particulars it proved untenable. It does, however, contain some fundamental ideas which to this day have enlisted the attention and speculation of prominent thinkers. Parts of his system are today outmoded, but there remains much which is still vital and suggestive. He has influenced thinkers not only in Germany but in France, Italy, Russia and England too.[1] His philosophy contains ideas which have stimulated political thinking of differing complexions. Even in his lifetime his school split into conservative, liberal and revolutionary groups. But soon the radicals gained the upper hand and contrived to remould Hegelian ideas to suit their own views.

What the conservatives found appealing in Hegel was above all his call for a strong state and rejection of revolution and democracy, as well as the important role he assigned to higher officials and a monarchical head of state. What the radicals of the left found especially congenial was his thinly-veiled pantheism and his doctrine of the unfettered onward march of reason and liberty. They also liked his idea that the national will could not be determined merely by the casting of votes; revolutionaries, of course, could never hope to realise their plans by normal democratic processes. (Hegel had a high regard for the French Revolution, and even in his old age he always celebrated with a bottle of vintage wine the anniversary of the storming of the Bastille.) Lastly, the liberals could take comfort from Hegel's support for many of their demands and from his doctrine that reason was bound to prevail in the end. There were, however, some liberals who strongly disliked him. The Rotteck-Welcker *Deutsches Staatslexikon*, the bible of the liberals, published an annihilating criticism of him, and Rudolf Haym, one of the greatest liberal scholars in the field of literature, wrote a book which attacked and sharply condemned him.

The markedly liberal, democratic or socialist-minded followers of Hegel were called the Young Hegelians, and first became known by their writings on religious questions, but they were also active in the field of literature and then turned to political and social journalism. In 1835, David Friedrich Strauss brought out his book, *Das Leben Jesu*, which caused a sensation. The author was a 27-year-old Swabian theologian, who with extraordinary erudition sought to show that the Gospel narratives did not rest on fact but largely on myths formed by the imagination of Jewish circles, and had later undergone important modifications. Natually enough, these theories were sharply attacked by Church circles and all posts in Germany were barred to Strauss, but he received a chair in Zürich, where a radical government was in power. The appointment caused popular disorders which brought down the

---

[1] Of the French philosophers, Victor Cousin in particular was a great admirer and personal friend of Hegel. Later Taine was strongly influenced by him, and in England Green, Bradley and Bosanquet. Of the Italians, Benedetto Croce, to name but one, can be mentioned. Hegel's prestige among Russian thinkers was extremely great.

Government, whereupon Strauss was pensioned off. He later wrote, among other works, a book denying Christian dogma.

Another disciple of Hegel, Ludwig Feuerbach, went even further. He was the son of a famous jurist who had played a large part in reforming the German penal code. In his book *Das Wesen des Christentums* (The Nature of Christianity), which appeared in 1841, Feuerbach declared all religions to be products of the human imagination, expressing in the form of gods and their commandments the peoples' ideals and their yearning for happiness. Human beings were, therefore, not the creations of gods, who were themselves products of the human mind. Feuerbach also worked out a system of ethics which set up as principles eudaemonism and altruism. He thus became the main founder of German positivism, and turned from Hegel's panlogism to materialism and socialism.

In the political and social fields, the *Hallischen Jahrbücher*, the organ of the Hegelian Left, was a highly influential paper. It was founded in 1838 by the philologist Theodor Echtermeyer and the philosopher Arnold Ruge, the latter being the moving spirit and the centre of a circle of prominent authors, including Strauss and Feuerbach. Great influence was also wielded by Bruno Bauer, a lecturer at Bonn, who at first attacked Strauss from the Hegelian standpoint but then sought to outdo him in radicalism. The hopes Ruge had placed in Frederick William IV were disappointed. After a temporary relaxation, Prussian censorship was once again tightened and so Ruge transferred his paper to Saxony, where the censorship was milder. Bruno Bauer and his circle, who called themselves *die Freien* (the free ones) now developed a criticism which not only exacerbated all conservatives and moderates but also had a disintegrating effect upon the extreme Left. The radical intellectuals were rather given to internecine disparagement. Bauer rejected the constitutional state, the representative system and other principles of liberalism and expressed his contempt for the bourgeoisie, the 'Philistines'. He also came out against the emancipation of the Jews. Ruge sought to give his publication a positive approach but let himself be strongly influenced by Bauer's limitless negation. Since the Ruge circle rejected above all the idea of God and replaced it by that of humanity, the new doctrine was called humanism. Ruge also issued a manifesto in which he declared democracy to be the goal of the age. Finally his periodical was banned and the Saxon parliament, to which he appealed, confirmed this decision by 52 votes to 8. He thereupon founded in Paris the *Deutsch-Französischen Jahrbücher*, which aimed at furthering cosmopolitanism, bringing about an understanding between the Germans and the French and setting them to work in partnership. Karl Marx was joint editor of this paper, as were Heine and other German émigrés. But Ruge won no support in French republican or socialist circles and the paper soon ceased publication.

Within a few years, many of Hegel's disciples had jettisoned important elements of his doctrines or had become violently opposed to them. His basic principle of the inexorable development of the mind in ever-changing and improving forms had grown more and more questionable and finally, as with Marx, had given place to materialism. But Hegelian views on religion and morality, state and society had also been interpreted in intellectual circles. This tendency reached its climax in a book which appeared in 1844 under the title *Der Einzige und sein Eigentum* (The Individual and his Property). The author, a Prussian private tutor, called himself Max Stirner, but his real name was Johann Kaspar Schmidt. He rejected the concepts of morality and justice, as indeed of any obligation or duty devolving on the individual. All who were zealous for the so-called 'good' seemed to Stirner to be mere supporters of illusory ideas, or *Pfaffen* (a derogatory term for parsons). While he does not reject the idea that the individual should by inclination do good to his fellow-men or subordinate himself to a community, he stresses that this must be an act of free-will. How a satisfactory communal existence can be organised out of the voluntary collaboration of innumerable egoists is a point on which the author has expressed himself only cursorily. Attempts have been made to declare him the precursor of anarchism or of the cult of the superman; the communists were pleased by his criticism of property and their opponents by his strictures on the uninhibited freedom of the individual. Stirner also founded 'Egoists' Associations' and many of his disciples held that they must go even further than their master. This movement never attained to any significance. All the same, both the literature and social criticism of the time suffered a negation of accepted principles in the fields of morality and justice, and the effects of this were far-reaching.

HISTORY, POLITICAL SCIENCE AND POLITICS

Niebuhr
One of the most notable scholars and statesmen was Barthold Georg Niebuhr (1776–1831). He was the son of the famous Arabian explorer, Carsten Niebuhr, and came from Frisian peasant stock. He spent ten years in government service in Denmark, where he gained a thorough knowledge of state finances which proved of great value to him in his study of Roman history. Then, in 1806, Stein summoned him to Prussia and gave him leading administrative posts there, in which he acquired deep insight into conditions in a powerful state. He also

lectured at the Universities of Bonn and Berlin and wrote works on Roman history which, in Macaulay's view, opened up a new epoch in historical research. His vast erudition and critical acumen enabled him to separate legend from history in his studies of ancient Rome. He described the Romans as free peasants who tilled and defended their own fields, until the lust of conquest brought about political and moral decline. For Niebuhr, a knowledge of the past was only possible on the basis of one's own political experience, that is by means of a comparative study. For the history of ancient Rome he used as his yardstick of comparison social conditions in his home district of Holstein and in England, a country where he had lived for some time and which he held in high regard. His political convictions are a mixture of conservative and liberal. The England of his day was his model for the shaping of Germany, and, on the other hand, in his distaste for the French Revolution he rivalled Burke. He was not against all revolutions – the Netherlands revolt, for example, or the Puritan revolution in England – but the French Revolution disgusted him by its cruelty and its greed for conquest. In the ancient world he condemned the Macedonian policy of force aimed against Greek liberty. The reactionary policy of the *Bund* aroused his abhorrence. His ideal state was a constitutional monarchy which conceded to education and ownership, the middle classes and the smallholders, a certain say in policy.

The unification of Germany was dear to his heart and he regarded the achievement of this as Prussia's mission. In this connection he considered Prussian annexations in Germany to be justified by so-called reasons of state. At the same time he considered history from an ethical standpoint, and demanded that the historian should always ask what he himself as a just man would have done. The influence of Kantian ethics is often apparent in him, and Protestantism too played a part in forming his aims. History seemed to him a means of educating a people on moral and national lines. For all his scholarship, Catholic religiosity and the Italian mode of life had no appeal for him, although he spent almost seven years in Rome as Prussian Ambassador to the Holy See.

Schlosser

Friedrich Christoph Schlosser (1776–1861) was, like Niebuhr, of Frisian origin. He first taught in Frankfurt, but the greater part of his life was spent at the University of Heidelberg. He possessed great erudition but was no match for Niebuhr in critical acumen. For a long time he was the most respected and popular historian in Germany. His roots were completely in the Enlightenment, and he hardly, if at all, shared in the complete change which came over the interpretation of history in the nineteenth century. At first he was mainly concerned with Church history, but he then turned his attention to universal history and wrote several works which were intended for the masses, such as his *Weltgeschichte für das deutsche Volk* and *Geschichte des 18. Jahrhunderts*. Schlosser preferred the history of civilisation to that of politics, and extolled the heroes of the mind in preference to those of the battlefield. His aim was to educate mankind into humane and rational politics. He was a follower of Kant, whose moral philosophy was, he claimed, also valid in politics, for there was only one moral law, namely the rules by which the 'pure and upright man' lives. In his obituary, his pupil Gervinus calls him a 'dyed-in-the-wool democrat', which was quite in keeping with his Frisian origin, but Schlosser preserved his independence and criticised any injustice without regard to nation, party or class. Admittedly he was prejudiced against the court and the nobility. He judged Napoleon more favourably than was usually the case in Germany; as a declared cosmopolite he had little sympathy for any pronounced nationalistic tendency. Although he admired the traditional freedom of the subject in England, her policy of colonial conquest aroused his loathing[1] and he thought that it was poisoning the pristine nobility of the English character. His historical method was increasingly criticised by experts and certainly left much to be desired. But Gervinus declared that of all the writers of the nineteenth century, Schlosser had exercised the widest and most lasting influence on the German people's moral view of the world and their political judgement.

Dahlmann

Prominent among the North German liberals was Friedrich Christoph Dahlmann. He was born in 1785 in Wismar, which at the time was under Swedish rule but belonged to the Holy Roman Empire. Dahlmann, like Arndt, always felt a strong attachment to Scandinavia, and to him the freedom enjoyed by the Swedish peasants was far more important than all the memories cherished in Swabia of the German emperors of old. He first taught at Copenhagen and then in Kiel from 1813, where he soon afterwards also became secretary to the Schleswig-Holstein Estates. As such he defended their constitutional rights and the German character of the two closely linked duchies against the absolutism of the Danish monarchy. In 1829 he became a professor at Göttingen, where he wrote his principal work of political science, *Die Politik auf den Grund und das Mass der gegebenen Zustände zurückgeführt* (Politics Traced Back to the Basis and Extent of Given Circumstances), which first appeared in 1835. Dahlmann had a great

---

[1] Cf. further his views on the English judicial atrocities against Scottish rebels in his *Geschichte des 18. Jahrhunderts*, 5th ed., 1864, Vol. II, p. 174.

share in working out the Hanoverian constitution of 1833, and in 1837,
as one of the 'Göttingen Seven', had to leave the country. He first
went to Jena, and in 1842 was appointed to Bonn. His historical works
on the revolutions in England and France had a great influence on
public opinion. They were written in a liberal spirit and demonstrated
the dangers of absolutism. When the 1848 revolution broke out,
Dahlmann was elected to the Frankfurt National Assembly.

Dahlmann's political convictions were modelled above all on Britain,
whose history he had studied thoroughly. He was convinced that the
British would succeed in overcoming the defects of their political
system, especially by the parliamentary reform of 1832.[1] As the title
of his principal work suggests, he was not guided by abstract speculations on the State but started out from a thorough, historical understanding of the given conditions. His *Politik*, of which, incidentally,
only the first volume appeared, contains a masterly exposition of political
development since antiquity, and pays special attention to the British
constitution. Dahlmann advocated a constitutional monarchy on the
English pattern because it seemed to him, and rightly, the most expedient
in the situation as it then was. Radicalism was not capable of initiating
a healthy constitutional development because it was based on a completely false conception of the stage of social development the German
people had reached.

Dahlmann considered the educated middle classes best equipped to
bring about progress towards freedom and culture. Neither absolute
monarchy and its officials nor the great masses and their leaders seemed
to him to be capable of this. As for national unity, it must be said that
Dahlmann could suggest no infallible method of attaining it. He
believed at the outset that only Prussia was suited to bring it about,
since Austria with her many nationalities and reactionary tendencies
could not take the lead, being herself threatened with dissolution.
But Prussia could unite Germany only as a liberal, constitutional state
and Dahlmann did not approve of the growing cult in Prussia of
Frederick the Great. He admitted that Frederick had been a great man,
but held the view that his rule had been too lacking in ideal content to
suit the character of the German people completely.[2] Dahlmann
looked on the partition of Poland as a great injustice.

He was convinced that only a monarchy could command sufficient
power for Germany to win respect, and even stated that she needed
power more urgently than liberty. This statement probably embodies
the view that the unity of Germany could only be attained by power,

[1] This view of Britain was shared by almost all moderate liberals, and also by
many conservatives, especially Stahl.
[2] Cf. Anton Springer, *F. Chr. Dahlmann*, Vol. II, 1872 pp. 402, 436.

as Bismarck's policy later showed. In general, however, Dahlmann was by no means a partisan of power politics, although he foresaw a warlike future. Besides, he considered kings for the most part as more peace-loving than the radical parties, which easily allied themselves to nationalism, whereas kings feared that war would lead to revolution.

Ranke

The Romantic School did much to awaken interest in and understanding of the past but the shaping of a critical method of writing history was not something they undertook. This was above all the work of the historical school founded by Savigny, Eichhorn and Niebuhr. It led to a large-scale development of historical research, which also greatly helped to strengthen national consciousness. It reached its climax with Leopold Ranke (1795–1886). His first major work appeared in 1824. He did not deny the importance of nationality, but was far removed from any tendency to pervert history for the aggrandisement of his own nation. He looked on the Latin and Germanic peoples as a unity, as a part of the western community with common origins and closely-related elements. For him the driving forces of history were general ideas and definite philosophies. The historian, he argues, must understand rather than judge these ideas. A statesman must of necessity be partial, whereas it is the historian's duty to overcome this partiality and appreciate the views of all sides. The abstract ideas of political doctrinaires had reference to an artificial state for which one would first have to create artificial men; but in the world as it was, differences existed between state and state which force alone could resolve. Not that Ranke cherished any predilection for power politics; he merely considered them to some extent inevitable. In his *Historisch-Politische Zeitschrift*, which he published for a few years, he criticised liberal-national aspirations, and some leading progressives took this very amiss. Unlike most politicians, he was not prepared to consider one side wholly in the right.

Droysen

The first half of the nineteenth century saw one trend in the writing of history which later had a strong effect on political opinions. This was the rise of the Prussian school of historians founded by Johann Gustav Droysen. Droysen was born in Pomerania in 1808, became professor at the Universities of Berlin in 1835 and Kiel in 1840, and played a great part in the Schleswig–Holstein movement as well as in the Frankfurt National Assembly. There had been politicians before Droysen who looked to Prussia for the unification of Germany, but it was he who tried to give this aspiration a broad historical foundation. While his principal works on this question did not appear until the second half of the century it is interesting to note that his early concern was with the history of ancient Greece. Hitherto the little Greek republics in their struggle with the Macedonian monarchy had been idealised. The Greeks appeared as the heroic champions of freedom and the Macedonians as armed aggressors, but Droysen sought to show that these small Greek states pursued a shortsighted and selfish policy. The military strength of Macedonia, he maintained, had brought national unification and spread Greek culture over the whole of the East. His presentation of the case led to the conclusion that small republican states with no military strength were not viable and were exposed to corruption. The parallel of the Greek situation with German particularism, and of Macedonia with Prussia, was obvious.

Politically Droysen was a liberal, but his emphasis on power put him at odds with the views of most other liberals. These latter tended to underestimate the importance of power and to detest the military character of Prussia. Droysen was no worshipper of military strength for its own sake but merely saw in it a necessity for the existence of states. Law and morality, too, he declared, could develop only in a state which was strong. In these views he was influenced by Hegel, from whom he later broke away. Like the other liberals who set their hopes on Prussia, he wanted her to be a constitutional state. Indeed, he coined the phrase about the merging of Prussia into Germany. He wanted to replace the federation of German states by one federal state and to strengthen the central power, which should devolve on Prussia. Droysen's liberalism irritated the ruling circles in Prussia. In 1846 he wrote a book about the wars of liberation and the immediately succeeding period. He sent the first volume to Frederick William IV, who, however, accepted it with only tepid thanks. When the second volume followed, he returned it to its author with some very ungracious words.

Raumer

Friedrich von Raumer (1781–1873) first occupied a high post in the Prussian civil service, but then devoted himself competely to the study of history. His most important work was his *Geschichte der Hohenstaufen* (6 vol. 1823–5). The author was far from sharing the Romantic enthusiasm for the Middle Ages; his ideals were impartiality and justice and his outlook was humane and temperate. As secretary of the Berlin Academy of Sciences, he made a speech on the religious tolerance of Frederick the Great, which aroused the strongest disapproval of Frederick William IV. Raumer gave up his post and was on all sides hailed as a martyr.

Rotteck

The most important leader of South German liberalism was Karl von Rotteck. He was born in 1775 at Freiburg in the Breisgau which was under Austrian rule at that time. His father was a famous professor who had been ennobled by Joseph II and his mother a Frenchwoman from Lorraine. As the father died early, it was the mother who was mainly responsible for bringing up the children. Karl read law and obtained his doctorate, but then went over completely to history. When he was only twenty-three, he was appointed professor of world history at the University of Freiburg. Of his historical writings, his *Weltgeschichte*, the volumes of which appeared between 1812–26, was the most widely read. More than 100,000 copies of the German edition were sold, and the work was also published in English, French, Italian, Danish and Polish editions. In this work, Rotteck portrayed the perniciousness of all power politics. The Spartans had sacrificed to the state all real enjoyment of life and adopted instead 'military pride and the illusions of patriotism'. During the war of liberation Rotteck had published a paper which whipped up patriotic feeling, but after the fall of Napoleon he no longer looked on the French as enemies. Shortly afterwards he wrote a pamphlet sharply criticising standing armies as a cause of militarism, wars and despotism and calling for their abolition and replacement by a national militia, which would include all the youth of the country, but would be called out by the national assembly only in emergencies. Local authorities should have weapons in readiness and appoint the officers, apart from those of the highest rank, who should be chosen by the Government. To repel a sudden attack, fortresses and a small standing army of professionals should serve. Rotteck condemned compulsory military service (except in emergencies) and exclaimed: 'A curse on the tyrant who invented conscription!'. This pamphlet was a highly effective contribution to the movement – which had for decades figured largely in the programme of German liberalism – against standing armies. Many other pamphlets appeared, both for and against their abolition or else proposing some middle course. The introduction of a militia in Prussia and other states went some way to meet the demands of the liberals, but they did not regard it as a people's army in the true sense.

In 1818 Rotteck was also made professor of natural law and political economy. His main works were his *Lehrbuch des Vernunftsrechts* (Manual of the Law of Reason), which appeared in 1829, and the *Staatslexikon*, which he started to publish in collaboration with Welcker in 1834. In the *Landtag* of Baden he was the spokesman of a pronounced liberalism and he championed many progressive demands. After the Carlsbad Decrees, the Government exerted great pressure and succeeded in preventing the election of Rotteck and other liberal leaders, but after the July Revolution this was no longer possible, and in 1831 the liberals triumphed. Rotteck was elected in five constituencies. In 1832, during the second great period of reaction, Rotteck and his fellow-fighter Welcker were deprived of their university posts, but they continued their activity in the Badenese *Landtag* with the greatest determination. Rotteck died in 1840, while Welcker still played a highly important role in the National Assembly of 1848–49.

Rotteck's principles made him a republican and a democrat, but he rejected violent revolution and mob rule and came out in favour of progress by legal means. He believed that in the circumstances then obtaining, a constitutional monarchy was preferable, provided it could be imbued with a republican spirit. His enemies compared him with Robespierre and the Jacobins, while Boerne despised him for rejecting force. Rotteck was a cosmopolite who supported the liberation of Italy from foreign rule. In 1829 he called France the hope of all European patriots. When the July Revolution broke out, he hailed it as the sublimest triumph of the law of reason and a boon for all Europe and the world. It was not, he said, the French, but German reactionary governments who were the enemies of Germany. But he disapproved of the plans of some German radical politicians to unleash a revolution in Germany with France's help. To appeal to France for assistance, he said, was excusable only in the most desperate extreme; the German people should win freedom by their own exertions. He did not wish for any unification of Germany which brought with it the danger of war with France or internal reaction. Unity was of value only when it went hand in hand with freedom; he would prefer freedom without unity to unity without freedom. He had no wish for unification under the wings of either the Prussian or the Austrian eagle, nor in the form of a general German republic; the path to a republic was paved with horror and uncertainty. Rotteck was no supporter of a strongly emphasised external unity, but of a genuine confederation of states and an intellectual union of the German peoples.

The Staatslexikon

The ideas of German liberalism during this period were brilliantly expounded in the *Staatslexikon* edited by Rotteck and Welcker. It was the result of a suggestion by Friedrich List, who was later a contributor. In all, sixty-nine experts were engaged on the work, mostly from countries in southern and central Germany. These were, with a few exceptions, the intellectual élite of German liberalism, though they did not include Dahlmann and Gervinus despite the fact that they had been invited to take part. Some foreigners contributed articles about their own countries. The work began to appear in 1834, and immediately ran into trouble with the censor. Prussia banned it from the outset. In 1843 it was completed in fifteen volumes, and the Prussian ban was lifted. Later on new editions came out. The *Staatslexikon* was, to quote Rotteck's own words in the preface, the creed of liberalism. Its aim was to further the spread of political education among all classes and to chart a middle course between reaction and revolution. Peace, freedom, justice, truth and the common good were seen by Rotteck to be best guaranteed in a constitutional monarchy with a truly popular representation. Although he himself stood for the sovereignty of the people, he considered this middle way to be the most reasonable in the existing circumstances. Welcker was essentially in agreement with him, and after Rotteck's death continued to edit the work jointly with Rotteck's son, who, however, himself died soon after.

The *Staatslexikon* discussed the bearing of these basic ideas on all departments of political life and also provided a most useful survey of the historical, political and economic conditions in all countries. Of fundamental importance was Rotteck's conception of a law of reason, largely based on Kant's philosophy of justice, though with a few modifications. The work was of the utmost value, not only to the teacher of political science but also to the practising statesman, deputy, official, journalist and, above all, every thinking citizen. When the initial difficulties had been overcome, the sales increased greatly, the *Staatslexikon* was constantly quoted in political books, articles and speeches and had an uncommonly strong influence on public opinion.

Naturally the contributors did not agree on all points. This was an advantage, because it meant that the articles published afforded closer acquaintance with varying shades of opinion. Even the two editors disagreed on many issues.[1] While Rotteck considered the French democratic constitution of 1791 as a model, Welcker had a particularly high opinion of English parliamentarianism. Rotteck's main objection to the English political system was the dominance of the aristocracy and plutocracy and the antiquated processes of law. Although Rotteck went further in his democratic views than most liberals, he was none the less completely right in compounding at that time for a constitutional monarchy and foreseeing that a revolution would be abortive. Despite his moderate views, he enlisted many convinced republicans as contributors, such as the jurist and publicist Philipp Jacob Siebenpfeiffer and other radicals, who lived abroad as political refugees. All the same, the *Staatslexikon* was on occasion violently attacked by extremists.

[1] Cf. H. Zehnter, *Das Staatslexikon von Rotteck und Welcker*, 1929, where the divergencies are discussed.

In the pages which follow, one or two conservative thinkers on politics and the state are discussed.

Haller

Karl Ludwig von Haller (1768–1854) came from an aristocratic Bernese family which produced many outstanding men. He was a grandson of Albrecht von Haller, who had won distinction as a naturalist, doctor, writer, statesman and political thinker. Karl began work in the service of the Bernese republic and was at first a liberal. He had the reputation of being a disciple of Rousseau and, indeed, a democrat and Jacobin. In 1798, partly for the tactical reason of preventing French interference in Swiss internal affairs, he drafted a liberal constitution for Berne, but this failed in its intended effect. After the victory of the Swiss democrats, who enjoyed French support, Haller fled abroad and was for some years in the service of Austria. Only when Napoleon again allowed the conservatives to return to office did he go back to Berne. He became a professor, wrote several books in which he set forth his completely changed political views and was elected to the Grand Council of Berne. But when he became a Catholic in 1820, he was excluded from all offices, as Berne was a strictly Protestant state. Haller now devoted himself to planning his principal work, *Restauration der Staatswissenschaft oder Theorie des natürlich-geselligen Zustandes*, which appeared in six volumes and was finished in 1834. For a number of years he lived in Paris and was in the French service until the July Revolution, whereupon he once again settled in Switzerland.

If the thoughts of the Genevan Rousseau paved the way for the French Revolution, it was the diametrically opposite views of the Bernese Haller which supported the counter-revolution. Both men held much in common, including the demand for a return to nature, but Haller directed his main criticism at Rousseau's theory of the social contract. Much as one may nowadays reject Haller's positive doctrines, one must concede that in this negative one he was right. The state has certainly not been expressly founded on contracts. Many proponents of the social contract theory have realised this fact and have therefore tended to assume that the character of the state has been contractual in a tacit or even retrospective sense. Haller started out from the idea that at all times great inequalities have existed between men, especially between those who were powerful and those who were not. States, he said, were not founded from the bottom upwards but from the top downwards, by individuals seizing power to which the many who were weak gladly submitted in order to receive protection and other benefits. The State had therefore arisen in a similar way to many other social phenomena, especially property. But the State did not rest merely on power but also on the divine order of things, and thus became a law which must be obeyed just as property, family circumstances or conditions of work compel heed.

So Haller does not represent the State as a unity proceeding from the concerted will of all, but as a conglomeration of many social circumstances which rest on power and protection. He does not conceive of the State as an organism which belongs to a higher sphere of public law, but only as a highly developed private law. Within certain limits a ruler can dispose of the State just as an owner can make over his property. This patrimonial conception of the State was, in fact, customary in the late Middle Ages. Whole countries or individual rights in a state could at that time be acquired by purchase or inheritance, and it could be pledged or divided up in the same way as private property. The old Germanic conception of law militated against the recognition of a higher 'public law' and opposed the view that the State could repeal privileges or confiscate property once it had been obtained. But even in the Middle Ages the idea of a higher state law was not entirely lacking.

Haller is by no means an adherent of absolute despotism, which allows a ruler to do what he likes. All authority, monarchical or republican, rests according to the Bible on a divine scheme of things. In consequence a ruler has both rights and obligations. God has enjoined justice and love upon all men. A ruler cannot therefore dispose arbitrarily of the liberty and property of his subjects, nor may he compel them to undertake military service. He can tax them only with the agreement of the Estates, who, however, are not representatives of *all* the people. Thus naked force shall not rule, but power which acts with justice and conscience. The subject may oppose any abuse of power, if necessary with the help of others and even by force; the Middle Ages, which Haller esteemed so highly, were full of feuds and violent self-help. Haller also approves of slavery, since Christianity had tolerated it. Besides, at that time slavery was legal in many countries – the U.S.A., for example – and a number of colonies.

Haller draws a distinction between seigneurial (patrimonial), military and spiritual principalities. The most original and widespread type is, according to him, the patrimonial state. He did not consider the existence of a large and powerful empire desirable and held that a breaking-up often had good consequences. But he levelled only mild criticism, sometimes none at all, at the expansionist policy of many kings. In general Haller regarded the smaller states in an idealistic light and could see no reason why they should be submerged in a large and poweful national state. Most of all he esteemed the Catholic Church, because it had realised a kind of cosmopolitan state. For this reason he considered the ecclesiastical states, which were all small ones, to be the freest and most beneficent of all. Haller was hostile to Protestantism and in the ultimate analysis held the Reformation responsible for the outbreak of the French Revolution. He also recognised the merits of a republic, but he always had in his mind's eye the type of an aristocratic republic, like that of Berne or Venice of old. In his last years Haller turned his attention to the social question and supported natural economy. He was against the building of railways and growing industrialisation.

The influence of Haller's ideas was manifold and extensive but not lasting.[1] The first volumes of his principal work aroused considerable attention and were translated into many languages. The literary opponents of the revolution found effective arguments in them. His disparaging view of the Reformation was shared by many writers, and a whole string of Protestant scholars and writers went over to Catholicism, among them Haller's most devoted disciple, the Berlin criminologist Jarcke. Frederick William IV and his circle, especially the Gerlach brothers, found him inspiring, whereas liberal circles detested his doctrines. There were also some prominent conservatives, such as Friedrich Julius Stahl, who viewed him with disapproval. In Austria his work was at first banned, probably because it was recognised that revolutionary conclusions might be drawn from it. The Romanticists were for the most part critical of him, although Adam Müller was an enthusiastic exception. Savigny called him an 'arrant product of Enlightenment' (*einen recht krassen Aufklärer*). In fact, for all Haller's hatred of the Enlightenment, his thinking was, as Stahl emphasised, closely akin to it. He was an individualist and a cosmopolite, regarded the State as a necessary evil and was against patriotism and national pride. In England, Carlyle based himself to a considerable extent on Haller's doctrines.

Adam Müller

The political ideas of Romanticism found a very talented exponent in Adam Müller (1779–1829). He was the son of a Prussian finance official, studied political science at Göttingen and for a long time worshipped at the shrine of Adam Smith, only to repudiate his doctrines later on. He became a friend of Friedrich Gentz, whose translation of Burke's *Reflections on the Revolution in France* he read. This work made a deep impression on him and contributed much to the development of his doctrines. In 1804 his book *Die Lehre vom Gegensatz* (The Doctrine of Opposites) appeared; in it, following Schelling, he developed the

---

[1] *Karl Ludwig Haller*, 1938, by the Swiss writer, Guggisberg, gives a very good account of Haller's influence on theories of the State.

idea of a polarity governing nature and intellect. He accepted an invitation from Gentz to go to Vienna and became a Catholic. He then lived in Dresden, where he made numerous contacts with the nobility and intellectual leaders and lectured on political science; these lectures appeared in book form in 1809. He next went to Berlin, where from the standpoint of feudal landed property he opposed Hardenberg's reforms and supported a conservative policy. In order to get him away from Berlin, Hardenberg sent him on a mission to Vienna. Gentz introduced him into the highest circles there, he was given various important commissions by Metternich and stayed on in the service of Austria, principally as Consul-General in Leipzig and finally as senior official (*Hofrat*) in the Imperial Austrian Chancellery. Müller also found time to write books and essays, and edit a journal. His views increasingly hardened against modern developments and liberalism, and he sought to give all political science a religious basis.

Of recent years Müller has sometimes been praised as the great exponent of the Romanticist view of the State.[1] Now he was certainly an intelligent writer, but he worked out no well-defined system of his own. Most of his ideas are taken from Burke, though Müller, with his predilection for the spirit of the Middle Ages, tints them accordingly. His ideals were the organic state, reverence for tradition, government by the landed aristocracy, the preservation of national individuality, the overriding interests of the community, the importance of the Estates and the avoidance of a powerful bureaucracy. He wanted Germany to keep her economy predominantly agrarian and to refrain from any extensive commercialisation.

Of Müller's position *vis-à-vis* the national movement, it must be mentioned that he once belonged to the *Christlich Deutsche Tischgesell-schaft*, a social circle which included leading Romanticists and worked for liberation from Napoleon's rule. Two main tendencies were represented: one, in which Major von der Marwitz was prominent, worshipped the Prussian power state of Frederick the Great, while the other had as its ideal an organic and harmonious inner life for the German people. Müller belonged to the second group. Even before his admission to the circle, he had given lectures on Frederick the Great and the Prussian monarchy and had criticised the King for his preoccupation with the Enlightenment and his machine state. Nor did he favour a policy of military strength and expansion for Prussia, although he did not reject war in principle. His later work in Metternich's service also revealed a distaste for aggressive nationalism.

[1] For example, by the Austrian political scientist, Othmar Spann (1878–1950).

Like many other Romanticists, Müller idolised the Middle Ages. He opposed liberalism because he saw in it a disruptive force which bred egoism. The ideas which he put forward about state and society were often ingenious but at the same time highly impracticable and even dangerous. His friend Gentz once took him to task in a private letter, saying that his judgements on existing conditions had often horrified him, and if they had not caused infinite harm, this was solely due to the fact that few of his hearers or readers could grasp what he really meant.

Stahl

The most important learned defender of conservatism was Friedrich Julius Stahl (1802–61), who came to the fore first as a theoretician and later as a statesman. He came of a strictly religious Jewish family in Bavaria, but while still young found himself under the influence of leading Protestant scholars, whose example imbued him with a Lutheranism of pietistic hue and Protestant neo-humanism. Out of deep personal conviction he received baptism in 1819. As a student, he joined a *Burschenschaft*, and as early as his second term was elected to the exalted office of spokesman, in which capacity he made a glowing speech for Germany's unity and freedom. In 1823 he was prosecuted for belonging to the *Burschenschaft* and suspended for two years.

In 1827 he took up residence as a lecturer at Munich University. In 1830 he published the first part of his *Philosophie des Rechts* (The Philosophy of Law), in which he rejected the unhistorical natural law and sought to prove that the concept of justice does not depend on human recognition. His arguments, which were influenced by Schelling, were theological and metaphysical and, in contrast to Hegel's pantheism, were based above all on the conception of a personal God. Morality and law were attributes of God's will. Reason alone cannot sustain the idea of moral obligation, and works only in a negative, not constructive sense. Stahl's ideas closely matched Luther's, especially his conviction of the power of evil in man. In 1837 the second part of the work, which dealt with political science, appeared. As early as 1832, Stahl was appointed a professor, first in Würzburg and shortly after that in Erlangen, and in 1837 he was elected by the city of Erlangen to the Bavarian *Landtag*, where he immediately played an important part and was distinguished for his integrity and political moderation. He maintained that the State was above the crown, the Estates and the parties. With an independent civil service alongside king and parliament there would be a better guarantee of justice and liberty than with a written constitution. Stahl fell into disfavour with the King; he was deprived of his post as lecturer in constitutional law and had to restrict himself to civil law. In 1840 he accepted Frederick William IV's offer of a chair in Berlin.

Stahl's theory of the State is that it is a divine institution for securing and promoting law and justice, morality and private and public welfare. This requires a constitution based on Estates and a monarchy. But Stahl rejects both the absolute power of ruler or people and Haller's and Jarcke's concept of the old patrimonial system based on the Estates. It is true that the ruler has supreme power in the State and it is the existence of the monarchy which gives the State an identity, i.e. unity and continuity of policy instead of the multiplicity and fluctuation of party movements. But the power of the ruler is limited by God's commandments, which are also the basis of the constitution. In contrast to Frederick William III, who in repeated declarations offered to concede to the Estates merely the right to advise, Stahl whould give them a 'judiciously-calculated' authority to take decisions. He proposes, however, to set considerable limits to this authority; thus, the Estates should be able neither to refuse the imposition of taxes nor to bring down ministers, although he would give them the right of impeachment. Laws would require the assent of the Estates and they should also control the national budget. Profession, not birth, should govern election to the Estates, which would then not be impregnable strongholds of class. Stahl's ideal was the English gentry. He does, it is true, assign an important role to the landed aristocracy, but he rejects the 'spirit of Junkerdom with its class pride, idleness, selfishness and insensitivity to ideal aims'.

Stahl sees in the political struggles of the day a contest between human and divine law, for which he used the words 'revolution' and 'legitimacy'. Liberalism and democracy, he declared, lead to revolution, even if not intentionally. Revolution is not necessarily violent but can come about through the undermining and collapse of the existing order. Although Stahl rejects liberalism, he none the less pays tribute to many of its principles and achievements. At times it seems as if he is struggling to reach a compromise between conservatism and liberalism. Particularly striking is his enthusiasm for the British constitution. He praises it as a masterpiece and declares that the British nation is outstanding in all fields for its seriousness, wealth, achievements and creative energy, and notably excels in manliness, though, he adds, its greatness rests on unique circumstances. In 1849 the King appointed Stahl a life member of the upper chamber, where he became the spokesman, and to some extent the intellectual leader, of the conservatives, which meant in particular the landed aristocracy. His dialectical skill in debate and his knowledge made him an outstanding parliamentarian and his utter selflessness and excellent character assured him of the respect of his opponents.

Leo

Another very talented and well-informed representative of the anti-liberal line was the historian Heinrich Leo (1799–1878), who was a professor, first in Berlin and then in Halle. In his youth he was a passionate *Burschenschafter* with revolutionary tendencies, a friend of the Follen brothers and a leader of the *Unbedingten*,[1] who approved of political murders and other crimes. Later, under the influence of the teachings of Haller, Burke and Hegel, he turned his back on these ideas and became an equally out-and-out supporter of the opposite principles. To begin with he was one of Hegel's disciples and supported freedom of thought against religious orthodoxy. Hegel's influence can be seen in his principal work, a history of the Italian states in five volumes published in 1829. In many respects medieval Italy seemed to Leo to realise his ideals; he translated Machiavelli's letters and found German history and politics 'eminently boring'. His Italian history also revealed a strong predilection for the papacy and its hierarchy, and in consequence Catholic circles in Germany expected – although wrongly – his conversion. Leo had some sharp criticisms to make of Luther and such Protestant heroes as Gustavus Adolphus.[2]

Politically, Leo experienced growing hatred for liberalism and democracy, although on occasion he also attacked monarchical despotism. Not until his old age did national problems exercise him more deeply, but all the same, he spoke out earlier in favour of national pride and keeping foreign religion and morals out of Germany. He once called the German people the born aristocrats among the nations. But he stressed that the Christian faith was more important than any community of language or blood, and that the Christian state represented the highest form of civilised community. Leo took his stand against liberal constitutionalism, saying that a king by the grace of God should not have to be dependent on the people and the Estates should have only advisory powers. A singularity of Leo is that he praised war as a specific against national degeneration. He considered economic progress harmful. He had a high regard for the landed aristocracy and for the peasants, while maintaining that trade on a monetary basis undermined moral and religious foundations and degraded man to a mere working animal. For this reason he wanted to keep the guild system and to limit industry. Leo was also an active journalist and often expressed his

---

[1] See p. 95.

[2] It is noteworthy that at this time numerous Protestant historians and political scientists held Protestantism largely responsible for Germany's national and social divisions. Many of them went over to Catholicism. In this they were partly swayed by the conviction that the Catholic Church offered a better protection against political revolution than Protestantism.

political views in terms as drastic as those he used in his historical works. In 1838 he wrote for the reactionary *Berliner politisches Wochen-blatt* an article on the railways, the construction of which had just begun. He warned of the 'approaching golden age in which the plutocrats will know no other church than the Stock Exchange and no other bible than their ledger'. Many of his exaggerations are positively outrageous, as, for example, when he writes: 'It is better that a hundred of the common rabble should perish than one man who is noble by birth or intellect", Elsewhere he declares that peace causes more unhappiness than war because it promotes a mechanistic, egalitarian order. No wonder the liberals opposed him bitterly and called him, not unfairly, the *enfant terrible* of the reaction.

13

THE EMERGENCE OF THE SOCIAL QUESTION
AND SOCIALISM

In the first half of the nineteenth century, some circles in Germany, seeing the widespread social distress in the country, concluded that the equality before the law broadly demanded by liberalism would not eliminate the formidable social inequalities which abounded. They saw the need for a great re-shaping of social conditions to match the ideals of justice and fraternity. They can be labelled 'early socialists' but socialism in this context cannot be equated with the later movement which goes by this name. Fichte's pamphlet *Der geschlossene Handelsstaat* (1800) belongs to the beginnings of early socialism. He develops a system which aims at obviating poverty by an extensive planned economy, i.e. by removing the freedom of choice to practise a trade and nationalising foreign trade. There is no question of nationalising production, which is what is understood by socialism today.

In the social development which led to the rise of capitalism and the growth of a proletariat, Germany was far behind England and France where socialist ideas first appeared and from there made their way to Germany. It was pre-eminently in France that they assumed greater significance.

The ideas of French reformers from Babeuf to Fourier and Saint-Simon were very varied. All they had in common was criticism of social conditions, especially the effects of private property, free competition and the collective inequalities between men. At the outset they held aloof from politics, and did not assume that in society there was a sharp class antagonism or that the class struggle was inevitable. Many of the early socialists looked to benevolent rulers or industrialists, the Church, the educated classes or co-operative associations (*Genossenschaften*) to remove poverty.

Socialist aspirations spread to Germany from France, England, Switzerland and Belgium in particular. In these countries there were

numerous radical German intellectuals, who were living abroad because
of political persecution, and also a large number of German artisans,
who during their wanderings had found favourable conditions of employment and settled down. Both groups became acquainted with the
ideas of early socialism and among them societies like the 'League of the
Outlawed' (1834) and the 'League of the Just' (1836) were formed. It was
from circles like these that Wilhelm Weitling came. He was born out of
wedlock in Magdeburg in 1808 and grew up amid the direst poverty.
He learned the craft of tailoring and in the course of his travels he
went to Paris, where he was admitted to the 'League of the Just',
which later became completely communist. In 1841 he went to
Switzerland, where he worked tirelessly as a communist agitator and
journalist; this led in 1844 to a six months' prison sentence and his
expulsion from that country. He continued his propaganda in Germany,
was repeatedly prosecuted and finally died in America. Weitling was a
very talented writer and a successful political organiser. His eloquence
was often spellbinding and he even wrote poems in prison. In his book
A Poor Sinner's Gospel he represented Christ as the harbinger of
communism and democracy. Many of his ideas were bizarre, as, for
example, his proposal to abolish property – which, after all, had
originally been stolen – by means of thefts carried out by the proletariat.

The German intellectuals who had fled abroad were particularly
taken with the ideas of Saint–Simon and his disciples, but were also
in touch with numerous other writers who tended towards communism. Many of Heine's most effective poems showed this influence.
About this time a group of talented poets who bitterly criticised the
tyranny of property came together in Germany. Herwegh openly
espoused communism and settled in Paris. The Young German movement was also in sympathy with other ideas of the Saint-Simonians –
those of Barthélemy Prosper Enfantin, for example, who celebrated
the freeing of sensual pleasure from the restrictions of religion and
morality, and was sentenced in Paris in 1832 to a year's imprisonment
for this.

The democratic-revolutionary movement, to which many members of
the *Burschenschaft* belonged, sometimes also led to social radicalism.
Georg Büchner (1813–37) studied natural science and medicine at
Strasbourg and Giessen, where he joined a secret revolutionary
society led by a clergyman named Weidig. As early as 1834 Büchner
wrote in the *Deutsch-Französischen Jahrbücher* that a political revolution in Germany was not possible without a social one. He founded a
Gesellschaft der Menschenrechte (Society for the Rights of Man) and
circulated among the Hessian peasants a pamphlet, the *Hessische
Landbote*, in which he proclaimed the class struggle and demanded a

fairer distribution of wealth, though, it must be said, without paying homage to communism. He fled to avoid arrest, became a lecturer at Zürich University but died soon after. He is principally known to posterity as a poet and dramatist. Weidig perished miserably in prison.

Moses Hess (1812–75), the son of a prosperous Rhenish merchant of the Jewish faith, met leading socialists in Paris at the end of the thirties and thenceforth devoted his life to preaching socialism, which for him meant a philosophically and ethically based liberation of the workers from exploitation by those of birth and wealth. In his view the existence of private property connoted selfishness and immorality. Its abolition would set man free and show him that the only true pleasure lay in work. Hess belonged to the Young Hegelians and disciples of Feuerbach, to whose journals he contributed.

In these years there were disastrous slumps which caused indescribable poverty. The plight of the Silesian weavers was so extreme that in a frenzy of despair they rose against the factory owners. About this time Heine wrote his *Weavers' Song*, in which the following lines occur:

> A curse on the King, the wealthy man's friend!
> Our woeful distress his heart cannot rend.
> And when the last farthing is wrung from our hand,
> He has us shot down just like dogs where we stand.

A number of leading political economists and experts made detailed studies in an attempt to identify the underlying causes of the current crises and the reasons for the rise of socialism, and suggested remedies for the distress. Even before this, Karl Rodbertus (1805–75) had begun to investigate these problems. He was a well-to-do Pomeranian landowner and in 1837 wrote his fundamental work *Die Forderungen der arbeitenden Klassen* (The Demands of the Working Classes). He tried to show theoretically that with a completely free economy the share of the workers in the gross national product, and hence their purchasing power, grows progressively less, which leads to social misery, economic crises and unemployment. From this he concluded that land as well as capital should become common property and that their yield should be shared according to work done. The State should run a planned economy and fix wages and conditions of work. Thus Rodbertus was a state socialist. He conceded the need for an interim stage, during which landowners and industrialists should retain a share in the gross national product, but his ultimate aim was a distribution exclusively based on work done. In later years he maintained connections both with Lassalle, the founder of Social Democracy, and conservative statesmen. His ideas may have influenced Bismarck's social reforms.

France's Christian socialists, notably Lamennais, influenced

Germany's political Catholicism, as the writings of Görres and Baader show. For the Protestants, Viktor Aimé Huber (1800–69) was prominent in his efforts to awaken social conscience. He was professor of literary history at several universities and in 1843 was summoned by Frederick William IV to Berlin. During visits to England and Scotland he got to know the circle of Christian social reformers which included Frederick Denison Maurice and Charles Kingsley, and adopted many of their ideas. The English co-operative societies also impressed him very much. He set out his social programme in 1844 in the *Evangelische Kirchenzeitung* as well as in books. He called upon the workers to help themselves by forming consumers', production and building co-operatives and later also supported their freedom of association. While Huber backed his demands by newspaper articles, the pastor Johann Hinrich Wichern (1808–81) devoted himself to practical social welfare. In 1833 he founded the *Rauhe Haus* (Rough House), an institution which cared for neglected children. He saw it as the Church's duty to take up the cause of the proletariat and to win them over to the Gospel by an 'inner mission'. Later he demanded a fair wage and shorter hours for the worker.

Thus, even in the first half of the century, many voices were raised for sweeping away the social evils which had sprung from the development of big business, but their practical effects were small. The radical demands for a complete reform of society were far from being based on a sufficient knowledge of the social facts or the practicability of far-reaching reform. The extremists had no clear, attainable goal in view, and many of them had quite fantastic schemes. Even those who thought along practical lines lacked much which could translate ideas into reality. Political and economic liberalism was gaining ground, and its arguments sounded very convincing. Even among the big industrialists who were liberals there were many, like Harkort and Mevissen, who were deeply concerned by social distress, although no means of overcoming it suggested itself to them.

Marx and Engels

Many circumstances combined to prepare the ground for the influence of Marx and Engels. Karl Marx was born in 1818 in Trier on the Moselle. His father, a Jewish lawyer, was baptised into the Protestant Church along with his family. The son studied jurisprudence, philosophy and history at Bonn and Berlin, and graduated as Doctor of Philosophy. He gave up his idea of settling down as a lecturer in Bonn: the fate of his friend Bruno Bauer had shown him what freedom of instruction really meant at Prussian universities. In 1842 he first became a contributor to, and then editor-in-chief of the *Rheinische Zeitung*, which had been founded shortly before by the leaders of the Rhenish liberals. At this time Marx was not yet a communist. The markedly liberal attitude and the high quality of the newspaper made an impression throughout Germany but led to its being banned by the Prussian Government as early as March 1843.

Soon after, Marx married Jenny von Westphalen, who became his staunch and lifelong companion. He went to Paris to join Arnold Ruge in bringing out the *Deutsch-Französischen Jahrbücher*. In this journal he declared that a purely political revolution in Germany was impossible; only a proletarian, social-democratic uprising could achieve liberation. The paper soon ceased publication and he now worked on the Paris *Vorwärts*. His attacks on the King of Prussia brought a complaint from Berlin, and the French authorities expelled Marx, though after a question in the Chamber this order was quashed. He now moved to Brussels.

Friedrich Engels, born in Barmen in 1820, was the son of a wealthy mill-owner and in 1842 went to Manchester, where his father had opened a branch. While in England he became acquainted with the socialists and wrote articles for *Northern Star*, edited by O'Connor, which was the main organ of the Chartists, and also for Owen's *New Moral World*. In the *Deutsch-Französischen Jahrbücher* he sharply attacked free trade and private property and criticised the fundamental concepts of Smith's political economy. In 1844 he met Marx in Paris and collaborated with him in writing a book attacking Bruno Bauer. 1845 saw the publication of *The Condition of the Working Classes in England*. The book caused a sensation. It was largely based on official sources and described an appalling state of affairs; but here and there, it must be said, Engels portrayed as normal conditions which were decidedly abnormal. Engels now stayed for some time in his native Barmen, but then went to Brussels where Marx was living and they both joined the League of the Just, later the Communist League.

In 1846–7 Marx wrote, in French, his book *The Poverty of Philosophy, a Reply to the Philosophy of Poverty of Proudhon*. In this he developed the historical and economic views which he had formed largely through his study of English political economy. Fundamental to this work is the Hegelian conception of irresistible progress to a higher goal, though Marx substitutes economic class interest for Hegel's 'world mind'. All ethical speculations and plans for an ideal society are brusquely rejected. The only motive force for social development which Marx will acknowledge is the opposition of the class interests of proletariat and bourgeoisie. At the same time Marx won over the German communists in England and other countries to his views and they entrusted him with the drafting of a *Communist Manifesto*, which he worked out in collaboration with Engels. After thorough discussion this was accepted and published in German at the beginning of 1848, shortly before the outbreak of the February Revolution.

The *Communist Manifesto* is an historical document of world-wide importance. In course of time it was translated into countless other languages and it has played a gigantic role in politics. It proceeds from the idea that the whole development of society, apart from that of primitive times, is the history of class struggles. The social organisation of antiquity and the Middle Ages is represented as a class system in which the upper classes again and again oppressed and exploited the lower. Now, in 1848, the bourgeoisie was in power and all other classes would quickly sink into a proletariat which would be exploited by the bourgeoisie. In those states which had reached the highest stage of development, the Government was merely an organisation for administering the interests of the bourgeoisie. Marx describes in the most downright terms the destructive activity of the bourgeoisie. It had stripped of their halo all professions hitherto looked up to with almost religious awe: doctor, lawyer, priest, poet and scientist – all had been transformed into paid workers. The sentimental veil had even been removed from the family relationship, which had been reduced to a purely financial one. On the other hand, the bourgeoisie had rendered great services to progress by destroying all feudal, patriarchal and idyllic situations, creating centralised states and nations and concentrating property in a few hands. But the unrestricted increase of productive capacity had caused commercial crises, whose periodic recurrence jeopardised the existence of bourgeois society and must in the end lead to its collapse, whereupon sovereignty would pass to the proletariat.

The manifesto paints the condition of the proletariat under the rule of the bourgeoisie in the most sombre colours. The spread of mechanisation was making the worker in his turn into a mere machine and robbed work of all attraction. Output was constantly increasing, wages were correspondingly shrinking and the position of the worker was growing less and less secure through economic crises and unemployment. The middle class would sink more and more into a proletariat through the superior competition of the big capitalists. Already the vast majority of the people were proletarian. In society as it existed it was impossible for nine-tenths of the population to own property. All this was leading inevitably to the revolution of the proletariat and its rise to power. Democracy would establish itself by its own struggles, would gradually wrest all capital from the bourgeoisie and concentrate all means of production in the hands of the state, which it controlled. The manifesto lists a number of measures which must be taken to attain this end.

It also proposes abolishing the existing form of marriage, though offering no clear alternative.

Communism would break down national differences and antagonisms between the peoples, although under the bourgeoisie these were already growing ever smaller. The main attention of the movement was at the moment focused on Germany, as she was on the eve of a civil revolution. In so far as the bourgeoisie adopted a revolutionary attitude, the communists would make common cause with them against absolute monarchy, feudal land ownership and the *petite bourgeoisie*. But they must always create in the workers as clear a consciousness as possible of the antithesis between bourgeoisie and proletariat, for after the fall of the reactionary classes the struggle with the bourgeoisie would at once begin. The manifesto closes with the words:

> The communists scorn to make any secret of their views and intentions. They openly declare that their aims can be achieved only by the forcible overthrow of every social order hitherto known. Let the ruling classes tremble at a communist revolution. In it, the proletarians have nothing to lose but their chains. They have a whole world to win. Proletarians of all lands, unite!

It is understandable that by its aggressive resolution and the fire of its language this manifesto exercised a massive effect. The prophecies of the speedy decline of the middle classes into the proletariat, the latter's progressive inpoverishment, the concentration of property in a few hands and much else besides have not come true. Statistics have inexorably burst these bubbles of the imagination. Marx and Engels were enmeshed in a vast error when they maintained that at that time nine-tenths of the population had no property and felt themselves to be proletarians. The idea, too, of a revolutionary coalition of democrats and communists with the bourgeoisie is strange. Just as unfounded was the view that national antagonisms between the peoples were dwindling. These and other ideas of the manifesto soon had a very fateful effect. Immediately after its appearance, revolution actually did break out. The communists followed the instructions in the manifesto, but soon discovered that the great mass of the people in England, France and Germany by no means felt themselves to be the proletariat or were resolved to bring communism to power by armed revolution. This fact forced them, and the extreme Left in general, to place their hopes not in democracy but in dictatorship, just as the Jacobins had done in the French Revolution. In this way the attitude of the radicals contributed more than any other factor to the failure of the revolution in France and Germany.

14

POLITICAL LITERATURE AND JOURNALISM

Besides scholars and journalists, poets played an important part in shaping public opinion. Books and periodicals for a limited circle of readers had fewer difficulties with the censorship than the press. Some writers contrived to put forward popular demands in a way which made it difficult for the censor to intervene, though as criticism became more open and more frequent, he usually acted more ruthlessly.

Ludwig Boerne (1786–1837) came from a Jewish family in Frankfurt; as a young man he lived in the age of Napoleon, who granted the Jews full civil rights in the territories he controlled. Boerne obtained a municipal post, but lost it after Napoleon's fall, when Frankfurt reimposed an earlier regulation barring Jews from public office. He now became a journalist and in 1817 started a journal, *Die Zeitschwingen* (Pinions of the Age). When this was suppressed he brought out another called *Die Waage* (The Scales), which also appeared for only a few years. Despite all the difficulties which the censorship put in his way, he contrived to pillory the forces hostile to freedom and justice and to enlist public opinion against them. When Jean Paul died in 1825, Boerne delivered a eulogy which was classical in its beauty. The situation in Germany filled Boerne with gloom; only the July revolution in France revived his hopes and he settled in Paris, where he wrote for Cotta. Much as he loved France and bitterly criticised conditions in Germany, he none the less looked on the latter as his native country claiming his passionate devotion. Indeed, in a periodical which he edited for French readers, he wrote that the relationship of Germany to France was that of genius to talent. Art with no patriotic or social aims was meaningless to him. This was why he taxed Goethe with having had no sense of fatherland or people. For a time he hoped that the French and German republicans would jointly open up the path to freedom and with this in mind took part in the Hambach Festival. He wrote a sharp rebuttal of Menzel's attacks on the French, but for all his delight in polemics he could not shake off an increasing melancholy.

Like Boerne, Heinrich Heine (1799–1856), whose fame rests on his poetry, was of Jewish origin and spent his youth under French rule, which gave him a life-long partiality for France, although he also loved Germany. He contributed articles to Cotta's journals and others. He attacked German reaction, princes, bureaucrats and Philistines with biting wit. He felt himself to be a fighter for freedom, though his views and feelings about what this meant changed. As a young man he followed the cult of Napoleon; later, his enthusiasm waned, but after the abortive revolution of 1848 he greeted Louis Napoleon's accession to power. England he regarded, on the one hand, as the land of freedom but, on the other, he condemned the power which the aristocracy and plutocracy enjoyed there, the habit of judging all things in terms of pounds, shillings and pence, the barbarity of British justice, the exploitation of Ireland and what he felt to be religious hypocrisy. The French appeared to him to be superior, and although their political system was also strongly tinged with plutocracy, they seemed to him the people who exemplified freedom. After the July revolution, Heine – like Boerne – settled in Paris, where he remained until his death. To be sure, he recognised more acutely than Boerne the darker side of conditions in France; indeed, in his judgement the French could not possibly be proper republicans and he called himself a monarchist. This attitude aroused great indignation among the German émigrés in Paris and he was called a renegade, which he certainly was not. He saw that it was easier to enthuse about freedom than to establish it. America, it is true, had a constitution, but was for him the land of Mammon, mob rule, the slave trade and lynch law.

Among French intellectuals there were many supporters of social reform who tended more or less to socialism. Heine showed warm sympathy for their aims. He also made the acquaintance of Marx, Engels and other German socialists, but he sensed the dangers which lie in mass communistic movements.

Heine's lyric art soon won him a wide circle of readers; even Metternich esteemed him as a poet. His satirical illumination of conditions in Germany likewise exercised a very great influence. The *Bund* took measures against him as one of the leaders of the Young Germany school.

Karl Gutzkow (1811–78), a Berliner, grew up in poor circumstances, studied theology and philosophy and was a member of a *Burschenschaft*. He was a keen student of the classics. He attended Hegel's lectures and received from his very hands a gold medal for a prize essay on the antique gods of fate. Fired by the July Revolution, he became a staunch supporter of Boerne, whose views he supported both in his literary works and political writings. He later wrote a biography of Boerne, in which he described the impact which the latter had had on German youth. He was indebted to Boerne for, among other things, a lofty conception of literature and journalism as a means of educating the nation to unity, freedom and culture. Gutzkow's rise to fame began with his work on the *Literaturzeitung*, which the publisher Cotta had founded at Boerne's instigation. At the time its editor was Wolfgang Menzel (1798–1873), one of the founders of the *Burschenschaft*. Menzel was a prominent literary critic and at the outset was in broad agreement with Gutzkow (who was known as his 'adjutant'), not least in his liberalism and his admiration for Heine and Boerne. Gutzkow's work on this paper and his own publications brought him into close contact with the group of writers and journalists known as Young Germany. He was closely associated with the house of Cotta, first with its founder, Johann Friedrich, and, after the latter's death at the end of 1832, with his son Georg. The elder Cotta was not only a great supporter of Young Germany and political liberalism, but also greatly strengthened the growing movement for the unification of Germany under the leadership of a liberal Prusssia.

Among the numerous works which Gutzkow wrote in the years which followed, his novel *Wally, die Zweiflerin* (Wally, the Doubter) caused a particular sensation. He and his friends were closely concerned with the problems of female emancipation and the radical criticism directed by the Young Hegelians at the Christian faith and religion in general. In this novel the heroine, Wally, chooses death because she has lost her faith and is convinced that without religion human life is wretched. Gutzkow attracted a large circle of prominent writers and with them he planned to bring out a new literary review on the grand scale. This threatened Menzel's position as a sort of Great Cham of letters and stung him to anger. Worse still, Gutzkow had criticised a book of Menzel's on the philosophy of history; he was particularly disapproving of Menzel's disbelief in the ultimate victory of humanitarianism and his prophecy that war would succeed war and that men would tear one another to shreds like uncaged beasts. In another review, Gutzkow reproached Menzel for setting his face against inspired new ideas in the interests of Philistine morality and taste. His former patriotism, he said, was now a mere outward cloak, and it is true that Menzel had changed in many respects. These remarks caused Menzel, in 1835, to attack Gutzkow and the whole of the Young German movement tooth and nail. He charged them with the grossest immorality, blasphemy and other scandalous practices. Soon after this the *Bundestag*, at Metternich's instance, embarked on a campaign against Young Germany; the movement was branded anti-Christian and blasphemous, deliberately trampling underfoot all morality, modesty and respectability. Heine, Gutzkow, Ludolf Wienbarg, Theodor Mundt and Heinrich Laube were named as the leaders. The *Bundestag* decided on the sharpest measures against these writers and their works.

The spirit of revolt animated a number of other writers of the time. One of the most talented was Georg Herwegh (1817–75), whose poems reveal, on the one hand, the most reckless spirit of attack on all the enemies of freedom and, on the other, deep tenderness and a feeling for nature. He yearned for one 'last, holy war' to set all peoples free and establish eternal peace between the nations; he scorned and condemned the princes, the nobles, the Pope and the priests. His greatest hatred was reserved for the Tsar, the oppressor of the Poles. His poem on the German fleet hymns Germany's coming role of a great power and a world-renewer, and from her rise to strength at sea he expects above all else the achievement of freedom.

No poet proclaimed the imminent revolution with such fire as Herwegh. When in 1842 he returned home from Switzerland, where he had lived as a refugee, his journey through Germany resembled a triumphal procession. Everywhere he was cheered to the echo by the young people. He was even presented to the King of Prussia, who, after a conversation with him, shook hands with the words: 'Let us be honourable enemies!'. But when the Prussian ministry banned a journal which he wanted to bring out, Herwegh wrote a very insulting letter to the King which got into the papers and resulted in his expulsion from Prussia. He went to Switzerland, then to Paris, and later, in April 1848, broke into Germany with a column of revolutionaries, but was defeated and again lived abroad. Even before this he had joined the communists.

Ferdinand Freiligrath (1810–76), who won distinction with his descriptions of nature and his translations of foreign poems into German, was even more significant as a poet. Although in 1842 he had said, in an argument with Herwegh, 'The poet stands on a higher level than a party rampart', he later declared himself a republican and friend of the proletariat. In the end he wrote the most bloodthirsty revolutionary songs. He too had to spend a great part of his life abroad for political reasons.

Political verse proliferated in the forties and there is room to discuss only a few typical poets. Robert Prutz (1816–72) wrote a poem accusing the liberals of talking a lot but doing nothing. Many of their weaknesses were acutely observed and sharply illuminated by him. He had sympathy with the social distress of the working masses, which many liberals completely overlooked. A tireless singer of political freedom and national unity was August Heinrich Hoffmann von Fallersleben (1798–1874), who had also won renown for his research in Germanic philology. In 1842 he lost his chair of German language and literature because of his political verse. He wrote many of his poems to be sung, often with a specific melody in mind. He gained unusual popularity and his songs were widely heard. The most famous of them is *Deutschland über Alles*, which later became the national anthem. To condemn this song as an expression of national megalomania is to misinterpret it completely. The poet by no means intends to convey that Germany is to rule over all, but that the Germans should love their native land above all else. That a country should mean more to its people than their private interests is a literary commonplace the world over, and to make so obvious a qualification explicit in the text would be pedestrian and misplaced. No poet was further removed from aggressive nationalism than Hoffmann, who in a subsequent verse proclaims unity, justice and freedom as national aims; the list of frontiers occurring in the first stanza merely outlines the geographical facts of the time.

Political poetry was also stirring in Austria, which was feeling the oppression of Metternich and his system. It began in 1832 with poems by Anastasius Grün (1806–76), whose real name was Anton, Count of Auersperg. One of his songs bore the title *Victory of Freedom* and another, dedicated to the censor, tells him he is worse than a blasphemer.

Among the Austrian poets, Nikolaus Niembsch von Strehlenau (1802–50), generally known as Lenau, expressed in his works a strong urge for freedom. Karl Beck, likewise a highly gifted poet, also wrote revolutionary songs. In his collection *Lieder vom armen Mann* (Songs of the Poor), which appeared in 1846, he gives expression to an early form of socialism which is lavish in sympathy for the exploited and threats towards the rich. Another prominent literary and political figure was the poet Moritz Hartmann (1821–72), who was born in Bohemia of Jewish stock. In 1848 he sat in the Frankfurt National Assembly. Closely associated with him was Alfred Meissner (1822–85), also a German from Bohemia. Like Hartmann, he combined in his poems a deep sympathy for the Czechs and a sense of his own German nationality.

The greatest name in Austrian literature is that of Franz Grillparzer (1791–1872), whose works are acknowledged German classics. His attitude to the German national freedom movement is as hard to determine as Goethe's. Even when he was eighty he wrote in his diary: 'I am not a German, but an Austrian, indeed, a Lower Austrian and above all a Viennese'. But culturally his work was certainly closely linked with the great corpus of German literature. He suffered much under the political conditions prevailing in the Austria of Metternich and the Emperor Francis. His deep melancholy was partly attributable to despair over public conditions. The censorship plagued him so much that he thought of emigrating, though he never took the decisive step. Before the revolution of 1848 Grillparzer had the reputation of being a liberal; after it, the liberal politicians looked on him as a reactionary. His political faith was primarily rooted in the ideal of many peoples living together in one fatherland. He watched the German national movement with concern, because it threatened to worsen relations between German and non-German peoples in Austria. Hence, he often gave sharp expression in his *Epigrams* to his anger at rising German nationalism. He felt in his bones that in the nationalistic principle – and not only in its application to Germanism – there lay a tendency to racial hatred which represented a threat to the existence of the Habsburg monarchy. It was this mood that inspired the lines:

> The path of modern progress leads
> From humanity
> Through nationality
> To bestiality.

15

NATIONAL AND INTERNATIONAL TRENDS
IN THE THIRTIES AND FORTIES

THE NATURE OF NATIONALISM

History shows that all states have sprung from long struggles for power between princes and peoples. Modern nationalism is an ideology which holds power, prestige and territorial extent to be the highest values and seeks to exalt one nation above others. It is not easy to decide in any given case whether striving to become a national state is morally and politically justified or unjustified and impracticable. Certainly there have been some situations in the past in which power has been the most important thing for a state and a nation, and at other times this has not been so. A dynamic and egocentric nationalism can only too easily develop into a substitute for religion with one's own nation as its idol. In the period dealt with in these pages, however, belief in Christianity and humanity had a moderating effect; moreover, the machinery of state and the technology which goes with it had not yet reached their ultimate sophistication. The struggle for power and prestige was often justified as the pursuit of a mission to bring freedom and civilisation to other peoples. The formation of ideologies is influenced by the conception of one's own national character as well as that of foreign nations. In all such judgements a grain of truth is mixed with a mass of error. The fact is that the ideology of a nation is neither uniform nor unalterable. Every people contains numerous groups which differ widely in their views on state, society and other nations. Only in a severe crisis, especially war, are these divergencies of opinion more or less composed, partly by pressure from above, partly by the sense of a common destiny.

The Enlightenment, with its belief in progress, assumed that the differences between peoples largely matched the stages of development they had reached. Romanticism and the historical school of law laid the main stress on the unfolding of the public mind, i.e. of the silent but continuous development of customs among wide sections of the

H

people. The traditionalists also based a country's individuality on tradition which had become historical but which they ascribed more to the mind of the State, i.e. to the activities of the leaders of the State, than that of the people. Hegel saw in the differences between the principal nations stages of development of the world mind or world reason. Fichte looked on the national mind not as a legacy of the past but a task for the future, as the ideal goal of a nation on the way to realising general human perfection.

The doctrine that there exists a national mind formed by history and environment has led to very varied political conclusions. Herder preached that only recognition of the individualities of all nations put together could enable humanity to develop. The peoples would then understand, esteem and help one another, and most of their differences would thereby gradually vanish, until the final goal of world citizenship was reached. For Rousseau, however, national unity demanded that every nation should express its own individuality, and, shutting itself off from others, cling to it, right or wrong; as examples he instanced the Spartans, Romans and Israelites of old. These ideas are admittedly hard to reconcile with his general views, for in another place he condemns the striving for power as an end in itself. This is just one of the contradictions between theory and practice which occur with Rousseau and the political parties inspired by his philosophy.

Concepts like the mind of the people, the mind of the nation and the character of the people have been interpreted in very different ways. The German Romanticists understood by these terms mainly the morals and customs which grow up among a people over a long period. They thought in this connection primarily of the lower and middle classes, particularly in rural districts, because they had supposedly preserved in their purest form the ideas and morals of an earlier day, and it was a fact that the upper classes largely preferred French to German and had absorbed much foreign culture. Rousseau the Romanticist condemned the tendency in the upper classes everywhere to ape the French and thus become estranged from a national outlook. Herder also enthused about the folk-songs of the classes untouched by foreign culture, but his idea of a synthesis of national characteristics was accessible only to an intellectual minority. A completely different conception of the national mind was to see in it not the historically developed mode of thinking and feeling of a people but only the forces conducive to the formation of a national personality. Even this concept could be interpreted in different ways. Whereas many thinkers saw the goal as the development of moral powers, of conscience and of reason, others saw it as the growth of power and prestige. Here the idealistic and the empirical view of human nature clashed. Rousseau relied on the 'people' to find the right way by intuition, adding that, in so far as this did not happen, pressure from the State should aid the process – which is what the Jacobins proceeded to do. Fichte wanted to educate youth for its new role and had in mind a sort of dictatorship of wise men.

To the modern empiricist, the 'people' is neither as uniform nor as infallible as Rousseau imagined. In many states there is not just one people, but several, with diverse languages and traditions as well as a multiplicity of religious faiths, classes, political parties and other groups, which in national questions may have very different and often irreconcilable convictions. The primitive way out is to regard the opinions and actions of the ruling classes as the character of the people or national mind, more especially as in the State today these classes are often in a position to neutralise those who think differently from them. That this conception can lead to the most fateful consequences needs no elaboration here.

RACE DOCTRINE

The most extreme form of nationalism is linked with the doctrine of an identity of nation and race. The premise was that mankind fell into various, clearly definable races. In the period under review, the doctrine of race played as yet no great part, although it was not altogether absent. Attempts were often made in the nineteenth century to distinguish between intellectually superior and inferior races. Gustav Klemm (1802–67) wrote a ten-volume *General Cultural History of Mankind* (1843–52) in which he distinguished between active and passive races, the former supposedly originating in the north and the latter in the south. In his view cultural progress rested on miscegenation; without this the people from the north would have remained barbarians and those from the south would not have risen above mediocrity. Kelmm's bold hypotheses were not scientifically demonstrable.

In 1848 Rotteck and Welcker's *Staatslexikon* published an article on the races of man,[1] written by Georg Friedrich Kolb (1808–84), a newspaper editor from Speyer, who took a critical view of the race doctrine. Of the assertion that there existed inferior races, he remarked that it was 'to some extent shameful for a friend of humanity to engage in argument against such sweeping and derogatory judgements'.

GERMANY'S RELATIONS WITH HER NEIGHBOURS

In this period most Germans felt themselves to be Prussians, Austrians, Bavarians and so forth, and only then Germans. In time past the German

[1] *The Races of Man*, Vol. XIII, pp. 389–408.

states had stood in widely differing relationships with neighbouring countries. South Germany traditionally maintained close ties with France and Italy, North Germany with Britain, the Netherlands and Scandinavia, and Austria and Saxony with eastern Europe. Some countries had suffered severely from French and Swedish wars of aggression, and in many circles these memories died hard. During the Napoleonic wars, many German dynasties were under an obligation to the French Emperor because he enabled them to expand their territories at the expense of small surrounding states. The peoples had shed much blood in Napoleon's cause, but at the same time the extension and modernisation of their political systems had brought them great advantages. In North Germany, Hanover was dynastically linked with Britain; the officials there were proud of having 'British and Hanoverian' in their titles. Hesse-Cassel had formerly been England's biggest supplier of troops, and both commercially and by sentiment Hamburg's outlook was thoroughly pro-British. Prussia was for a long time in close relations with France; moreover, the French refugees of an earlier day, the Huguenots, had brought her uncommonly great economic and cultural benefits.

A preference for things foreign had long been very marked in Germany. The courts and aristocratic circles preferred speaking French and anything from abroad was much more highly esteemed than its native counterpart. Besides this, enthusiasm developed for England's national example as well as her literature; other foreign cultural elements, too, were early recognised in Germany. Thus it is not surprising that Francophobia, which prevailed among some Germans during the wars of liberation, was relatively soon overcome. Jahn's 'Teutomania' lived on for a time in the *Burschenschaft* and among professors, but was for the most part rejected by educated people.

In the first half of the nineteenth century, the Germans regarded many of the Slav races with a sympathy which, in the case of the Poles and their struggle for freedom, amounted to enthusiasm. There were German scholars, like Schlözer and Herder, who prophesied the rise of the Polish nation and welcomed it. Only in the course of long national struggles did relations between Germans and Slavs grow worse again.

The National Struggle for Power
The struggle for national unity always contained the desire to gain more power, though not necessarily by military means. This aim was helped by the example of those nations who had already won unity and strength. Germany's neighbours, France and Russia, both had a

strong military tradition and were able to muster more powerful armies than the German Confederation with its diffusion of sovereignty. Towards the end of the thirties, the *Bund* comprised somewhat under 40 million inhabitants, considerably less than Russia, but slightly more than France with 33·5 millions.

Though German liberals were in principle peaceable, they did not rule out war completely, as, for example, when its aim was liberation. They hated Russian absolutism and loathed the Tsar as the 'butcher of Poland'. They were well aware that he regarded a liberal Germany as a threat to his own régime. He often intervened in German affairs and brought pressure to bear on the princes who were related to him in order to block any political progress. One section of the democrats cherished the plan of establishing Germany's freedom by a war against the Tsar, if possible with the help of France.

Many Germans had the feeling that other nationals looked down on them because they were not powerful. There was no general German nationality and passports showed merely the bearer's citizenship of one particular German state. An Englishman or a Frenchman could hardly take a state seriously when its population was no bigger than that of a small town in his own country.

Finally, there were not a few who wanted a policy of strength in order to secure a leading place in Europe for Germany. The publisher Friedrich Perthes (1772–1843) wrote at the end of the twenties that many seemed to be completely sacrificing the German nation out of a 'mania for illusory national renown, because they were discontented all the while Germany was not playing a great role in Europe or even dominating it. But these self-same men would recoil in horror if they had to give up and accept what would have to be given up and accepted if we were to be politically dominant in Europe'.[1]

Germany and France

In 1840 the centenary of Frederick the Great's accession was celebrated in Prussia. His prestige, which had suffered as the result of historical criticism, was now reviving and thus contributed to the rise of Prussian nationalism which later spread to German ideology generally. It was generally forgotten that Frederick had grievously impaired Germany's unity, though in 1847 the Rotteck-Welcker *Staatslexikon* published an article on him, sharply condemning much of his policy, while approving of some of his reforms. But the glorification of Frederick was scarcely

---

[1] *Friedrich Perthes Leben*, Vol. I, p. 275. Heine, as is well known, drew a grim picture of the German nationalism which he could see arising. He probably had in mind the Teutonism rife in the group round Menzel, who had been his mentor in the *Burschenschaft*.

compatible with Francophobia, for the King read only books written in French, which he spoke much better than German, and regarded Prussia and France as natural allies.[1]

The later differences between Germany and France arose less from Friderician ideology than from the Rhineland question. Many Germans contested the Allies' decision in 1815 to leave Alsace to France, and some even demanded that other territories which had once belonged to the Holy Roman Empire should form part of Germany. The problem of Alsace had two facets. From the fact that its inhabitants were predominantly German-speaking, one could take the view that their nationality was German, but, on the other hand, it was also a fact that they wanted to remain French, and this was fairly generally recognised in Germany. The liberals put this attitude down to the circumstance that France offered her citizens more freedom than Germany, where the *Bund* and the two great powers were pursuing a highly reactionary policy. They assumed that when freedom triumphed in Germany, the Alsatians would voluntarily join her.

In France there was a widespread and passionate conviction that the Rhine territories must be recovered from Germany. On this subject the views of the French writer Edgar Quinet are typical. He began as an enthusiast for German philosophy and literature and a convinced cosmopolite, and married a German woman. After 1830 he saw the German national movement as a dangerous threat to the security of France and the return of the German Rhine provinces as indispensable.

A German politician who occupied himself with the Rhineland question was Johann Georg Wirth (1798–1848)[2], a republican who had been arrested for taking part in the Hambach Festival and author of a book written at a time when Franco-German tension was at its most acute. In it Wirth opposed the inclination of many German republicans to an alliance with their political friends in France based on the transfer of the Rhineland to France in exchange for armed help in setting up a German republic. In any case the plan was purely theoretical, since neither the French nor the German republicans were strong enough to carry it out. In Wirth's view the Russians were aggressive and expansionist, whereas the Germans in modern times had grown decidedly averse to power politics. The author counted the 'Germanic tribes' severed from Germany in the Netherlands, Alsace, Lorraine and German Switzerland as having German nationality and hoped for their re-unification with Germany, but he repeatedly emphasises that these changes must be brought about not by conquest but by the voluntary

[1] Cf. *The Development of the German Public Mind*, Vol. II, 1962, Chap. 16.
[2] Vide supra, p. 145–148.

agreement of these peoples. Nor was the application of the principle of nationality to be interpreted solely in favour of the Germans. Germany should restore to the Poles the areas which had remained Polish, and France was likewise to receive those territories which did not yet belong to her but which were really French.

A noteworthy examination of the Rhineland question by Georg Friedrich Kolb appears in the *Staatslexikon* (Vol. II, p. 565) and is probably the best presentation of the liberal view. The article appeared when the excitement had died down.[1] It first describes the position of the Rhine provinces in the old *Reich*, the latter's extraordinary fragmentation and the misery caused by 'despotism', which, incidentally, he doubtless exaggerates. The union of the left bank of the Rhine with France is, in contrast, represented as highly beneficial. The Congress of Vienna is criticised because it had recently split up the Rhine provinces. The Rhinelanders on German soil were decidedly German-minded, and besides, compared with the earlier French régime, things there were much improved. But the Alsatians, Lorrainers, Dutch and Swiss did not want union with Germany; even the Alsatians, who had remained thoroughly German, definitely wanted 'foreign rule' to continue. Language was no touchstone for nationality either in the west or the east. Prussia, and Austria even more, contained very large Slav populations which would have to go if language were regarded as the decisive factor. Reunion of the lost territories with Germany could be initiated only if liberal and reasonable principles prevailed in the countries of the *Bund*, and any *Anschluss* must be voluntary. Indeed, the article repeatedly and sharply condemns all national conceit *vis-à-vis* other peoples and 'declamations about patriotism and nationality' which disregard liberty.

Germany and England

Whereas South Germany and the Rhineland gravitated towards Paris, North Germany had always had close relations with England. In the latter half of the eighteenth century, an enthusiasm for English literature spread in Germany and the preference for French culture subsided. Cultural exchanges flourished; the English in their turn grew interested in German literature. It became fashionable for them to pay visits to Weimar. Goethe's *Conversations with Eckermann* afforded much information about English visitors and the impression they gave and received. At the same time there was still a widespread conviction that German literature was immoral and irreligious. Ultimately it was Carlyle who was its great populariser. He read widely and made German

---

[1] The author expressed the same ideas in his contribution on *Natural Frontiers* (Vol. IX, p. 404), which he wrote in mid-1840.

works known by translations, essays and praise which was often effusive. His own views were strongly influenced by German Romanticists, philosophers and reactionary journalists like von Haller and Adam Müller. His essay *The Moral Phenomena of Germany* (1845) contains many interesting comparisons between conditions in the two countries. Another writer and politician on whom German literature exercised a great influence was Edward Bulwer, later Lord Lytton. He dedicated his novel *Ernest Maltravers* to the Germans, whom he called a nation of thinkers. German universities attracted many English students and researchers who became celebrated scholars – John Kemble, Lord Acton and John Austin, for instance.

Some impressions of Germany are given in a work which appeared anonymously in 1836 in two volumes. The author, Edmund Spencer, found much in Germany that was better than in England – for example, the Prussian judicial system and the training of teachers. Although the *Zollverein* had hitherto brought Germany great advantages, he said, it would in the end prove a doubtful blessing since its protective tariffs were pampering her industries. The Prussian military system and the Government's dependence on Russia were harmful and both were also criticised by the Germans themselves. The movement for unity and freedom might well lead to a revolution one day. The Germans, added Spencer, were lovers of order, ponderous, serious thinkers and pertinacious in pursuing their aims, but they had little idea of making money, a trait which was so strongly developed in England. They differed from the French by their lack of *esprit*, of the mania for innovation and particularly of any vanity. But there were young officers who boasted of the successes of the Prussian army at Waterloo. Although the Germans were sober and thoughtful, they were also capable of lapsing into boundless enthusiasm which worked like an infectious disease.

Another Englishman, Bisset Hawkins, a doctor, professor and inspector of prisons, gave in a book on Germany published in 1838 many statistical comparisons with other nations. He paid a handsome tribute to German particularism and the princes, who opened up to their peoples many more advantages in the way of schools, scientific institutes, galleries and parks than other states. The people lived very frugally, but not in poverty. Censorship was admittedly a great evil. The author had a special word of praise for German scholars, who were masters of many languages and subjects and thought on cosmopolitan lines.

16

THE SCHLESWIG-HOLSTEIN QUESTION

The movement for German unity and freedom became increasingly involved with the Schleswig-Holstein question. The two duchies, which lie between Denmark and Germany, gave rise to a serious European problem in the nineteenth century. Schleswig, once a fief of Denmark, did not belong to the *Bund*, unlike Holstein, a former fief of the Holy Roman Empire. The King of Denmark was Duke of both states, and was a member of the *Bund* through the Holstein connection.

In the Middle Ages the Danish kings set about building a large empire. At times they ruled England and parts of northern Germany and other Baltic countries. They also maintained close relations with German princes and their vassals. In her struggle with Sweden, Denmark depended on German help; alone, she could not have sustained these interminable wars. The Danish Estates repeatedly chose German princes as their king: first Eric of Pomerania, then Christopher of Bavaria and finally Christian of Oldenburg (1448), whose descendants still reign today. The nobility dominated the Estates and compelled the kings to grant them privileges which were considerable even in modern times. Of these dispensations the declaration of Christian I in 1460 – that Schleswig and Holstein must always remain united – was especially important, but as early as 1544 they were, with the agreement of the Estates, divided between the three sons of Frederick I. This led to further parcellings out, and 229 years passed before the duchies were once again united under their Duke, the King of Denmark.

The Danish kings who came from Oldenburg were at first surrounded by German nobles, soldiers, officials and clergy. Thus German became the language of the upper classes, the army, the clergy and the scholars to a marked degree. At the outset the kings spoke as little Danish as George I did English. Later, they learned the native tongue, but for a long time were still more German than Danish. The first prince to be brought up in a completely Danish way was Frederick, who in 1784 became regent for his mentally deranged father and in 1808 came to the throne as Frederick VI.

The Reformation helped the spread of High German, which was used in Danish churches and schools by German Lutheran clergy and supplanted Low German, previously predominant among the people. Although in the churches of North Schleswig Protestantism furthered the use of Danish, the general effect of the Reformation was to make the population of Schleswig (until then purely Danish) into a mainly German-speaking people. A third nationality was also represented in the duchies – the Frisians, who were pro-German and spoke a language related to Dutch. One of the main reasons for the spread of German in Schleswig was that the Danish and Frisian dialects spoken there did not lend themselves by vocabulary or idiom to the expression of the more lofty ideas needed for sermons, nor were there any hymns in these dialects. The Frisian tongue was especially hard hit because there was no Frisian version of the Bible, and so church services were held in German. Simple, everyday topics were discussed by the peasants in Frisian; beyond that, German was used instead.

Many leading ministers in Denmark, like the Bernstorffs, came from Germany. Denmark's foreign policy was handled in close concert with the so-called 'German Chancellery', which administered Schleswig-Holstein. In both duchies German was the official language, and international treaties were also drawn up in German. Until 1772, German was the language used in the Danish army, whereas the navy both spoke and felt Danish. As in other countries, national aspirations stirred when the vernacular developed into a written language. The first Danish grammar was published in 1668, and in the eighteenth century Danish literature began to flourish, though even in the nineteenth century many leading Danish authors still wrote in both Danish and German. Under the Bernstorffs, German writers – Klopstock and Schiller, for instance – received help from the Danish court and the nobility in the duchies, and this at a time when the upper classes in Germany reserved their esteem for French literature.

For a very long time most of the inhabitants looked on themselves as neither Danes nor Germans but Schleswig-Holsteiners. History had welded them together and given them, along with an almost national consciousness, the feeling that they formed a bridge between Germany and Denmark. The duchies were administered in the German language by the 'German Chancellery' in Copenhagen, they had their own laws and institutions and were largely independent of the Danish government. But this changed when Danish and German national movements started up beyond the borders. Both in Denmark and Germany national sentiment was awakened by the deep humiliation suffered in the Napoleonic era. Through her alliance with France, Denmark had been exposed to bombardment by the British fleet, and when peace was concluded she lost Norway to Sweden and sank to being a third-class power in Europe.

It now seemed vital to the Danes that they should retain the duchies or at least assimilate Schleswig. There were many who dreamed of a union of all Scandinavian nations. However, all plans to incorporate the duchies aroused the opposition of the knights and intellectuals there; they jealously defended their German character and their independence, and later strove for a close union with Germany. The University of Kiel in Holstein was their stronghold and Professors Dahlmann and Falck their leaders. Dahlmann was at the same time the Permanent Secretary (*Syndikus*) to the landowners in the Estates. Apart from their national grievances, these aristocrats and intellectuals also had political and financial objections to the Danish régime; they were indignant over monarchical absolutism which denied them their historical rights and they complained about Danish taxation. When in 1829 Dahlmann left Kiel, where he had taught for sixteen years, he said that about half the clergy and officials, especially the younger ones, sympathised with his views.

A few months after the July Revolution in France, a pamphlet circulating in the duchies caused a considerable stir. Its author was a Frisian, Uwe Lornsen, born in 1793 and a member of the Jena *Burschenschaft*, who had for years occupied a senior post in the German Chancellery in Copenhagen. He was promptly removed from his post of Governor (*Landvogt*) of his native island of Sylt and arrested. In 1838 he committed suicide in Switzerland. Lornsen demanded a joint *Landtag* for the duchies and a mere personal union with Denmark. His pamphlet helped to get liberal demands met, at least in part, but they were far from being fully satisfied. In 1831 the King granted all his lands, including both duchies, separate provincial assemblies which, however, had only advisory powers. In 1836, Orla Lehmann, son of a German father and Danish mother, came out with the demand that Schleswig should be closely linked with Denmark, his ultimate goal being to have the duchy incorporated and made fully Danish. Denmark's frontier was to be, with the exclusion of Holstein, the Eider. The 'Eider Danes' were prepared in case of need to give up Holstein. The counterpart to this on the German side was the New Holstein Party, founded by the democrat Olshausen, which wanted to associate Holstein closely with Germany and leave Schleswig to the Danes. In Olshausen's view, the linking of the duchies hindered progress towards freedom, but he later changed his mind. The Danish conservatives wanted to keep all territories together under the Danish crown, but were prepared to grant the Germans certain special rights.

Danish plans to separate Schleswig from Holstein and to ensure the Danish language wider currency and adoption as the official language were sharply opposed by the Germans, who pointed to the fact that the duchies had been closely united for four centuries. Another controversial issue was the right of succession. The German view was that the duchies did not form part of Denmark and could pass only to a male heir (agnatic succession), not to a female heir as in Denmark (cognate succession). The Germans declared that their demands were fundamental constitutional rights based on privileges granted to the Estates. The Danes sought to prove that these special rights lapsed in 1660 when the King instituted monarchical absolutism in Denmark. The question of the succession was important because it could be seen in advance that the male line of the Danish royal house would die out with the son of the new king, Christian VIII. The Germans held that in this case the duchies would fall to the nearest male collateral line – the dukes of Augustenburg, who were pro-German. The Danes claimed that the same right of succession held good for the kingdom as for the duchies. The King had these controversial questions examined by a commission and in his letters patent of 1846 broadly associated himself with the Danish viewpoint.

This declaration by Christian aroused a storm of indignation in the duchies and in Germany. He therefore issued a second pacific declaration which, however, failed in its object. In 1847 he gave orders for the drafting of a new constitution but died on 20 January 1848 before it was completed. The new constitution, published by his son, Frederick VII, satisfied neither the Danish nor the German liberals. Soon after this, revolution broke out in Germany and the problem of the duchies entered a new phase.

17

THE OUTBREAK OF THE GERMAN REVOLUTION

THE BEGINNINGS

On 12 February 1848 Friedrich Bassermann proposed a motion in the Baden lower house which in its ultimate intention aimed at creating a national legislative institution in the Diet of the *Bund*. The demand had already been raised earlier, but this time it had an electrifying effect, coming, as it did, only ten days before a revolution in Paris which culminated in Louis Philippe's flight to England and the proclamation of a republic.

These events set Germany ablaze. Within a few days demonstrations and disorders had spread over most of the small states in the west and south and a little later over those in the north and east as well. In the smaller states of the *Bund* the revolution took place without much bloodshed. The demands were mostly for a constitution, a national German parliament, jury courts and freedom of the press. Many princes, realising the futility of resistance, complied at once; the armed forces of the lesser states were not capable of suppressing the new movement unaided. The general pattern was for the rulers to dismiss those ministers and officials who had made themselves unpopular during the period of reaction and to appoint in their place men who enjoyed general confidence. Ludwig of Bavaria, who even before this had made himself utterly unacceptable through his liaison with Lola Montez, abdicated.

Not that the outbreak of the revolution in these smaller states was completely without violence, but it sprang more from social than political causes. Thus there were risings in many country districts. Some were in those parts where land was scarce and the peasants were cramped on minute holdings – the result of division and re-division over the years by the laws of inheritance. Besides this there were still many oppressive feudal services to be rendered. In the south-west the rebellious peasants actually destroyed a few castles and burned the records of their servitude.

On 5 March fifty-one respected politicians gathered together in Heidelberg and demanded the speediest possible setting-up of a national parliament. The meeting resolved to summon a larger preliminary assembly, known as the *Vorparlament*, to prepare the elections. Later it was often regarded as a fatal error that the revolution did not depose the princes, and cause republics to be proclaimed in all the states, or even a single republic throughout Germany. It must, however, be said that this would have called for a considerable measure of agreement on the type of republic to be set up. In France the radicals proclaimed a republic and carried the masses with them, but a violent controversy immediately arose over whether the republic should reflect the conservative and moderate liberal convictions of the great majority or the views of the radicals. Since these proponents of a 'red republic' were in a minority, they could not achieve their ends by democratic means but only by a dictatorship. They were defeated in an attempt to seize power. The unrest caused by the radical left played a considerable part at the end of 1848 in the choice of Louis Napoleon as president of the republic, thus paving the way for the Second Empire. It can be assumed that the proclamation of a republic and a coup by the extreme left in Germany would not have solved her internal problems any better than was the case in France.

While many German intellectuals regarded the princes as the main obstacle to national unity, most of them were convinced for a number of different reasons that the monarchical principle could not be completely set aside, as it afforded a better guarantee against external and internal dangers than a purely republican constitution. The moderate liberals also reached this conclusion because they felt that their aims were threatened both by communism and the Russian brand of conservatism. They also believed history showed that national unity had always been achieved by powerful kings. Above all else they saw in Britain, who at that time was reaching the zenith of her power and wealth, proof positive that king and parliament could work fruitfully together. Among the humbler folk, who were largely under the influence of tradition, the Church and the aristocracy, the rulers were not infrequently popular. At this time there were Badenese peasants who declared: 'We want a republic with the Grand Duke'. After the outbreak of the revolution in Vienna, the American Ambassador, William Henry Stiles, wrote that the workers were calling for a republic with the Emperor. It depended very much on special circumstances whether large sections of the people would turn to the left or the right.

THE VIENNA RISING

The revolutions in France and Germany caused Metternich the greatest alarm, for he could see his whole system collapsing. In Italy the national movement was drifting towards war with Austria. In Vienna a hard core of liberals had been forming for some time. They were squarely opposed to Metternich's policies and demanded reforms; they included many aristocrats, influential officials and respected citizens and had the vigorous support of many writers. Even in the Imperial family Metternich had powerful opponents, such as the Archduchess Sophie and Archduke John. The liberal aristocratic party, led by the Lower Austrian provincial marshal Count Montecuccoli and Baron Anton von Doblhoff, prepared petitions calling for the setting up of Imperial Estates. On 13 March the Estates of Lower Austria met. The house in which they sat was besieged by thousands of students, townsfolk and workers. Dr Adolf Fischhof, a young Jewish doctor, made the opening speech; he demanded freedom of the press, jury courts, freedom of instruction and fraternal collaboration between the nations of Austria, and he was loudly cheered. The Estates now went jointly to the Hofburg to present their petitions to the Emperor. When the military ruthlessly intervened, the crowds got out of hand and it was left to the *Bürgerwehr* (the national guard formed by the bourgeoisie) to restore order. That same evening Metternich bowed to the inevitable and resigned. The arming of the students and the setting up of a civic guard were approved.

Next day the lifting of the censorship was announced and on 15 March the ailing Emperor promised a constitution. On 31 March a provisional press law came out but it was not satisfactory, so the Government withdrew it and replaced it by a more comprehensive measure. The first responsible ministry took over the conduct of affairs in 21 March.

THE BERLIN RISING

The events in Vienna became known in Berlin on 16 March, where they led to the granting of important concessions which were announced on 18 March and well received by the public. All seemed to be going well when, apparently by accident, two shots were fired from a body of troops on the march. This led to bitter clashes; hundreds of barricades were erected and there was much bloodshed. Although the struggle reached no military decision, the King ordered the withdrawal of the troops in order to restore peace. The next day a long column of street-fighters marched to the royal castle. The King bared his head in token of respect to their dead. On the advice of his new Foreign Minister, Baron Heinrich von Arnim, he also, rather reluctantly, went on a solemn ride round Berlin, wearing an armlet in the black, red and gold which the conservatives had hitherto regarded as revolutionary colours. On 21 March he issued a proclamation 'To my people and the German nation', in which he declared that henceforward Prussia would be merged in Germany.

THE VORPARLAMENT AND HECKER'S REVOLT

The reconstruction of the various governments had repercussions on the Diet of the *Bund*, which now repealed its reactionary decrees and tried to play its part in the developing situation. The *Vorparlament* met in Frankfurt on 31 March as a result of the decisions taken at the Heidelberg meeting. It comprised more than 500 members, including many deputies from the various *Landtage* and other prominent politicians; the representation of the different states did not, however, reflect their importance. The south-west, for example, sent a strong contingent, while Austria had only two members. The *Vorparlament* resolved that the national assembly to be elected should alone have the power to determine Germany's future constitution. The proceedings were sometimes stormy, as a group of extremists led by Friedrich Hecker and Gustav von Struve urged the setting up of a republic. The *Vorparlament* left behind a committee of fifty to which Hecker and Struve were not elected.

Meanwhile, in Berlin, the Rhenish industrialist and liberal politician Ludolf Camphausen had become head of the Government and a few days later the Second United Diet met and approved a decree on fundamental rights of freedom and created an electoral law which introduced for the future Prussian Popular Assembly a universal, equal and secret franchise.

After the close of the *Vorparlament*, Hecker (a brilliant agitator) and Struve went ahead with their plans to set up a republic by any possible means – even rebellion; they counted on support from armed columns from France and Switzerland. In Paris Georg Herwegh, who stood very close to communism, was the moving spirit. In many places in South-West Germany and the adjoining countries there were republican and communist groups who made extensive preparations for the rising. The leaders were hoping that at least some government troops would make common cause with them, but in this they were disappointed, as the insurgents themselves created no sort of military impression. They were poorly armed, many only with scythes; they lacked ammunition and food; there was no question of strategy, and military discipline was rejected as undemocratic. Furthermore, there was a deep rift among the democratic republicans which had already appeared in the *Vorparlament*. In a letter to his wife after the collapse of the risings, Robert Blum, the most prominent of their leaders, wrote: 'Hecker and Struve have betrayed the country in the eyes of the law – that in itself is trifling; but they have betrayed the people by their crazy revolt; the people have been checked in their victorious career; that is a dreadful crime'.

On 20 April Hecker's main forces were routed after a short engagement. In France soon afterwards a new National Assembly was elected and the moderates won an overwhelming victory. Thus even in Paris the radicals suffered a heavy defeat and for their fellows in Germany, who had been counting on their help, this was a grievous disappointment.

SCHLESWIG-HOLSTEIN

The revolution also brought the German–Danish conflict to a head.[1] In Denmark, the Eider Danes demanded the immediate incorporation of Schleswig into Denmark. In Schleswig-Holstein, on the other hand, a meeting of deputies of the Estates demanded the incorporation of Schleswig into the *Bund,* a common constitution for the duchies, the general arming of the people and full freedom of the press and assembly. A new Government, dominated by the Eider Danes, was formed in Copenhagen. On the German side, a provisional Government was formed in Schleswig-Holstein on 24 March and included the democrats, who were recognised almost everywhere in the duchies. The Provisional Government issued an 'Address to the Danish Nation' in which it expressed its willingness to leave the future of north Schleswig to a popular plebiscite. Since the Danish authorities refused to have any dealings with rebels and were mobilising, the Provisional Government requested Prussian help. Frederick William IV was very loath to intervene, since he regarded the rising against the Danish king as a revolutionary act, but his Minister for Foreign Affairs, Baron Arnim, prevailed on him to change his mind; by this policy Arnim was hoping to regain Prussia's popularity in Germany. Prussian and other federal troops were despatched to the duchies. At the same time, Danish troops moved into Schleswig and threw back the Schleswig-Holstein vanguard with heavy losses, only to be driven off in their turn by German federal troops. Since Germany had no battle fleet, the Danish navy was in a position to inflict heavy damage on her trade. In order to make sure of adequate compensation, the Prussian

[1] Vide supra, p. 233ff.

commander-in-chief, General Wrangel, crossed the Danish frontier and levied contributions.

The diplomatic climate in Europe did not favour German plans in Schleswig-Holstein. Tsar Nicholas I was outraged that his brother-in-law, Frederick William, was supporting 'rebels'. In England, public opinion was completely on Denmark's side. It was feared that Schleswig's entry into the *Bund* would harm English trade and also lead to the building of a German fleet, and the Danish blockade of the German coast did in fact revive German demands for a navy. France and Sweden supported Denmark's claims.

Palmerston, the British Foreign Secretary, tried to mediate and proposed a partition of Schleswig by nationalities, but neither the Danish nor the Schleswig-Holstein Provisional Government, which latter had been first to suggest this solution, was now prepared to accept it. Prussia was left to bear the weight of the war virtually single-handed; she had scant support from the other states of the *Bund* and her own King wanted a speedy end to hostilities. So the Prussian troops withdrew, which caused jubilation in Denmark but great indignation throughout Germany. The King now sought an armistice through Sweden's good offices and, to all intents and purposes, the war was suspended.

POSEN

Meanwhile, Prussians and Poles in Posen were increasingly at logger-heads. The Congress of Vienna had laid down that the Poles' nationality was to be recognised in this territory and for most of the time Prussia had gone a long way towards discharging this obligation. The national liberal movement in Germany saw making reparation to the Poles for the injustice they had suffered as one of their main duties; this was repeatedly stressed, in the *Vorparlament* as well. When the revolution broke out in 1848, liberal-minded Germans and the Poles themselves were both aware that Russia was their greatest enemy. Many of them thought that a war with Russia was probable, since the Tsar could tolerate a free Germany as little as he could the liberation of the Poles. For these reasons the Prussian Foreign Minister, Baron Arnim, and other ministers in the Government were strongly in favour of good relations with the Poles and ready to make them considerable concessions. On the other hand, reactionary militaristic circles in Germany looked on the Tsar as their friend and were against any anti-Russian attitude.

The King of Prussia had promised the Poles a 'national reorganisation' of Posen and had sent as his commissary General von Willisen, a cultivated, just and very pro-Polish man. In Posen a Polish National Committee had been set up which behaved very injudiciously, expelling Prussian officials, confiscating public funds, tearing down the Prussian coat of arms and trampling it underfoot and organising armed bands. Germans and Jews were insulted and maltreated. Another committee was promptly set up to safeguard German interests, and on this side too there were many fanatics who indulged in excesses against the Poles, not infrequently with the backing of Prussian officials. General von Willisen now hoped to reconcile Poles and Germans; he made considerable concessions to the former and concluded a treaty with them. But this policy, which issued from the Government in Berlin, was thwarted by the commander of the Prussian troops in Posen, General von Colomb, with the help of court intrigues.

Towards the end of April Government policy changed and partition was mooted. The Germans, together with the German-speaking Jews, made up 36–40% of the population. The German areas were to be incorporated in the *Bund* and the Polish ones to form a separate autonomous territory. Willisen was recalled and General von Pfuel was sent to Posen with full powers to carry out the demarcation. Pfuel, like Willisen, was a very humane and just-minded man and well disposed towards the Poles, but not even he could overcome the passionate nationalism on both sides. Von Colomb's policy of naked force was largely responsible for a serious but ultimately abortive rising by the Poles. The planned partition did not in itself conflict with the principle of self-determination but it soon ran into great difficulties. The Poles refused to hear of partition, demanding the restoration of the Polish state within its old borders and declaring that only then could there be any negotiations about a separation of territories. They therefore refused to co-operate in the projected demarcation and since this meant that only the Germans gave evidence before the commission, the demarcation turned out to be completely unfavourable to the Poles. Pfuel himself had considerable misgivings over the justness and practicability of these frontiers. Not only national but also military considerations played their part in this. Like most towns in Poland, Posen, the capital of the province, had been founded by Germans and was still predominantly German, whereas the surrounding district was Polish. Now the strongest Prussian fortress against Russia was in Posen, and if this area had been incorporated into an autonomous Polish state, Prussia would have lost her most important line of defence in the east.

Although in 1848 very many Germans were serious in their support for the Poles in their struggle for freedom, the first practical problem to arise led to a worsening of relations between the two peoples. On neither side could one completely absolve the romantic radicalism, which, impatient of the slow march of considered actions, hoped to attain its aims overnight by violence as heroic as it was blind. The liberation of Poland by a great struggle with Russia presupposed the help of an established great power, which Germany was far from being at this juncture, as well as a relationship based on complete trust between Germans and Poles. The Austrian Poles, who at that time enjoyed far fewer national rights than those in Prussian territory, later contrived by a sensible and farsighted policy to secure for themselves national freedom and great influence within the Danubian Empire. Mieroslawski, the leader of the Polish dissidents in Posen, wanted to drag Germany into a war with Russia to be provoked by raids by a Polish corps operating from Posen. On strategic grounds alone such a plan would have been highly dubious, since a large Russian army was standing ready on the frontier. The fact that Mieroslawski denied Germans the right of self-determination and refused any agreement over demarcation could hardly fail to antagonise them.

THE PRESS

The censorship, which for decades had assiduously stifled every free word, was abolished by the revolution. As a result, not only did the existing papers improve and thrive, but countless new ones of every kind were founded.

Shortly before the revolution, the *Deutsche Zeitung* was started in Heidelberg by a group of liberal professors and politicians. Its editor-in-chief was Georg Gottfried Gervinus, one of the 'Seven Men of Göttingen', and he had many eminent contributors to call on. Its leading articles brilliantly mirrored the liberal principles of the day. 'Hereditary monarchy surrounded by democratic institutions' – to use the phrase of the French politician Odilon Barrot – was praised as the ideal constitution. Freedom was the supreme goal, but freedom linked with national dignity. The efforts of other oppressed nations to win liberty were sympathetically appraised and the restoration of Poland was even considered as a duty devolving on Germany. Consequently the paper considered war with Russia to be inevitable and for a long time it advocated extensive concessions to the Poles over Posen. But when the Poles would not recognise the right of the German districts in Posen and West Prussia to self-determination, and national fanaticism flared up on both sides, the paper's attitude changed. On 19 April 1848 a leading article declared that Germany had been mistaken; the Poles had spurned the outstretched hand and now wanted to rob the

Germans. Arndt even wrote a letter to the paper representing the Poles as racially inferior.

Developments over Schleswig-Holstein were attentively followed and the paper reflected the German standpoint. It is worthy of note that its articles repeatedly stressed that thanks to the French Revolution Alsace had associated itself closely with France and Germany could not therefore demand its return.

Another high-class paper was the Berlin liberal-democratic *National-Zeitung*, which was founded after the revolution by some respected citizens of the Prussian capital. The paper was associated with a club which met once a week and discussed editorial policy as well as questions of the day. The editors-in-chief were Friedrich Zabel and Ewald Matthäi, who had both begun as theologians. Bernhard Wolff, who took over the business management, also set up the first telegraphic news agency for the press and business men. He had a powerful intellect and a flair for organisation.

In its first issue the paper declared that it intended above all else to represent the national viewpoint, i.e. Germanism in the noblest and purest sense. This would not be a narrow Teutonism but would tend towards humanity. The paper undertook to combat the traditional German vices of servility and philistinism. Instead of rigid dogmas, the *National–Zeitung* supported a practical policy which took account of the realities of life. A glance at the leading articles in the months which followed will show that these principles were actually observed. In international politics the paper sought above all else to foster friendship with France and England, whereas it regarded Russia as an enemy. It did not consider a war against Russia as a hopeless enterprise, since the Russian Empire, for all its numerical superiority, suffered from considerable internal defects, but it recommended in the main a defensive attitude on Germany's part. Events in Posen were dealt with exhaustively and impartially and Prussian policy hitherto was sharply condemned. When differences broke out between Prussians and Poles, both sides were exhorted to become reconciled. Unlawful German activities often came in for criticism. On the other hand the paper could not approve of the Polish refusal to agree to any partition at all, and said that demarcation difficulties could be overcome by an exchange of minorities.

In the Schleswig question, too, the paper supported an ethnic demarcation. It welcomed the Italian rising against Austrian rule and called upon Austria to free Lombardy and Venetia. It was utterly opposed to German claims on Alsace and Lorraine, saying that a free Germany must be a just Germany.

The proceedings of the Prussian National Assembly were followed with critical attention and its shortcomings realistically commented on; the conclusion reached was that it was not equal to its task. In social matters the paper supported the just demands of the workers and criticised the fact that they were excluded from the national militia. The paper was later prosecuted by the Government for its democratic attitude during the revolutionary period and was compelled to change its tune very considerably, which lost it much of its popularity and half its readers. It was only saved by Wolff, who made a lot of money out of his telegraphic agency; he bought the paper and kept it alive during the period of reaction, after which it once more went from strength to strength.

In addition to the *National-Zeitung*, two old-established papers, the *Vossische Zeitung* and the *Spenersche Zeitung*, continued in being, though in a rather modernised form. The *Neue Preussische Zeitung*, founded just before 1848 and better known as the *Kreuzzeitung*, kept going during the revolutionary period. Its first editor was Hermann Wagener. The *Kreuzzeitung*, although conservative, did not always take the official line but often indulged in vigorous polemics, even against Prussian statesmen and foreign governments.

Of the other Prussian newspapers, the old *Kölnische Zeitung* edited by Karl Brüggemann (1810–87) was by far the most outstanding. As a young student, Brüggemann had belonged to the *Burschenschaft*, and at the Hambach Festival had made a rousing speech calling for the unification of Germany. He was arrested, handed over to Prussia and in 1837 condemned to death for high treason, but the sentence was finally commuted to life imprisonment. He was released in 1840. The *Kölnische Zeitung* was highly thought of for its financial as well as its general news. At the beginning of 1848 it had a circulation of 9,500, which rose within a year to 17,400. This shows how limited was the readership on which a paper of this kind could count even when, as in this case, it enjoyed a world-wide reputation.

A near neighbour of this paper was the *Neue Rheinische Zeitung*, of which Karl Marx was the founder (in 1848) and the first editor. In 1842 he had been the editor of the rapidly suppressed *Rheinische Zeitung*. In 1848 he belonged to the left wing of the democratic party and the new paper was called 'the organ of democracy'. Friedrich Engels, and later the poet Ferdinand Freiligrath, were also on the editorial board. Marx poured scorn on the Frankfurt National Assembly for advocating a monarchy, but he was also hostile to nationalism. The circulation rose to 6,000, but with the dawn of reaction the paper was mercilessly harried and Marx expelled from the country.

In Austria, too, a large number of new papers of the most varied types and policies arose after the revolution. Only a few days after it broke out, *Die Constitution*, founded by Leopold Häfner (born 1820), made its appearance. Häfner was a small, hunchbacked man with a huge moustache. He came from the lower classes but had studied law. Without any higher education or money, and quite unknown to the public, he none the less exercised a mesmeric influence and his paper caused a sensation. After only a short time, some 15,000 copies were being printed, and the circulation at times reached 25,000. Friedrich Ebeling, a writer who knew Häfner personally, called him a Marat and wrote of the paper: 'It was the ceaseless rattle of the guillotine; its lines dripped human blood, its logic was that of the sword, its means were revolution and its end revolution'.

Among the anti-radical papers, *Die Presse* was prominent; it was run by August Zang and Dr Leopold Landsteiner, the former an adroit businessman and the latter an excellent journalist, who had both acquired considerable political experience in Paris. The paper called itself the journal of pure democracy but incessantly counselled caution. The senseless cry for freedom, it said, would lead to nothing. The paper, which cost only one kreuzer, was cheaper than its rivals but offered its readers more and consequently enjoyed a wide circulation, despite furious attacks from the radicals. Zang looked on his enterprise first and foremost as a good piece of business and he was called, not unjustly, the father of press corruption.

A paper which pursued an honourable political line was founded under the name *Ost-deutsche Post* by Ignatz Kuranda, a Bohemian German of Jewish birth who had formerly run the excellent journal *Die Grenzboten*. In 1848 he became a deputy in the Frankfurt National Assembly and later sat on the Austrian Imperial Parliament (*Reichsrat*). In his considered view, a monarchy was the best form of government for Austria at that time provided it was linked with political freedom. The Germans in Austria, he said, were the champions of liberty and prevented a relapse into absolutism, but if ever the Slav majority should reach predominance, then it was the Germans' most sacred duty to act as the Italians and Croats had done against their oppressors. Kuranda was a highly-educated, utterly unselfish and intelligent man, but in an age of violent political passions his temperate language did not secure the same effect as that of demagogues and political opportunists, and as a result his paper never attained a wide circulation.

18

THE NATIONAL ASSEMBLIES

THE FRANKFURT PARLIAMENT

On 18 May 1848 the National Assembly was opened in the Free City of Frankfurt amid popular acclaim up and down the country. About this time other parliaments were meeting in the member states of the *Bund*: four days later in Berlin the Prussian National Assembly began its sittings and on 22 July the Austrian *Reichstag*, representing a number of nations, also met. Besides these there were, in other states of the *Bund*, popular assemblies whose demands were often hard to reconcile with the idea of national unity. The attempts of the Frankfurt Assembly to establish its precedence over the other parliaments failed, hardly a good omen for the cause of unity.

The Frankfurt Assembly was elected on a non-uniform and often broad franchise. The basis varied according to the law prevailing in the different states represented. For the most part election was indirect. Just as in other European countries, no real political parties yet existed; even in France these were slow to emerge. This was bound up with the doctrine of Rousseau which had decisively influenced the French Revolution – that parties caused more harm than good: the people (so the argument ran) knew what they wanted, and all that was needed was to establish what this was. Therefore, the deputies sent to Frankfurt had often been chosen for their personal prestige, with no over-nice scrutiny of their precise political views. Many constituencies set great store by being represented by a nationally prominent personage, and in Catholic countries the Church had a great influence when candidates were selected. As a result, the National Assembly included a very large number of eminent men, mainly recruited from the liberal professions and the upper middle class. Not a single working man and only a few members of the unpropertied classes were elected, and this could be put down to the fact that no effective workers' organisation yet existed. All the same, there were many members, mostly intellectuals, who stood for democratic principles, demanded social reforms or inclined to socialism. There was a strong representation of university professors and schoolmasters, judges, public prosecutors, lawyers, journalists and senior state officials. Thus the total of those with an academic background was high. Many deputies had played a leading part in the popular assemblies of their own states and not a few had been persecuted for their efforts in support of freedom and unity. Whatever the Assembly's failures, they did not stem from any lack of political experience and it is equally mistaken to regard its members as, in the main, impractical theorists or abstract philosophers.

The Political Spectrum

The 'clubs' or party groups which formed in Frankfurt were the germ cells of subsequent parties. The Right Centre was the forerunner of the national liberals and from the Left emerged the Progressive Party and the Social Democrats. It is noteworthy that in 1848 no clear division between democrats and socialists yet existed. A Catholic group also grew up and later became the Centre Party.

The Organisation of the Executive

The National Assembly elected as its president the Minister President of Hesse-Darmstadt, Heinrich von Gagern, who was a moderate liberal. At the very outset of the revolution, Gagern had proved himself an authoritative figure, possessing, as he did, outstanding qualities as a statesman. An order of business was adopted and committees nominated. The fact that several members had secured seats in both the Frankfurt and Berlin Assemblies gave rise to a resolution, which was adopted, that all provisions in the constitutions of the component German states must be aligned with those of the constitution to be established in Frankfurt, thus according supremacy to the Frankfurt Assembly.

The war with Denmark made the setting up of a Central Power for all Germany a matter of urgency. Denmark possessed a fleet which was causing severe harm to German maritime trade. Without warships of her own, Germany could do nothing in reply. The German mercantile fleet was, even at that time, of considerable size, and so it was not surprising that a strong movement had grown up within Germany for the building of a navy. Money was collected on all sides and negotiations to buy warships were opened with foreign firms. The National Assembly agreed almost unanimously to allot six million thalers for a navy, the employment of which would be controlled by the future Central Power. An intensive debate now opened over the setting-up of this Central Power. A few moderate liberal politicians at first sought to tailor the Diet of the *Bund*, which had been renovated on liberal lines, for this role, and even before this plans for a directorium of three rulers had been discussed.

The National Assembly studied the question of a provisional directorium in detail and the proposals made fluctuated between monarchical and republican forms. The constitutional committee proposed a directorium of three to be nominated by the governments and appointed by them after approval by the National Assembly, to which they would be responsible. But the democrats wanted the executive to be formed solely by a decision of the National Assembly without any assistance from the princes or governments. Gagern finally declared in favour of the National Assembly's itself choosing a vicar of the empire (*Reichsverweser*), which was, he said, a 'bold stroke' (*kühner Griff*) but the most expedient thing to be done. Until the definitive formation of a governmental power, the *Reichsverweser* was to administer affairs for all Germany with the help of an imperial ministry responsible to the National Assembly. With the founding of the provisional Central Power, the Diet of the *Bund* was to cease its activity. Gagern proposed as *Reichsverweser* Archduke John of Austria, who was very popular in Germany. He received 463 votes, which gave him an overwhelming majority. After a few difficulties had been smoothed out, the election was recognised by all Germany governments and accepted by the Archduke. His ministry included the Austrian statesman Anton von Schmerling (the interior), the Prussian General Eduard von Peucker (war), the Hamburg deputy Heckscher (foreign affairs), the Württemberger Robert Mohl (justice), the Prussian Beckerath (finance) and Duckwitz from Bremen (trade). At its head was Prince Karl von Leiningen, a half-brother of Queen Victoria.

The Imperial Ministry began work at once. The War Minister issued an order to all German troops to give three cheers for the *Reichsverweser* and acknowledge him as their supreme commander. Most states complied, but in Prussia and Austria a watered-down form of words was used, and Hanover failed to pay any form of military homage. It was soon apparent that in military and financial matters the Imperial Government was completely dependent on the governments of the *Bund*.

The Polish Question

Some of the most important debates in the National Assembly concerned the Posen question,[1] which, from 24 July onwards, was thoroughly thrashed out in several sittings. Before the house was a report from its committee on international affairs. This proposed the admission of a

---

[1] Vide supra, p. 123 & 242.

part of Posen into the *Bund*, which was what the Diet of the *Bund* had already decided upon, so that the Assembly might then approve the election of Posen deputies to Frankfurt, to recognise a provisional partition of Polish and German territory but to suspend a final decision. The report further proposed that, on the one hand, Prussia should undertake the protection of Germans in the Polish areas, even if these should become independent, and that, on the other, the protection guaranteed by the National Assembly on 31 May to all non-German races in Germany should be extended to Poles in German territory. This provided for unhampered national development and equal rights for their language within their own territory as far as church, schools, literature, administration and justice were concerned.[1] The great majority of the deputies recognised that the partitions of Poland had been a grievous injustice and that they must do all they could to make restitution. The democrats and the Catholic party were completely on the side of the Poles; they were against the partition of Posen or the admission of a part of it into the *Bund*; many, indeed, demanded steps to restore an independent Poland. A number of liberals also strove to be fair to the Poles, though they were not prepared to hand over 400,000 Germans and German Jews, as well as the fortress of Posen, to them.

In sharp contrast to the attitude of the other democrats was a speech made by Wilhelm Jordan, at that time a man of the Left and a successful poet. This speech was vigorous and impressive and is frequently quoted by critics of the Assembly who tax it with a narrow-minded nationalism. Jordan pointed out that some parts of Posen were originally German and had been conquered by the Poles; that the Germans had founded many cities there; that demarcation of German territories was necessary and that Germany's security demanded that these should include the fortress of Posen. He was conscious, he went on, of swimming against a strong current of German public opinion, but it was a current which was losing impetus. Much as he sympathised with the tragic plight of the Poles, it was impossible to put the clock back. In his view Germany did not need the existence of a Polish state for her protection, the Poles could never win back their eastern territories from Russia, and a war with Russia was not desirable for Germany. One should not hate the Russians, for hatred between nations was a barbarism quite irreconcilable with nineteenth-century civilisation, though one ought to hate the system under which Russia was groaning. The setting-up of an independent Poland would entail a life and death struggle with Germany, for the Poles would lay claim to the German Baltic coast. In politics one should observe a healthy national egoism and put the power

[1] It is perhaps worth noting that England, for example, had for centuries suppressed the Celtic languages in Scotland, Wales and Ireland.

and weal of the fatherland above all else. Jordan conceded that the rights enjoyed by the Germans in Poland rested on conquest, but what was done could not be undone, and in any case the conquest had not been merely by the sword but also by the plough. In the west the Germans had lost territories to conquerors, in the east they had themselves been conquerors. They had expanded because they had made the land doubly, even trebly fruitful. When Poland had been partitioned, it had already been a corpse; Rousseau had said at the time that it was the greatest of all miracles that such a state could have existed for a single moment. Prussia and Austria had jointly carried out the partition because they could not abandon Poland completely to Russia. Prussia had freed the Polish peasants from serfdom, had educated Poles up to civilisation and humanity and thus created the foundations for a new Poland, and this could only be welcomed. He was for the Polish people but against the Polish aristocracy and clergy, who were fomenting the movement against Prussia for their own ends. Jordan's arguments were sharply criticised by other speakers.[1]

The report was eventually adopted with the usual majority of the liberals over the democrats, but the partition of Posen was not carried out, for the Prussian National Assembly also had a say in the matter. It first decided to hold its own investigation into the question, and then, on 26 October, dropped all ideas of partition. It decreed, however, that the rights promised to the Poles should be granted to them throughout Posen. This led to a conflict with the Frankfurt National Assembly, which claimed that decisions of individual states should not conflict with those of the Central Parliament, but the further course of events prevented any rearrangement.

It is understandable that German politicians, according to their party and their individual outlook, should cherish more or less national prejudices and in many cases put the interest or the prestige of their country before anything else, for this was in keeping with the spirit of the age. Many of them may well have lapsed into a nationalistic excess of patriotism, but to assume that in the middle of the nineteenth century dangerous nationalism was a monopoly of the Germans can imply only gross ignorance of history or blind national hatred.

The September Rising

The war with Denmark over Schleswig-Holstein came to a standstill in the summer of 1848. England, Russia, France and Sweden in general

---

[1] Sir Lewis Namier, in his work *1848: The Revolution of the Intellectuals* (1944) used this speech and other utterances to represent the liberals of 1848 as 'in reality forerunners of Hitler'. Cf. pp. 33, 56, 57, 69, 73, 84, 87, 88, 124.

supported the Danish viewpoint. The whole affair had long since become tedious to Frederick William of Prussia, and on 26 August he concluded an armistice at Malmö which granted very favourable terms to Denmark. This aroused great indignation in Germany, a particular objection being that the Imperial Ministry had had so little influence on the treaty. Admittedly the *Reichsverweser* had given Prussia full powers, but he had then been completely excluded from the negotiations. The *Reich* ministry declared that Prussia had exceeded her powers. On 5 September the National Assembly voted by 238 to 221 to stay the execution of the armistice and the Leiningen ministry resigned. But the Opposition did not succeed in forming a new government, and so the National Assembly had to beat a retreat: on 16 September it was resolved to put no further obstacles in the way of the armistice.

These circumstances damaged the prestige of the National Assembly and the republicans exploited this to bring about a revolution which aimed at setting up a democratic socialist republic. Intensive agitation began, and on 18 September there were violent street battles in Frankfurt. Federal troops were called in and the rising was put down. Two members of the Assembly, Felix, Prince Lichnowsky and General Hans von Auerswald, were killed and both troops and insurgents had many dead and wounded.

The revolutionary party had made preparations for risings in many other places. On 21 September Struve crossed the frontier from Basle with a small band of sympathisers, weapons having been sent on ahead. In Baden, where he was greeted by cheering crowds, he proclaimed a socialist republic, called up all men capable of bearing arms, confiscated state funds and forced Jews and rich people to pay him money. Though the movement quickly spread, Struve was defeated at Staufen by Badenese troops; he himself escaped.

The September rising did much to strengthen reaction, as was soon to be evident in Austria and Prussia.

THE PRUSSIAN NATIONAL ASSEMBLY

The elections in Prussia on 1 May were to seats not only in the Frankfurt Assembly but the Prussian National Assembly as well. Even in its composition the Prussian Assembly differed very much from the Frankfurt Parliament. In the case of the latter the voters often attached importance to giving their mandate to a person of distinction and prominence without always scrutinising too closely his political alignment. The level of education was higher in Frankfurt than in Berlin. The ordinary people had greater influence in Berlin than in Frankfurt; the lower middle class was more strongly represented in the

Prussian capital, with correspondingly fewer aristocrats. Many of the judges and officials in the Berlin Assembly had radical convictions. A considerable group termed themselves *Bauern* (farmers), though some of these cultivated only very little land and were more farmworkers than landowners. A small number of members could neither read nor write.

The comparatively big influence wielded by the Left in the Prussian Parliament rested partly on the capability and prestige of its members. The leading figure among the radicals was the redoubtable Benedikt Waldeck, a senior judge, who came from Catholic Westphalia and whose popularity had won him the sobriquet of *Bauernkönig* (King of the Peasants). Both his character and his learning compelled admiration, even from his opponents. Ranged alongside him were Johann Jacoby, a Jewish lawyer from East Prussia, and the public prosecutor, Temme.

Ludolf Camphausen, a prominent liberal from the Rhenish bourgeoisie, was Prime Minister, and now laid before the Prussian National Assembly a draft constitution on the French and Belgian model which provided for two chambers. The draft was handed over to the constitutional committee, of which Waldeck was the chairman, and there remodelled in a democratic sense.

The summer months passed very stormily in Berlin. Unemployment was rife and there were many radical agitators working to inflame and spread a mood of revolution. The civic militia either could not or would not fufil their task of keeping order. The fact that the citizens were armed embittered the workers and on 14 June they stormed the arsenal and seized the weapons stored there. These persistent excesses forced Camphausen's resignation. Another Rhenish industrialist, David Hansemann, was the key figure in the new ministry. Rudolf von Auerswald became Prime Minister. Many democratic members found the disorders highly distasteful, since they were obviously playing into the hands of reaction. An attempt was made by a series of measures to relieve unemployment and carry out reforms in order to calm public opinion, but with only temporary success. The future depended not only on how things turned out in Prussia but also in the neighbouring states, more especially the Habsburg Empire.

19

FURTHER REVOLUTIONARY MOVEMENTS
AND REACTION

AUSTRIA AND HUNGARY

The revolution of 1848 had unsettled the Habsburg Empire. In Vienna it was not the Government which ruled but the National Guard and the Academic Legion, which decided many legal and administrative matters without reference to the law. The National Guard, like the old militia (*Bürgerwehr*), consisted of armed middle-class citizens. The workers were excluded from it but they supported the Academic Legion – mostly students – and thus gave its activities the character of a mass movement. On 25 April the ministry published a draft constitution which did not go far enough for the democrats. The Government now announced its intention of dissolving the students' central committee and the National Guard, whereupon these bodies, supported by the masses, pressed their demands by action rather than words and forced the ministers to grant a *Reichstag* elected on a democratic basis. Shortly afterwards the Emperor and his family fled to Innsbruck. When the Government tried in vain to break up the Academic Legion by force of arms, the barricades went up and the revolutionaries formed a committee of public safety with which the Government dared not meddle. This committee, under the presidency of Adolf Fischhof, functioned in an exemplary manner; it preserved peace and order and the mass of unemployed were given building and excavation work to keep them occupied.

In Bohemia, too, a period of intensive political activity set in. On 11 March a great rally of Czechs was held in Prague; the usual constitutional demands were voiced and there was also a call for the unification of Bohemia, Moravia and Austrian Silesia within the framework of the monarchy, with the Czechs and Germans enjoying complete equality. The Emperor did promise to grant parity between the Czech and German languages, but he wanted the question of unification to be laid before the coming *Reichstag* for a decision. In the event, the

Estates of Moravia and Silesia formally protested against union with Bohemia.

The leading intellectual among the Czechs was the historian, Franz Palacky. When invited to join the committee which was preparing the ground for the Frankfurt National Assembly, he declined in a letter dated 11 April and managed to prevent the holding of elections in the Czech districts of Bohemia. He declared that the Bohemian territories were linked with the German only dynastically, and without prejudice to their independence and sovereignty. The plans so far announced in Frankfurt, he wrote, would inevitably lead to a weakening of the Austrian Empire, the preservation, integrity and strengthening of which was a vital interest not only of the Czechs but also of all Europe, indeed of humanity and civilisation. The Habsburg monarchy protected eastern Europe from the spread of the vast might of Russia, which was striving for universal sovereignty. He was wholeheartedly a Slav and no enemy of the Russian people, but no one was more decidedly against Russian domination than he. Singly the Danubian nations were not strong enough to resist Russia. 'Truly, if the Austrian Empire had not long since existed, then in the interests of Europe, in the interests of humanity itself, one would have to hasten to create it.' Austria had, unfortunately, severely weakened herself by not granting full equality to all her nationalities and religious communities, but it was still not too late to translate this principle of justice into reality. The efforts being made in Frankfurt were incompatible with the existence of Austria. Instead of an *Anschluss* of Austria with Germany, Germany should, rather, unite herself with Austria on the basis of full equality for all nations or, if this were impracticable, Austria and Germany should form independent states and then conclude a permanent alliance for joint defence and, if possible, a customs union.

On 2 June a congress assembled in Prague under Palacky's chairmanship to which representatives of all the Slav nations within the Empire were invited, as well as a few guests. Its aim was the unification of all Slavs to counterbalance both the German National Assembly and the Hungarian *Reichstag*. Palacky argued in support of his Austro-Slav viewpoint, while Michael Bakunin, a Russian, and Libelt, a Pole from Posen, took up an attitude hostile to Austria. It was soon apparent that there were considerable differences among the Slavs. Finally, a proclamation to the peoples of Europe was decided on in which the Slavs' love of peace and freedom was contrasted with the militaristic expansionism and despotism of the Latin and German races. Austria should be transformed into a federation of nations with equal rights. The deliberations ended prematurely when riots broke out.

The Czech students in Prague tried to play the same role as the

Academic Legion in Vienna and when Alfred, Prince Windischgrätz, who commanded the troops in the city, refused their demands the barricades went up. When Windischgrätz appeared, shots were fired, one of which killed his wife, who was standing at a window of their house. Windischgrätz finally reduced the city to complete submission by bombardment.

The Italian rising against Austrian rule enjoyed great sympathy among the liberals and democrats in many countries, notably England and France, as well as in Germany. The Hungarian Diet refused to authorise the despatch of troops to fight in Italy. At the outset the Austrian Government declared its readiness to free Lombardy completely and allow Venetia to become a free and independent state under an Austrian prince, but various diplomatic démarches failed, as this offer did not satisfy the Italians. In July Field-Marshal Radetzky inflicted a crushing defeat on the Italian forces and on 9 August an armistice was concluded. Radetzky's victories were greeted with enthusiasm among wide circles in Austria. They revived faith in the future of the Empire, though it must be admitted that the influence of military circles on politics was now strengthened.

Developments in Hungary confronted the monarchy with its hardest test. When the news of the revolution in Paris and the fall of Metternich reached Hungary, the radical Magyar deputy, Kossuth, made demands for what amounted to the separation of Hungary from Austria and the former's complete independence; hitherto she had already enjoyed internal autonomy.

All that the Crown and its advisers could do was to meet Kossuth's demands to a very large extent, though they did stipulate that Hungary should pay a reasonable share of interest on the common national debt. On 23 March an independent Hungarian ministry was formed, headed by Count Ludwig Batthyany and including Szechenyi, Déak and Kossuth. On 16 April the King and court came to Pressburg (Bratislava), where a number of new laws received the royal assent and were published. As well as some fundamental political innovations, they contained some highly beneficial social provisions, largely inspired by Déak. But Kossuth, who was Finance Minister, was totally unwilling to make any contribution to the national debt and soon afterwards he authorised the printing of Hungarian banknotes. He provoked the hostility of the Slav peoples in Hungary by his emphasis on Magyar predominance. Both the Serbs and the Croats sought to make themselves as independent as possible of Hungary and clashed with the Government. The Croats found an energetic leader in Joseph, Baron Jellačič, the Ban of Croatia. Pillersdorf had lost the confidence of the revolutionary faction and resigned. In July a government was formed

I

which was predominantly liberal; at its head was the aged Baron
Johann Philipp von Wessenberg, who also took over foreign affairs,
and he was supported by Doblhoff (interior), Bach (justice), Krauss
(finance), Hornbostel (trade), Schwarzer (public works) and Latour
(war).

The Reichstag

The *Reichstag* was opened on 22 July in Vienna. Most of the members
were Slavs, many of whom understood only a little German. The
Czechs formed the backbone of the Right and the Germans of the Left.
In the Centre were mustered the Tyroleans and other elements loyal
to the Emperor. The business of the Assembly was conducted in German.
The Italians were allowed to address the chamber in their own language
and, on application by a minimum of ten members, any matter which
was to be put to the vote could be translated into any other desired
language. At the *Reichstag's* request the Court returned to Vienna on 12
August. The most urgent question facing the *Reichstag*, and one forced
on its attention by countless petitions, was that of freeing the peasants
from feudal dues and services as well as the patrimonial justice of the
landowners, to all of which they were still subject. On 7 September the
relationship of servitude and patrimonial justice were annulled. All
dues were to be abolished in return for moderate compensation. The
peasants had thus achieved what they wanted and most of them now
lost interest in the *Reichstag*.

Meanwhile political sentiment among the middle classes had swung
round. They were weary of the constant disorders, angry at the assumption of the role of national leaders by callow students and irritated
by the windy rhetoric and agitation of journalists. Business was bad
and unemployment rife, and poverty provoked the workers to riots
which the middle-class civic militia put down by armed force. This
reinforced class hatred and gave agitators a chance to inflame the
workers' passions still more. There was a strong impression that the
more prudent deputies were powerless against the demagogues of
the street and the press. Not only did the middle classes fear a social
revolution, but their consciousness of being Austrian made any extreme
republicanism or nationalism unpalatable. Grillparzer's change in
attitude from what it was in pre-revolutionary days to what it later
became was typical. To give full rein to national aspirations – and this
also applied to the Germans in the Empire – must inevitably lead to
Austria's collapse. German students and many German intellectuals
proudly displayed the black, red and gold colours which symbolised
German unity, and despised those who sported the Habsburg black and
yellow. They sympathised with all Austria's enemies, even if these

hated the Germans. In order to join the German *Reich* many would gladly have left most of the non-Germans in the Danubian Empire to go their own way. The fact that millions of Germans lived intermingled with Slavs, Hungarians and Wallachians was shrugged aside. This, many thought, could easily be sorted out as between good republican neighbours. The cautious attitude of Palacky and his following, which comprised the majority of the Czechs, had at the outset found a ready response from many German Bohemians, as he himself recognised. Meanwhile a radicalism had developed among the Germans of the Left which was directed against his conservative viewpoint and the danger of a Slav majority, and at the same time, there were radicals among the Slavs who contributed to hostility towards the Germans.

War between Hungary and Croatia

The conflict between Hungary and Croatia now threatened to erupt into open warfare after attempts at mediation between the Hungarian Government and the Austrian Court had foundered on Kossuth's profound mistrust of the Habsburg Empire and its statesmen.

On 11 September Jellačič crossed from Croatia into Hungary with 36,000 Croatian troops; simultaneously the Slovaks and Wallachians rose against Hungary, which was already locked in combat with the Serbs. At this critical moment Kossuth tried to win over the Austrian people as allies against the 'treacherous court' for a joint struggle against absolutism. A deputation of Hungarian members of parliament and magnates travelled to Vienna to establish contact with the *Reichstag*, but the Slav majority in the *Reichstag* refused to see them, and therefore they were all the more enthusiastically greeted and fêted by the democrats of Vienna. After secret negotiations with a few conservative Hungarian magnates, the Court decided to send General Count Lamberg to Hungary. He was to take over supreme command of all troops, both Hungarian and Croatian, end the civil war and have a new Hungarian Government formed. Despite the resistance of the Prime Minister, Kossuth succeeded in mobilising the Hungarian *Reichstag* against the Lamberg mission. The *Reichstag* prohibited Lamberg from taking over command of the Hungarian armed forces, saying that if he did so he would be a traitor. This move stirred up such fanatical feeling that on the next day Lamberg was brutally murdered.

An Imperial decree now dissolved the Hungarian Diet and annulled its unratified measures. The Emperor appointed General Recsey as Prime Minister and Jellačič as commander-in-chief of the Hungarian forces. The Diet transferred the executive power to the defence committee, of which Kossuth was president, and he thus exercised supreme power.

The October Revolution in Vienna

When the War Minister, Count Latour, wanted to send Austrian troops to Jellačič as reinforcements, the Viennese democrats did all they could to prevent it. On 6 October street fighting broke out, in which the rioters gained the upper hand. Latour was murdered and his body barbarically mutilated. This was the beginning of the Vienna October revolution. Many ministers and deputies fled the city, as did the Emperor and the Court, who went with a strong military escort to the Moravian fortress of Olmütz. Political control was assumed by Felix, Prince Schwarzenberg, with the military backing of his brother-in-law Windischgrätz. On 23 October the latter began the siege of Vienna, and despite a brave defence the city finally surrendered. Jellačič and his Croats also had a part in this. The hopes of the democrats that Hungarian troops would save Vienna was not realised. After the city's capture, military courts were set up and condemned to death, among others, Robert Blum, the leader of the Left in the Frankfurt National Assembly. His execution aroused vast indignation in democratic circles in Germany.

The Austrian Court now decided to induce the ailing Emperor Ferdinand to abdicate and replace him by his 18-year-old nephew, Francis Joseph. The new Emperor was supported by a newly-formed, unified and energetic ministry under Schwarzenberg. Franz, Count Stadion, a moderate, was appointed Minister of the Interior, Alexander Bach, originally in the opposition, became Minister of Justice and a business man from Elberfeld, Karl Ludwig Bruck, Minister of Trade. The *Reichstag* was moved from Vienna to Kremsier, a small country town near Olmütz. Schwarzenberg read out to it a programme in which the Government supported 'honestly and without reserve' a constitutional monarchy. In March 1849 the Government published a constitution which was to come into force later. In contrast to the draft constitution of the *Reichstag*, this was to apply to Hungary as well. The whole Empire was declared to be a single customs and commercial area, which was an extremely practical move. A number of other Imperial decrees were published which would have achieved considerable progress if they had not very soon been modified or repealed. At all events the measure passed by the *Reichstag* for freeing the peasants from all feudal obligations was carried through. The *Reichstag* was then dissolved.

RADICALISM AND REACTION IN PRUSSIA

The victory of the revolution in the Berlin street fighting and the strength of democracy in the Prussian National Assembly had created an impression that reaction was impossible. In fact, however, the circles which clung to the feudal-absolutist and militaristic traditions of Prussia were more powerful than the champions of reform believed. In the first flush of national and libertarian enthusiasm, the traditional forces had been overpowered or had lain low, but gradually the nobility, which controlled the administration and the army, realised clearly what was at stake for their class. Moreover, there was a rift between large sections of the bourgeoisie and the workers, partly by reason of communist propaganda and partly through the terrorist activities of radical elements, largely drawn from the unemployed. Lastly, there was an upsurge of Prussian national sentiment against the German brand represented by the Frankfurt National Assembly.

In the course of 1848 it became clear that radicals and revolutionaries were not pursuing a uniform aim. While the enthusiasm of the intellectuals and some sections of the middle class was mainly for political freedom, that of the lower middle class and the proletariat was for social reforms which would serve their interests. The master craftsmen and their apprentices were by no means in favour of economic freedom in the liberal sense such as the intellectuals and well-to-do were demanding. Their ideals often bore a guild, reactionary hue. The workers were split; some were ensnared by downright communistic propaganda, while others pursued the aim of organising themselves in order to achieve better living conditions. Marx and Engels had proclaimed the dictatorship of the proletariat in the Communist Manifesto and in reality had nothing but scorn and mockery for liberalism and democracy. But Marx gave the word to support any movement directed against an existing government, hoping that this would provide a chance to foment revolution. The dividing lines between democracy, republicanism, socialism and communism were consequently very blurred, and at democratic congresses, demonstrations and disorders people whose aims were utterly dissimilar often worked together. In the eyes of the communists, the republicans and democrats constituted groups whom they hoped to convert or carry along with them, and in this they quite often succeeded. On the other hand, this now led many citizens to equate democracy and a republic with communism and socialism, and this was a useful weapon for the forces of reaction. The leaders of communism were, moreover, by no means proletarians; Marx and Engels themselves came from the bourgeoisie, and Engels was even a capitalist. But there were also many other non-proletarians who were enthusiastic about social revolution. One of the most active agitators for communism was the student Gustav Adolf Schlöffel, who published the journal *Der Volksfreund*. His father was a Silesian manufacturer, Friedrich Wilhelm Schlöffel, who sat in the Frankfurt National

Assembly and was a republican. The theory of socialism also inspired Karl Rodbertus, who was a wealthy landowner, and even, for a short time, a Prussian minister. A communist leader from the ranks of the proletariat was Wilhelm Weitling, who also published a journal in Berlin at this time. In it, however, he supported moderate policies, probably because he had no liking for violence. The policy of the Berlin compositor Stephan Born was practical and sober. Although he looked on himself as a disciple of Marx and was in constant touch with him, he put forward in his paper *Das Volk* a programme of comprehensive social reforms which had nothing Utopian about them and were later almost completely achieved. The Leftist groups in both the Frankfurt and Berlin Assemblies often adopted an attitude which grievously offended orthodox Prussian national sentiment. The democratic deputies were hostile to militarism in any form, Junkerdom and traditional Prussian patriotism alike. Their condemnation of the partitions of Poland and their support for the cession of extensive Prussian territories to the Poles were particularly irritating in their effects. The plan put forward in the Frankfurt National Assembly and the Prussian Government for dissolving and merging Prussia into Germany could not but deeply wound Prussian patriots. The black, red and gold flags and cockades tended to disappear more and more and were replaced by black and white ones.

It was very much in the interests of the nobility and those circles of army officers and officials largely drawn from it to combat the forces unleashed by the revolution. They founded various newspapers and enjoyed the support of one which was already in existence: the *Neue Preussische Zeitung*, popularly known as the *Kreuzzeitung*, because its title page displayed the Iron Cross (*Kreuz*). A league of landowners was formed, which, when in session, was known to the public at large as the *Junker Parliament*. The civic guard also changed its character, because bleak economic conditions of the day forced many democratic citizens without private means to retire from it in order to earn a living.

The Constitutional Crisis

In Schweidnitz on 31 July some trifling incident gave rise to a clash between the civic militia and the army and many citizens were killed or wounded. Doubtless the army was to blame and the ministry took this into account. Besides this, the Government had recently threatened officials with dismissal if they acted against the new system of government. The Left in the Prussian Assembly now demanded the removal of reactionary officers from the army, and this led to a conflict over competence, for the King exercised authority as Commander-in-Chief. After further grave disorders the Auerswald–Hansemann administration, which sought in vain to mediate between the Crown and the National Assembly, resigned. The King now appointed General von Wrangel Commander-in-Chief of the troops in and around Berlin, a sinister omen. He made the aged General Ernst von Pfuel Prime Minister and War Minister, but was very much mistaken if he was expecting Pfuel to lend his good name to give respectability to reactionary policies. Pfuel was a highly cultivated, progressive man, who worked in precisely the opposite direction. He even achieved a solution of the conflict which had brought down the previous government by issuing on 25 September, to everyone's surprise, an order to the generals 'not to tolerate reactionary tendencies in the army and to foster to the full extent of their powers good relations between the civil population and the military'. The King approved a series of progressive measures passed by the National Assembly, one of which ensured the protection of personal freedom (habeas corpus). Hunting rights were abolished without any compensation.

Meanwhile, after long consultations, the constitutional committee had discussed the Government's draft constitution and altered it in some essential respects. Their recommendations showed what form of constitution the majority of the deputies had in mind. On the one hand it was recognised that the constitution rested on an agreement between the King and the representatives of the people, which disposed of the republican view that sovereignty lay with the people alone. On the other hand, the rights of the King were very limited. In the plenum it was resolved, by 217 votes to 124, to delete from the King's title the words 'by the grace of God' a resolution which wounded the King deeply. The rights of the nobility were to be restricted. The committee recommended that the King should take an oath to respect the constitution – this had long been the legal practice in many German countries – and should possess only a very limited and suspensive veto.

The great majority of members did not want a fresh revolution, although they believed that if one broke out they could master it – a fatal miscalculation. Those who supported appeasement were under pressure from the radicals and the street mob.

From the end of September onwards there were constant disorders in the streets of Berlin which the civic militia (*Bürgerwehr*) could put down only with difficulty. Some of them refused to intervene. In the fighting ten workers were killed, many were wounded and the militia itself had some losses. The militia, consisting mainly of members of the middle class, was thus set at odds with the workers. At the end of October a democratic congress intending to unite all republicans took place in Berlin. The debates were so stormy that the chairman, G. Fein, soon resigned and the journalist Ludwig Bamberger – subsequently a

member of the *Reichstag* – was voted into the chair. He too relinquished
the post soon after and left the congress. The main antagonism was
between democrats and socialists, and within each of these groups there
were also considerable divergencies of opinion. Weitling declared:
'Democracy and military rule both amount to the same thing: only in
the immediate setting up of a communist state is there any sense'. The
Leftist deputy Temme later declared in his memoirs that the congress
had probably been the most injudicious, arrogant and crude ever held in
Germany. Bamberger wrote a leading article in May 1849, in which he
bemoaned the fact that at all German democratic congresses and in all
newspapers and assemblies, squabbles over 'questions of principle'
formed the main occupation of German democrats.

The Prime Minister Pfuel resigned after refusing the King's demand
to declare a state of siege in Berlin. In the streets there were constant
disorders, ministers and deputies were insulted and threatened and the
militia had to intervene. The King now entrusted his uncle, Count
Brandenburg, with the formation of a new ministry. Its leading spirit
was Otto, Baron Manteuffel, a moderate conservative official who played
an important role in the Government for ten years. The National
Assembly objected and sought the appointment of a ministry in which
the Parliament could have confidence. An all-party deputation was
received by the King, who listened to a respectfully-worded address but
refused any discussion, whereupon the Leftist deputy, Johann Jacoby,
called out to him: 'It is the misfortune of kings that they will not
hear the truth'. On 9 November the King transferred the Assembly to
the provincial town of Brandenburg on the grounds that in Berlin it was
under pressure from the street. The Assembly declared this to be
illegal and continued its deliberations. On the next day Wrangel's
troops marched into Berlin, the civic militia was dissolved, their
weapons called in and a state of siege proclaimed. The members of the
Assembly who had remained in Berlin decided that the Government
was not entitled to levy taxes while Parliament could not meet un-
molested in the capital. The sittings were broken up by the troops.
There were some disorders but the efforts of the democrats to unleash a
general revolution were unsuccessful.

The question of what was next to be done was hotly disputed among
the leading statesmen. The ministers and other influential figures like
Radowitz advised the King against a *coup d'état* and the dissolution of
Parliament. It was not only strictly conservative observers who took
the view that the Prussian Parliament had put itself in the wrong by
adopting the motion to refuse to levy taxes. The Frankfurt National
Assembly, which had previously urged the Prussian Government to
conciliate Parliament, now pronounced its decision to refuse to raise

taxes null and void, though at the same time it had recently been hoping for the appointment of a more popular ministry in Berlin. Several leading members of the Frankfurt Parliament, notably von Gagern, hurried to Berlin to prevent a reactionary catastrophe. Gagern also sought to prepare the King for his election as Emperor by the Frankfurt National Assembly. To be sure, the group of Frankfurt deputies which wished to make the King of Prussia head of the German *Reich* did not wish by that token to secure the hegemony for Prussia, whose militaristic traditions, Junkerdom and close connection with Tsarism by no means met with their approval and were odious to wide circles of the German people. The belief that Prussia must be merged in Germany meant, for those in Frankfurt who supported it, that Prussia must not remain a centralised state but should be broken up into its provinces or at least very considerably loosened up. There should be *Landtage* in the individual provinces but the Parliament for all Prussia should vanish and hand over its tasks to the German Parliament.[1] In any case there existed a strong rivalry between the Assemblies in Frankfurt and Berlin and so the crisis in the Berlin Parliament obviously called for a thorough discussion and agreement between the leaders in both bodies.

For many Prussian statesmen, even those who were conservative, the ideas of Gagern and his friends were very tempting. The suppression of all liberties and a military despotism on the Austrian pattern would, of course, have competely wrecked such plans. It was therefore important to find some middle course between the demands of the extreme conservatives and the liberals. Any immediate changeover to a policy of repression would not only have made an understanding with Frankfurt impossible but it would have strengthened those elements which were working in many places towards a fresh revolution. Gagern's plans foundered on the difficulty of reconciling the traditional mould of the Prussian State with his ideas. Prussia had probably advanced further along the path to a well-defined nationality than most other states. Anything tending to loosen the structure of the State would have given full scope to the forces of subversion. To old conservatives like the Gerlachs, born and bred in the tradition of the Estates, the German National Movement was written off as the 'German swindle'. The sense of being Prussian was even more strongly marked in men like Bismarck. It will be seen how he sought to reconcile the Prussian and German concepts of nationality.

The December Constitution
The Prussian Government finally decided to dissolve Parliament and to proclaim on 5 December a constitution which was imposed (*oktroyiert*),

[1] Cf. especially Meinecke: *Weltbürgertum*, pp. 374 ff.

though it was subject to revision by the two newly-elected chambers in agreement with the Government. The King had long resisted any such move and the compromise was largely the work of Count Brandenburg's ministry, in which Manteuffel played a key role. The constitution was surprisingly liberal. It adopted almost verbatim many provisions in the draft earlier worked out by the parliamentary constitutional committee but added clauses which strengthened the royal power and the rights of the Government. A new article, No. 105, laid down: 'When the chambers are not sitting, in cases of emergency and on the collective responsibility of the ministry decrees can be enacted which shall have the force of law; but they are to be laid before the chambers for ratification immediately they next meet.' These emergency powers were at once invoked. The privileged legal position enjoyed by nobles and officials and the landowners' patrimonial jurisdiction over their peasants in Silesia were repealed and oral proceedings in public with a jury were introduced for criminal cases. The franchise for the second chamber was no longer for 'every Prussian' but for 'every independent Prussian'.

The new Parliament was opened in February 1849 with a majority of moderates. But when, on a motion by Rodbertus, the second chamber accepted the Frankfurt constitution for the *Reich* and protested against the continuance of the state of siege, it came into conflict with the Government and was dissolved in April. The Government now made fresh use of its emergency powers and introduced the triple-class franchise, whereby the electorate was divided into three classes, each of which produced a third of the taxes and had to choose in open election the same number of electors. This system put the richer voters at a great advantage and the poorer at a corresponding disadvantage. The democrats declared it to be illegal and abstained from voting. At the next election the conservative party gained a majority, the liberals were more weakly represented and the democrats completely absent. The second chamber contained many state officials. With this Parliament the revision of the constitution was carried through. The King raised constant difficulties and took his oath to respect the constitution only after long hesitation.

20

THE CONSTITUTION OF THE *REICH* – CHOOSING AN EMPEROR – THE END OF A CHAPTER

GROSSDEUTSCH AND *KLEINDEUTSCH*

The thorniest constitutional problem was how far and in what form Austria, herself a large and mainly non-German empire, was to be associated with Germany. Over the question 'Austria or Prussia?' the parties divided into two main currents of opinion which later came to be known as *grossdeutsch* and *kleindeutsch*. The first group, largely made up of Southern Germans and Catholics, wanted Austria to fill the leading role, while the second supported Prussian hegemony. Deep-rooted feelings prevented any rationally negotiated solution; only the path of force remained open and this Bismarck later took.

THE FUNDAMENTAL RIGHTS

At the end of December 1848 the fundamental rights (*Grundrechte*) of the German people were proclaimed as an Imperial Law. These were no mere statements of abstract principles but represented an effort to eliminate countless violations of liberty, equality and humanity – violations hitherto rife and without redress in the states of the *Bund*. Such attempts at removing abuses had the incidental effect of furthering national unity, for the people at large were far more interested in questions like this than in constitutional matters, which did not affect most of them and on which they were often not competent to pass judgement. The new law laid down that no state might adopt any measure which conflicted with these basic rights. Every German received common civil rights along with his particular ones; that is to say, he was now a citizen not only of Prussia or Austria but also of Germany. This gave him the right to live where he chose, acquire property, carry on a trade, accept employment, belong to a municipality or parish (*Gemeinde*) and vote at elections. No state might treat citizens of another German state less favourably than its own. Emigration was to be free and not subject to any tax. All men were equal before the law; the nobility was abolished as an estate. No German might accept a decoration from a foreign state. Public offices were open to all with the necessary educational qualifications. Military service was universal and could not be discharged by proxy. No one could be arrested without legal sanction and the preferment of a precise charge, and he had to be given into legal custody. The capital penalty was severely restricted and corporal punishment abolished. House searches and the confiscation of papers required a warrant. The privacy of correspondence was guaranteed. Anyone might express his opinions freely by the spoken or written word and censorship and similar restrictions were forbidden. Press offences were to be heard before juries. Everyone enjoyed full freedom of belief and conscience. The possession of civil rights did not depend upon membership of any specific religious denomination; equality was thus granted to Jews as well. Every religious community was autonomous, none was to enjoy special privileges and there was to be no established church. The civil validity of marriage was to depend solely on the completion of a civil act; the church ceremony might take place only after this. Difference of religion was no civil bar to marriage. Scientific research and teaching were unrestricted. Except for religious instruction, education was to be supervised by the State and no longer by the clergy. Anyone who could prove that he possessed the necessary aptitude could set up a school or teach in one, and sufficient schools were to be built everywhere. Elementary education was to be compulsory and free, and in other public educational institutions those without means would not have to pay anything. All Germans had the right to assemble peaceably and without weapons and to belong to societies – even soldiers, provided that military discipline was not prejudiced. Property was declared inviolable and could be expropriated only in the general interest and in return for fair compensation. A law of copyright was introduced. Land could be transferred to another owner or divided up, and entailment was to be abolished. All feudal rights, such as patrimonial justice and police, services and dues and hunting rights were terminated without compensation; other rights could be redeemed. Everyone might hunt on his own land. All jurisdiction was in the hands of the State. The exercise of judicial powers was completely removed from any governmental control; political offences were to be heard before a jury.

Although the codification of these fundamental rights freed the people from many fetters of the feudal and absolutist past, they were not accepted by all states as legally binding.

In many states one of the greatest obstacles to economic and social progress arose from the restrictions on trade imposed by the guilds and other institutions. The mood of the artisans who formed a large section of the urban voters was opposed to any progressive reform. They indulged in much propaganda, held conferences and swamped the National Assembly with petitions. Many of them were against factories and machines and non-guild labour.

The National Assembly included many experts in the field of economic and social policy, and some of these cherished progressive social aims. The Assembly's economic committee performed very creditable work, as its reports and recommendations show, but it was hampered by having to take account of particularism, which was still strong, and had to be content with a mere supervisory role in the most important economic questions of the *Reich*, leaving their final settlement to the individual states.

It was widely hoped that the building of a German fleet would broaden Germany's horizons and overcome the narrow philistinism of the small states. Herwegh's view (already quoted) was that with a fleet of her own Germany could reach the status of a world power. Support was manifested by many voluntary collections, but actually building the navy was far more difficult than its enthusiasts ever dreamed. The *Reich* ministry therefore contented itself with modest plans, and even these for the most part came to nothing. One of the obstacles was the attitude of Prussia and Austria. Austria had her own fleet, which was reserved for use in Adriatic and Mediterranean waters, and declared that she had thereby discharged her obligations. Prussia wanted to build a fleet of her own to serve her own policies and was therefore not in favour of a German fleet. A fleet would, moreover, have demanded far more money than the *Reich* Government had at its disposal. It depended on contributions from the individual states, which were disinclined to make them. The same obstacle faced the setting up of an Imperial military force, since the contributions requested for this purpose were in almost every case not forthcoming. That other naval powers, Britain in particular, should seek to prevent the building of a German fleet is understandable, but this antagonism has often been exaggerated by German historians.

THE IMPERIAL CONSTITUTION AND THE CHOICE OF AN EMPEROR

On 19 October the debate on a constitution for the *Reich* began. The events of the next few weeks in Austria, especially the unification of all the lands of the Habsburg monarchy into one vast state on 27 November, disappointed the *grossdeutsch* party's hopes both of an association of the German parts of the Austrian Empire with the rest of Germany and of

Austria's predominance in Germany. The inclusion of the whole Habsburg monarchy, with its non-German majority, in a federal German state was out of the question, as it could not be reconciled with the founding of a German national state. The draft of the Frankfurt constitution laid down that no part of the German *Reich* could be united into a state with non-German territories, and that links between the *Reich* and such lands would have to be confined to a personal union of crowns. Gagern proposed that the countries of Germany should form a close association (*engerer Bund*) and that the latter should then conclude a permanent and indissoluble confederation with the whole Austrian monarchy (*weiterer Bund*). This idea, which had been canvassed before – by Austria in fact – met violent opposition, and Gagern found himself obliged to withdraw provisionally his amendment on these lines. For a time, moreover, the Left considered the break-up of Austria both desirable and inevitable, and this would have made possible the incorporation of her German territories in the new state.

The ruthless suppression of the Vienna rising aroused great bitterness against reactionary Austria, though Prussia's prestige also suffered through her own constitutional conflict. In any case, a swing to the *kleindeutsch* view ensued among the parties and in consequence the Austrian Schmerling resigned from the Imperial Ministry of which he was President. Gagern succeeded him and Eduard Simson, a highly respected jurist of Jewish origin, was elected to Gagern's previous post of President of the National Assembly. Gagern laid his *kleindeutsch* programme before the Assembly, which approved it by the narrow margin of 261 votes to 224. At this time the Austrians often voted with the Left. The main point of Gagern's programme was once again a Prussian-led *engerer Bund* and a *weiterer Bund* including Austria. Although it was known that Frederick William of Prussia was disinclined to become emperor, it was hoped that his intimates and ministers would get him to change his mind.

Events soon showed that Gagern's programme would run into considerable difficulties. The Austrian Prime Minister Schwarzenberg, wanted to weld the whole multinational Habsburg empire into one compact state and at the same time maintain Austria's predominance in Germany. The plan for Prussian hegemony met strong resistance from a number of states in the *Bund*, especially those in the south. The Prussian Government managed to persuade the reluctant King to agree to a circular despatch (23 January 1849) to all German governments, which went a long way towards meeting the views of the Frankfurt Parliament and Gagern's programme. It was proposed from a number of sides that the leadership of the federation to be formed should not be entrusted to an emperor but to a directorium, which Austria and Prussia would preside over by turns and in which the bigger states of the *Bund* should also be represented. A note of 9 March 1849, addressed by Schwarzenberg to the Austrian plenipotentiary Schmerling, now demanded the admission of the whole Austrian Empire into the *Bund*, with Austria as permanent president of the directorium. It was clear from this note that Schwarzenberg was aiming not only at a renewal of the German *Bund* but also at its domination by an Austria which had returned to absolutism and in which two-thirds of its subjects were non-German.

This proposal aroused the greatest indignation among the deputies. Schmerling's answer to Schwarzenberg was a request to be relieved of his post. Welcker, hitherto a zealous *grossdeutsch* enthusiast and a vehement opponent of Prussian hegemony, moved the immediate adoption of the draft constitution and the offer of the crown to the King of Prussia as hereditary emperor. The motion was defeated by a small margin. Gagern and his ministry resigned but carried on official business until a new ministry was formed. A majority for the choice of emperor was made possible by the fact that the liberal 'hereditary emperor' party promised a small group of democrats a democratic franchise as a reward for their support, though the majority of the Left steered clear of this compromise, which seemed to them a betrayal of democratic principles. In any case, concessions like these made it difficult for a prince of strongly monarchical convictions to accept the imperial dignity.

The Frankfurt Parliament's draft constitution formed a well-reasoned whole which, even though it failed to secure adoption at the time, remained an important model for later German constitutions.[1] It left individual states with wide autonomy. The *Reich* would completely control foreign affairs, diplomacy, the decision on war and peace and the supreme command of the army and navy. In legislation the *Reich* was to have a very extensive competence. The *Reichstag* was to consist of two houses, one representing the states and one the nation as a whole, the first being composed of representatives of the various countries and elected half by the governments and half by the chambers. A law would need the assent of both houses. The Government would have only a suspensive veto. There would be an Imperial Court of Law (*Reichsgericht*) which was to decide mainly constitutional and political issues but not civil or criminal cases. The executive power and internal administration were to be divided between the *Reich* and the constituent countries. The implementation of Imperial Laws would lie with the

[1] Cf. the detailed study in Ernst Rudolf Huber, *Deutsche Verfassungsgeschichte*, Vol. II, pp. 817 ff., and, on the franchise, pp. 787 ff.

Emperor and the Imperial Government and the ministers would be responsible to the *Reichstag*. Regulations governing election to the People's House were laid down in the Imperial electoral law. All male Germans of good character aged twenty-five and upwards would have the vote. Election was to be secret and direct. On 28 March the National Assembly chose Frederick William as Emperor by 290 votes, with 248 abstentions and 29 deputies absent. A deputation left for Berlin to offer him the crown and was received in audience on 3 April. Simson, who led the deputation, addressed the King, who made an impromptu reply, thanking the National Assembly for the confidence with which they had honoured him but declaring that he could make no decision unless the princes and Free Cities signified their assent and the constitution was approved by the governments of the individual states. The deputation was considerably taken aback, though various influential personages at court, and even the heir to the throne, did not regard the King's answer as final. On the very day of this meeting a despatch went out to the Prussian diplomats accredited to the German courts which sounded more promising. It contained the statement that, since the *Reichsverweser* wished to lay down his office, the King was provisionally prepared to direct German affairs and also to take over the permanent presidency of a federal state made up of countries which had voluntarily joined it. The King's somewhat ambiguous attitude was rooted in a number of causes. Personally, he hated democracy and revolution, and he was confirmed in this by the influence of Austria, Russia and the German kings. The great majority of his ministers, however, favoured his unconditional, or at least conditional, acceptance of the offer, and so did the two Prussian chambers. On 14 April, twenty-eight governments representing almost all the small states declared collectively under pressure from public opinion their agreement with the Frankfurt constitution and the choice of emperor. The four kingdoms shrouded themselves in silence and Austria brusquely dissented. Thus the approval of at least some of the governments was given, even though that of the most important was lacking. The Frankfurt deputy Beckerath, who was an intimate of Frederick William, tried to make him change his mind, but the King replied: 'If you could have addressed your eloquent words to Frederick the Great, he would have been the man for you; I am no great ruler'. One must, of course, bear in mind that, with the exception of Britain, all the great powers and many of the smaller ones were against a unified Germany led by Prussia, while Russia and Austria were against a democratic – or even a moderately liberal – Germany. On 28 April, the Prussian Government finally informed the *Reichsverweser* and the National Assembly that the King declined their offer, but added that it was still possible to reach a negotiated agreement on the constitution. The number of members in the Frankfurt Assembly sank steadily, since first Austria and then Prussia withdrew their deputies. Many moderates departed of their own accord, and consequently it was mostly Leftist deputies who remained. The Gagern ministry finally resigned on 10 May. The radical majority in the Assembly now decided on the election of a provisional *Reich* regency. Meanwhile a revolutionary movement spread in many areas. The rump Assembly withdrew to Stuttgart on 30 May, but there it was soon prevented by military force from continuing its sittings.

FURTHER RISINGS AND THE END

For months a fresh revolution had been expected by the radicals; many preparations were made but there was no unity of aim, no central direction and a shortage of arms. The property-owning middle class was alarmed by the active communist propaganda and the many riots which broke out, but among the petty bourgeoisie, broad sections of the workers, Gymnasts and intellectuals the revolution had many supporters. Disorders occurred in the Rhineland; arsenals were stormed, barricades set up and in many places the militia (*Landwehr*) mutinied. The *Bürgerwehr* and the military restored order. Things looked serious in Saxony; a hundred barricades went up in Dresden and Richard Wagner was one who helped to build them. The King fled from the capital, and the battles in the streets were finally won by Prussian troops, who gave no quarter. A large part of the country, however, was unaffected by the revolution. Soon afterwards troops mutinied in Baden, the Grand Duke fled and a revolutionary government was set up. In Bavaria, too, there existed a strong movement for recognising the democratic constitution which had already been achieved in Württemberg. In the Swabian and Franconian provinces of Bavaria the movement assumed a particularly threatening form and revolution broke out in the Palatinate. Many soldiers went over to the rebels and a revolutionary government was formed which ordered arms and ammunition from abroad. The setting up and control of the civic militia (*Volkswehr*) ran into great difficulties, especially as the leaders were at loggerheads. At the end of May the insurgents suffered a reverse at the hands of a Prussian general, and in June the Prince of Prussia, Frederick William's eldest brother, arrived with strong Prussian forces and finally conquered them. Those who could not make good their escape were brought before a military tribunal which left some bitter memories behind. In the years which followed a stream of emigrants left for America.

WAS THE REVOLUTION BOUND TO FAIL?

The question of why the huge movement of 1848, which countless Germans had served with so much enthusiasm, exertion and sacrifice, finally collapsed has met with the most varied answers. Many have believed that the struggle between monarchy and democracy or the class struggle between bourgeoisie and proletariat ended in the victory of the stronger. Impartial consideration of all the factors leads one to conclude that the obstacles which had accumulated over centuries along the path to unity and freedom could not be surmounted in a short time. Those nations who reached their goal earlier had taken generations to do so, and they were helped by natural and historical circumstances from which the 1848 movement in Germany did not benefit.

Such questions lend themselves to infinite argument. It is not intended to examine here more than one or two views which later changed the modes of thought and action of many of those concerned, for quite a number did learn by experience. Unity and liberty were generally the main avowed aims, but in some situations it often turned out that these concepts were variously understood and that for the most part they could not be realised simultaneously and completely but only piecemeal, one after the other, and even then differently from what had been hoped. There were many who held that freedom should come first and then unity, while others thought it possible to reverse the order. Differing ideas of what unity meant often proved to be at variance with one another. In theory, everyone was above all else a German, but in practice he was primarily a Prussian or an Austrian or a Bavarian. Particularism went very deep and could not be uprooted overnight. Religious, economic and other interests also played their part. The Austrian Germans were worst off, for they faced the question whether they belonged first and foremost to the multinational Danubian Empire, in which they were only a minority, or to the German national state still to be founded, in which mighty Prussia would always be Austria's greatest rival.

The draft constitution of the Berlin Assembly, even more than the Frankfurt one, had many democratic features. It deserves every credit when viewed from the standpoint of human rights and morality, but rather less when looked at from that of politics (which, after all, is the art of the possible), for its radical-democratic tendency provoked the resistance of both the monarchy and the aristocracy, and this proved the undoing of the whole work. This is one of those instances where asking a little less would have secured much more, for more moderate demands would more easily have met with the approval of the established powers and could have been expanded and improved as opportunity offered. The radical deputies were, however, convinced that they were strong enough to maintain their demands, even by means of a fresh revolution.

During the preliminary work in the Assembly it was a widely-debated question whether the constitutions should be drawn up in agreement with the German governments or solely according to the will of the representatives of the people. The moderate progressives were inclined to let the governments have their say, but the radicals dismissed this out of hand as an infringement of the sovereignty of the people. In consequence when the rulers unexpectedly found their hands strengthened – mainly through the activities of street-corner demagogues who would not be bridled – the result was that the forces of reaction had also gained strength and rejected the provisions of the constitutions.

The German parliaments set particular store by removing from royal titles the phrase 'by the grace of God', and this was taken in very bad part by the rulers. In England, for example, no one ever seems to have been concerned over this, for the words 'dei gratia' still appear today on the coinage along with the monarch's name and this does not seem to have impaired British liberty in any way.

This comparison with developments in England prompts the question of whether the Prussian democrats and liberals of 1848, despite their mainly admirable attitude, were not making a crucial error by, in a highly difficult situation, preferring uncompromising adherence to general principles to tactics of caution and compromise. One of the outstanding republican leaders of 1848, Dr Heinrich Bernhard Oppenheim, confessed twenty-four years later in his biography of Waldeck:[1] 'Certainly at that time a constitutional legal position could have been established if one had remained content with securing positive rights instead of infuriating and uniting all opposing forces by abstract dogmatism.'

British constitutional history shows that in England no general principles were laid down in advance but that decisions on individual cases were taken as they arose, and allowance was also made for custom. In any event the general conditions obtaining there were much more favourable than in Germany. As long as the British fleet ruled the seas, England had no need of a powerful army, and militarism in the continental sense could not develop, although this by no means excluded the exercise of power politics. In Prussia the military nobility were very strong and opposed parliamentarianism. That is not to say that all senior officers were reactionary; many were not interested in politics and some – like Generals von Pfuel and Willisen, who have already been mentioned in these pages – were supporters of markedly progressive

[1] Vide p. 254.

and humane ideas. Many younger Prussian officers from the nobility fought on the side of the republicans.[1] The attitude of the King constantly wavered. He was no lover of violence and his chief adviser Radowitz was utterly opposed to any breach of the constitution. The great majority of the ministers and other statesmen, indeed even Prince William, the King's brother, were prepared to come to an understanding on the constitutional issue, partly because the prospect of the Imperial Crown or at least of Prussian leadership was tempting.

The radicals, however, were sadly mistaken if they believed that a fresh revolution would put them in power. There were, it is true, parts of Germany where republican sentiment was widespread, especially in the south-west and on the Rhine; after all, it was here that Germany bordered on the French and Swiss republics, with whose German democrats there was a busy traffic. Considerable numbers of troops in these areas went over to the insurgents or sympathised with them. But there were also large areas of Germany where the situation was quite different, and in addition there was the internal cleavage of particularism. It is understandable that Badenese or Palatine troops had no wish to fire on their relatives. Germans from the north and the south, on the other hand, looked on each other as foreigners and had no such misgivings about fighting each other. The September rising in Frankfurt was partly suppressed by Austrian troops, who, because they were Czechs, did not understand the shouts of the insurgents inviting them to come over to their side. Whether Pomeranians and Swabians could easily communicate is doubtful. The democrats often tried to maintain good relations with the military by inviting soldiers to their meetings and fraternising with them over a glass of wine or a tankard of beer, but the military authorities soon contrived either to prevent this or to make it very difficult by transferring billets to outlying districts or arranging for exercises to be held while the meetings were on.

It was a long-cherished wish among the republicans to form a popular militia (*Volkswehr*). In the siege of Vienna, armed workers played a great part. But an army which was really well trained, equipped and led could not be created overnight. It took a long time, unremitting effort and special knowledge and skills. The Poles and Hungarians had at their disposal in their revolutions large numbers of troops trained by former governments. The German revolution did not last long enough to influence the army. When the German and Austrian republicans took up arms, they lacked strategically trained and seasoned forces and had to appoint Polish generals, who scarcely spoke a word of German. True, there were also native officers in their ranks but none of them possessed the capability and authority which the highly difficult situation

[1] Cf. Valentin, *Geschichte der deutschen Revolution 1848–9*, Vol. I, p. 500.

demanded. When the democrats refused to reach an understanding with those circles which controlled the military, they were making a grave mistake which finally proved fatal.

The main obstacle to national unity lay in the existence of two German great powers and four German kingdoms of medium size, all of which were resolved to acknowledge no other ruler than their own monarch. In this they could rely on the support of those sections of their peoples who really counted. Innumerable attempts at compromise showed that, at the most, only a loose confederation of states could emerge, and this was far removed from the ideal of national unity. This question could be solved only by force of arms. History shows that national unity has always and in all places been attained through war.

The goal of national freedom could be reached only through an understanding between the monarchical and the parliamentary power. Here the moderate liberals wanted to follow England's example and take the path of peaceful compromise. The democrats had the example of the French Revolution before their eyes (or, more exactly, of its Jacobin phase). In fact, the path of violent revolution did not lead to freedom but to a military dictatorship, first Napoleon I's and later Napoleon III's.

Finally, the creators of a united, free and powerful Germany would also have to come to terms with the other great powers. The main obstacle was Russia. The system prevailing there could not possibly tolerate a liberal Germany, the existence of which would have been a constant incitement for Russia's own peoples, especially the Poles, to rise against the Tsar's rule.

All these problems were left unresolved when the revolution came to an end.

21

AFTER THE REVOLUTION

AUSTRIA AND PRUSSIA IN THE STRUGGLE FOR UNITY

The high aims of the revolution had come to nothing but the struggle for unity and freedom went on. It was Frederick William IV, no less, who issued a manifesto on 15 May 1849 in which he held out to all Germans the prospect of unity and freedom on the basis of the *Reich* constitution worked out by the Frankfurt National Assembly, with a few modifications. The new draft was to be laid before a *Reichstag* for examination and approval. This could mean only one thing – a Federal State under Prussian leadership and in a close treaty relationship with Austria. This plan had been vigorously sponsored by Gagern and Radowitz, and negotiations beteween Prussia and Austria had begun after the Austrian revolution had been put down. Frederick William charged his friend Radowitz with their continuation. Radowitz dealt with relations with Austria in a memorandum which proposed an indissoluble alliance governed by international law and amounting to a 'union' between the Austrian monarchy and the German Federal State. Permanent peace was to prevail between them; any outside attack on either partner would be jointly repulsed and as far as possible a common economic area was to be created. Matters affecting the union were to be handled by a directorium under Austria's presidency, and the German Federal State was to be headed by the King of Prussia, supported by a college of princes.

These proposals were put before both the Austrian Government and a conference of German governments. The Austrian Prime Minister, Schwarzenberg, flatly rejected them; the idea of Prussian dominance in Germany was quite unacceptable to him. Much depended on the attitude of the secondary states. Bavaria was completely on the side of Austria, and on 26 May Prussia, Saxony and Hanover concluded the Three Kings' Alliance, which from the very outset was of doubtful viability. The plan was welcomed by many former members of the

Frankfurt Parliament in the *kleindeutsch* or 'hereditary emperor' party who had assembled in Gotha. At the end of September Austria and Prussia concluded the *Interim*, which gave them jointly the powers of the *Reichsverweser*. Soon Bavaria declined to join a union under Prussian leadership and in February 1850 Bavaria, Württemberg, Hanover and Saxony formed the Four Kings' Alliance, which aimed at reforming the *Bund*. Austria for her part wanted to join the new *Bund* along with all her lands and at the same time demanded admission to the German *Zollverein*, but this was unacceptable to Prussia.

On 20 March 1850 the Parliament provided for in the Prussian plan met at Erfurt, its lower house having been elected on the basis of the three-class franchise. The four Kingdoms were not represented at Erfurt, and so to begin with one had to rest content with a German Union consisting of Prussia and the mainly smaller states; the founding of a broader union between Germany and Austria did not come about. While the Erfurt parliament was still sitting, Austria invited all German states to send plenipotentiaries to Frankfurt to revive the old *Bundestag*. Schwarzenberg was, incidentally, prepared to recognise the Main as the dividing line between the Prussian and Austrian spheres of influence, which realistically reflected the existing situation.

These démarches paralysed the Prussian initiative in Germany, which was hampered still more by setbacks in Schleswig-Holstein. Partly under Russian pressure, Prussia was forced, in the Treaty of Berlin (July 1850), to leave the duchies to the Danes. At about this time the great powers meeting in London settled the succession in the whole Danish monarchy, including the duchies, in favour of the Danes.

Prussian policy grew more and more reactionary and was sharply criticised by German liberals and democrats. Finally a serious conflict broke out between Austria and Prussia over Hesse-Cassel. The Elector and his minister, Hassenpflug, had pursued a policy which was regarded by the state Diet as a breach of the constitution and met with a refusal to vote taxes. The Elector and his ministers fled the country. Austria and Bavaria decided, in the name of the *Bundestag*, to come to his aid, a step which Prussia opposed. Both Prussia and Austria mobilised and a major European war seemed imminent. Both Governments asked Tsar Nicholas, who sided with Austria on most issues, to mediate. Tension increased to such a pitch that on 8 November there was a clash between advanced units near Bronzell in Hesse.

Negotiations led to a personal discussion at Olmütz between the Prussian and Austrian Prime Ministers at the end of November. Shortly before this, the Tsar had threatened to go to war with Prussia if she did not comply with Austria's demands on all points. The Prussian Union was dissolved, the Diet of the *Bund* was recognised and the people of Schleswig-Holstein were forced by the threat of military intervention to cease their resistance to Denmark. The only concession on Austria's part was the reform of the federal constitution, but this came to nothing. The *Bund* soon became the main instrument of political reaction in Germany once more. Austria repeated her demand for admission to the *Zollverein*, but gained only a commercial treaty and the promise of later negotiations on entry. In September 1857 Prussia succeeded in considerably extending the *Zollverein* by a treaty with Hanover. She was also able to lay the foundations of a navy of her own when in December 1853 she obtained from Oldenburg some territory on which the naval base of Wilhelmshaven was built. She was also able to acquire some ships which had been ordered by the provisional *Reich* Government in Frankfurt and now came up for auction.

THE PERIOD OF REACTION

The victory of Austria and Russia at Olmütz meant a triumph for the reactionary forces in Prussia and all the rest of Germany. Before Olmütz, the conservative Government of Prussia, headed by Count Brandenburg and under the influence of Otto von Manteuffel, had not been completely opposed to progress; indeed, in many respects it had been moderately liberal. As late as 2 March 1850 Manteuffel, in the teeth of determined opposition from the feudalists and after overcoming the King's initial refusal, had put through a beneficial measure enabling peasant holders of land to become proprietors. But it was not long before the reactionary Court clique, notably the Gerlachs, succeeded in destroying Manteuffel's influence in these matters. It is true that when Brandenburg died in December 1850 (soon after Olmütz) it was Manteuffel who succeeded him as Prime Minister – he could hardly be dispensed with at the time – but the key post of the Interior went to F. O. W. von Westphalen,[1] who stood well to the Right.

The King regarded with suspicion and dislike those officials whose sense of justice and concern for the common weal resisted arbitrariness and corruption, and the ministry carried on an underground struggle with the Gerlachs and other members of the 'shadow government' who often dominated the vacillating King. True, Manteuffel succeeded in foiling the clique's plans to set aside the constitution and replace it with feudal monarchical institutions, but the spirit of reaction prevailed over much of the scene. Freedom of the press and the whole system of association and assembly were strangled, liberal judges and officials were persecuted and free political activity hindered. Elections

[1] Brother of Karl Marx's admirable wife.

were heavily influenced by the Government, and many officials who were mere puppets of the ministry were put into the lower house. In church affairs and education orthodoxy was all-powerful. The fundamental rights proclaimed by the Frankfurt Parliament were declared null and void. All the same, many important liberal rights which flowed from the Stein–Hardenberg reforms were still preserved in Prussia. Moreover, many people in high places disapproved of the new trend and did their best to check it. Georg von Vincke, the spokesman for the old liberals in the lower house, waged a brilliant campaign against the leaders of the ultra-conservatives. In both chambers protests against the Government's actions were often raised, though for the most part they fell on deaf ears. One of Westphalen's decisions which was a flagrant injustice caused a small group of moderate conservatives, with the prominent jurist Bethmann Hollweg at their head, to break away and form an independent group. Bethmann Hollweg founded the *Preussische Wochenblatt*, which did battle with the *Kreuzzeitung*. Radowitz and Bunsen, who stood high in the King's esteem, influenced him from a distance on similar lines. The heir to the throne, Prince William, and his wife Augusta, who resided in Koblenz, followed the state of affairs with much concern, and many critics of government in high circles gathered round them. In April 1853 the Prince called on Manteuffel to rid his Government of reactionary elements.

In Austria things were even worse. The suppression of the revolutions in Vienna and Hungary had cost much bloodshed and despotism had ousted justice. After the rebels had been punished there had at first been a period of transition and, as in Prussia, a relatively liberal constitution was proclaimed, though its coming into effect was deferred for the time being. The Government also carried through important reforms with a double motive: to win over large sections among their own peoples and to make an impact on German public opinion, thus helping Schwarzenberg in his struggle for Austrian predominance in Germany. In drafting these reforms he enjoyed the assistance of highly competent experts, but the state of emergency continued and freedom of the press was stifled.

Schwarzenberg probably never took the new constitution very seriously and he had no objections to the tendency towards absolutism which soon set in. The youthful Emperor was in the hands of reactionary generals. One of the most influential and capable statesmen, Karl Friedrich, Baron Kübeck, the son of a tailor, had forsaken his liberalism as a result of the revolution and in many respects shared the view of Metternich, who had now returned. After Olmütz the supporters of naked absolutism were in the ascendant; the constitution, proclaimed but never implemented, was suspended at the end of 1851, and many of the reforms only recently announced were repealed. Schwarzenberg died not long after.

His successor was Count Buol-Schauenstein, but the leading spirit was the Minister of the Interior, Alexander Bach, who was later ennobled. At the time of the revolution he had been an important leader of the Left. For some time he exercised power jointly with Kübeck, and on the latter's death in 1855 he came to the head of the Government. The prevailing policy was called the 'Bach system'. It was based on the omnipotence of the bureaucracy and the police, the influence of generals and aristocrats on the Emperor, government by the cabinet and, above all, on the Church, the Jesuits and clericalism. The collaboration between Church and State found expression in the concordat of 1855. All political freedom was held in suspicion and suppressed, Hungary and her dependencies were fragmented and subjected to a centralised, Germanising administration. The mainly German and Czech instruments of this policy were called 'Bach's Hussars'. The Croats and other nationalities in Hungary were deeply wounded in their national pride and the large number of officials and troops led to a considerable increase in the national debt.

The victory of reaction was not confined to Prussia and Austria. In 1851 the restored Diet of the *Bund* appointed a committee which promoted the spread of reactionary measures throughout Germany and was popularly known as the 'reactionary committee'. A few small states, like Coburg-Gotha, Saxe-Weimar and Brunswick, did their best to escape the pressure. In Bavaria, Maximilian II sought to alleviate the reaction and a considerable liberal opposition remained in being in the chambers. In many countries people only reluctantly followed the contemporary trend, whereas in others anything which smacked of liberalism was harshly persecuted. The fundamental rights were everywhere abolished and along with them, in many cases, the principle of equality before the law. The democratic and liberal constitutions of the revolutionary period were modified. The *Bund* issued regulations aimed at preventing the 'abuse' of the freedom of the press and of association, and the influence of clericalism increased markedly.

ECONOMIC DEVELOPMENTS

In the reactionary era following 1850 there were parts of Germany and Austria where the economy (and, incidentally, the arts and the sciences) flourished. The extraordinary economic growth, which was not confined to Central Europe, was far from being primarily due to the governments, although these contributed much to it. Europe was now benefiting above all from the spread of the idea of a free economy and its realisation in institutions and laws. Germany owed her economic advances mainly to railway construction and the *Zollverein* as well as to the progress of economic unity and freedom. These goals were not attainable in the sphere of politics because of the reaction; but on the economic plane this was far from being the case.

Between 1857 and 1861 a standardisation of German commercial law was achieved. In 1853 the *Zollverein* was extended to Hanover and Oldenburg, so that it now embraced almost all German states. In the same year the *Zollverein* agreed on a trade treaty with Austria and in 1857 a currency treaty followed. In the fifties, regular sailings began from Hamburg and Bremen to North America and a whole string of large banks was founded. Other factors which stimulated the economy were England's adoption of free trade and the removal of French protective tariffs in 1860 by a commercial treaty between England and France, as well as big finds of gold in California and Australia. Coal and iron production in Germany was given fresh impetus by the construction of railways. With the growth of industry the position of the workers had also to be settled. In 1853, a law was passed in Prussia prohibiting the employment of children until they had completed their twelfth year and other socio-political measures followed. In 1858, a number of prominent supporters of economic liberalism and national unity founded a 'Social Economic Congress' which held conferences every year. These proceedings greatly furthered the spread of the spirit of free economy.

In the fifties the peasants' remaining feudal services and obligations were removed or made redeemable. Improved communications created huge new markets. Scientific research, particularly in the field of chemistry, made possible a much better use of the soil. The period from 1850–75 was the most prosperous ever known by German agriculture, though it was later hard hit by overseas competition.

Economic and scientific developments had their repercussions on political outlook. The growth of heavy industry led to the strengthening of those circles inclined to liberalism, particularly the supporters of a free economy, who were usually progressive in their political views as well. Liberalism also spread among artisans and peasants, as election results demonstrated. The prominent liberal leader F. H. Schulze-Delitzsch, organised the co-operative trading system which was a boon to ambitious workers. The peasants had liberalism to thank for their emancipation from many of the relics of feudalism and as a result voted liberal in many districts. In the regions east of the Elbe, however, the peasants were still very dependent on the aristocratic landowners.

POLITICAL SCIENCE

The study of history was enriched during the period of reaction by many valuable works, which had a largely political background and were intended to further national unity and freedom. These were mainly detailed studies begun in the fifties and completed only later. Among historians Ranke, Droysen, Gervinus, Häusser, Sybel, Strauss and Mommsen were prominent, and of these Ranke alone had stood aloof from the German movement; the others had been powerfully influenced by its ideas.

In the period after the revolution of 1848 Friedrich Julius Stahl, to whom reference has been made, maintained the position as the leading conservative theorist which he had achieved in pre-1848 Germany. Stahl took a prominent part in the founding of the right-wing Prussian journal, which became known as *Kreuzzeitung*. In 1849 he was elected a member of the Prussian Union parliament at Erfurt. He was in close alliance with Bismarck and the Gerlach circle. But earlier than the Gerlachs and Bismarck, Stahl grasped the importance of adapting the conservative creed to the realities of the new situation. In spite of all reservations towards liberalism, Stahl was prepared to move some way towards constitutionalism, though of a particular kind. Ministers were to be dependent not only on the confidence of parliament, but also on that of the crown. Similarly, Stahl was not quite negatively inclined towards German unity at a time when the unification movement was in the hands of anti-conservative forces. But he emphasised the need for building the unity of the nation on what already existed, such as the dynasties. Like other political scientists, Stahl did not always manage to maintain consistency between theory and practice. However critical he was of the Junkers, as a member of the Prussian upper house Stahl often defended aristocratic privileges by equating them with the public interest. As a synodal councillor he had attempted to strengthen Lutheran orthodoxy.

On the liberal side many important works on political science, mainly with a historical perspective, appeared during the epoch of reaction. Robert von Mohl, the former *Reich* minister, published a three-volume *Geschichte und Literatur der Staatswissenschaften* (1855–58) which revealed an unrivalled expertise and served as a text-book for generations. Between 1857 and 1863, Rudolf Gneist, a professor at Berlin University, brought out his work *Das heutige englische Verfassungs- und Verwaltungsrecht* (English Constitutional and Administrative Law Today) – also in three volumes – which threw much light on conditions in England. Most studies of this kind were intended to sharpen understanding of domestic politics.

The Deutsche Staatswörterbuch

The Rotteck-Welcker *Staatslexikon* reproduced the world of ideas of liberals and democrats before the 1848 revolution.[1] In the period from the reactionary era to the founding of the *Reich* there appeared a similar publication, the *Deutsche Staatswörterbuch* (11 vols, 1857–70), edited by J. C. Bluntschli and K. Brater. Johann Caspar Bluntschli, who came of an old-established family in Zürich, where he was a prominent political figure, was appointed to the University of Munich in 1848 as professor of civil and constitutional law and in 1861 to the chair of constitutional and international law at Heidelberg. Karl Brater was at first mayor of Nördlingen and then became leader of the Bavarian liberal party, which supported German unification. Bluntschli was a member of the upper chamber in Baden. He wrote numerous works on jurisprudence. He justified the publication of the *Staatswörterbuch* on the grounds that while the old *Staatslexikon* of Rotteck and Welcker matched the still youthful inclinations and views of German liberalism in the twenties and thirties, political science had meanwhile made great progress through political experience. Although he edited many of the most important articles in the *Staatswörterbuch* personally, the task of organising the undertaking devolved largely upon Brater – 142 experts, many of them the leading scholars of the day, contributed to the work.

The *Staatswörterbuch* not only provides an excellent survey of the liberal views of the time but it also furnishes important material on the conditions prevailing in all other states and among all other peoples. It is notable that its general tone is cosmopolitan. Thus, one article stresses that there was no distinct form of government which could be called specifically German: the German nation displayed democratic, aristocratic and monarchical elements, one or other of which was prominent or subdued according to the conditions of the time. But, in general, the form of the German state combined the ancient conception of a powerful state with the Germanic view that moral limitations are confined to that sphere of life which pertains to the state and that the freedom of the individual must be asserted. But if the quietist tendencies of the masses are exploited, this combination may lead to gross distortions. The work contains two articles on Poland, one by a German and the other by a Pole, so that both viewpoints may be given expression. The contributors were for the most part German and Austrian professors and senior officials, but they also numbered many Swiss as well as individual Frenchmen, Belgians, Russians and Hungarians. By reason of the number and variety of contributors, the views represented are not altogether uniform but they fit into the general picture of liberalism.

[1] Vide, p. 202 ff.

Bluntschli was a declared opponent of the mechanistic mentality which was at the core of both monarchical and democratic absolutism. He conceived of states, peoples and nations as spiritual organisms which nature and history had moulded in numerous and varied forms. Even those forms which differed from one's own ideas must be understood, but also, he added, opposed if they did not match the level of social and moral development already attained. Thus absolutism, which Bluntschli completely rejects for his day, may have been necessary at earlier stages. Bluntschli also displays a desire to reconcile conservatism and liberalism, in so far as they both shun extremes and radicalism. His outlook was conditioned by his Protestantism and the political struggles in which he had taken part in Switzerland. A constitutionally limited monarchy seemed to him best for Germany and other states of that day, but he did not altogether disapprove of republics. He also drew a distinction between differing forms of constitutional monarchy. The first state to develop this had been Britain, and then France and Germany had followed. But in each state this had happened under special conditions, and although the British and French models had had a strong influence on German constitutions, foreign institutions could not be imposed *en bloc* on other nations. In particular, Bluntschli took the view that British parliamentary rule could not be imitated in Germany because there the given social preconditions in England did not exist. The English gentry and their traditions were the preconditions of parliamentary rule, while in Germany the highly educated, responsible class of officials gave its own special character to constitutional monarchy. These arguments were often used later by Bismarck to combat liberal attempts at securing parliamentary rule; Bluntschli had set them out in the *Staatswörterbuch* before Bismarck became a minister. Bluntschli, however, never argued the need for monarchical government on the grounds of foreign policy or military expediency, nor did he demand for it any overwhelming preponderance of power as was the case with Bismarck's constitutions for the North German Confederation and for the German *Reich*. Bluntschli's endeavours were not directed at an international power system but at creating an international code of law.

In the *Staatswörterbuch* Bluntschli also dealt with questions of race, and this reflected the spirit of the times. Here he based himself largely on Gobineau, whose book appears to have made a deep impression on him. To Bluntschli the noblest race appears to be the Aryans, whom he sees as the creators of science, intellectual liberty and the constitutional state, though as warriors they had let themselves be led astray into arrogance and the oppression of others, which could only be condemned. Bluntschli gives second place to the Semites, who had displayed *par excellence* submission to the will of God, fostered the religious spirit and created Christianity. Besides, Aryans and Semites had originally been related and had only later separated. The Aryans had developed constitutional monarchy, and the Semites theocracy. The other races were far behind these two, but it was the Aryans' task to educate the less gifted peoples to a humane outlook. Hence, for Bluntschli, racial disposition does not appear immutable. He also holds that the peoples today are mixed; the Teutons contain more Aryan blood, and the Slavs and Celts from the lower strata less. There is no call to criticise these views here. Reflections on racial disposition were found at that time in many writers,[1] even, to quote but one example, in a scholar like Ernest Renan, who wrote in detail about the racial spirit of the Semites. But in general these views played no important part either in learning or in European politics.

The *Staatswörterbuch* also published two articles on the Jews. Professor Wuttke dealt with their historical role and Bluntschli with their legal status. Both were in favour of equal rights for the Jews, and Wuttke declared that from the way a Christian behaved towards Jews one could tell how far he was really civilised.

Konstantin Frantz

Another of the more important political writers was Konstantin Frantz (1817–91). He came from Northern Thuringia; his father was a Protestant parson and his mother was of Huguenot extraction. After extensive studies, in which Schelling and Fichte exercised a deep and lasting influence on him, he published many works, of which only the political will be considered here. In the forties he carried out surveys for the Prussian Ministry of Culture, notably on the Polish question. Instead of trying to Germanise the Poles or to oppress them, he said, they should be won over to Prussia, so that in them she might have a defence against Russia and Pan-Slavism. Frantz declined the offer of a university chair in order to keep his independence. He was convinced that there would be a very real threat from Russia in the future, and he was in favour of an alliance between Germany and other European countries, including Britain. He was in sympathy with the efforts of the socialists in France, whose fundamental ideas he considered very progressive. He also held the view that on many points the socialists agreed with the conservatism which inspired him. In the fifties his work aroused the interest of leading statesmen in various countries, and he himself was now once more employed in the Prussian consular service, though his views developed increasingly in conflict with those of Bismarck.

[1] There is no history of racial belief, but the book by Bieder, himself a believer, contains much that is worthy of note.

Frantz rejected the idea of the power state. After the Peace of Paris of 1856, he came out in favour of an alliance, directed against Russia, between Prussia and Britain. He supported the further development of the *Bund* into a great central European alliance, such as Schwarzenberg had also proposed during the period of reaction. The liberals' fanatical cult of Germanism (*Deutschtümelei*) and striving for centralisation repelled him, as did their constitutionalism, in which he could see nothing but the rule of the bourgeoisie on the French pattern. His ideal was the 'trias', namely, three federations – Austria, Prussia and southwest Germany. These three federations should unite into one confederation for affairs of common concern. Furthermore, entry to each of the three regional federations should be open to smaller neighbouring states like Switzerland, the Netherlands, Scandinavia, Poland and the Balkan countries. Frantz was equally opposed to absolutism as to liberal parliamentarianism. He had visions of parliaments composed of representatives of the various Estates (*Berufsstände*) which should also send delegates to a German Federal Council (*Bundesrat*).

After the First World War people recalled the theories of Frantz and a discussion arose over whether they ought not to have been preferred to those of Bismarck. But they contained, along with some seminal ideas, others which were quite Utopian, and times had already changed far too much for them to be of any great use.

THE NATURAL SCIENCES

Since the greatest progress had probably been made in the realm of the natural sciences, man was often regarded first and foremost as a natural being and this led to the application of scientific methods to the political and social sciences. This tendency reflected the spirit of the age and was found in many peoples. One consequence was the emergence of the view that there were hereditary racial characteristics which conditioned the nature of peoples.

In a much more far-reaching way the cultivation of the natural sciences influenced the philosophical concept of the nature of man by leading to the spread of materialism, i.e. the doctrine that mind is merely a product of material processes. Even in antiquity philosophical materialism had weighty supporters and it was fostered in the seventeenth and eighteenth centuries by English and French thinkers. It was not unknown in Germany either, but to begin with made no headway there. Not until the middle of the nineteenth century did its great advance begin, and this was due above all else to the collapse of philosophical idealism. The rise of ethical materialism was naturally linked with economic and political processes as well as with the shaking of religious faith. Among the scientists, Moleschott, Vogt and Büchner were especially active in propagating materialistic ideas. Büchner's work *Kraft und Stoff* (Force and Matter), which appeared in 1855, enjoyed an uncommonly wide circulation. In 1859, Darwin's book on the origin of species by natural selection was published; this overthrew one of the main objections to materialism, namely purpose in nature. Man now appeared more than ever a member of the animal world, even if the most highly developed one. The concepts of right and wrong, good and evil were questioned: after all, one could not accuse an animal of being immoral if it devoured another. Spinoza had already reached this conclusion.

Materialism was now often linked with socialist ideas. In Feuerbach's words: 'Man is what he eats', by which he intended to demonstrate the influence of food on morality. Marx set out his theory of historical materialism, according to which all history consisted of a series of class struggles which ended in the victory of the exploited but more numerous class. The accompanying explanation claimed that this was in no way a question of morality but the natural course of events, in which the stronger gained the upper hand. The application of the theory of materialism to politics stirred up great opposition and the reactionary governments disciplined some of the guilty professors. Büchner lost his chair at Tübingen, as did Moleschott at Heidelberg. All the same, this theory could also be invoked in favour of the militarily stronger and thus serve to suppress revolutions. It is notable that Bismarck, who ordinarily had little time for philosophy, found a kindred spirit in Spinoza.

SCHOPENHAUER

A startling phenomenon in the intellectual development of Germany from about the middle of the nineteenth century was the growing influence of pessimism, whose main proponent was Arthur Schopenhauer (1788–1860). Schopenhauer's works had appeared before this time, but neither they nor his lectures had made much impact. Only towards the middle of the century did extensive interest in his doctrines awaken, and he then became the most widely read philosopher and a strong influence on many leading figures such as Nietzsche (in his early period) and Richard Wagner. To Schopenhauer the world presents the picture of a dreary, torturing nightmare. The absolute is the raw, restless, insensate greed for life, that will which is particularly manifest in the sexual urge and, in fact, in the whole of the life of the emotions. Schopenhauer can find no colours harsh enough to paint the horrors of hell. Human malice, narrow-mindedness and blindness are over-powering and ineradicable, man's innate character is unchangeable and his perfectibility and progress alike are non-existent. History is worthless nonsense. Only isolated, higher beings like the genius and the saint stand out from the undistinguished masses. They can conquer the dull, egoistic greed for life by selfless devotion to philosophy, art and music as well as by pity. They stand beyond good and evil, see through the play-acting of the world and live in solitude.

Schopenhauer was by disposition splenetic and suspicious. He suffered from fits of nervous depression; there was a history of insanity in his family. His writings contain many contradictions. He sharply contested belief in God, rejected the Old Testament and Judaism as optimistic and egoistic, but regarded true Christianity as pessimistic, since it preached the hopeless depravity of human nature and the impossibility of its redemption by its own efforts. He sought to Aryanise primitive Christianity by declaring it to be Indian, though without citing any ethnic authority. He also levelled serious criticisms at the Jews, although he had a high regard for Spinoza and on many counts favoured equal rights for the Jews.[1]

He writes in the most scathing terms about all national aspirations. National pride he calls pride in its cheapest form. Every pitiful blockhead who has nothing in the world to be proud of fastens on it as the last means of proving himself to be something. An intelligent man, on the other hand, will clearly recognise and despise the faults of his own nation. The Germans for the most part had no national pride, except for those who ridiculously affected it, especially the democrats. National character consisted mainly of evil traits which assumed a particular form in every country. Every nation mocked all the rest, and all were justified in doing so.

Schopenhauer's father , a rich Danzig merchant, had a strong predilection for French and English culture and hated Prussia. The son was brought up as a Voltairean and was intended to become, if possible, a Frenchman or an Englishman. For this reason he was made to travel widely even when a child, and he spent some years in France, with the result that when he returned home he could scarcely speak any German. He always retained a relatively high opinion of French and English culture. True, he called France the vainest of all nations, which talked incessantly of 'la gloire', and he passed disparaging judgement on her language and literature. As against this, he praised her achievements in the field of science, her moralists and, most of all, her unworldly Trappists, members of that strictest of all monastic orders. He heaped

---

[1] Schopenhauer's few intimate friends included three men of Jewish extraction: Dr Julius Frauenstaedt, Dr David Asher and Dr Martin Emden, who contributed much to the spread of his teachings—especially Frauenstaedt, whom he called his 'Arch-Evangelist'.

praise on the English, whom he admired for a number of reasons and particularly for their emancipation of the slaves. But he thought very little of the Anglican Church, which, he said, existed mainly to provide an occupation for the younger sons of the aristocracy. The priests, with popular education in their hands, had contrived that the majority of the people could not read. The national characteristic which seemed to him eminently German was ponderousness. Phlegm was the root of stupidity, and of lack of energy, liveliness and imagination. To imitate the French and the English was the most sensible thing that Germans could do. The only advantage they possessed over other nations was the German language, but he took them sharply to task for misusing it by cultivating a high-flown, precious and hyperbolical style as well as misty imprecision.

Schopenhauer directs his fiercest attacks against all German philosophers after Kant, saying that they had been at pains to impress by an arrogant incomprehensibility. From youth upwards the Germans had been trained to understand words rather than concepts. Hegel in particular had been a complete charlatan. 'The honourable word "enlightenment" ', says Schopenhauer, 'has become a kind of term of abuse; the greatest men of the previous century – Voltaire Rousseau, Locke and Hume, those heroes, those ornaments and benefactors of mankind – are slandered. . . .'

Among his papers was found a declaration that he despised the German nation for its effusive stupidity and was ashamed of belonging to it. In other places he pokes particular fun at the fanatical disciples of Germanism (*Deutschtümler*). All the same, he did on occasion concede some virtues to the Germans. They had produced a few quite exceptional men, they possessed the noblest and most sublime language, they were free of national pride – a proof of their honesty – and finally it was among them that most atheists were to be found.

His misanthropy made him by nature an opponent of democracy. He defended the monarchical system as especially suitable for Germany, whereas in his view parliamentarianism seemed to suit conditions in England. In his will he bequeathed all his money to the fund for Prussian soldiers disabled in the struggle against the 1848 revolution. His manuscripts, copyright, library and works of art he left to two of the Jewish friends already mentioned. His political views matched his basic conception of human nature. Thus he regarded all wars as evil. They sprang from rapacity but were inevitable because men, being beasts, could be held in check only by force.

Schopenhauer, who, it may be mentioned *en passant*, had many characteristics in common with the Romanticists, was not the only representative of pessimism. He was followed by a whole string of philosophers of the same cast of mind. This argues against his pessimism's springing from purely personal motives: tendencies of the age must also have played their part. One main reason was probably the shipwreck of idealistic philosophy, especially Hegelianism, which, of course, Schopenhauer bitterly attacked, but certainly political reasons were also a factor. It has often been assumed that the failure of the 1848 revolution released a great wave of pessimism. Schopenhauer himself disputed that his fundamental views were in any way responsible for this, but it may well be significant that for a considerable time he was the most widely read and admired philosopher in Germany and that it was precisely that philosophic thought in Germany which followed on from him which produced a whole school of pessimism.

RICHARD WAGNER AND POLITICS

Richard Wagner was neither active in politics nor a serious student of them, although his work had an indirect effect on political sentiment. His operas are full of symbolic happenings which bear elemental human features and can be politically interpreted. Thus Bernard Shaw has treated the 'Ring' as a proclamation of socialism. This is probably too extreme a view, for Wagner belonged to no party and did not concern himself with economic or political problems. He was completely the artist, and shared the tendency of the Romanticists to retreat from reality into the realm of dreams. Reality, the rule of human egoism, the urge for power and the striving for profit moved him to passionate protest. His intuitive view of the world was stimulated by his reading of philosophical works and fluctuated between optimism and pessimism, between Feuerbach's atheism, Schopenhauer's view of life and finally Christian mysticism, between nationalism and a generous cosmopolitanism, between revolutionary protest against authority, property and sexual morality and praise of an ideal monarchy and the middle-class virtues of a medieval city. Wagner's greatest influence falls predominantly in the period before the founding of the *Reich*. Only the last decade of his life during which he wrote his 'Parsifal' comes within the period of the Bismarckian Empire. His friend in need who helped him to realise his aims was Ludwig II of Bavaria.

In Wagner's artistic work the idea of release from the distress of life, from human passions and spiritual tempests is paramount. The means to this end are partly a Rousseauesque return to nature, symbolised in Siegfried, and partly self-abnegating love, pity, vegetarianism, the protection of wild animals, renunciation, asceticism and re-birth. Although these things lie outside the sphere of politics, many of Wagner's ideas have influenced his disciples in a political respect too. Romanticism, by the stress it lays on intuition and tradition, often lessened esteem for cool reason and led youth astray by its exaggerated praise of heroism. It is understandable that many German nationalists made a cult of Wagner, even though the moral lessons of his dramas are diametrically opposed to the aims of nationalism. Wotan, indeed, is punished with destruction for striving for power and violating solemn promises. While Wagner's racial beliefs and anti-Semitism exercised a strong and widespread influence, it must be said that he by no means assumed that Jews cannot attain to spiritual re-birth. Indeed, many Jews played a leading part in popularising his operas and others formed a large part of his following. The French Count Gobineau, who developed the doctrine of Aryanism, knew Wagner and found zealous supporters in the composer's circle. The most influential propagator of racial doctrine in Germany was Wagner's son-in-law, Houston Stewart Chamberlain, who, although of English origin, had an uncommonly good command of German. Chamberlain's racial doctrine was diametrically opposed to Wagner's idea of redemption by compassion, which he took over from Schopenhauer.

22

THE RISE OF BISMARCK

Otto von Bismarck (1815–98) had occupied himself with politics early
on, but neither his civil service career nor his activity in four parliaments
appealed to him, and he turned to the management of his estates. His
speeches in the Prussian Assembly and the Erfurt Parliament showed
him to be a pronounced Junker, though of quite a special kind, a
monarchist but no supporter of absolutism, and a man who placed
being a Prussian above being a German. By nature passionate, he
thirsted for struggle, action and power, and with all this he had an
extraordinary ability to judge men and political situations which was
quite uninfluenced by any party slogans and sprang above all from his
own observations and a wide study of history. For him, nature and
history were filled with conflict; without conflict there was no life. The
State had to defend its vital interests and extend its power in order to
escape eclipse. Yet he by no means advocated the pursuit of unlimited
power for the State, either at home or abroad. For every state nature and
history had laid down certain limits which must not be overstepped.
Despite his own liking for power politics and the extraordinarily great
qualities which he could command in their prosecution, he was by no
means inclined to overestimate the political possibilities open to him. He
was equally far removed from the outlook which could seek to resuscitate
a superannuated past as he was from the striving after goals which might
lie in the remote future. For him politics was the art of the possible
and his acumen, the lessons he had drawn from history and his instinct
told him what was possible. In the uncertainty which is inseparably
linked with politics he always had several options open and the corresponding means in readiness.

Even under Frederick William IV, Bismarck could have become a
minister, but he felt the time was not yet ripe. In 1851 he became
Prussian delegate to the Bundestag in Frankfurt, in 1859 Ambassador

in St Petersburg and, in 1862, in Paris. All these posts afforded him an excellent training for the conflicts to come. In Frankfurt he considered it his prime task to lessen Austria's dominance in Germany. His aim was first to secure for Prussia equality of status, and then, step by step, supremacy. For tactical reasons he sought to prevent for the time being any evolution of the *Bund*. Even at that time he was thinking of an eventual military show-down – perhaps in concert with France and Russia – with Austria.

THE CRIMEAN WAR

In the Crimean War (1853–6), Prussia and Austria were courted by both Russia and the western powers. In Prussia the King, with the support of the conservatives, pursued a policy of neutrality, while the liberals and even the heir to the throne wanted to work, at least on the diplomatic plane, with the western powers. A few liberals hoped that a war with Russia would lead to the unification of all Germans.

Austria vacillated for a long time. The Tsar offered to place the Balkan peoples under a joint Russo-Austrian protectorate, but Francis Joseph refused, because he feared that Russia would have the greater influence on those peoples which were related to her by language and religion. Napoleon III was prepared to leave large areas of the Balkans to Austria if she would surrender Italian or Polish territories in return. Bismarck put up the most determined resistance to such plans, for the restoration of Poland would, in his view, permanently weaken Russia's power and do great harm to Prussia. The Tsar was exasperated by Austrian diplomacy, condemning the ingratitude shown for the help which he had given Francis Joseph in 1849 in the war against Hungary.

After the defeat of Russia, the Crimean War was concluded by the Peace of Paris. Prussia was much criticised by the western powers for having remained neutral and the victors did not even wish to allow her to take part in the Congress of Paris. Finally, on a motion by France, she was invited after all, though admittedly after the main points had been settled, for a discussion on the Straits Convention, of which she was a signatory.

Austria suffered most damage from the Crimean War. Since she had given the western powers some help, she was able to take part in the Congress from the outset, but her interests were not looked after to the extent that she had hoped and her policy during the war had attracted Russia's hostility. What a contrast her position offered with that of a minor state like Sardinia, whose Prime Minister, Cavour, was not only able to attend the Congress but even to voice complaints against Austria

- and all because his country had taken part in the war against Russia!

THE 'NEW ERA' IN PRUSSIA

In 1857 Frederick William IV became incurably ill and mentally unbalanced, and as a consequence his brother William provisionally acted for him. William's political views were moderately conservative and he himself declared his intention of steering a middle course between Right and Left. The feudal-absolutist *Camarilla* which had surrounded his brother mistrusted him deeply and tried for a long time to prevent his formal appointment as regent. William had shown sympathy for liberal and national aspirations in so far as they did not undermine monarchical rule, especially in military matters. Several visits to England and his friendship with Prince Albert had had their effect on him. His wife Augusta, the highly cultivated grand-daughter of Charles Augustus of Weimar, was progressively minded and their son, Frederick William, married Princess Victoria, the daughter of Albert and Victoria, in 1858. In the same year William became Regent. His first act was to dismiss the existing reactionary government and summon the *Landtag*, and in its presence he took an oath to respect the constitution. Prince Karl Anton of Hohenzollern was the new Prime Minister, but the real leader was Rudolf von Auerswald, a liberal. Some of the other ministers were also moderate liberals, so that the new cabinet represented an unmistakeable swing in a liberal direction. The Regent also developed a government programme which seemed to confirm this and it became customary to call the change which ensued the 'New Era'. Fresh elections were held and ended in the rout of the reactionaries who had owed their seats solely to the rigging of earlier elections. This time the liberals had avoided putting up radicals as candidates, and they won a handsome majority. The swing of the pendulum in Prussia had its effect on other states in the *Bund*. In Bavaria, where the reactionaries were just then planning a coup, they likewise lost their dominance and Maximilian II declared that he wanted peace with his people.

In the following year Napoleon III, in concert with the King of Sardinia, went to war with Austria as a first step towards creating a free and united Italy. The Austrian army suffered two heavy defeats, but could have continued the war, since it possessed some strong fortresses in Italy. The *Bund* refused to go to Austria's assistance, and the two Emperors soon concluded an armistice, which was followed by the Peace of Zürich. Austria lost Lombardy but retained Venetia. The war caused great excitement in Germany and it was widely believed that Napoleon would soon embark on the reconquest of the Rhine provinces, but views on whether Germany should go to Austria's aid and on what conditions were divided.[1] While South Germany was completely pro-Austrian, the central and northern states were less so. It was not forgotten in Germany that in the Peace of Basle (1795) and the struggles which ensued, Prussia had left Austria in the lurch and in 1806 had been defeated in her turn by the French army and grievously oppressed for years. The democrats and liberals had, it is true, always had great sympathy for the Italian national movement and condemned Austrian absolutism; but, after all, Italy's ally, Napoleon III, had also come to power by a bloody *coup d'état* and wanted to tear up the treaties of 1815. At first the Prussian Government sought to mediate and was even prepared to support concessions to the Italian freedom movement. Later Prussia mobilised and occupied positions to protect her Rhine frontier against attack. Any intervention on Austria's behalf was, however, only to be granted on condition that Prussia was given supreme command of the federal forces. The Austrian Government now feared that this would lead to Prussian hegemony in Germany and preferred to lose its commanding position in Italy rather than in Germany. The official Prussian policy of making the granting of military aid contingent on a significant growth of her power in the *Bund* was also widely supported in liberal circles, who expected this to lead to substantial progress towards national unity.

The great success of the Italian liberation movement also brought about a fresh and powerful upsurge of the national movement in Germany. A German National Association (*Nationalverein*) was founded to which numerous distinguished liberal politicians belonged. Rudolf von Bennigsen was elected its president. He came from an old family of the Lower Saxon nobility and in the Hanoverian *Landtag* had been a prominent opponent of reaction and the rule of the aristocracy. Bennigsen was the pattern of the genuine liberal, utterly devoted to the ideals of the constitutional state, liberty and national unity but without lapsing into radical illusions. His aim was by no means a completely unitary German state but a federalistic reform of the situation in Germany and the preservation of a moderate particularism, though under the direction of a strong central power – in other words, a liberal Prussia. This, in essentials, had been the aim pursued ten years before by the Frankfurt National Assembly, with its constitution for the *Reich* and the fundamental rights. Power politics, such as Bismarck was planning, would have seemed to him an outrage on the German

---

[1] Vide Mittelstädt, *Der Krieg von 1859. Bismarck und die öffentliche Meinung in Deutschland*, 1904.

people.[1] Another founder member of the National League was Hermann Schulze-Delitzsch, an extremely effective orator and agitator.

The National League quickly assembled a considerable number of respected liberal spokesmen, mostly from North and Central Germany; it found far fewer supporters in the South. It also had the full support of one of the princes – Duke Ernest of Saxe–Coburg–Gotha, a brother of Prince Albert of England.[2] Even before this the Duke had cherished plans for a similar league and had communicated them to his friend Gustav Freytag, the well-known writer. He looked on part of his sovereign rights as the property of the German nation, with himself merely as their steward. Most German governments considered the National League a threat to the State, but were unable to take any decisive steps against it.

The Italian movement for unity had meanwhile made further progress, and in 1860 Napoleon received Savoy and Nice from Sardinia in return for his support. Switzerland protested vigorously against this cession of territory, since the Congress of Vienna had decided on the neutrality of parts of Savoy. When the French Government thereupon declared that at this point France had reached her natural frontiers, there was great excitement in Europe, because people thought they detected here a hint that Napoleon now intended to annex the left bank of the Rhine. Napoleon was not aiming at a war but seeking a settlement of the Rhine frontier in agreement with Prussia and Russia, so he let it be known in Berlin that he would ensure for Prussia a rich compensation in return – possibly the acquisition of Schleswig-Holstein and a worthy position in the *Bund*.[3] In South Germany the conviction prevailed that Prussia had either already secretly ceded the left bank of the Rhine or that it needed only a Bismarck ministry to be formed for it to be handed over to France in return for the annexation of Hanover and Mecklenburg.[4] These rumours were false, but they originated in the fact that Bismarck really did wish to win over Napoleon for support against Austria. That he tried to tempt him by hints of this nature is known from several sources. William, the Regent of Prussia, was, however, totally opposed to such plans. In the middle of June 1860 a meeting followed between Napoleon and William in Baden which was also attended by the Kings of Bavaria, Württemberg, Saxony and Hanover as well as a number of other German princes. The Emperor

---

[1] Cf. Hermann Oncken's masterly biography of Bennigsen, Vol. I, p. 319.

[2] Cf. Duke Ernest's memoirs, *Aus meinem Leben und aus meiner Zeit*, Vol. III, 1889.

[3] Cf. Sybel: *Die Begründung des deutschen Reiches*, Vol. II, p. 261.

[4] Cf. Bernhardi's memoirs: *Tagebücher: Aus dem Leben Dr. v. Bernhardis*, E. v. Bernhardi (ed.), Vol. III, pp. 335, 338.

admitted that there was a party in France which had designs on German territory, but declared that he personally in nowise shared their views and was for peace. The Regent emphasised that he would never permit a territorial adjustment at Germany's expense.

At this meeting there was also a discussion between the Regent and the other kings on the reform of the *Bund*, and Maximilian of Bavaria urged William to reach an understanding with Francis Joseph. The two did, in fact, meet soon after in Teplitz and there was a discussion which, though friendly, could not bridge the great gulf between them. All the same, their relations grew rather more cordial and this made it possible for them to collaborate on a few important issues, such as the situation in Hesse–Cassel and Schleswig–Holstein. Once again the reform of the *Bund* was on the agenda and about this time various schemes were worked out by both *grossdeutsch* and *kleindeutsch* interests. In essence Austria wanted to preserve the old *Bund* as a loose union of sovereign states and progressively extend its sphere of influence. She maintained her claim to permanent presidency. Prussia for her part wanted either equality with Austria in directing the whole *Bund* or a division into a North German Prussian, and a South German Austrian sphere of influence. But the most commonly canvassed scheme harked back to the Erfurt Union policy of setting up a firm federal state under Prussian leadership which should then conclude a further federation with Austria. Prussia refused to consider an extension of the competence of the *Bund* on the ground that a mere federation of states was not sufficient but that a federal state was necessary. The medium-sized German states supported the 'trias' idea, by which they would have a part to play as a third force. They were predominantly pro-Austrian. The difference between the two great powers was also intensified in the commercial field. Prussia eased trading conditions with France, whereas Austria and the South German states supported stronger tariffs.

About two years later than in Prussia, Austria experienced a 'new era' as well, absolutism being abandoned and a constitution introduced. After a transitional stage there appeared in 1861 the February Patent, which created a larger *Reichsrat* with a lower house made up of members elected from each *Landtag*. The Prime Minister was Anton von Schmerling, and Count Rechberg remained Foreign Minister. Austria's changeover to constitutionalism and the leading position occupied by Schmerling, who had distinguished himself in the Frankfurt National Assembly, aroused great hopes in the *grossdeutsch* circles of most of the countries in the *Bund*. Many of the *grossdeutsch* supporters had a democratic or liberal outlook, and it did not agree with their convictions that Austria, whom they wished to stay within the *Bund*, should be under absolutist rule while in Prussia constitutionalism prevailed. It is significant that even Heinrich von Gagern, who had been the leader of the *kleindeutsch* movement in the Frankfurt Parliament, later went over to the *grossdeutsch* view, though he did want a central power evenly balanced between Austria and Prussia. Julius Fröbel, too, who in November 1848 had been condemned to death in Vienna along with Blum, now collaborated with the Austrian Government. As a republican champion of the *grossdeutsch* idea in 1848, he had sat on the extreme left of the Frankfurt Assembly. Even during the revolutionary period he had reached the conviction that the existence of Austria as a great power was an utterly indispensable bulwark against the barbarism of Russia and that the many nationalities making up the Danubian State would stay together only within the framework of a monarchy. In the final rising of 1849 he fought against the Prussian troops and then fled, first to Switzerland and later to America, where for seven years he grew better acquainted with republicanism in practice and changed his views. He returned to Europe, and in 1861 drew up a memorandum on the reform of the *Bund* which aroused great interest in Austrian governmental circles and was later made the basis of an official plan.

PRUSSIAN ARMY REFORM

During the Italian war, Prussian mobilisation had revealed a number of anomalies in the composition of the army. Its size was still based on the population figure for 1815 of ten millions, though this had meanwhile grown to eighteen millions. In consequence, and despite the universal liability to military service, many young men every year remained completely exempt. On the other hand, the first reserves (*Landwehr ersten Aufgebots*) – that is, men between twenty-five and thirty-two who had already done their service – were recalled and this meant that thousands of fathers of families became front-line troops. Moreover, during the campaign against the Badenese rebels in 1849, the Prince Regent had observed that the *Landwehr* executed tactical manoeuvres less skilfully than the regiments of the line and so suffered heavier casualties. He had therefore worked out a plan to increase the annual call-up and the number of regiments as well as to incorporate the younger age-groups of the *Landwehr* in the active field army, but to use the older men only to garrison fortresses. The setting up of the new regiments required $9\frac{1}{2}$ million thalers annually. The three-year period of service was to be retained. To the Regent these reforms appeared indispensable but the liberal War Minister von Bonin was dubious whether they could be put through on this scale. The Regent therefore replaced him by General Albrecht von Roon, who was no supporter of a liberal constitution.

At the beginning of 1860 the bill for army reform was introduced into the *Landtag*. It was referred to a committee which elected the liberal leader Georg von Vincke as its chairman and the retired Major-General Stavenhagen, who was wholly on the side of the liberals, as its *rapporteur*. Stavenhagen stated that the separation of the *Landwehr* from the field army was an insult to the former and a betrayal of the most sacred traditions of the Prussian people. Furthermore, he reported that the three-year period of service was unacceptable, two years being adequate and more economical. The committee recommended that the bill be thrown out, whereupon the Government withdrew it for the time being and then reached the questionable conclusion that certain reforms could be carried through on the basis of existing legislation. It was able to induce the *Landtag* to make a provisional grant of 9 million thalers and, in the belief that approval was certain to be forthcoming later, began to raise the new regiments. In the following year the deputies approved the estimates for the new scheme, though with a token cut, but demanded the drafting of a new bill in which they hoped that the ministry would take account of their demands.

When the 'New Era' began, the liberals, under Vincke's leadership, had decided on a policy of caution and avoided the doctrinairism which had proved the undoing of the revolution. When the army bill was brought in, the former Prime Minister, Otto von Manteuffel, said that if the liberals showed sense in handling this issue, they would be safely ensconced in power for years. But army reform raised questions which were soon to lead to a serious constitutional conflict, though this was, of course, by no means the fault of the liberals alone. The feudal, absolutist and clerical forces of reaction were both active and powerful and contrived to influence the Regent. They also tried to win over the workers, founding for this purpose a Prussian Popular Association (*Volksverein*), in whose programme, it is true, German *Einigkeit* (concord) – not *Einheit* (unity) – was laid down as the aim, but with the rider: 'There must be no denial of our Prussian fatherland, no sinking into the morass of a German republic, no theft of crowns or nationality fraud . . . no weakening of the army, no parliamentary rule and no constitutional ministerial responsibility, a personal monarchy by the grace of God, not of the constitution', and so on. It was natural that even among the liberals a stronger line should increasingly be taken. Two out-and-out democrats, Waldeck and Schulze-Delitzsch, were returned at by-elections and many politicians who had been active in 1848 as republicans were soon mustering in the *Nationalverein*.

Frederick William IV died at the beginning of 1861 and his brother became king at the age of sixty-three. To emphasise his divine right, and despite all attempts by his ministers to dissuade him, he had himself

solemnly crowned in a manner which for many liberals contra-
dicted the spirit of a constitutional monarchy and also helped to sharpen
political antagonisms. About the middle of the year, a new liberal party
of a more radical tendency was formed, the German Progressive
Party (*Deutsche Fortschrittspartei*), whose leaders included brilliant
scholars like Virchow and Mommsen and fearless political fighters like
Johann Jacoby and Schulze-Delitzsch. Its electoral manifesto rejected
the watchword of moderation, which had prevailed during the previous
election, and called for energetic measures. At the general election of
1861 the party won over 100 seats, thus becoming the strongest liberal
group in the lower house. The Government submitted to the Parliament,
which was dominated by the various liberals, a new army bill which
included many of the provisions previously attacked by the Opposition.
These measures – the three-year period of service, a considerable
increase in the strength of the regular army linked with a diminution
of the role of the *Landwehr* and the high resultant costs – had been
sharply assailed in the liberals' electoral propaganda. The Opposition
had no great love for the regular army, since it was in the main officered
by aristocrats who were blindly devoted to the King. The *Landwehr*,
on the other hand, was more popular, for it had mostly middle-class
officers, who, after a short period on the active list, followed a civilian
profession and were open to the influence of public opinion. Quite a
number of military experts considered the three-year period of service
excessive, and the suspicion prevailed that its main purpose was to drill
the soldiers into being utterly docile tools of royal policy. Besides this,
the military budget was greatly inflated by the new provisions, which
necessitated a considerable increase in direct taxation. The Government, which for the greater part still consisted of moderate liberals,
sought to allay hostility to the army bill by making concessions in other
directions, but these did not go far enough to induce the liberals to
agree to the bill. There were heated debates in which the Opposition
demanded the repeal of the reforms already undertaken and an adjustment of the budget. Their attitude seemed to be tending more and more
towards a call for parliamentary government, i.e. the principle that it was
for the majority to decide on the ministers and their policy. In the end
the Government asked to be allowed to resign, but the King refused.
The liberal ministers tried to get the King to make important concessions
to the Opposition but were thwarted in this by the stand taken by
Roon, who influenced the King in a reactionary sense. The King
therefore dismissed his liberal ministers, replaced them by conservatives and dissolved the lower house. In the elections which followed
the liberals and the parties close to them gained an overwhelming
majority. Once again there were violent struggles which for the most

part centred round the budget. The Opposition, however, seemed ready to reach an understanding with the Government if the latter would concede the two-year period of service and even Roon was, on certain conditions, not averse to a compromise, but the King flatly refused and declared himself ready to abdicate if his ministers sided with the Opposition. He wanted to pass on the crown to his son Frederick William, who stood close to the liberals, but the Crown Prince was against his father's abdication.

BISMARCK COMES TO POWER

In this critical situation Roon advised the King to summon Bismarck, with whom he (Roon) was in constant touch. He had urged this course before now, but William I had had misgivings about appointing a man with the reputation of being an out-and-out reactionary as his minister. He now sent for him and told him he had decided to give up the crown if he could not find a minister to represent his policy against the Opposition. Bismarck persuaded the King to entrust him with the task, and on 22 September 1862 he was appointed Prime Minister. At this time it was far from certain that the hope of German unity and of a strong central power which yet preserved a federal structure would be realised; the situation in Germany was confused, and the King of Prussia had been ready to abdicate. Little more than eight years later this same King was crowned Emperor of Germany in Versailles and a German *Reich* was founded. This is the measure of Bismarck's achievement. Along the path to his goal he had to overcome much opposition, in particular the King's resistance – shared by his immediate family – to a militaristic policy; the jealousy of powerful statesmen; the mistrust of great powers; the apprehension of many German princes; the opposition of Prussian liberals and the distaste felt by influential conservatives for the revolutionary tendencies of his policy.

Bismarck's appointment as Prime Minister aroused indignation among the Prussian liberals and further increased the detestation of subordination to Prussia felt in the rest of the *Bund*. Even the National League sharply opposed Bismarck, and many of its leaders saw in his position of power a great danger for Germany. To their surprise he tried to persuade some moderate liberals to join the Government, but in vain. The deputies had taken their stand on a two-year period of military service and the King on three: this difference could not be bridged. Bismarck hinted that he would try gradually to bring the King round, but even this did not help. The lower house refused to approve the supplementary estimates for the army and navy and demanded a vote on the budget, which Bismarck withdrew before the end of the year. In committee the Prime Minister said that the great questions of the day would not be decided by speeches and majority decisions but by 'blood and iron', which aroused a fresh storm of indignation. The session was closed and Bismarck declared that the Government would pass the payments for the army and national welfare even without the formal consent of the lower house. There was, he said, a loophole in the constitution which allowed the Crown to act thus; this considerably sharpened the constitutional conflict.

The upper house, a few provincial diets and the Prussian *Volksverein* did, it is true, welcome the Government's attitude, but the educated and propertied classes, along with the middle class, overwhelmingly rejected Bismarck's policy. Thus it was that the members of the municipal council of Berlin and other cities, as well as the most prominent and respected Rhenish and Westphalian industrialists, submitted addresses to the King in which they expressed their fears. On 22 January 1863 the liberal deputy Virchow, supported by more than 200 members, introduced in the lower house an address to the King which was directed against Bismarck. After a three-day debate it was adopted by 255 votes to 68, of which latter only 11 votes came from the feudal party and 57 from the Old Liberal and Catholic factions, who, while sharing the opinion that Bismarck had infringed the constitution, wished to express this conviction in a rather milder form. It can be seen that the real reactionaries had only a handful of votes at their disposal. Numerous further divisions yielded far greater majorities for the liberals whenever the Old Liberals and the Catholics threw in their lot with the Progressive Party. It must, of course, be remembered that the three-class franchise introduced in 1849 by the reaction gave a much wider suffrage to the more heavily taxed than to those without means, who in consequence had little influence in elections. Among the liberal deputies there were many state officials and individuals dependent on the Government in other ways, especially judges, civil servants, army officers, municipal officials and professors. Bismarck now introduced a whole series of measures against those with liberal views, measures calculated to harass them and make a mockery of the conception of a constitutional state. There were many who took their grievances to the courts and won. The Government consequently withdrew some of their sanctions but introduced others in their place, while the liberals raised a fund to help the victims of Government measures. The triple freedom of association, public assembly and the press was severely curtailed, the press law of 1863 being beyond all doubt unconstitutional. A few days after it was issued, the Crown Prince, speaking in Danzig, stated that he regretted the estrangement between Government and people and had neither known of nor had any hand in the decrees which had caused it. The King was greatly incensed at this speech and was considering a severe punishment for his son, but Bismarck dissuaded him. The King's unpopularity was underlined by the cities' deliberate withholding of formal greetings, addresses of sympathy and similar expressions of loyalty. When the time then drew near for fresh elections to the lower house, Bismarck took measures which he himself, in private, termed election-rigging (*Wahlschwindel*).

This election took place in October 1863, and despite all the machinations of the Government less than forty of the candidates returned supported it. The liberals underwent radicalisation by the Progressive Party's gaining seats, while the moderate Old Liberals suffered a complete defeat. Bismarck realised that his tactics hitherto were not going to achieve his ends and now toyed with the idea of introducing universal franchise as soon as the time was ripe. The example of France under Napoleon III showed that under universal franchise the Government came off well, because great masses of peasants, workers and small craftsmen were under the influence of government officials, the landowning aristocracy and the Church. The industrial proletariat was still relatively undeveloped in Germany and the better-paid workers voted mostly for the Progressive Party. August Bebel, a master turner from Dresden, who later became the outstanding pioneer of social democracy, campaigned in 1865-6 with the writings of Schulze-Delitzsch against the 'Heresies of Lassallean Communism'. Bismarck, however, was not offended by Lassalle's socialism and had several conversations with him, in the course of which universal suffrage was discussed. Bismarck was considering winning over the workers by social reforms. He had detailed studies prepared of their living conditions and drew up a comprehensive programme for the protection of labour and national welfare. But in these plans Bismarck ran into strong resistance from leading officials who were filled with the prevailing theory of the free play of forces and hostile to state intervention. Therefore, to begin with, Bismarck had to defer his socio-political plans. Incidentally, the more far-seeing liberals also realised the need for social reforms. The big Berlin machine manufacturers, who all belonged to the Progressive Party, came out with a declaration in favour of the workers' right of association.

Meanwhile discussion of federal reform had made further progress. Bismarck sharply combated the policy of Austria and was convinced that there would inevitably be a military showdown with her. He declared that if there were a war with Austria, Prussia would ally herself with foreign powers, by which he meant France and Russia. Soon afterwards, in January 1863, the Poles rose against Russian rule and both sides fought grimly. While England, France and Austria protested to the Russian Government against its brutality in Poland, Bismarck ranged himself on Russia's side and concluded a convention with her for mutual aid in suppressing the rebellion. Public opinion in Germany and Austria was outraged at Bismarck's step. The *Nationalverein* repudiated Prussian policy towards the Poles as something condemned by all Europe and a threat to the honour of the German nation.

Meanwhile, the chief Austrian Minister, Schmerling, was preparing a comprehensive scheme for a complete reform of the *Bund*. It was based above all on the ideas of Fröbel, which have already been mentioned. The plan proposed a wide extension of the *Bund*'s authority; it was to be provided with a parliament consisting of a council of princes and an assembly of delegates from the parliaments of the various states. A federal directory of five members under the presidency of Austria and the setting up of a federal court were also proposed, and the whole scheme was to be submitted for approval to an assembly of all German princes in Frankfurt. Francis Joseph visited William of Prussia in Bad Gastein and laid the plan before him, but William would not commit himself. In the middle of August 1863 nearly all the princes assembled in Frankfurt, though William was a notable absentee. At this *Fürstentag* twenty-four votes were cast in favour of the Austrian plan and Prussia subsequently agreed to negotiate if three preliminary conditions were accepted. These were the right of Prussia and Austria to veto any declaration of war by the *Bund*, the alternate presidency of Prussia and Austria, and the setting-up of a German parliament elected by direct popular suffrage. This latter idea was Bismarck's and to begin with it made William uneasy. The Austrian Foreign Minister, Count Rechberg, refused Prussia's demands, but when he tried to form a separate federation with the larger German states, the latter made it clear that while they did not want a federation without Austria, they did not want one without Prussia either. In consequence the Austrian plan was doomed. In any case one must concede that Prussia's demands were justified. Whether an effective federal state with a directory and headed by two great powers which had long been fundamentally hostile would have been a practical possibility is very doubtful. The initiative in Germany soon passed to Prussia.

23

BISMARCK'S THREE WARS

The international treaties concluded between 1850 and 1852 about the duchies of Schleswig and Holstein aimed mainly at strengthening the position of the King of Denmark within the whole monarchy and settling the succession accordingly, though the rights hitherto enjoyed by the Estates, the German *Bund* and the Germans living in the duchies were also acknowledged. Nevertheless, in 1854 and 1855 measures governing the constitution were issued in Denmark by royal decree without consultation with the Estates of the duchies. The Germans, who, except in North Schleswig, outnumbered the Danes throughout both duchies, were completely subordinated to the Danish majority in the newly-created Parliament. The decrees undoubtedly infringed those Danish treaties with Prussia and Austria which contained provisions intended to safeguard the rights of the duchies. The protests of the Schleswig–Holsteiners, Prussia, Austria and the *Bund* were therefore justified. But the Danish Government did not stop here; it took many measures to punish both duchies for their rebellion and to make Schleswig Danish in language and outlook. Many German officials, professors and clergy were dismissed. The democrats (the Eider Danes) were, incidentally, far more intolerant than the conservatives.

In the years following the Crimean War, German national consciousness began to stir more strongly. Even Frederick William IV expressed in the presence of the Danish Ambassador his anger at events in Schleswig–Holstein, which he termed revolutionary and an affront to Germany. Prussia and Austria both took up the complaints of the Schleswig–Holsteiners, if only because their rivalry for predominance in the *Bund* drove them to win over public opinion in the member states to their side. The *Bundestag*, too, protested against measures affecting Holstein, which formed part of the *Bund* and, when Denmark ignored this, threatened military intervention. Negotiations dragged on for years and nationalist feelings ran high on both sides. The King of Denmark might perhaps have been willing to meet Prussian and Austrian demands by agreeing to a personal union which would have given the duchies complete autonomy, but in the face of the Eider Danes he was powerless.

Matters reached a climax in 1863. The King issued a decree on the status of Holstein which infringed Danish undertakings to the German powers. The Diet of the *Bund* therefore decided to send German troops into Holstein. Soon after, the Danish Parliament adopted a new constitution which applied to Schleswig as well. Then, in November 1863, Frederick VII died. Now that the male line was extinct, the problem of the succession became acute. The Treaty of London of 1852 had designated Prince Christian von Glücksburg as heir, but the Germans in Schleswig-Holstein took the view that in the duchies, as distinct from Denmark, only the male succession was legal, a view which is today regarded as correct. They claimed Prince Frederick of Augustenburg, who was closely related to the dynasty which had reigned hitherto, as the sole rightful heir. 'Der Augustenburger', as Frederick was known, was very popular in the duchies and in many circles in Germany. He had the reputation of being a liberal and was on terms of friendship with progressive German princes like the Crown Prince of Prussia and with liberal politicians. Even William of Prussia, who was locked in conflict with the liberals, was convinced that Frederick was the rightful heir, a standpoint from which Bismarck could not make him budge for some time.

Over the Schleswig-Holstein question Bismarck was so cool, even antipathetic, towards the German nationalist view that on one occasion William asked him: 'Are you not also a German?'. Bismarck's whole attitude was that of a Prussian, and he preferred the King of Denmark as ruler of the duchies to a German prince who, probably through fear of the Hohenzollern state, had joined the Opposition to its leadership in Germany. Later, when taxed by the liberals with trying to dispose of the constitutional question by plotting wars, he admitted in private conversation that his foreign policy was conditioned by domestic considerations. The acquisition of the duchies was for reasons of power politics very tempting to Prussia and – he was convinced – essential for the unification of Germany. In particular, the Holstein harbour of Kiel had helped Prussia to build up her sea power, which even the liberals found desirable. It was a stroke of luck for Bismarck that in Austria, after the failure of Schmerling's plans for a reform of the *Bund*, Rechberg's policy of collaboration with Prussia had prevailed. This change sprang largely from Austria's fear that Napoleon III was planning a fresh attack.

Bismarck agreed with Austria on joint action based on the recognition of the Treaty of London whereby Prince Christian entered on the succession in Denmark and the duchies. The Diet of the *Bund*, on the other hand, wanted to make Frederick of Augustenburg Duke of Schleswig and Holstein. Prussia and Austria now proposed the occupation of Schleswig as a pledge for the fulfilment of Denmark's treaty obligations and when the Diet of the *Bund* refused, the two powers acted independently. They presented an ultimatum to Denmark, demanding the immediate repeal of the constitution of November 1863. England tried to persuade Denmark to comply and even Palmerston, no partisan of Germany in the controversy, sharply criticised the policy of Denmark, who he accused of a breach of treaty and of misrule in Schleswig which recalled Russian tyranny in Poland. At the same time the British cabinet did consider armed intervention against the German powers, but this idea was dropped, as no other power was willing to join in.

When the Danes rejected the ultimatum, hostilities began. Palmerston ordered preparations to be made for landing British troops in Denmark but at a cabinet meeting any military intervention was voted down by a great majority. By the end of December 1863 federal troops – Saxons and Hanoverians – had occupied all Holstein without meeting any Danish resistance. Everywhere the population called for Augustenburg as their ruler. On 1 February 1864 Prussian and Austrian troops crossed the frontier into Schleswig and after a few engagements occupied it completely. Here, too, the German population wanted Frederick as their ruler. In Copenhagen crowds raged against the alleged 'betrayal', and even the Queen and one of her daughters were exposed to the grossest insults. The German troops thrust on through Schleswig into Denmark proper, where the Danes resisted stoutly but vainly. A conference held in London in April achieved nothing. Austria and Prussia demanded the independence of the duchies from Denmark, on the basis of a personal union under the Danish King. Christian IX would have gladly agreed, but his ministers declared that this would be followed by the proclamation of a republic in Copenhagen. Austria and Prussia thereupon proposed Frederick of Augustenburg as ruler. Austria associated herself with this demand because she feared that otherwise Prussia would annex the duchies. Bismarck apparently concurred, but secretly he was only prepared to accept Augustenburg on conditions which would have made him a vassal of Prussia.

Various attempts at compromise made during the war foundered on the obstinacy of the Danish politicians. In the end it became clear that England would not give Denmark military help. In July Christian dismissed the Eider–Danish ministry and summoned the moderate

Count Bluhme, who immediately began negotiations with Prussia and Austria. A preliminary peace was signed in Vienna in August, followed by the final instrument in October. Denmark had to cede the two duchies and the little territory of Lauenburg to Prussia and Austria. The duchies had to bear the whole cost of the war and assume a part of the Danish national debt; the calculations were very much in Denmark's favour.

It now had to be decided what was to happen to the duchies. Austria continued to support Augustenburg's candidacy as did almost all the German governments, the great majority of politically-minded Germans and, of course, the German population of Schleswig-Holstein. Bismarck, however, was working to bring the duchies under Prussian sovereignty, although William of Prussia and the Crown Prince resisted this because they felt they had no right to them. The long negotiations with Austria, who continued to support Augustenburg, were not a very great success. When Bismarck revealed his plans for annexation to his Austrian ally, she demanded compensation which he could not grant. Almost to the last moment the King, and even more the Crown Prince, resisted war with Austria. Early in October 1865 Bismarck visited the French Emperor in Biarritz to ensure the latter's neutrality, and although Napoleon gave no definite promise he received him cordially enough. Bismarck also formed connections with Italy. His intention was to bring about a war, but by diplomatic and military threats to force Austria into the role of aggressor.

THE WAR WITH AUSTRIA

The mere idea of an armed conflict with Austria aroused the greatest horror throughout Germany; no party wanted anything to do with this 'fratricidal war'. But Bismarck was undeterred. On 8 April 1866 he concluded a treaty with Italy and on the following day he proposed to the *Bund* the setting-up of a German parliament elected by universal suffrage. This was intended to create an atmosphere favourable to Prussia but it by no means lessened the aversion to war in all the German states, including Prussia. In the liberal press, at meetings of the National League and in the German parliaments hardly anything else was heard but expressions of mistrust and indignation at Bismarck's policy. At many meetings of municipal councils, chambers of commerce and voters the Prussian Government was implored not to go to war. Even the conservative party did its utmost to prevent the outbreak of hostilities. Ludwig von Gerlach, in the columns of the *Kreuzzeitung*, warned against Bismarck's disastrous policy and this mood was shared in the highest circles. King William remained on his knees for hours at a time praying that there would be no war. Queen Augusta and

Elizabeth the dowager Queen, the King's brother, Charles, leader of the feudal Court clique, as well as the Crown Prince and his wife also pleaded with Bismarck. The call-up of the Prussian *Landwehr* led to riots in many places. Bismarck stood almost entirely alone, a target for hostility from every quarter. A young man made an unsuccessful attempt on his life and then committed suicide, which led even educated circles to do no more than deplore the fact that the bullets had missed their mark. Queen Victoria and the British Government, as well as Tsar Alexander, all urged peace. But Bismarck finally got his way because the Austrian Government played into his hands. Prussia now demanded the setting-up of a new *Bund* without Austria, the summoning of a German national assembly and the disarming of those states who supported Austria. When these demands were refused, Prussia sent her troops into the territory of Austria's allies.

In the south the Austrian forces did succeed in defeating the Italians, but in the north her troops and those of her German allies were beaten by the Prussians. Austria asked Napoleon to mediate and ceded Venetia to him for transfer to Italy. Napoleon now initiated negotiations with Prussia as Austria's intermediary. Bismarck took them seriously and offered Austria very favourable terms, even going so far as to propose the division of Germany into two spheres of influence, but no agreement was reached on this basis. Subsequent negotiations were made difficult by William's insistence on harsh peace terms. While Bismarck intended to annex completely several German states which were especially important for Prussia, he did not expect any cessions of territory from the other German states or, indeed, from Austria herself. He hoped by this means to avoid the growth of fresh bitterness and an eventual war waged by the conquered states to regain the territories they had surrendered. It was only by the intervention of the Crown Prince that William could be induced to comply with Bismarck's views. Many generals never forgave Bismarck for robbing them of the chance to win fresh laurels.

By the peace treaty signed in Prague in August 1866 Austria and Saxony ceded no territory to Prussia, but had to pay moderately computed reparations. Austria agreed to the dissolution of the Germanic *Bund* as well as to the setting-up of a North German and South German *Bund*, which Bismarck had previously agreed on with Napoleon. Saxony undertook to join the North German *Bund* and to place her army, posts and telegraphs at its disposal. Prussia took over Schleswig-Holstein. At Napoleon's instance, North Schleswig was to decide by a plebiscite whether it wished to join Denmark, but this provision was not implemented. In Germany, Hesse-Cassel, Hanover, Frankfurt, Nassau and a small part of Hesse-Darmstadt were annexed by Prussia.

These territories not only afforded Prussia a very considerable enlargement but also provided a bridge to her Rhenish-Westphalian territories from which they had hitherto separated her. The South German states had all taken part in the war against Prussia, but they lost no territory, having merely to pay reparations. The South German *Bund* provided for in the treaty did not come into being. Any possibility of fusing the southern states with the North German *Bund* was prevented by Bismarck's agreements with Napoleon. Fear of France led the southern states to conclude secret offensive and defensive alliances with Prussia, and they pledged themselves to leave the supreme command in the hands of the King of Prussia in case of war.

THE END OF THE PRUSSIAN CONSTITUTIONAL CONFLICT

Prussia's victories and the progress made towards national unification also helped to solve her constitutional conflict, which had now been going on for four years. Even during the war fresh elections for the Prussian *Landtag* had been held. The liberals lost many seats, since their open hostility to the war and its cost appeared unpatriotic. The conservatives had been hostile to Bismarck's plans for unification and annexation because they feared that these would damage Prussian traditions, do harm the monarchical principle and help liberal aspirations, but after Prussia's victories many of them changed their attitude, since they had close ties with the army. However, the opposition parties still had an overall majority. There were many liberals who, in the interests of national unity, wanted to reach an understanding with the Government. Bismarck was prepared to give his blessing to a measure for an indemnity, by which the *Landtag* could retrospectively approve the expenditure incurred. For a long time the King opposed this step, which he looked on as an admission that a wrong had been committed. Reactionary circles, which had been strengthened by the wartime elections, were likewise opposed to any understanding with the liberals, and, moreover, cherished hopes of altering or repealing the constitution. Bismarck finally succeeded in overcoming the King's opposition and the indemnity measure was adopted by a large majority. The Progressive Party was split over this issue; most of its members refused to enter upon an understanding with the Government, with which a smaller liberal group led by Twesten and Lasker sided. These two members formed a new party which they first called the National Party and later the National Liberal Party. Its aim was to support the Government in national affairs and at the same time to realise liberal principles within the country. Many other members joined the National Liberals, especially those from the territories just annexed by Prussia as well as from the non-Prussian states of North Germany. This was soon shown in the 1867 elections to the *Reichstag*, the *Zollparlament* (Customs Parliament) and the Prussian *Landtag*. The National Liberals grew in strength while the numbers of the Progressives dwindled. Soon afterwards a new party, which supported Bismarck's policy, broke away from the conservatives. It first styled itself the Free Conservative Party and later the *Deutsche Reichspartei* (German Imperial Party), and included many prominent figures, especially former high officials. The National Liberals and the Free Conservatives formed two centre parties which often took the same line and supported compromises between the Government and the politicians further to the Left.

THE NORTH GERMAN *BUND*

In accordance with the peace treaty, Prussia joined with the states of northern and central Germany to form the North German *Bund*. After the governments had worked out a draft constitution, elections were held in February 1867, on the basis of universal manhood suffrage, for the new Constituent *Reichstag* of the North German *Bund*. This in its turn was to decide on a constitution, which was then to be laid before the parliaments of the federal states for approval. The election revealed a fairly wide dispersal of votes. The National Liberals, with 79 seats, formed the biggest single party. Then came 59 Old Conservatives, 39 Free Conservatives, 27 Old Liberals, 19 Progressives and several smaller groups.

In none of the states was the majority of the people inclined at the outset towards annexation by Prussia, but when this had actually come about, a considerable section in many states subsequently approved; partly because they saw in it progress towards national unity, partly for other reasons and often out of mere indifference. It was hardly surprising that in Hesse-Cassel and Nassau the election results proved unmistakeably nationalistic, that is to say, positively for union with Prussia, for both countries had previously suffered under very bad governments. What was surprising was that in Hanover the majority approved of the new order, for in this country there was a strong particularist movement – known as the 'Guelphs' after the dynasty which had for so long ruled the land – which was sharply anti-Prussian. In Schleswig–Holstein, on the other hand, two-thirds of the electorate, mostly in Schleswig and South Holstein, voted against annexation by Prussia because they were attached to Frederick of Augustenburg, and the people of North Schleswig did the same because the felt themselves to be Danes. There was strong anti-Prussian feeling in the former imperial city of Frankfurt, whose inhabitants had always been pro-Austrian and could not bear the Prussians. When the city was occupied, the Prussian general imposed a heavy war levy on it, though this was later reduced.

The particularism which came out against union with Prussia was the result of historical development, by which not only a strong national consciousness but also an aversion to Prussia had grown up in the territories concerned. Prussia's militarism and Junkerdom were generally loathed, and, besides, union with her entailed conscription and considerably higher taxes, all of which aroused great apprehension in the annexed countries.[1] Even the progressive aspects of Prussian policy, such as freedom to trade, freedom of movement and the equality of the Jews, were far from welcome to many people. That Catholics were not over-anxious to be linked with Prussia is understandable, but there were also orthodox Lutherans to whom the Prussian union of the two Protestant confessional churches was unpalatable.

A draft constitution, which Bismarck had worked out and discussed point by point with representatives of member states, was laid before the North German *Reichstag*. Bismarck often stressed that he was no friend of absolutism, whether monarchical or parliamentary, but he set great store by creating a strong central power, if only because of the international dangers which threatened. He was convinced that Germany's prime need was a militarily and diplomatically strong and durable government which was not at the mercy of the uncertainties of parliamentary struggles for power but could alone be founded on the authority of the Prussian kingdom. But he did not intend in this to rely merely on his compeers east of the Elbe, with whom he was, in fact, to a large extent bitterly at variance. In his considered view, the broad masses of the people must be won over as allies against the liberal bourgeoisie, as Napoleon III had tried to do fifteen years earlier and Disraeli was doing at this time in England. He therefore proposed universal equal franchise for elections to the *Reichstag* – a revolutionary proposal in the eyes of many conservatives and liberals. At the same time he wanted to limit the political power of the people's representatives and this at once led to a violent controversy in the *Reichstag*. Finally, the problem of particularism was still unsolved. Although Bismarck considered a strong central power controlled by Prussia essential, he was, unlike the radical democrats, no unitarian. He was prepared to

---

[1] Eduard Pfeiffer's book *Vergleichende Zusammenstellung der europäischen Staatsausgaben*, 1877, shows with a wealth of statistics that after the founding of the German *Reich* the financial burden on the taxpayer was everywhere doubled or trebled.

concede important rights to the other states of the federation, out of regard for both the time-honoured prerogatives of their princes and the feelings of their peoples, who by no means wanted to be Prussia's subordinates. Bismarck was also well aware that the future attitude of the South Germans, among whom hatred of things Prussian had considerably increased since 1866, would depend on the concessions he made to the individual states in the North German *Bund*.

The draft constitution was debated by the Federal Government at the turn of the year and many amendments were proposed; Prussia accepted eighteen in which no matters of principle were involved but rejected the rest. In essence the draft provided for the setting-up of a federal council (*Bundesrat*) made up of nominees of the governments and under the direction of Prussia, which controlled only 17 of the 43 votes, although of the thirty million inhabitants of the federal states, twenty-five millions were Prussian. The King of Prussia was to appoint the Federal Chancellor, the only federal minister, and was commander-in-chief of the combined armed forces of the *Bund*. In his hands lay the decision on peace or war and the conduct of diplomacy. In these matters only very limited rights were left to the princes and their parliaments. Liability to military service was extended to all the states of the *Bund*, which meant significant extra burdens in services and taxes. The *Reichstag* exercised jointly with the *Bundesrat* the right to enact legislation and to vote the budget, though here their powers were in practice very limited where military expenditure was concerned. All matters affecting the common interests of member states fell within the *Reichstag's* competence, while the individual parliaments took decisions on matters which were the particular concern of their own countries. The finances of the *Reich* were to be secured mainly by customs duties and indirect taxation and, if these proved insufficient, by contributions from the member states.

The *Reichstag* was opened by King William, who read a speech from the throne in which he called upon the members to approve the draft constitution. When the President was elected, all the liberal parties joined in a tribute to the memory of the Frankfurt National Assembly by choosing Eduard Simson, the liberal jurist of Jewish extraction who had presided with distinction in the Church of St Paul and who, it will be recalled, had headed the deputation which offered the King of Prussia the imperial crown. As vice-presidents the Duke of Ujest, a Free Conservative, and Rudolf von Bennigsen, the leader of the National Liberals, were chosen. There followed a detailed discussion on the draft. Numerous members criticised it strongly and demanded a strengthening of the power of the *Reichstag*. Bismarck opposed this, stressing that one could not create an ideal constitution and should rest content with what was feasible at the time and hope for improvements in the future. That degree of freedom which was compatible with the safety of the whole should be realised. In particular, where military matters were concerned, parliamentary influence must not be so great that the stability of the army depended on fluctuating majorities.

The other controversial issue was the responsibility of the *Reich* Government, and here the *Reich's* federal character posed a problem. The ministers of the *Bund* could not be responsible simultaneously to the *Reichstag* and a multiplicity of federal princes and parliaments. The democrat Waldeck, the most out-and-out defender of the sovereignty of the people, would have preferred to abolish federalism altogether on this score. Bismarck showed that he was by no means rigidly opposed to all concessions and on many points he met liberal demands or agreed to a compromise. Thus, von Bennigsen was enabled to carry the principle of the responsibility of the Federal Chancellor, who had to countersign all the proceedings of the Government. As a result of Bennigsen's motion Bismarck himself had to take over the office of Chancellor, which he had not originally intended to do. On the military budget a compromise was reached: Bismarck relinquished his demand for the exclusion of the *Reichstag*, and the army's peace-time strength as well as the estimates for the next four and a half years were approved. The subsequent appropriation was to be voted as a federal measure. The Progressive Party hoped that this would lead to a reduction in the size of the army. Despite Bismarck's objections the liberals carried the principle of the secret ballot at elections for the *Reichstag*. They could not get him to agree to the payment of members, since he held that this would only breed professional politicians and doctrinaires, for which reason he adamantly opposed it. Other concessions to the liberals were an annual budget, a considerable extension of the competence of the *Reichstag*, guarantees of regular meetings and parliamentary liberties.

In the years which followed up to the founding of the German *Reich*, numerous liberal demands were realised. Here a great part was played by Rudolf Delbrück as head of the Federal Chancellor's Office (*Bundeskanzleramt*). The most important innovations were freedom of movement and of trade in all countries of the *Bund*, the abolition of attachment of wages (*Lohnarrest*) and imprisonment for debt, the introduction of the right of association for employees and employers, the regulation of the co-operative trading system, unified weights and measures, as well as posts and telegraphs, the setting-up of a supreme court for commercial cases and the creation of a new penal code. Bismarck followed up an idea embodied in a motion put down by the liberal member Karl Braun of Wiesbaden about the consolidation of the

German *Zollverein*, to which, of course, the South German states also belonged, by means of federal organs. A Federal Customs Council (*Zollbundesrat*) and a Customs Parliament were set up. The latter, which consisted of members of all German states elected on the basis of universal suffrage, met until 1870 under Simson's presidency and can be regarded as the forerunner of complete unification. The new customs union was a much more solid structure than the old, which had been able to modify tariffs only if unanimity was achieved and was often shaken by violent crises. Along with this the South German states and Hesse conducted, partly between themselves and partly with Prussia, military negotiations which aimed mainly at the introduction of universal military service and the reform of army institutions on the Prussian model. Hesse and Baden even concluded a close military agreement with Prussia, and though the other states did not go so far they made radical improvements in their military systems.

Despite all attempts to prepare for the accession of the Germans in the south to the North German *Bund*, majority opinion in the two largest states in the south by no means favoured such a step. In Württemberg the party which supported the link-up (the *Deutsche Partei*) controlled only a fifth of the seats in the *Landtag*, where the Democratic People's Party, which campaigned vigorously for a militia on the Swiss pattern and loathed Prussian militarism, was in a majority. In Bavaria, hatred of Prussia was even stronger, for one thing because the country was predominantly Catholic-clerical, whereas Württemberg was a Protestant stronghold. The anti-Prussian interests in Bavaria formed the Patriotic Party, which was particularly strong among the peasants. Their opponents in the *Landtag* were the liberals, who consisted mainly of Protestants and the intelligentsia in the larger cities, where massive demonstrations for union with the north were sometimes held.

At the instance of Britain and Russia and after long negotiations, the three rulers of the biggest states annexed by Prussia received substantial sums by way of indemnity. But since the ex-King of Hanover and the ex-Elector of Hesse-Cassel continued to intrigue against Prussia, their fortunes were confiscated and used by Bismarck as a fund for influencing the press and similar activities for which he did not have to render any public account.

There was a long and bitter controversy over parliamentary freedom of speech. The constitution of both the *Reich* and Prussia contained provisions protecting members of parliament from prosecution on the grounds of political statements. Despite this, the Prussian Minister of Justice, Count zur Lippe, by interpreting the constitution in a different sense, caused the deputies Twesten and Lasker to be prosecuted.

True, the courts repeatedly acquitted them, but the Minister persisted in trying to secure a conviction and finally had his way. In the Prussian *Landtag* Lasker succeeded in putting through an authentic interpretation of the provision. This led to the quashing of the conviction and the resignation of the Minister. In any case he had not been acting on behalf of Bismarck, who, on the contrary, got the *Reichstag* to approve an adequate constitutional provision for political freedom of speech for members.

The liberal trend in many countries was strong and led to many reforms. In Saxony measures for a fundamentally improved franchise, the introduction of jury courts and the abolition of the death penalty were all approved. Baden passed legislation on schools, the press and ministerial responsibility, and in Prussia, too, numerous bills were introduced and made law. One of the leaders of the Progressive Party, the prominent scientist Rudolf Virchow, proposed a motion in the Prussian lower house on 21 October 1869 for cutting military expenditure and opening diplomatic negotiations for general disarmament. The motion was heavily defeated. The two liberal parties proposed the introduction of universal suffrage for the Prussian Parliament just as it existed for the *Reichstag*.

THE WAR WITH FRANCE

In the first half of his reign Napoleon III enjoyed military, diplomatic and economic successes which filled France with a proud sense of pre-eminence. But then came the years in which his foreign policy ran into difficulties and his prestige dwindled. One of his worst miscalculations was his attempt to exploit the American Civil War to found an empire in Mexico. With the victory of the North this venture became hopeless and came to a bloody end.

After the war in Italy the Emperor began to temper his dictatorship with liberal reforms. This step coincided with Bismarck's triumph in his first two wars, which understandably caused deep concern in France. The unification of Germany ran counter to one of the fundamental principles of French policy and Prussia's military successes offended the military ambitions of powerful circles in France. Napoleon himself, however, hoped to reach a peaceful understanding with Bismarck and was prepared to make him far-reaching concessions, though he expected territorial compensation in return. At the same time he began massive rearmament and gave Marshal Niel the task of reorganising the French army.

The further the concentration of Germany proceeded, the more urgent in the eyes of French statesmen was a settlement of the question of compensation. Napoleon himself was aware of the enormous obstacles to the cession of German Rhenish territories, since German national sentiment must inevitably be opposed to it. There were times when he would gladly have dropped the whole idea, but influential French statesmen left him in no doubt that public feeling at home made this impossible. His minister Drouyn de l'Huys, in particular, kept hammering home the point, assisted by the Empress Eugénie. When the war of 1866 broke out, Napoleon believed that a long struggle lay ahead and that French diplomacy could therefore intervene decisively. This view proved wrong. It may also be mentioned that in conversation with French diplomats Bismarck dropped occasional hints of possible cessions, perhaps at the expense of the Bavarian Rhenish Palatinate, but these were probably never intended seriously.

Prussia's arch-opponent, Drouyn de l'Huys, resigned and Napoleon decided to set out his own considered views in a circular dated 16 September 1866 to French embassies abroad. This document pointed out that the Emperor's policy had fundamentally improved France's security, and that whereas Russia and Austria had hitherto kept Germany within the anti-French camp, the rise of Prussia had now opened up to her the possibility of firm friendship with France. The national movements in Germany and Italy matched the French principle of nationality and would draw their countries closer to France.

French policy vacillated. In December Benedetti the French ambassador had a fresh interview with Bismarck, asked for a decision from the King on Belgium and Luxemburg and proposed a Franco-German alliance. France was now prepared to recognise not only the North German *Bund* but also the extension of Prussian hegemony to Southern Germany. Attention was then focused on Luxemburg, the acquisition of which was to constitute the first step towards the conquest of Belgium. In 1815 the great powers had transferred sovereignty over Luxemburg to the King of Holland as compensation for his German possessions, and Prussia was authorised to garrison the fortress there for protection against attack from France. But Luxemburg did not belong to Holland and joined the German *Bund* and, later, the *Zollverein*. The King of Holland was prepared to transfer it to France for a financial consideration, but when Prussia and Germany protested, he withdrew the offer. Since the German *Bund* no longer existed, a congress of the great powers was held, which declared Luxemburg neutral. Prussia withdrew her garrison and the fortress was dismantled.

The possibility of war between France and Prussia continued to lour like a thundercloud and it needed no more than a trifling cause to make the threat a reality. Napoleon was reluctant to go to war, whereas many of his statesmen and generals would have been prepared to fight before Prussia grew too strong. The highly efficient War Minister, Niel, was, it will be remembered, directing massive rearmament, but this ran into fierce resistance from the Opposition and Niel died in 1869, shortly before war came.

After the 1869 elections, Napoleon decided on a considerable widening of the powers of Parliament. Early in 1870, Emile Ollivier was entrusted with the formation of a liberal ministry. A referendum was held and the new constitution approved by a substantial majority. All the same, fears of a revolution persisted – even with the Empress, who considered successes in foreign policy essential if Bonapartism was to be preserved. Napoleon continued to work tenaciously for peace. He even requested the British cabinet to suggest that Prussia should disarm, and he also got the French Parliament to reduce the call-up of recruits.

Bismarck kept all his options open, even though he was on the whole convinced that the political unification of Germany could hardly be achieved without war with France. At all events he sought to delay the outbreak of hostilities until diplomatic, military and psychological conditions looked as auspicious as possible. The army reform which he had been summoned to carry through was yielding a greater striking power with every year that passed. Besides this there was the experience gained in two wars to be turned to account. Bismarck was, moreover, hoping to be able to sway the mainly anti-Prussian mood of Southern Germany towards his policies. Finally, he attached great importance to making France appear responsible if war should prove inevitable. It was easy to find a pretext for fighting, since both sides were very sensitive where their prestige was concerned.

In fact, it was for reasons of prestige that the war of 1870 did break out. Conditions in Spain at the time were very confused. After Isabella had been banished the Government cast round for a new ruler and their eyes finally lighted on Leopold, hereditary prince of Sigmaringen, who belonged to the Swabian and Catholic branch of the Hohenzollerns, though he was more closely related to the Bonapartes than to William of Prussia. In 1866, Napoleon III had successfully proposed Leopold's brother, Charles of Hohenzollern, as Prince of Rumania whereas William, who, by virtue of an agreement of 1851, was head of the whole Hohenzollern family, had been uneasy. William now also opposed Leopold's candidature for the Spanish crown and Leopold himself was disinclined to accept the honour. But they were at last persuaded by Spain and Bismarck to acquiesce. The candidature aroused the sharpest opposition in France and led to threats of war. On 6 July 1870 the French Foreign Minister, the Duc de Gramont, declared that France could not permit a foreign power to set one of its princes on the throne of Charles V and thus upset the equilibrium of Europe and imperil France's interests and honour. This comparison between nineteenth-century Spain and the empire on which 'the sun never set' sounded odd. The Spain of 1870 was more like a South American republic in which military pronunciamentos and civil strife constantly recurred. A study of the utterances of French ministers, diplomats, members of parliament and newspapers of the day reveals above all else a pre-occupation with 'national honour'. But there also existed a peace party, which had no time for excessive and touchy nationalism. Prussia's military successes had disgruntled the French army, which was looking for a chance to prove itself superior. The Emperor was criticised for having been too compliant towards Bismarck. Besides, up to 1868 Spain had long been ruled by a branch of the House of Bourbon and was closer to France than to Germany. On the face of it, a German prince on the throne of Spain seemed a threat to French security; at any rate, this provided a pretext for agitation.

It is today beyond doubt that from the outset Bismarck had secretly and vigorously backed the candidature of Leopold. What end did he have in view? Even if he did maintain in his memoirs that he was primarily seeking economic advantages for Germany, this sounds most unlikely, for he usually left such considerations to others. But he was right when he wrote: 'No Spanish government, and least of all a foreign king, would wield enough authority in the country to send even one regiment to the Pyrenees out of love for Germany'. So there was never any question of strengthening the Prussian armed forces. The most probable explanation is that Bismarck was seeking an opportunity to provoke France's jealous concern for her prestige and thus unleash a war which would fire the hearts of the South Germans, who were very hostile to Prussia, and fuse them into one nation with the Germans of the North. It is a commonplace that one of the factors leading to the formation of nation-states has been the participation by various tribes in common wars; another has been conquest. It must be said that Bismarck, true to his nature, was not at the outset bent on war at all costs, but only when the French Government made demands which could not but be seen as a grave injury to Prussian prestige.

The danger of war caused Leopold to withdraw his candidature only a week after it had been announced; William of Prussia heartily concurred, for he would have been very reluctant to consent to the arrangement. The French Prime Minister Ollivier thereupon declared the matter settled, but Gramont, in collusion with the war party, went further and demanded that William should also guarantee that the Hohenzollern candidature would never be renewed and that in addition he should write a letter to Napoleon which could be interpreted as a

L

kind of apology. William rejected this somewhat impudent demand for a guarantee for the future, but quite without heat. It had been a severe blow to Bismarck that Leopold had stood down and that war would now probably be averted, but when the report of the King's conversations in Ems with the French Ambassador Benedetti reached him, he suddenly saw how he could carry his policy through after all. He made a summary of the essentials of this report without adding anything and published it. Such was the origin of the 'Ems telegram'. It was skilfully calculated to inflame French public opinion by giving the impression of a brusque dismissal of the French demand, whereas the original document had left a continuation of the negotiations in Berlin open. The omission of important passages certainly distorted the sense. No historian could risk doing this to a document without being justly accused of falsification. As Bismarck himself later wrote, he was by this means waving a red rag before the Gallic bull and getting it to charge in a blind frenzy. If the French Government had kept its head, it could, with the help of the despatches from its ambassador, have uncovered Bismarck's game and possibly brought about his fall. Late in the evening of 13 July and on the next day the contents of the Ems telegram became widely known. At the same time a council of ministers was held in Paris under the chairmanship of the Emperor, at which he and the great majority of his ministers, especially Ollivier, were for peace, whereas Gramont and the War Minister called for mobilisation, which was approved after a debate of some hours. The Emperor now proposed a European congress which should establish the principle that members of dynasties which ruled over great powers could not ascend foreign thrones. The majority accepted this proposal with delight. Even Gramont, who at first raised objections, finally agreed and thought that by this expedient the guarantees for the future from William of Prussia need not be insisted upon. The call-up of the reserves was deferred. Peace seemed saved.

The postponement of mobilisation had meanwhile caused such a stir among the army and the people at large that a government which came out in favour of peace must inevitably fall. Moreover, fresh reports came in containing the text of the Ems telegram and sensational but untrue accounts of the events in Ems. A further meeting of ministers was called, and, with Gramont and even Ollivier now calling for war, the Emperor was no longer able to carry his proposal for a congress. Mobilisation was decided on at midnight.

On 15 July the Government informed Parliament that war was now inevitable. Thiers objected on the grounds that Prussia had accepted France's main demand. He warned against undue haste and demanded that the despatches be produced. A war with Prussia, he said, would be calamitous and they would live to regret their precipitancy. Ollivier thereupon declared that war was necessary, that the French Ambassador had been shown the door, and that by what Thiers had called touchiness he, Ollivier, understood a sense of honour. It was unnecessary to produce the despatches. At this, Gambetta called for at least the production of the one according to which William of Prussia was supposed to have refused to see the Ambassador. Ollivier replied that not only was this refusal a fact, but that it had also been communicated to all the countries of Europe and given wide currency by the press. He could, he said, assume the responsibility with a light heart and in full knowledge of the justice of the cause he defended. This war had been forced on France. Later in the debate, Ollivier stated that the King's refusal to receive the Ambassador had been conveyed in the politest possible terms, and that the Ambassador himself was not conscious of any offensive intention and had telegraphed in this sense. This startling statement was punctuated with numerous interjections from the Opposition and considerably weakened any justification for the war. Thiers accused the Government of having brought about the war by unnecessary demands after Leopold's candidature had been withdrawn. In any case, the other European powers should have been given time to mediate. Jules Favre, too, declared that the Government was responsible for the war and called for production of the despatches, but the motion was rejected by a decisive majority. In the evening session, the Government's military estimates were voted almost unanimously.

If the Government had produced the despatches or agreed to mediation, then it would at once have been evident that William had not really insulted France but that it was Bismarck who had given this impression in the Ems telegram. The King, although he was taking what at his age was a very strenuous cure, had received Benedetti several times and treated him with marked courtesy. True, he had broken off personal negotiations but this was no bar to their resumption through the normal channels, as Bismarck himself subsequently admitted.

Napoleon later declared that he had not wanted war, but had been forced into it by 'public opinion'. This was certainly his real conviction and also that of many other French statesmen. But it must be added that in this instance so-called 'public opinion' by no means reflected the wishes of the great majority of the French people, but rather the nationalistic hunger for prestige of certain influential groups which were particularly centred in Paris. These were drawn from army officers, some sections of the civil service and the intelligentsia, and stunt journalists. They had it in their power to spread a feverish

chauvinism, summed up in the slogan: To Berlin![1] Some peace demonstrations took place but were broken up. The precondition for the influence of nationalistic circles on the masses lay in the widespread
tradition of revolution and the cult of Bonaparte, whose magic phrase
'la grande nation' was still potent and swamped all sensible thinking
in a flood of rhetoric. Bismarck's and Moltke's military triumphs later
created a similar tradition in Germany, which eventually enabled
nationalists and militarists to plunge their own country and others
into the most abject misery, though this was not possible during
Bismarck's time in office: he was far too cautious and farsighted for that.
It is a curious feature that, before the war of 1870, France's striving
for prestige often found expression in the naive idea that she would
soon beat Prussia, make peace and then clasp hands with her.

When William learned that France was mobilising he ordered that
Prussia should follow suit. In Germany, France was seen as the aggressor
and on all sides such conduct in a neighbour aroused a sense of deep
indignation. Both the particularist patriotism of the North German
states, which inspired the conservatives, and the hope of at last achieving
full unification, especially marked among the liberals and democrats,
spread a vast enthusiasm and martial outlook far and wide. Bismarck's
activity in bringing the war about was not known at the time, and it was
many years before this information began to circulate; even if it had
been known, this could scarcely have held the prevailing mood in check.

In the southern states the situation was less clear-cut, especially as
the interpretation of the conditions of their military alliance with
Prussia was a matter of controversy. The opponents of Prussia maintained that their states had the right to declare themselves neutral.
In February 1870 the particularist Patriotic Party in Bavaria had
brought down the Prime Minister, Prince Hohenlohe, who supported
union with North Germany. When France decided on war, the Bavarian
Government did, it is true, mobilise but at the same time made peace
proposals. The committee which debated mobilisation voted by six
to three for Bavaria's neutrality. The Government declared that
Bavaria's agreement with Prussia was binding if, as seemed probable,
an attack on German territory should take place. Part of the Patriotic
Party joined the nationalists and the majority approved the credits
requested 'should war prove inevitable'. In Württemberg, too, the
Government mobilised and the Parliament passed military estimates,
though some influential members declared that in a situation similar to
Bavaria's they would have voted for neutrality. The war, they said,

---

[1] Malcolm Carroll, however, in his detailed study *French Public Opinion*
(pp. 25, 31, 33, 42), says that neither public opinion nor the Ems telegram was
decisive for the outbreak of war and cites evidence for this.

was merely a consequence of the work of 1866, i.e. of Bismarck's policy. In Baden the *Landtag* was not summoned at all, so sure was the Government of its approval.

The French Government had believed that South Germany would stay neutral, though they doubtless intended to march in and occupy the territory. The Foreign Minister Gramont had, moreover, seized on a pretext to threaten Baden with the most frightful devastation. There could be no question of a real neutrality such as the South German opponents of the war envisaged.

The course of the war needs no description here. The French armies were successively beaten, Napoleon III taken prisoner and Paris conquered. Eleven months after the outbreak of war the Peace of Frankfurt was concluded, by which France ceded Alsace and Lorraine and gave an undertaking to pay five milliards of francs in reparations, which she proceeded to do with surprising alacrity. Of all these conditions, Prussia's annexation of Alsace and Lorraine had the most fateful consequences, for it poisoned political relations between France and Germany. At first Bismarck was against this measure, but in the *Reichstag* he defended it with the military argument that the two provinces formed a projecting wedge which made it possible for French troops to invade South Germany before help could reach her.

Many in Germany wished for milder peace terms, because otherwise they foresaw evil consequences. Many, too, were opposed to the annexations for economic reasons, as, for example, the cotton magnates and ironfounders, who feared competition from Alsace-Lorraine. But such misgivings had little chance of consideration in the face of a vehement 'national' demand. The great majority of voices called for the annexations on the grounds of justice and national security, and prophesied that the mainly German-speaking Alsatians would soon feel themselves to be Germans again. Only a few could foresee that German administration would put the greatest difficulties in the way of the moral reclamation of considerable sections of the Alsatians by treating them as second-class citizens. France, if she had won, would probably have annexed the German Rhine provinces and used the same arguments as Bismarck – that they were essential for national defence.

Prussia's victory led to the elevation of William to German Emperor. He had long held out against accepting this honour, because he considered the style 'King of Prussia' far more glorious than any imperial title, and it took all Bismarck's skill and cunning to overcome his objections. The act of proclamation as emperor bore an almost exclusively royal and military character, which was symbolic of the pattern of the new empire. Bismarck's services were rewarded by

William by the conferment on him of the title of prince and the grant of extensive domains.

THE CROWN PRINCE AND THE WAR OF 1870–1

During the Franco–Prussian war Frederick William, the Crown Prince and later Emperor, kept a diary which was by no means intended for the public eye. He was commander-in-chief of all South German troops along with a Prussian corps, with his friend, Lt-Gen. von Blumenthal, at his side, and in the course of the campaign this army won some notable successes. In many passages the Crown Prince expressed his loathing for the war. Near the beginning he wrote that the great powers should call a halt to the slaughter in the name of Christian and civilised humanity. On 7 September 1870 he wrote:

Despite all the victories and the exaltation they bring, I ask myself every day how this mutual slaughter in the manner of wild beasts can still be possible in the face of all the Christian doctrines of virtue and morality which are daily preached. I cannot bear to dwell on these contradictions; if I did I should go almost out of my mind....

He brooded on whether the demoralisation nourished by warlike passions would grow still worse after the war and hoped that there would be a revulsion of feeling. The princes and governments, he went on, had a duty to grapple without delay with the problems of the inner development of a liberal state and a truly national life and the *Volkszeitung* was setting out some excellent views on this subject which followed his own line of thought. Later the Crown Prince often quoted from this democratic paper, whereas he scarcely mentioned any others.

During the siege of Paris he stayed at army headquarters at Versailles. At the time there were considerable differences of opinion over the best way to reduce Paris. Moltke and the General Staff considered an effective bombardment of the city possible only if sufficient heavy artillery were brought up, which was not practicable. Storming the outlying forts would take a heavy toll of life, and it was therefore best to starve Paris out. Bismarck fought this view, saying it would prolong the war and maintaining that the King and his generals were influenced by humanitarian motives inspired by Queen Augusta, the Crown Prince, his English wife and other high personages. Humanity, said Bismarck, had no place here; rather one must make the inhabitants suffer in such a way that they would force the authorities to surrender. Bismarck also considered it a mistake to lay siege to Paris, and expressed the opinion that it would have been better to occupy as large an area of France as possible. The siege did, in fact, enable the republicans

Gambetta and Freycinet to form large new armies in unoccupied France. They fought bravely, and though this did not prevent a German victory it caused further heavy losses. Paris was under siege for four months and when, after all, heavy artillery was at last brought up, the city soon capitulated. It was mainly the forts which were bombarded; the number of civilians killed by artillery fire was very small.

The bombardment of Paris is dealt with at length in the Crown Prince's diary. On 8 January 1871 he wrote:

I confess that at every shot fired into the city my heart turned over, because I thought of the innocent people who have to suffer under this evil of war; in particular, I cannot dismiss from my mind the thought of the children who may possibly be hit.

It was, he said, a real cross for him to do his duty in these circumstances and he only hoped that peace might bring some progress which would atone, at least in part, for the horrors of what was then happening. He had learned, he added, that his distaste for this bloody trade was well known in France and that he had the reputation of letting forbearance and mercy prevail wherever possible. He went on to condemn any expression of national arrogance and Francophobia in Germany. He called such utterances 'the babble of the mob' and said they must be fought. He himself would do all in his power to bring about reconciliation, agreement and mutual understanding.

With views like these Frederick William often came into collision with Bismarck, whose policy, he said, was bringing Germany into disrepute with other nations, for while at the outset all Europe had been convinced – and indignant – that Germany had been attacked, the longer the struggle lasted, the more was sympathy swinging over to France and hatred developing for Germany. On 31 December 1870 the following entry occurs:

'We are considered capable of any baseness and mistrust of us is daily on the increase. This is not the result of the war alone: it is to this pass that the theory of blood and iron, invented by Bismarck and practised for years, has brought us! Of what use to us is all the power, all the martial glory and glitter, if we are met at every turn by hatred and mistrust, if every step forward we take meets grudging suspicion? Bismarck has made us great and powerful, but he has robbed us of our friends, of international sympathy and – of our own clear conscience. I still stand by the view that Germany without blood and iron but using her just influence could have made "moral conquests" and become united, free and powerful. She would then

have achieved a superiority quite different from that gained solely
by force of arms, because German culture, German science and the
German nature could not but win us esteem, love and – honour.
This bold and violent Junker wanted it otherwise.'

When the elections for the Prussian lower house drew near, the Crown
Prince was most anxious that the people should not be misled by their
country's successes in the war and should return only such men as had
a truly liberal development of the state at heart. A few days later, he
recorded that he had read with real pleasure the leading article on the
elections in the *Volkszeitung* and its exhortations to hold fast to the
liberal principle in all circumstances matched his own innermost
thoughts.

The founding of the *Reich* and the elevation of his father to be its
emperor were greeted with great joy by Frederick William, but he
often stressed that it must be a free state which stood at the head of
civilisation and fostered all noble ideas. The *Volkszeitung*, he wrote,
strikingly exposed the shortcomings of the constitution as well as the
lack of fundamental rights and adequate control by the *Reichstag*. This
was unfortunately true but he hoped that all shortcomings could be
made good. When he came to power, an era would dawn in which one
would be honourably subject to a liberal constitution. The *Volkszeitung*
was right in considering a really retrograde step impossible, since the
whole people had taken part in the national movement. On this confidence he based his hopes for such time as was left for him and whose
claims he intended to meet. Above all, the social question must be
solved. At the peace negotiations it was of prime importance to be
moderate and demand no territory which was really French. The
annexation of German-speaking areas was justified, but they should be
granted autonomy. He also had doubts whether their inhabitants would
soon feel themselves to be Germans again.

We know today that not only the Crown Prince but also his mother
Queen (shortly afterwards Empress) Augusta and others who stood
close to them wanted a lenient peace and a speedy reconciliation of the
two peoples. Remarks made by Bismarck to his intimates show that he
never ceased to regard this court circle with mistrust and aversion and
did everything he could to work against them. Many of the generals,
even more strongly than Bismarck, rejected humane impulses in the
war and in this respect exercised a strong influence on the King–
Emperor William I, who at the end of the war was seventy-four and
lived to see his ninety-first year. How utterly different might have been
the course of world history if his son had come to power considerably
earlier! Even if he could not have worked miracles, he would all the same

have done much to heal the wounds of the war. True, this is what Bismarck also wanted but his resources were inadequate.

ALSACE-LORRAINE

The annexation of Alsace–Lorraine was the main cause of the deep gulf which was opened up between France and Germany by the war. Before 1870 there was no strong movement in Germany for the incorporation of Alsace-Lorraine. During the war the mood in Germany changed because France was considered the aggressor, and recovering the provinces which had formerly belonged to the Holy Roman Empire thus seemed fully justified to many Germans. The right of self-determination was by no means recognised by international law. Napoleon III, it is true, had proclaimed it as a guiding principle and supported it in a number of cases, but he had also made some exceptions. The English liberals had at various times supported the principle for the Italians, Poles, Hungarians and the inhabitants of Schleswig, but it was not granted by Britain to the Irish, Indians and many other peoples. Lord John Russell had declared that England intended to retain Canada only for as long as Canada wished. But risings by French-Canadians and semi-native groups were put down by force. In the American Civil War English public opinion was divided over whether the Southern states had the right of self-determination. France, in the course of her colonial expansion which was soon under way, was far from granting this right to the peoples concerned and would certainly not have granted it to the Germans if she had been victorious in 1870. Given this absence of any clear-cut ruling under international law, many liberals and even some declared democrats in Germany held that it was permissible to incorporate Alsace-Lorraine into the *Reich*. They were also convinced that the Alsatians in particular, who were for the greater part German-speaking, would soon accept the idea. In the case of the Lorrainers, there were bigger doubts. The generals' demand for Metz and other French territories on the grounds of their strategic importance for the defence of South Germany aroused in Bismarck and many others considerable misgivings, which, however, these military 'demigods', as Bismarck termed them, ignored.

Over annexations without the consent of the inhabitants the liberal-minded Grand Duke Frederick of Baden, for example, and the later Field Marshal von Loë had serious doubts. Some editors of leading newspapers, like Leopold Sonnemann, proprietor of the *Frankfurter Zeitung*, who as a deputy in the *Reichstag* voted against the incorporation of Alsace-Lorraine, and Dr Heinrich Kruse of the *Kölnische Zeitung* voiced similar views. Kruse had earlier come out against the annexation of North Schleswig. On the orders of the military, the deputy Johann Jacoby, editor of the democratic paper *Zukunft*, was confined to a fortress because of his attitude, though Bismarck intervened and he was released. The democratic *Volkszeitung*, which has already been mentioned in connection with the Crown Prince's views, opposed any peace terms such as annexations which made reconciliation between France and Germany difficult.

In later years Bismarck himself repeatedly described the annexations as a serious mistake, even in conversation with the French Ambassador in 1879. One of the leading liberals, Max von Forckenbeck, President of the *Reichstag* and Chief Burgomaster of Berlin, also opposed this policy. Julius von Eckardt, a Balt, declares in his memoirs that annexations must inevitably set up an insurmountable barrier between France and Germany, make a Franco-German alliance impossible and force Germany into the arms of Russia, which would lead to the most brutal Russianisation of the Balts. The attitude of the German social democrats was at first coloured by the conviction that Napoleon III alone bore responsibility for the war, although even then Bebel suspected that Bismarck had laid a trap for the Emperor, but when on 24 November the *Reichstag* was informed that hostilities would be continued on account of Alsace-Lorraine, Bebel and Liebknecht declared that the war had assumed the character of one of conquest and called for an immediate peace. The party followed their lead and issued a pointed manifesto on these lines. The members of the party executive were arrested and charged with high treason. Bebel and Liebknecht were given prison sentences of two years. There were many other German politicians who rejected annexation as being a violation of the right of self-determination, but they could make no headway against the storm of public opinion. Even among the social democratic workers such a mood prevailed that Bebel protested against the 'national paroxysm' and Liebknecht was so sickened by the 'patriotic frenzy' that he considered emigrating to America.

THE EFFECT OF THE WARS ON THE PUBLIC MIND

Bismarck's wars exercised a powerful influence on the Germans and many other nations. Various forms of this influence must be distinguished, namely the immediate effect of the wars on the psychology of those who took part in them, the subsequent mental assimilation and the change in the spirit of the age. At first every war induces outbreaks of passion, patriotic enthusiasm, hatred of the enemy and other emotions. In a war, a closer knowledge of its causes is concealed from the people at large and any more profound weighing up of the rights and wrongs of the case is ruled out, because they do not know the facts and because a really impartial frame of mind is hardly possible. When injustices and acts of cruelty are committed during a war, legal investigation of the incidents is not always practicable. In any case, bitterness towards the enemy remains and the nations concerned receive into their ideologies many legends which often actively persist for years. Critical consideration of the war and its causes, as well as support for a rapprochement, mostly comes later. Finally, wars have an effect not only on those who take part in them but also on other nations, whose judgement, while less one-sided, is not uninfluenced by their own national ideologies.

War psychology lasts longest in military circles, where it is systematically fostered. The mercantile classes are among the first who seek to overcome it, in so far as they are concerned with world trade. The attitude of the other professions, classes and social groups depends on a variety of circumstances. In a fully-developed, centralised national state, however, the 'national interest' is the most potent factor. Since the French Revolution, modern nationalism, which saw the unity, strength and prestige of the nation as its supreme goal, spread ever wider. It must be said, of course, that in the ideologies of the political parties it was mixed with other aims. The strongest emphasis on nationalism was found, among others, in officials, writers and journalists. In Germany the spread and intensification of nationalism met extremely strong obstacles, notably particularism, which represented a kind of territorially limited national sense and was strongly buttressed by dynasties and historical memories. Another obstacle was Germany's cleavage into two religious communities, whereas each of the other peoples which attained to national unity was predominantly of one faith which was regarded as the state religion. A nationalism developed all the same among the Germans, but it was one which reached its full development only through the foundation of the *Reich*. Before this, observers both in and outside Germany often noticed a lack of national pride, whereas later they were not infrequently struck by an excess of it. At all events, for a long time there was energetic opposition, especially in the south, to Bismarck's national policy, as the elections to the *Zollparlament* proved.

Even after the founding of the *Reich*, this spirit was by no means extinguished. The Empire and the form of its constitution were admittedly approved with some reservations, but many were hoping to modify it along lines of their own. Bismarck's struggle with the Centre was directed above all at the enemies of his nationalistic power politics, and his hatred of the liberals of the left was largely aimed at their tendency towards internationalism and their hostility to a strong army. Many of his old opponents made their protest in print. The historian and publicist Gervinus, one of Germany's first liberal mentors, had urged his people not to consider themselves merely a nation of thinkers and poets but to go in for politics and combine freedom with power. In his view, foreign policy would compel the country at large to feel itself to be a single whole and overcome petty internal squabbles. In 1848 he had supported the *kleindeutsch* programme and would not even have flinched from war with Russia and Austria in order to unite Germany and restore Poland. Bismarck's founding of the *Reich* was a keen disappointment to him. He rallied the remnants of his powers to set down what he felt and thought about it, and the document[1] was published soon after his death in 1871. He declared that the new empire conflicted with the federalistic and peaceful nature of the Germans, that annexations made after 1866 should be reversed and that Germany should not develop into a powerful centralised state under a military dictatorship. Instead, she should form a truly federal state which should adopt a purely defensive attitude and strive to initiate an era of peace and disarmament. He agreed with the peace concluded with France, but German chauvinism and unbridled Franco-phobia filled him with disgust.

Gervinus was not alone in criticising at the very outset Bismarck's founding of the *Reich*. A whole chorus of voices echoed his views,[2] and throughout the Bismarck era there was always a strong opposition to the Chancellor's system. Against this it must be said that his extra-ordinary successes weakened the principles of many of his critics and won them over to his régime. Although, once the *Reich* had been founded, he followed a policy which sought to preserve peace and shunned the pursuit of prestige at any price, his activity in office – though this was not his intention – greatly helped the rise of a dangerous nationalism, the most pernicious manifestations of which appeared only after his fall. It is going too far to accuse him of an unparalleled destruction of Christian and moral principles in politics. Bonaparte, Frederick the Great, Cromwell and Richelieu and numerous other 'great men' went further than he in violations of accepted justice and they have many admirers even today. German democrats saw no injustice at all in the deposition of German princes. The argument that the standards of private morality do not apply to questions of world history has been advanced or adopted by many statesmen and political theorists in all the great nations.

[1] Vide his literary remains, especially his memorandum on peace addressed to the Prussian royal house, 1872.
[2] A good description of this tendency is to be found in Hans Kohn's *The Mind of Germany*, 1961, p. 157.

In discussion inside Germany, the demand for securing her frontiers by the annexation of Alsace-Lorraine was justified on the grounds that in the course of history the French nation had again and again shown itself incapable of resisting the urge for war which prevailed in leading circles. Napoleon III and French statesmen laid the blame for war on this occasion on 'public opinion'. In Germany it was argued that throughout history the French nation had cherished a strong desire for martial glory and hegemony in Europe and therefore bore a share of responsibility, and the utterances of leading French politicians and historians could be adduced in support. Thus, the French War Minister Niel had declared on 23 December 1867: 'The French people has from time immemorial been very proud and the army is its image. Gallic blood runs in its veins and it cannot long endure a danger which threatens it: rather should there be war at once'. Two of the most important French historians and statesmen, Thiers and Guizot, have expressly confirmed the unusual proclivity of the French nation to war.[1]

On the other hand, much could be quoted to show that a pacific attitude existed among broad sections of the French people. It was precisely among the intellectuals, where nationalism was widely spread, that there were many who had a deep interest in and admiration for German culture, and evinced great sympathy for the German movement towards freedom and unity. A whole series of leading scholars and writers were of this cast of thought. The *Revue des deux Mondes* and other periodicals possessed a brilliant group of contributors who were predominantly Germanophile. Ollivier, too, who headed the Government in the summer of 1870, was well disposed towards Germany and her national movement. The outbreak of war aroused the utmost consternation in these circles; many of them cast about desperately for a just peace while many others were in two minds. Victor Hugo, who was in Paris during the siege and bombardment, was moved to write a poem in which he hymned Germany in lines of incomparable splendour and fervency. He did not allow a single angry word to creep in; none of the foremost German poets has ever composed such a magnificent hymn to Germany's greatness, justice and beauty. To France he directed only the words 'Ma mère!' But the subsequent distress of his mother, the harshness of the conquerors and the rising flood of hatred soon swept him away into other poems in which he demanded bloody revenge. France must first hurl the Germans to the ground and plant her foot on them before she could become reconciled with them.

A particular admirer of German culture was the well-known scholar Renan. When, in 1843, he began to know more of Germany through

[1] The quotations can be found in my book *Nationality in History and Politics* p. 376.

the works of Goethe and Herder, he had felt, as he put it in 1870, as if he were entering a temple, but from 1870 onwards everything which he had hitherto considered a glory worthy of the godhead made no more impression on him than faded and yellowing paper flowers. Only a year before the war he had seen in Germany the model for a radical reform of French cultural and political conditions. He hoped for the fraternal union of the Gallic and Germanic spirit, with an assured peace and Alsace-Lorraine the chosen mediator. His dream was of a spiritual, moral and political alliance with Germany and England, to conquer the Slav threat or even civilize Russia. The outbreak of war was a shattering blow to him and the German demand for Alsace-Lorraine drove him to despair. An exchange of letters took place between him and the German scholar David Friedrich Strauss, which showed that, although they shared the same fundamental convictions, they could still not reach an understanding. Strauss clung above all to the cession of Alsace-Lorraine to Germany because, so he argued, the French people, through the urge for prestige and glory which had grown up among them, would always remain a danger to peace, even without the annexation of these territories. Napoleon III, he wrote, had 'repeatedly added fuel to the national passion for pomp, glory and conquest in order to lead his nation astray and divert its attention away from the moral and political depravity within'. While paying homage to French cultural achievements, he criticises the 'general decay and disintegration of all moral bonds, both in literature and among the people'. Strauss's letters are, however, strongly tinged by the German war ideology.[1]

During the war and after it, many other writings appeared which saw the deeper cause of the conflict and the course it took in qualities inherent in the national mind of the two countries; naturally enough, the author's own country usually came off better than the enemy's, which was often portrayed as being positively barbaric or completely corrupt. But there were also some people who really strove to be impartial, such as Hippolyte Taine and Gabriel Monod, both historians of integrity.[2] While Taine considered that everything hinged on the attitude of the Alsace-Lorrainers at that particular point of time, Treitschke based himself on the national spirit (*Volksgeist*), which had developed throughout history and was an unconscious factor; according to this, the Alsatians belonged to the Germans even if the present

---

[1] See his collected works.

[2] Taine's and Treitschke's views are appraised in detail in W. Bussmann: *Treitschke*, pp. 341 ff. On Monod's book, *Allemands et Français*, cf. Hillebrand's *Frankreich und die Franzosen*, p. 364. Hillebrand also discusses other French comments.

generation disputed the fact. (Incidentally, no other scholar has done so much to intensify German nationalism as Treitschke). From conversations with his German friend Karl Hillebrand and his own researches, Taine concluded that for sixty years German scholars had been teaching their people to regard themselves as the chosen race. Both Taine and Renan examined critically the unhappy political conditions in France which had contributed to the débâcle. As early as 1859 Renan had reached the conclusion that the tradition of the great Revolution had worked perniciously on the national mind. After the defeat of 1870 he made this view the basis of his book *La Réforme Intellectuelle et Morale.*[1] Taine came to similar conclusions, which he set out in his great work *Les Origines de la France Contemporaine* (six volumes, 1876–94).

Of the German participants in this controversy, Karl Hillebrand deserves particular mention. He had lived for a long time in France and had had the opportunity to make thorough observations. In his book on France,[2] he decisively rebuts the accusations made against the private morals and way of life of the French, but, in common with Renan and Taine, finds much that is unhealthy in their political life. He recognises the enormous influence of the French spirit on mankind, and even considers the traditions of the old French monarchy admirable, despite the great harm it had done Germany. On the other hand he finds much to criticise in the Germans, and he was consequently attacked as unpatriotic. At the very beginning of his book, he remarks (pp. 4 ff.) that since the forties the demon of arrogance had been stirring in the sphere of German learning, claiming for the Germanic races the role of the chosen people, talking of 'German virtues' and occasionally beginning to look down on the Romance and Slav races. Hillebrand gives one or two examples of this – that Gothic architecture, for instance, which originated in Northern France, was held to be Old German. He admits that since the sixties a distinct reaction against national conceit had set in among distinguished scholars. There could be no question of the French nation being in a slough of despond comparable with that of Germany after the Thirty Years' War. One had no need, he went on, to go back very far to find conditions in Germany beside which the notorious corruption of the Second Empire paled into insignificance. This ought to cool down somewhat the Germans' pride in their own virtue and to some extent shake their belief in innate racial superiority.

[1] The views of Renan are reproduced and critically examined in my book *Nationalgeist und Politik*, pp. 78 ff. Taine's conception of the French Revolution has been criticised by many French historians but contains a very important core of truth.

[2] *Frankreich und die Franzosen*, 1874.

How much better had their grandfathers known France and England! Napoleon III, whom Hillebrand respects as a benefactor of Europe, had been swept into the war by the 'nation' against his better judgement and his own wishes. But this 'nation' had not been the whole French people, merely certain sections whose voice passed for that of public opinion, such as sensation-mongering journalists and many Parisian politicians, who contrived to carry the whole country with them and tyrannise it. In this way the people had had a part in unleashing war, but without realising what they were doing. Alsace-Lorraine had been incorporated into Germany for reasons of security, and in the firm conviction that the succeeding generation there would be Germany's, body and soul. But Hillebrand thinks that the peace treaty went too far and that nearly all true liberals in Germany criticised and regretted the annexation of Metz.[1]

[1] *Op. cit.*, p. 329, 330.

24

THE *REICH* UNDER BISMARCK

THE BIRTH OF THE *REICH*

The German *Reich* came into being when the southern states joined the North German *Bund*. Bismarck was quick to negotiate with the South during the war of 1870–1, in order, as he said, to prevent an evaporation of national enthusiasm before the *Anschluss* took place. He well knew that there were still considerable difficulties to overcome and was prepared to make appropriate concessions. In this respect he was much more farsighted than many liberals and democrats, who would have preferred to dethrone more princes and form a single state. Even the Crown Prince of Prussia, whose advisers were mostly liberals, toyed for a time with such plans but later dropped them. Bismarck was utterly opposed to applying any pressure which he felt might lead to a 'latent civil war', and so he was very cautious in his negotiations with the South. Baden had long been ready to join the North; the strongest resistance was put up by Bavaria, but Württemberg soon decided to join, thus forcing Bavaria's hand. Bismarck even managed to get Ludwig of Bavaria to sign a letter (drafted by Bismarck) inviting William of Prussia to become the German Emperor. In return Ludwig received large sums of money from Bismarck out of secret funds, but he soon regretted his agreement. Certain special rights were reserved for the two southern states, notably administration of their own post and telegraph services and excise taxes. Bavaria was further allowed the control of her own army in peacetime, whereas Württemberg, like Saxony before her, had to rest content with a War Ministry of her own and the appointment of officers by her king. In addition, a few provisions were included in the constitution of the *Reich* which gave the Federal States a bigger say in foreign policy.

The treaties with the South German states were approved by the latter's *Landtage* and the North German *Reichstag*, though the two-thirds majority required by Bavarian law was only just obtained.

Bavaria's agreement was made considerably easier by a move which Bismarck made towards a rapprochement with Austria. What he did was to inform the Austrian Government in very friendly terms of the conclusion of the treaties. The Bavarian Foreign Minister Count Bray-Steinburg announced this in the lower house and hailed it as a political act which would lead to an alliance with Austria – i.e. to a realisation of the *grossdeutsch* idea – another instance of the masterly fashion in which Bismarck was able to influence popular opinion.

The constitution of the *Reich* was based on that of the North German *Bund*, which was altered in only a few points. The number of Prussian seats in the *Bundesrat* was not increased, although the remainder rose by fifteen. Thus, in theory, Prussia could be outvoted – except where changes in the constitution, military affairs or modification of the laws governing customs and excise were concerned – but this happened only infrequently. The princes were unwilling to be subject to any alien sovereignty and in this they were for the most part supported by their peoples or those circles which were influential at home. Bismarck therefore vested sovereignty neither in the Emperor nor in the nation but in the *Bundesrat*, so that the twenty-two allied princes and the senates of the three Free Cities had a share in it, but at the same time Prussia wielded an extraordinarily great, indeed a decisive influence. The *Reich* had only one minister, the Imperial Chancellor (*Reichskanzler*), who might at the same time be head of the Prussian Government and often was. He was appointed by the Emperor and could remain in office all the while he enjoyed the monarch's confidence. Laws needed the assent of the *Bundesrat* and the *Reichstag*. It was not the *Reichstag* but the *Bundesrat*, whose Foreign Affairs Committee was presided over by Bavaria, which shared the right of decision on a declaration of war, except in the case of attack from without. The *Reichstag* could, however, refuse to vote the credits for a war.

BISMARCK'S FOREIGN POLICY

Bismarck's three successful wars had aroused fears in Europe that Prussia-Germany would follow a similar policy of expansion throughout the continent. But this was far from Bismarck's thoughts; he repeatedly stressed that now that the previous excessive fragmentation was a thing of the past, the *Reich* would pursue a policy of peace. Germany, he declared, was now satisfied, and there was no territory which could lead her into a war of conquest. In particular, the recovery of lands which had once belonged to the Holy Roman Empire was far from being an aim of German policy. This was in complete contrast to the former *grossdeutsch* conception and the subsequent Pan-German ideal. Bismarck was equally averse to interference in the affairs of far distant lands, among which he numbered Turkey and the Balkans, and if he did concern himself with them this was not part of a policy of conquest but to prevent war between Russia and Austria. This standpoint was equally far removed from that of Napoleon III – who, though not himself warlike, waged war for the sake of national prestige in Russia, Italy and even Mexico – as from that of William II, who held that no important decision the wide world over might in future be taken without Germany. Bismarck disposed of the main dogma of any nationalism – that national honour was the highest goal – with the words: 'I have no sympathy for any honour which begins where sound common-sense ends'.

The Chancellor was true to his conception of the State. He did not worship the revolutionaries' idol, the nation, but based his policy on the viable, historically evolved State. The mere fact that outside the *Reich* there existed millions whose language was German or one of the related tongues, or whose union with Germany would have offered advantages to the *Reich*, was in his eyes no reason at all for aiming to incorporate them. Just as little did he cherish the notion, prevalent among nationalists in many countries, that they had a mission to rule less civilised people and to spread their own language and culture by conquest. The Germans or Prussians did not seem to him an ideal people or a particularly noble race. He often credited them with unflattering qualities even though he also on occasion paid tribute to their merits. His policy towards the Poles, Danes and the French inhabitants of Alsace-Lorraine did not aim at suppressing their language but at getting them to learn German as the official language of the country, which was quite indispensable in a predominantly German state, and to educate them into loyal citizens. All other nation states have done the same.

Above all Bismarck was convinced that man cannot create and control the tide of time but can only sail and steer on it. Nor did he believe that policy can be conducted with an eye to the distant future; to him the future was always uncertain. Some measure of power and prestige was certainly necessary for a state, but Bismarck decisively rejected wars for power and prestige where no vital interests were at stake. Hence he could not agree at all with William II's world, colonial and naval policy, which must inevitably founder because it utterly misinterpreted the given situation. Bismarck's diplomatic strength rested above all else on his extraordinary gift for thinking and feeling himself into the minds of other peoples and their statesmen and on his ability to foresee how complicated and obscure situations would develop.

For him, politics was the art of realising what was possible in the given circumstances.

Bismarck considered a French republic to offer greater prospects of peace than a monarchy. Many French politicians sought to meet the need for enhanced national prestige by a large-scale colonial expansion. Bismarck supported the extension of France's colonial empire in the hope that this would preclude any thought of a war of revenge against Germany.

Bismarck felt himself to be first and foremost a Prussian and only then a German. This largely explains why he always set particular store by good relations with Russia, which was in keeping with the old dynastic bonds between the two countries and their common interest in preventing the emergence of an independent Poland. Not that Russia was always easy to handle; her statesmen were only too aware how much Bismarck owed to Russia's backing when the *Reich* was founded. An inflammable Pan-Slavism existed which had aimed at the destruction of Austria ever since the Crimean War but which was also often directed against Germany. The persecution of the German Balts by the Pan-Slavists could not be prevented, but Russian hostility towards the Danubian monarchy, which Bismarck would gladly have won as an ally, was far from suiting his plans and so he sought to engineer a rapprochement between the three empires. This began with an exchange of visits between the three emperors and was followed in 1873 by treaties between them. These treaties are usually referred to as the Three Emperors' League (*Dreikaiserbund*), though the only real defensive alliance was concluded between Germany and Russia, Austria confining herself to an assurance of her friendship. Bismarck's aim in this was twofold: to prevent Russia and Austria from going to war with each other and from allying themselves against Germany.

In 1875 a European crisis blew up because the German General Staff wanted to counter France's unusually massive rearmament by a preventive war. Bismarck was probably not in agreement with this but he did at least seek, by means of newspaper articles and other threatening utterances, to frighten the French off their plans. At France's request, Britain and Russia brought influence to bear on the German Government, whereupon the Russian Chancellor Gorchakov made it appear that Russia had preserved the peace, to Bismarck's great indignation. About the same time a further crisis broke out in the Balkans. Turkish maladministration, Pan-Slav propaganda and Austria's designs on Bosnia and Herzegovina led to uprisings in these provinces. Disraeli sent the British Mediterranean fleet to cruise off Constantinople, which only increased Turkey's intransigence. There were fresh risings and outbreaks of violence in the Balkans, the Sultan was deposed and met a violent end and Serbia and Montenegro declared war. Pan-Slavism was driving the Tsar towards a war against Turkey, which was declared in 1877. After some initial successes the Turks were defeated and the preliminary peace treaty of San Stefano (March 1878) imposed stiff conditions on them.

The establishment of Russian domination in the Near East aroused the opposition of the other powers. In Britain in particular feelings ran high and an Anglo-Russian war seemed imminent. Austria too now came out against Russia and called for an examination by the powers of the peace conditions and a European congress. Finally Bismarck declared his willingness to act as the 'honest broker'. In June 1878 the Congress of Berlin met. It disclosed some very violent differences and Bismarck later remarked that without him the congress might have broken up on every single day. Even before it met Britain had received Cyprus from Turkey. Austria occupied Bosnia-Herzegovina. The idea of a large, independent Bulgaria under Russian protection was dropped, but Russia and the Balkan states received many concessions at Turkey's expense. Russia was very disappointed and thought Bismarck ungrateful because he seemed to have forgotten her help towards German unification. Putting the decisions into effect caused further difficulties for a number of years, since Turkey was extremely loath to implement them and the great powers for the most part did not work together but placed their own interests first.

The Congress of Berlin marked the start of a positive race between the powers to acquire large colonial empires and set up protectorates even over advanced states. Bismarck looked indulgently on this competition, for one thing because it bred antagonisms and offered him the chance to use his influence. He did not, however, consider the acquisition of colonies by Germany desirable. In his view, colonies could not be administered without a powerful navy, which Germany could not afford, since it would have to be built at the expense of the army, and he did not consider the German bureaucracy fitted to administer colonies. But German entrepreneurs now acquired land in various parts of the world, especially Africa, and at the same time a colonial movement grew up within Germany. Bismarck had no objection to merchants' administering their overseas possessions at their own expense and the *Reich* was prepared to offer them protection. But in the British colonies bordering on German settlements violent opposition to their new neighbours arose. So in 1884 Bismarck took joint steps with France to settle the Congo question and regulate the procedure for taking over ownerless territories. At the time relations between Britain on the one hand and France and Russia on the other were highly strained, and Bismarck succeeded by diplomatic means in overcoming Britain's resistance after he had put her under pressure by his veto over financial control in Egypt. But his backing for the German colonial movement was probably conditioned by considerations of domestic policy and was soon dropped. He more than once declared that he considered war with Britain an impossibility.

The growing Russian hatred of Germany and Austria had rendered the Three Emperors' League ineffective as a practical instrument. The Tsar and the German Emperor were still amicably disposed towards each other, but after the Congress of Berlin Bismarck felt that the time had come to make a treaty with Austria to guard against a Russian attack. He thought of such an alliance in terms of a permanent constitutional provision subject to approval by Parliament, but this the Austrian Foreign Minister, Count Andrássy, would not accept. The aged German Emperor held out stubbornly against any alliance with his old enemy, Austria, as being a betrayal of Russia. Bismarck had the greatest difficulty – he even had to threaten resignation – in getting him to agree. The Dual Alliance was concluded in 1879 and acclaimed in both empires alike. Many other countries also saw in it a great safeguard for the peace of Europe: the British Foreign Secretary, Lord Salisbury, declared it to be highly welcome. Bismarck now hoped to induce England to associate herself with it, but soon afterwards the liberals came to power in England and their leader, Gladstone, detested Bismarck, had no sympathy for Austria and inclined to the side of Russia and France.

In 1882 the Dual Alliance became the Triple Alliance by the entry of Italy. Bismarck had not been aiming at this, for he mistrusted Italy and there was at the time considerable tension between France and Italy after France had set up a protectorate over Tunis, which Italy would gladly have kept for herself. The Italians turned to Austria and Germany. In the Triple Alliance the signatories gave mutual assurances of aid in the event of attack by two other great powers, i.e. France and Russia. But the treaty was not directed against Britain, as Italy – if only because of her long coastline – wanted peace at all costs with her. Germany and Austria considered any hostilities with England to be as undesirable as they were unlikely. The alliance promised Italy help against an attack by France alone. Bismarck also brought about, in 1883, a secret defensive alliance between Germany, Austria and Rumania. Austria had a secret pact with Serbia. In 1881, a fresh *Dreikaiserbund* was signed between Germany, Russia and Austria, which provided, in case of war, for benevolent neutrality between the three powers, and reached an agreement on Balkan policy. This alliance was renewed in 1884. It was at the outset kept secret from the public, in

Russia because of fear of the Pan-Slavs, and in Austria-Hungary
in order not to provoke the Magyar Russophobes.

Peace seemed ensured by this treaty. Both Alexander III, who had
become Tsar after the assassination of his father, and his Foreign
Minister von Giers were peaceably disposed, although this Tsar also
had Pan-Slav leanings. Bismarck would have liked to achieve a permanent
settlement of Balkan problems, based on an Austrian sphere of influence
in the West and a Russian one in the East. This matched the realities
of the situation, since the Russians were in occupation in Bulgaria,
which they treated just like a colony, while Austria was exercising a
concealed protectorate over Serbia, though it must be said that she did
not copy the Russian example of brutal intervention in internal affairs.

In Bulgaria the National Assembly had elected as ruler Prince
Alexander of Battenberg, a relative and favourite of the Tsar, but the
Russian officers and officials behaved so much as if they were masters
of the country that the Bulgars rose in revolt and in company with the
prince shook off this despotism. Alexander thereby incurred the Tsar's
displeasure but was counting on British and Austrian support. He was
related to the British royal family, and, with the support of Queen
Victoria, the German Crown Prince and his wife were planning to marry
their daughter Victoria to him. But Bismarck imposed an absolute veto,
even after Alexander had abdicated in 1886. Russian attempts to seize
power foundered on the resistance of the Bulgars. In 1887, the national
assembly elected as their ruler Prince Ferdinand von Coburg-Kohary,
who came of a German family, lived in Austria and was a Hungarian
officer.

These events greatly increased tension in Hungary, especially as at
the same time militaristic nationalism, typified by such figures as the
generals Boulanger and Déroulède, was flourishing in France. In
Russia, hostility towards Germany and Austria reached its peak;
Russian and French chauvinists were fraternising and calling for war.
In Germany and Austria too many voices were saying that a decision
by force of arms was inevitable. In Germany the liberals and the
Centre were particularly anti-Russian, as were the Magyars in Austria–
Hungary. In both Empires the general staffs were working towards war
and Bismarck was hard put to it to prevent an outbreak. He declared in
the *Reichstag* that the *Reich* had no interest in Bulgaria or Constanti-
nople. He sought to damp down the martial ardour of the Hungarians
and the general staffs and negotiated with Russia. The result was the
'Reinsurance Treaty' of 1887, in which Germany went so far to meet
Russia that one might well wonder whether it was compatible with
Germany's treaty obligations towards Austria-Hungary and Rumania.
The Reinsurance Treaty was kept strictly secret. Another considerable

feat of Bismarck's was to persuade Britain to conclude agreements with Austria and Italy for preserving the status quo in the Mediterranean and the Black Sea.

During the period of tension in 1887 and 1888, Bismarck published in the semi-official organ *Die Post* the following principles governing Germany's attitude to war:[1]

1 Germany should never begin a war in the belief that one might otherwise be forced on her.

2 The conduct of political affairs must not be subordinated to the views of the General Staff.

3 Neither Swiss nor Belgian neutrality would ever be violated by Germany.

4 Germany set the greatest store by preserving her reputation for strictly observing treaties concluded with the aim of keeping the peace.

Bismarck's relations with Britain fluctuated. He was always sympathetically inclined towards her, especially when, as a young man, he once confessed that he would gladly have been a statesman in a free country like Britain. If he did consider parliamentarianism on the British pattern impossible in Germany, he attributed this to the special conditions obtaining there: the fragmentation of the parties, the overhanging threat from two great powers and the absence of a social class which was prosperous and schooled to politics for generations. A fully parliamentary system also made it impossible to conclude binding treaties for military support, since majorities in Parliament changed and no government could bind its successor to take up arms, possibly in the face of public opinion. Hence all attempts to achieve a firm military alliance between England and Germany inevitably came to nothing. The only hope lay in a relationship of trust based on an identity of views. Even when Bismarck was in control this was difficult, and under William II it became impossible.

BISMARCK'S DOMESTIC POLICY

In the first *Reichstag*, elected in 1871, the National Liberals were the strongest party. They drew their support from the middle classes, the academic intelligentsia and the national movement. They represented liberal demands, in particular that for a parliamentary régime, but were in certain cases prepared to place the interest of the national unitary state above the principle of liberty. The party's national wing was more willing to do this than its liberal wing. This dual attitude

[1] Cf. Bülow, *Denkwürdigkeiten*, II, p. 79.

gave the party a very advantageous tactical position, for on national issues they could vote with the Free Conservatives and on liberal issues with the Progressive Party. Hence there was talk of the two souls of National Liberalism. The party was recruited from all parts of Germany, and this gave rise to many differences of attitude. The South Germans, for instance, could not come to terms with the brusque demand for unity made by Treitschke, a Saxon by birth and a Prussian by choice. Moreover, the great majority of National Liberals came from non-Prussian territories or from those which had belonged to Prussia only since 1866. Among their leaders, Eduard Lasker, who hailed from the old original Prussia, and Rudolf von Bennigsen, a former Hanoverian, were prominent. While Bennigsen was fairly far to the right in the party, he had close ties of friendship with members of its left wing, especially Lasker. He was eminently a moderate who did his best to smooth out differences within the party and between the party and Bismarck. Lasker, a lawyer of Jewish extraction, came from Posen and in this predominantly Polish province he had, as he said, come to recognise Prussian rule as a blessing for his country. He was the most assiduous and indefatigable worker and the most quick-witted speaker in the party, or, in Bamberger's words, its Chief of the General Staff and Sergeant-major rolled into one. Bismarck once confessed that whenever he had considered resigning, it was Lasker who had given him cause to do so.

The Progressive Party embodied the radical liberalism which had formed in the Prussian *Landtag* in the conflict over the army bill. This party had grown up in East Prussia among the liberal bourgeoisie and had a considerable following there. About half of its members in the *Reichstag* were returned from the older Prussian provinces. The Progressive Party received relatively more votes than the National Liberals from the petty bourgeoisie.

The roots of the conservatives lay above all in the Junkerdom east of the Elbe and in Prussian army and official circles. Almost all their members were returned by the older Prussian provinces. When the *Reich* was first founded they were not on good terms with Bismarck; they had disapproved of many of his actions since 1866, had many criticisms to make of the *Kulturkampf* and not a few of them hated him for personal reasons. Their subsequent rise occurred during the period when he and they buried their differences and was probably due in part to the pressure exercised by the government machine in their favour. Some of them had broken away and called themselves Free Conservatives and in the *Reichstag* went under the style of the *Deutsche Reichspartei*. This party numbered many former senior officials, great landowners and other notabilities among its members. In many respects they were open to liberal ideas and shared the views of the National Liberals. A similar party, to which numerous Prussian ministers belonged, had been formed under the name *Liberale Reichspartei*, but it soon broke up and its members joined the National Liberals.

From the very outset the Centre enjoyed considerable influence, which grew even stronger as time went by. It mainly represented a large section of the Catholics within the *Reich* and was the chief target of Bismarck's so-called *Kulturkampf*.

The rise of the Social Democrats was slow while Bismarck was Chancellor. Harassed as they were by the measures taken against them, they did not obtain any significant number of seats until these measures were lifted. If Bismarck wanted to rule with the *Reichstag*, he was forced to rely on the National Liberals for support. He did, it is true, do his best to tailor their ideas to his own pattern and render their left wing ineffective or even sever it. Since he could not do this to the extent he wished, he later sought other allies, but at the outset the unleashing of the *Kulturkampf* offered him an excellent means of imposing his leadership on the great majority of liberals.

THE KULTURKAMPF

In July 1870 the doctrine of papal infallibility was proclaimed at the Vatican Council. It called forth vigorous protests in many countries, especially among liberals, who mistakenly saw it as a claim by the Pope to world domination and a deliberate attempt to stifle all intellectual freedom and modern culture, whereas the infallibility in fact applied only to the realm of doctrine. All the same, there was no disguising the fact that making this declaration might well have unfortunate consequences. Many Catholics, including some prelates and eminent scholars, strove for a long time to prevent it. The term *Kulturkampf* – i.e. cultural struggle against the Catholic Church, was coined by the Progressive deputy Virchow, a scholar of distinction. Gladstone, who was Prime Minister at the time, wrote two papers attacking papal policy, for which Bismarck sent him a letter of thanks, and an earlier Liberal Prime Minister, Lord John Russell, greeted Bismarck's policy with enthusiasm. But it cannot be taken for granted that Bismarck entered on this struggle because he feared that the papal declaration threatened intellectual liberty and culture, or, indeed, the German State; his real campaign was, rather, directed solely at the Centre Party, which had been founded at the end of 1870 and proposed to represent Catholic interests above all else.

This party's programme demanded denominational schools, federalism within the *Reich*, provincial autonomy, social reforms and cuts in military obligations and the period of service. The party also admitted non-Catholics, and many leading figures who were Protestants joined. It was made up of the most diverse elements, whose political persuasion ranged from the monarchical to the democratic. Many peasants, workers and members of the petty bourgeoisie belonged to it, as well as numerous men of title, big landowners and industrialists, senior officials, scholars and clergymen. It by no means embraced all Catholics, many of whom joined other parties. The first move to found the party was made by Peter Reichensperger, who had been active in politics as far back as 1848. The party soon acquired an outstanding leader in Ludwig Windthorst, formerly a minister in the Hanoverian Government. As a parliamentarian he was in a class of his own and Bismarck cordially detested him. This was not surprising, for the Centre was the most weighty successor to the old *grossdeutsch* party, which had resisted Bismarck's policy tooth and nail. Even in 1866 the majority of the Germans were firmly against war with Austria. When Bismarck's policy scored some successes, it carried many along with it and intimidated many others. But it is doubtful whether, even when the climax of 1870 was reached, the German people welcomed the Hohenzollern empire as unanimously as was often claimed. In many German states there was still aversion to union with Prussia, and this was often manifested in a highly demagogic fashion, especially in Bavarian elections.

Bismarck's attitude towards the Centre certainly sprang from political considerations, and these were not only connected with the party's antecedents but also with its subsequent outlook. It championed the cause of Poland and Alsace-Lorraine and maintained close contact with the Guelphs, from whose ranks it had recruited its greatest leader. On the other hand, it cannot be denied that the Centre had good reason for misgivings over Bismarck's policy. Not a few liberals rejoiced in the 'Protestant empire' of the Hohenzollerns and looked down on the German Catholics with a certain contempt. The widespread dislike of Prussia, be it noted, did not spring primarily from religious motives but was directed above all else at her militaristic and absolutist character. To many, Bismarck's constitution for the *Reich* appeared a piece of mere sham constitutionalism.

The *Kulturkampf* began immediately the *Reich* was founded. Bismarck refused the Centre's demand that a few fundamental civic rights provided by the Prussian constitution be incorporated in the *Reich* constitution. Furthermore, in July 1871 he dissolved the Catholic division of the Prussian Ministry of Education. He then introduced a number of measures aimed at the Centre. A Prussian law put the management of primary schools under state control even if they often did remain in the hands of Protestant or Catholic clergy. The *Reichstag* adopted a measure which forbade Jesuits and members of similar orders to take any part in education or ecclesiastical tasks. Foreign Jesuits could be expelled and native ones restricted to specified domiciles. The Centre's comment was that in this way innocent Germans were being subjected to the same treatment as discharged convicts. The *Reich* broke off diplomatic relations with the Holy See. In Prussia the new Minister of Education, Adalbert Falk, introduced draft measures which were enacted in May 1873, and are known as the 'May Laws'. In future the clergy was to be drawn only from German citizens, and their instruction was laid down along very precise lines to train them in a national, anti-Catholic spirit. The Government was given the right to veto the appointment of clergy of whom they did not approve, the disciplinary powers of the Pope over German clergy were removed and it was made easier to leave the Church.

The Prussian bishops offered passive resistance to this legislation, whereupon the Government retaliated with severe punishments. The clergy followed their bishops' lead and were likewise persecuted. The struggle was waged with the utmost bitterness. Further measures laid down that any priest who continued to administer an office which had been withdrawn from him should suffer restriction to specific localities and might even be expelled from Germany with the loss of citizenship. In order to break the power of the Church, compulsory civil marriage was introduced, there were soon vast areas with neither priest nor church services, and baptisms and church weddings could not be held. But the great majority of the Catholic population could not be deterred from supporting their clergy. Things reached such a pass that, as in the days of the French Revolution and the persecution of the Puritans in England, the clergy organised itself clandestinely and discharged its pastoral duties in disguise. After a Catholic workman made an attempt on Bismarck's life in 1874, the laws against the Catholic Church were made even more stringent, but to no avail. Anti-Catholic or anti-Church measures were, moreover, not introduced in all the states of the *Reich*. Besides, among both the liberals and the conservatives there were deputies who thoroughly disapproved of Bismarck's measures, which ran so counter to the spirit of a constitutional state. The election of 1874 showed that the persecutions had only strengthened the Centre. Bismarck gradually realised that his policy could not achieve its ends. He sought to lay the responsibility for certain especially repugnant measures at the door of others, but he had committed himself so deeply to the *Kulturkampf* that he could not simply call a halt to it without damage to his own prestige.

BISMARCK AND THE CONSERVATIVES

Although Bismarck himself came of Junker stock and saw eye to eye with them on some important issues, he also had a number of points of difference with them. Personal jealousy played a part. He himself once said: 'They are angry that I have become a prince but at the same time they are angry if I do not invite them to dine.' The differences were sharpened by the *Kulturkampf*. The orthodox Protestants were just as offended as the Catholics by the laws which restricted the rights of the Church to supervise schools and made civil marriage compulsory. Even more resented were the attempts to reform rural government and the upper house. The owners of manorial estates still wielded decisive power in the *Landgemeinden* (rural communities) as well as in the *Kreistage* (district assemblies) and provincial assemblies, especially in the eastern areas. Westphalia, the Rhine province and the newly-conquered territories, on the other hand, enjoyed local self-government. It was now urgently necessary to bring the system in Prussia into line and up to date, and by vesting the administration of justice in a central judiciary, to establish the idea of a fully constitutional state. Even in the days of the North German *Bund*, Bismarck had wished to overhaul the legal system but he had left the task to the Minister of the Interior, Friedrich, Count Eulenburg. In the *Landtag* of 1872, a new *Kreisordnung*, initially for the six eastern provinces, was adopted by a large majority but the upper house threw out the measure. At the time Bismarck was ill on his estate at Varzin, but still planning his reform of the upper house. However, Eulenburg anticipated him and prevailed on the reluctant King to appoint twenty-five new members to the upper house, which then passed the measure. Although this marked a considerable step forward, the landowners none the less retained a large measure of control in rural areas. Further projected reforms foundered in 1876 on the opposition of the upper house.

In 1873 the conservatives split into two factions; the 'new' conservatives wanted to keep in contact with the Government, while the more numerous 'old' conservatives vigorously opposed it. At the elections to the *Reichstag* and *Landtag*, both groups lost a large number of votes as they lacked government backing.

The struggle of the Old Conservatives against Bismarck proved futile and after ten years they gave it up. They revised their programme and formed the German Conservative Party. They now took their stand on the *Reich* constitution, particularly federalism, accepted constitutionalism and the changes in district and provincial administration, and demanded denominational schools and an end to the *Kulturkampf*. They also called for limitations on freedom of movement and trade, an attack on high finance and a social policy favouring industrial workers. This new course proved its worth. At the elections of 1877 and 1878, they gained seats instead of – as in 1874 – losing them.

BISMARCK AND THE LIBERALS

In the first few years of the *Reichstag*, the state of the parties was such that only the liberals could command a majority. Backing for Bismarck from the National Liberals had already begun in the North German *Bund*, and it is customary to label the decade from 1867 to 1877 a liberal epoch. But then the situation changed: the liberal vote decreased, that of the conservatives rose, the *Kulturkampf* came to an end and the Chancellor could rely increasingly for support on the conservatives and the Centre, as well as on the liberal right wing. One of the main reasons for this turn of events was Bismarck's change-over to a protectionist policy, but the fact that the Social Democrats won more and more seats also played a part.

Even in the liberal era there were many points of friction between Government and Parliament, especially in the sphere of army policy. Under the constitution the *Reichstag* had a measure of control by giving or withholding its approval when the army estimates were debated, though the Government sought to limit these powers as far as possible. Memories of the Prussian constitutional conflict led the Kaiser to demand a fixed long-term army grant. The North German *Reichstag* had passed the estimates for the four years up to 31 December 1871, which was extended in 1871, by a narrow majority, for a further three years. In 1874 the Government demanded a further long-term grant. This unleashed sharp opposition from the liberals, who once again supported an annual vote. Their leaders, Eduard Lasker and Eugen Richter, a Progressive, wanted to win for Parliament the exclusive right to control the budget. At the time, Bismarck was seriously ill; Moltke defended the Government bill, pointing out that France was making strenuous exertions to set up an army superior to Germany's and in any case her peace-time strength was far superior. The Free Conservatives and National Liberals moved for a reduction in the army establishment and the Progressive Party and the Social Democrats pressed for fundamental reforms. The danger of a fresh constitutional conflict loomed, the Emperor talked of an army crisis and Bismarck threatened to resign or dissolve the *Reichstag*. He also put it about that the liberals wanted to render the *Reich* defenceless which would induce France to embark on a war of revenge. Many deputies feared that if the *Reichstag* were dissolved they would not retain their seats. Fourteen members left the Progressive Party and were prepared to support the Government measure. Finally Bennigsen suggested a compromise: that the credits should be granted not indefinitely but for seven years, the so-called *Septennat*. He managed to win over Bismarck and the Emperor, and the measure was adopted by a handsome majority.

The founding of the *Reich* opened the way for legislation to promote Germany's economic unity. The *Zollverein* and the building of railways required large economic areas and aided this trend. The *Reichstag* enacted a number of laws by which any remaining differences between the member states of the *Bund* were evened out. When the *Reich* was founded, there were seven different currencies and thirty-three banks which issued notes. The creation of a uniform currency based on gold was achieved by several measures passed between 1871 and 1875.

The introduction of a uniform code of justice for the whole *Reich* was also urgently needed. The civil and criminal codes in the states of the Bund had many anomalies. Over a large area of the country the 'common law' (*gemeine Recht*) – based on old German codes such as the *Sachsenspiegel* and Charles V's penal laws of 1532, Roman and canon law – still prevailed. Even in one and the same state several conflicting laws might exist side by side. Many provisions were out of date, others very modern. In 1851 a penal code had been adopted in Prussia which was excellent in many respects but which, as a product of the period of reaction, punished political offences severely. At that time the legal immunity and payment of deputies were suppressed. Since then the liberals had waged an incessant campaign against this limitation of parliamentary privilege. In the North German *Reichstag* they secured all their demands except for the payment of deputies, about which there were in any case divided views within their own ranks.

In 1870, the liberals in the North German *Bund* moved the extension of immunity to the *Landtage* of the states of the *Bund*, abolition of humiliating penal servitude for political offences committed with no dishonourable intention, jury courts for political cases, the abolition of the death penalty, a speedy revision of the military penal laws and other reforms. While the total abolition of the death penalty was not approved, the measure passed by the North German *Reichstag* represented a considerable step forward, and was converted into an Imperial Law when the *Reich* came into being.

The reform of the penal code was only one part of the judicial reform achieved in a number of measures in the early years of the *Reich*. The new constitution had limited the *Reich*'s competence in legal matters, since the particularism prevailing in many states resisted its extension. In November 1871 Lasker moved that the *Reich*'s authority should be extended to the entire civil and criminal law, judicial proceedings and the organisation of the courts. The *Reichstag* adopted the measure by a large majority, but the *Bundesrat's* attitude was one of disapproval because the South Germans and the Saxons voted against it. The motion was put again in 1872 and 1873 and received even greater majorities in the *Reichstag*. In the *Bundesrat* there was now a complete change of heart and in December 1873, it came out almost unanimously in favour of Lasker's measure. A commission of prominent jurists was set up to work out a civil code, and in the years which followed justice was standardised and reformed by a series of laws. The liberals, especially those who were South Germans, criticised the code of criminal procedure as being permeated with the Prussian spirit, and found much that was unacceptable in the drafts of a press law as well as in a supplement to the criminal code. Thus, for example, a provision making incitement to class hatred illegal was almost unanimously defeated. Bismarck and the *Bundesrat* met the liberals over many points and dropped the clauses which they found particularly objectionable. Over some bills Bismarck negotiated in private with Bennigsen, Miquel and Lasker and reached a compromise which the *Reichstag*, with the votes of the National Liberals, adopted. The Progressive Party and the Centre voted against it and a sharp conflict broke out between the two liberal factions.

THE ECONOMIC CRISIS

May 1873 saw a crash on the Vienna stock market. Its effects, which spread to several other countries, were especially devastating in Germany from October onwards. A measure agreed between the Government and the *Reichstag* regulated the circulation of bank-notes and limited it considerably, but one thing conspicuously lacking was any mention of a *Reichsbank*. At the instance of Lasker, the *Reichstag* decided to set up a committee to fill this gap. The *Reichsbank*, a cross between a private and a state bank, was opened in 1876.

In the first six years of the *Reich*, its customs policy was dominated by the spirit of free trade. Delbrück, with his outstanding expertise and great influence on Bismarck in economic matters, was its main proponent. Duties on iron were completely removed and those on machines and other iron goods were due to be taken off, when the economic crisis brought growing criticism of the policy of free trade.

The general election of 1877 brought a decline in the strength of the liberal parties, though united they could still command a majority. But this was not often the case, since their left wing was greatly offended at Bennigsen's compromises with Bismarck. The conservatives, on the other hand, were growing stronger and Bismarck now looked to their ranks and to a section of the National Liberals for a reliable majority to back his policies. But this assumed that the left wing of the National Liberals would break away from the party, since it was by no means prepared to submit to Bismarck's leadership. A reliable majority in the *Reichstag* was urgently required if the *Reich* finances, imperilled by heavy military expenditure, were to be stabilised. Moreover, the long-drawn-out economic crisis increased both the attacks on economic liberalism and the call for higher duties. Matters of finance and economy were in the hands of officials who inclined towards liberalism, but Bismarck now began to make himself independent of them and frequently advanced his views with great ruthlessness. As early as 1876 Delbrück resigned – an act in accord with his economic liberalism, which was closely related to his political liberalism. The liberals were opposed to any considerable state intervention in the economy, they supported free trade and backed a policy of direct taxation voted annually. Bismarck, on the other hand, preferred indirect taxes on luxury goods – which, incidentally, the constitution largely empowered the *Reich* to levy, the right of direct taxation being reserved to the individual states.

In March 1877, after a clash with the head of the Admiralty, General von Stosch, Bismarck went on indefinite leave. He retired to his country estates for ten months and there formed fresh plans. But before he finally decided to tackle the question of liberal economic policy, he tried to tempt Bennigsen, leader of the National Liberals, to accept a ministerial post, calculating that this would detach the left liberals from the party and pave the way for a coalition of the liberals of the right with the conservatives. Bennigsen, however, wanted to avoid a split in the liberal ranks and was, moreover, very disinclined to become a mere tool of Bismarck's policy, to which his isolated position would probably have reduced him. He therefore insisted on ministerial posts for two liberals of the left and measures to preserve the *Reichstag's* right to vote the budget. Bismarck was not prepared to accept conditions which would have severely curtailed his power.

Bismarck's long stay at Varzin gave him the chance to grapple in detail with financial and economic problems. Up till now he had left them almost entirely to departmental ministers, who supported free trade. Long before this he had nursed an inclination towards decisive state intervention in the economic field. He later declared in the *Reichstag* that in 1877, soon after Delbrück's resignation, he had grown convinced how harmful to the German economy was the free trade system which had come in since 1865.

The agrarians were complaining of the fall in the price of corn, which

M

resulted mainly from the great improvements and lower cost of international transport, which made it possible to import bulk goods from distant countries where production costs were low. Moreover, many countries were still suffering in 1877 from the economic crisis which had arisen in 1873 and dealt industry a heavy blow. A number of countries sought relief by imposing protective duties before Germany had recourse to them. In any case, Bismarck was interested in duties for financial and political reasons as well. He hoped to strengthen the economy of the *Reich* by high receipts from customs and taxes on luxury goods like tobacco, and thus be able to dispense with matricular contributions from the member states of the *Reich*. He also considered agriculture and the iron industry vital in the event of war if the *Reich* were to be as little dependent as possible on imports. The farmers of the Elbe, who were those most interested in corn duties, dominated the conservative party on whose support Bismarck particularly relied. The Centre, too, which he would gladly have won over, was predominantly protectionist.

In February 1878 Bismarck returned from his long 'leave'. The National Liberal party called for Parliament's full right to vote the budget and its left wing for a considerable extension of the Government's responsibility to Parliament. In the same month, in the course of a *Reichstag* debate on the tax proposals, in which an increase in the tobacco tax was prominently mooted, Bismarck revealed that his real aim was to create a monopoly such as already existed in France, Austria and Italy. But no majority in the *Reichstag* could be obtained for this, and the budget deficit was reduced to a very low figure by cuts in expenditure and other measures.

THE ANTI-SOCIALIST LAW

Soon after, two attempts were made on the life of the 81-year old Emperor, in the second of which he was seriously wounded. Little could be discovered about the motives of the would-be assassins; they were said to have cherished socialist views and the Government therefore laid the blame at the door of the Social Democrats, even though their complicity was highly improbable. Immediately after the first attempt Bismarck had had a sharp anti-socialist measure drafted, but it had been put together very hastily and was rejected by the *Reichstag* by a large majority. When the second attempt was made immediately after, he tried to exploit public indignation by casting suspicion not only on the socialists but also the radical liberals and their press as fomenters of revolution. The *Reichstag* was dissolved on 11 June 1878 and elections fixed for 30 July. During this interval the Congress of Berlin was held and Bismarck, as its chairman, mediated between the great powers and earned considerable prestige as a peacemaker. In the electoral campaign all possible means of provoking the opposition were used, but the results fell short of Bismarck's expectations. It is true that the conservatives' representation was markedly stronger and the liberals' correspondingly weaker, while the Centre's strength was unchanged, but the Government did not secure a safe majority. In September 1878 a fresh anti-socialist bill with some extremely severe provisions was introduced. Reichensperger, a leader of the Centre, argued that the bill was unacceptable, for socialism, on Bismarck's own admission, possessed an inner core of justification and the measure might also hit social reformers. It would give the socialists a highly effective pretext for agitation. August Bebel, leader of the Social Democrats, flatly rebutted the assertion that any responsibility for the attempts on the Emperor attached to his party and gave a detailed account of how assiduously Bismarck had wooed the socialists as allies against the liberals back in the sixties. In committee Lasker succeeded in putting through a number of modifications aimed at preventing abuses and arbitrary actions, but Bennigsen opposed him, and the National Liberals and conservatives reached a compromise to which the Government gave its blessing. In the course of a major speech, Bismarck discussed the parliamentary principle and stressed that it functioned well in Britain because there were now only two parties in that country, whereas in Germany there was a whole series of parties, each filled with blind *esprit de corps* and incapable of working together. The anti-socialist bill was finally approved in the face of the votes of the Progressive Party and the Centre.

Immediately after it had become law, the Social Democrats came under heavy fire. Their meetings, associations, newspapers and pamphlets were banned and many agitators were expelled from Berlin and other cities. Sometimes the party moved faster than the police. The central organisation was transferred abroad and the party's activities in Germany continued underground. At subsequent elections the socialist vote at first dropped but after a few years it rose substantially, and when the Government barred from the *Reichstag* two Social Democrat members who had been expelled from Berlin, the house rejected a motion for their arrest and prosecution by a large majority.

Early in March 1878 the Government introduced two bills modifying industrial regulations to meet continued pressure from the *Reichstag*. One of these bills provided safeguards intended mainly for young workers. The house approved the measure and made the introduction of factory inspectors compulsory. Windthorst, leader of the Centre, was for meeting Social Democratic demands, which were to some extent justified, as far as possible, whereas Bamberger, for the liberals, opposed the idea. Broadly speaking, the call for a substantial measure of protection for the workers – particularly for a Sunday rest-day – came from the Catholic Church, and it was taken up by the Protestants as well. In 1878, a court chaplain named Stöcker founded a Christian Socialist party whose programme, as he himself said, had been put together from the demands of the Social Democrat and Catholic workers' movements. There were also many liberals, such as Max Hirsch, who campaigned for adequate protection for the workers. Over and above this there was a significant spread of ideas on social reform among academic political economists like Brentano, Schmoller and Wagner, whom their opponents called *Kathedersozialisten* (theoretical socialists).

PROTECTIVE TARIFFS

Before the elections of 1878, the majority of the *Reichstag* was utterly averse to the introduction of tariffs. In March of that year an economic association (*Volkswirtschaftliche Vereinigung*) had been formed, headed by the Württemberg politician von Varnbühler, which came out in favour of protection, though at the time it numbered only some sixty members. In the new *Reichstag*, no fewer than 204 members – the majority of the house – were in the *Vereinigung*. Most of them belonged to the Centre; the Conservatives and Free Conservatives were well represented and rather fewer were National Liberals. Varnbühler now sent Bismarck a letter asking him to state his attitude to economic policy. This Bismarck did, and he emphasised in a memorandum of December 1878 that he aimed at a comprehensive increase in duties and indirect taxes with the country's fiscal interests foremost in his mind. Tariff reform, he said, was also justified on economic grounds. On the other hand, he claimed that direct taxation in Germany was too high. Duties of from 5–10% *ad valorem* made very little difference to the selling price and would be borne mainly by the exporter. Of much greater importance in this whole question, he said, were the railway tariffs, which would have to be revised. This memorandum caused a stir both at home and abroad. Although there were free traders and protectionists in all parties and professions, the liberals were quite overwhelmingly for free trade and the conservatives and the Centre for tariffs. The large towns, trade organisations, most professors of national economy and many high officials disapproved of Bismarck's policy. It was clear that it was the masses who would be hardest hit by the duties and indirect taxes. Those who were in favour of tariffs were above all the landowners and big farmers, ironfounders and other manufacturers, to many of whom the duties proposed by the Government seemed too low.

In the course of an exhaustive *Reichstag* debate on tariffs in February

1879 Eugen Richter, a progressive, produced statistics to show that the economic policy pursued hitherto had by no means worked out as unfavourably as Bismarck sought to show. On the contrary, it had led to an extraordinary growth of Germany's industry and exports. Bismarck defended himself against the criticism that he had himself framed the policy he was now disowning by arguing that in the past he had put his trust in Delbrück, the leading German authority, and left him to run affairs. Delbrück himself argued that the existing crisis could not be put down to free trade. Many countries, he said, both free trade and protectionist, were in similar straits. Despite the swelling ranks of protectionist members, Bismarck was hard put to it to raise sufficient votes to carry his tariff policy, and was forced to negotiate with both Bennigsen and Windthorst. The liberals insisted on safeguarding Parliament's right to vote the budget. This would be threatened if the *Reich* revenue consisted entirely of customs duties and indirect taxes as the Chancellor intended. The Centre aimed at breaking the predominance of the liberals, whom they detested as the principal supporters of the *Kulturkampf*. They were particularly anxious to bring down Falk, who had waged a ruthless war on the Catholic Church. Under Windthorst's skilful leadership the Centre had won considerable influence and had every hope of playing a decisive role by forming a coalition with the conservatives.

A solution was finally made possible by a clause suggested by von Franckenstein, one of the leaders of the Centre. This provided that the *Reich* should retain part of the new revenue and return the rest to the individual states. They, in their turn, were to make their matricular contributions, which Bismarck had wanted to abolish, as soon as the state of *Reich* finances made this necessary. The clause satisfied both the federalistic demands of the Centre and the parliamentary demands of the liberals. Bismarck promised the Centre a change in his policy towards the Church. Falk had to resign and was replaced by von Puttkamer, who supported denominational schools, which the Centre also wanted. The tariff bill, the Franckenstein clause and the increase in tobacco duty were all passed with the votes of the conservatives, the Centre and a few National Liberals. The great majority of the liberals voted against the measures. The duties on iron and rye were, incidentally, approved by only a narrow majority; the *Vossische Zeitung* pointed out that the increase in the duty on rye, which weighed heavily on the poorer people, was passed by the votes of 119 nobles and 67 members from the middle class, the corresponding figures for the 'noes' being 28 and 132. This duty favoured above all the Junkers east of the Elbe.

The course of events led to a crisis in the National Liberal party. To begin with, fifteen members of the right wing who sided with

Bismarck broke away. Then a bigger group from the left wing split off in protest against Bennigsen's policy of compromise with Bismarck. Three ministers in the Prussian Government who were close to the liberals resigned and were replaced by conservatives. The swing from liberalism was also apparent in the Prussian *Landtag*. In the elections in the autumn of 1879 the liberals suffered heavy losses while the conservatives were able to register gains. Neither in the *Reichstag* nor in the *Landtag* was sufficient taxation voted to cover the cost of the imminent army expansion and social insurance. Bismarck's attempts to reform *Reich* finances were unsuccessful, and this did much to embitter him against the opposition parties and the *Reichstag* itself.

Bismarck's break with the liberals made the winding-up of the *Kulturkampf* especially important. The new taxes were feasible only if the Centre voted in favour of them, and when the bill had gone through the Centre persisted in its hostile attitude and opposed every major government bill. In the spring of 1878 Pope Pius IX died and was succeeded by Leo XIII, who wanted peace between the Church and the *Reich*. For a long time negotiations between Bismarck and representatives of the Holy See led to no practical results. It was hard for Bismarck to bring himself to repeal the anti-Church laws, for this would be bound to appear to the country at large as a heavy defeat for his policy. Besides, he wanted to induce the Pope to bring pressure to bear on the Centre and make it more favourably disposed towards him. The party, however, was by no means prepared to have its policy dictated by Rome and it consequently viewed the negotiations with no little suspicion. In the end Bismarck adopted the expedient of not removing the anti-Church legislation by treaty but of gradually mitigating it unilaterally, by empowering the Government to ignore some of its provisions. 'Peace Laws' of this kind were enacted in 1880, 1882 and 1883. The Pope also made concessions. The *Reich* resumed diplomatic relations with the papal curia, and the final reconciliation was greatly helped when Bismarck proposed the Pope as mediator in a dispute between Germany and Spain, and, what is more, in a manner which recognised his temporal sovereignty. After further negotiations, measures were passed in 1885 and 1887 which met the principal demands of the Church, and the Pope thereupon declared that the struggle was over. This did not, however, mean that the Centre always supported the Government.

In the spring of 1880, the *Reichstag* debated a fresh army bill designed to offset the increase in French and Russian effectives. Once again Bismarck demanded approval of the estimates for seven years (the second *Septennat*). The bill was passed with the votes of the conservatives and most of the National Liberals, whereas the whole Centre, along with the Progressives, Social Democrats and a few smaller groups, voted against it. The Government also called for a prolongation of the anti-socialist law of 1878. The *Reichstag* committee agreed to the proposal but limited the prolongation to three years. The bill was passed by a comfortable majority, though only a handful of the Centre voted for it.

There was a general election in the autumn of 1881, which Bismarck hoped would give him a majority to carry through his financial and social reforms. Once again he marshalled the officials and newspapers under his control in a ruthless campaign to weaken the Opposition as far as possible. In his eyes, the real enemies were the left-wing liberals, whom he looked on as republicans. But no amount of electoral agitation could prevent a marked increase in Opposition strength. The two conservatives parties lost ground and the National Liberals forfeited fully half of their seats. In contrast, the number of left-wing liberals and Democrats returned rose considerably and the Centre and Social Democrats also had some gains. Thus Bismarck failed in his aim of creating a majority of conservatives and right-wing liberals. It was some consolation that the Centre no longer opposed government bills in principle, but even if it did sometimes vote with the Government, it was not a reliable prop.

It was in the electoral campaign of 1881 that anti-Semitism, represented by Stöcker and his Christian Social Party, first played a part. Bismarck supported Stöcker because he fought the hated Progressives, but he got few votes and no seats. After the election Bismarck refused in cabinet to countenance anti-Semitism directed against the Jews in general, saying that he was only against those Jews who were Progressives. On a later occasion he defended himself against the charge of anti-Semitism, declaring that he much enjoyed the company of Jews and that, in fact, his principal companions on his estates were two Jews – Cohen, his doctor, and Philipp, his legal adviser. As far as election-rigging went, Puttkamer, now Prussian Minister of the Interior, was notoriously active – so much so that, out of fifty disputed seats, no fewer than thirty-six were for Prussian constituencies. Puttkamer maintained that in an election officials must support the Government, and since the Emperor also backed this principle in a decree, the Progressive Party protested vigorously in the *Reichstag*. Bismarck himself declared that, while officials should not agitate against the Government or tolerate lies about it during an election, they had the right to vote against it.

SOCIAL INSURANCE

In the eighties Bismarck introduced a series of measures for social insurance. Even in the sixties he had given thought to the idea of winning over the workers as allies against the liberal bourgeoisie in this way, but the time was not then ripe. The rise of the Social Democrats now induced him to work at setting up a large-scale scheme of workers' insurance financed by the state and the employers. He hoped by this means to make the workers content with their lot and to counter the effects of socialist agitation. While his main motive was political, humanitarian considerations also played a part, though not a primary one, as is shown by his opposition to shorter hours, better working conditions and higher wages for the workers. The conviction that both welfare and insurance were necessary had already spread to many circles, such as sociologists, senior officials, the clergy and even some enlightened employers. The liberals, however, feared that compulsory insurance organised by the state – which they called state socialism – might encroach on civic liberty, and they therefore preferred voluntary insurance with private organisations, such as was widespread in England. Moreover, many categories of worker in a number of German states were already covered by regulations which provided benefits in case of illness, accident and so forth.

As early as the spring of 1881 Bismarck laid an Accident Insurance bill before the *Reichstag*. Its provisions considerably extended the numbers of those who would benefit. A *Reich* institution was to be set up to manage the scheme, but both the Centre and the left-wing liberals feared that this would unduly strengthen the power of the *Reich* Government, and consequently wished the organisation to be handed over to the individual states. The bill was so mutilated by the *Reichstag* that Bismarck did not submit it to the *Bundesrat* for ratification. In May 1882 a second bill was laid before the *Reichstag*, but the members did not find it suitable and it was not until 1884 that a third measure, incorporating many improvements, met with the approval of the *Reichstag* and became law. Administration of the scheme was not vested in the *Reich* but in autonomous trade societies. The contributions, which were payable solely by the employers, were graded according to categories of danger and levied. Bismarck's pet ideas of a state organisation and a regular state subvention were dropped. By their elected representatives, the workers shared in the autonomous administration of the scheme and this gave them much useful training and experience in practical social reform. Supplementary measures extended accident insurance to other occupations, including agriculture. In 1883 a bill for sickness insurance had been brought in and made law. Insurance was obligatory but the worker could choose which of the existing sick-funds he wished to join. Broadly speaking, any worker who fell ill received free treatment and sick pay.

Old age and disablement pensions were next tackled. This was the most difficult operation, as there were no statistics or practical experience to work on. For a long time it had been Bismarck's cherished plan to meet this and other social expenditure, without affecting the workers' pockets, by introducing a tobacco monopoly. In 1882 a bill to set up a monopoly was introduced but decisively defeated. It was a highly unpopular plan, which had already contributed to Bismarck's setback at the 1881 elections. Because of the special difficulties arising, the question of old age and disablement benefits was subjected to a searching public inquiry. Late in 1888 a pensions bill was brought in which was passed by the *Reichstag* in May 1889 with a bare majority of 20 (185 votes to 165). The conservatives and liberals for the most part voted with the Government, and the Centre and left-wing liberals against, as did all the Social Democrats. The measure provided that all manual and most white-collar workers in all occupations, including agriculture, should receive a pension at seventy or, if they lost two-thirds of their fitness for work, a disablement pension.

The whole scheme of insurance marked a magnificent advance in social reform; it aroused admiration – and some hostility – in other countries and in the course of time was copied by most of them. The first two insurance acts were the work of a senior official, Theodor Lohmann, who was highly critical of the Prussian-style, militaristic *Reich*. He was also opposed to Bismarck's idea of using social insurance for political ends and broke with Bismarck in 1883. The old age and disablement pensions scheme was worked out by the minister von Bötticher. It is worth noting that the Social Democrats poured scorn on the bill and fought it vigorously in the *Reichstag*. The left-wing liberals, too, showed small appreciation of the measure, notably Bamberger, who was a dyed-in-the-wool disciple of the Manchester school and labelled the scheme a 'misfortune' during the debates.

THE LIBERALS AFTER THE LIBERAL ERA

The 1881 election had not fulfilled Bismarck's hopes that, with the National Liberals fragmented, all the conservative elements in the various parties could be welded into a reliable majority for the Government. The parties closest to him, such as the conservatives and the remnants of the National Liberals, could not form a majority, and although the Centre sometimes supported the Government wholly or in part, it kept its independence.

The liberal left, Bismarck's *bête noire*, was growing in importance. Its members were on good terms with the Crown Prince, the death of the old Emperor could not be long delayed and Frederick William would then, as Emperor, certainly grant them considerable influence.

Bismarck therefore sought to discredit some of the members of the Crown Prince's entourage. The National Liberals passed through a severe crisis. In 1883 Bennigsen, who had led them for years, left politics in a state of utter despair at the situation. Eduard Lasker, worn out by decades of overwork, was invited to be guest of honour at a celebration in America where, in 1884, he died of a stroke. The American House of Representatives resolved to send a message of condolence to the *Reichstag* on the death of this prominent champion of liberal ideas but Bismarck refused the American Ambassador's request that it be conveyed to the *Reichstag*.

Various attempts were made within the ranks of the liberals to bridge gaps between the various groups. The Progressive Party and the Liberal Union (*Liberale Vereinigung*) – the former left wing of the National Liberals, usually known as the *Sezession* – joined forces in 1884 to form the *Deutsche Freisinnige Partei*. In its programme constitutional questions were well to the fore; it rejected state socialism and adopted a moderate position on army matters. The *Freisinnigen* had high hopes of the Crown Prince, who had told their leader Forckenbeck in 1879 that he had greeted 'with joy' his call for a great liberal party. But there were still great antagonisms within the party.

The National Liberals, too, were in self-reforming mood. As Bennigsen had retired, Johannes Miquel now became their leader. In his youth an enthusiastic follower of Marx, he had later broken away, joined the National Liberals and won himself a great reputation as a financial expert and administrator. He was, in fact, one of the best brains of the party and belonged to its right wing. In 1884 a number of National Liberals from South Germany assembled in Heidelberg and adopted a programme, drafted by Miquel, which laid special emphasis on economic policy, particularly for agriculture, thus marking a swing to the right by the party, which was just what Bismarck had wished.

In the general election of 1884, the hopes of the *Freisinnigen* were dashed: they lost about a third of their 100-odd seats. The National Liberals registered a few gains and the conservatives a considerable number. The Centre held its ground almost unchanged. But the Social Democrats, despite the sharpest government measures against them, managed to double their seats to twenty-four. The previous opposition from the *Freisinnigen* to measures for social insurance now brought heavy retribution; many of their former supporters had obviously gone over to the Social Democrats. The Centre was now the party which held the balance: it could ally itself at will to either the left or the right. Combined with the *Freisinnigen*, the Social Democrats and a few smaller groups, it could offer highly effective opposition to the Government and defeat its measures. In common with the left liberals and the democrats, it championed the rights of Parliament and opposed any extension of the power of the Government and the army. Along with the Right it supported higher tariffs and middle-class interests. When the Centre backed the rights of the individual states against the *Reich*, it reflected the feelings of broad masses of the people. It also spoke out for workers' welfare and oppressed minorities. The parliamentary battles with the Chancellor engendered a mood which led to petty actions on both sides.

In 1885 Bismarck intensified his policy against the Poles living in Prussia, even though he declared that he had no desire to rob them of their nationality but merely to prevent German territory becoming Polish. Moreover, he demanded that the Poles should acquire a know-ledge of German as being the official language. At the outset many Poles from Russia and Austria who had settled in Prussia were expelled. The Polish members, backed by the Centre, the *Freisinnigen*, the Social Democrats and the members for Alsace-Lorraine, put down a question on the matter to the Chancellor. Bismarck's attitude was that this was an internal Prussian matter which did not concern the *Reich* and had this confirmed by an Imperial message to the *Reichstag*. The following year he laid a bill before the Prussian Parliament to place a substantial sum at the disposal of the Government for settling German farmers and workers in the provinces of West Prussia and Posen. The Centre, the *Freisinnigen* and the Poles opposed this measure just as they did others which were directed against the Poles. But in the lower house the conservatives had a majority and the bill was passed. A renewal of the anti-Socialist law was approved, though for only two years instead of the five for which the Government asked.

ARMY BILLS

In November 1886, because of the possibilities of foreign complications and the tense international situation, Bismarck laid a bill before the *Reichstag* providing for an increase in the peace strength of the army by a little under 10% to 468,409 non-commissioned officers and men. (The comparative figure for France was 471,000, to be raised by 44,000, and 547,456, without officers, for Russia.) The German army establishment was again to be fixed for seven years (third *Septennat*). While it was generally agreed in committee that an increase was justified, getting the agreement of the majority depended on reducing the term of the act to three years. In the debate in January 1887 Bismarck first gave an assurance that Germany was far from wanting war, for one thing because she was asking for nothing which could be won by the sword. She belonged, he said, to the satisfied states. Her policy during the preceding sixteen years had proved her love of peace. She had become completely reconciled with Austria. Friendship with Russia had always existed and even on the day he was speaking, it still existed beyond any shadow of doubt, whereas the Opposition press teemed with incitements to war with Russia over Balkan questions which were no concern of Germany's. No less honest and strenuous, he went on, had been Germany's efforts to reach a reconciliation with France, but here the task of peace was much harder and the future less certain. Any question of a preventive war had always been far from his thoughts. He had firm confidence in the pacific disposition of the existing French Government and was convinced that a large part of the French people also wanted peace. History showed, however, that in France critical decisions had always been taken by energetic minorities, not by parliamentary majorities or the popular will. In France in particular one could never tell how long a government would survive. This was a consequence of parliamentary rule. At any time a French government with a policy leading to war might take the helm. Since 1870, France had doubled her army and trebled her reserves. The French Parliament had voted the necessary funds with alacrity. Therefore, in a fresh war, France could certainly be victorious. The attempt by the existing majority in the *Reichstag* to make the strength of the German army dependent on fluctuating majorities and parliamentary resolutions would not succeed. If it did, the Government would appeal to the country to find out what it really thought.

The house divided, and the period was reduced from seven years to three, and even then by only a slender majority. Bismarck immediately rose and read out an Imperial order dissolving the *Reichstag*. Fresh elections were held, in which the Conservatives and National Liberals formed a coalition, known as the *Cartel*. Bennigsen agreed to accept a seat once more. It became known that before the final division, the Pope had advised the Centre, through the papal nuncio in Munich, to vote for the *Septennat*, as this would help considerably to get the anti-church laws from the *Kulturkampf* removed, but Windthorst had passed on this message to only a few. At the big party rally of Rhineland Catholics, he declared that in his message the Holy Father had enunciated the principle that in secular matters the Centre Party, like all Catholics, could vote with complete freedom of conscience. That, he said, was something to be clung fast to. The conference promised the party full support, and this included backing for its attitude to the army bill. Besides, Windthorst doubted whether the international political situation was as critical as the Government made out.

The elections brought a resounding victory for the *Cartel*, which won 220 seats and thus gained a majority. The Conservatives took 121 seats, the National Liberals 99 and the Centre 98, whereas the *Freisinnigen* now had a mere 32. The gains of the *Cartel* parties were partly due to their collaboration both when putting up candidates and when second ballots were held.

Bismarck's hope of a majority in the *Reichstag* had at last been realised, though not for long. In March the army bill was passed by the *Reichstag*. The members of the Centre, despite the Pope's wishes, for the most part abstained. Soon after, a Church law was passed in both Prussian chambers and finally ended the *Kulturkampf*. The most important provision was the admission, subject to the approval of the Minister of Education, of religious orders devoted to spiritual welfare, the practice of Christian charity and the education of girls. The National Liberals and *Freisinnigen* voted against the measure but could not prevent its going through.

In December 1887 a new army bill was laid before the *Reichstag* to recognise the existing effectives and thus increase the field army by half a million men. Up to 1860, the first reserves (*Landwehr ersten Aufgebots*), consisting of older soldiers and mainly officered by middle-class men with civilian jobs, had formed part of the army proper but had then been withdrawn from it since they were not considered wholly reliable. The *Landwehr* was now once more incorporated in the fighting forces and the period of service increased. About 278 million marks would have to be raised by the flotation of a loan. All the major parties agreed to these proposals. When the bill was debated in the *Reichstag* in February 1888 Bismarck again stressed that Germany had not the faintest intention of disturbing the peace but that to preserve it in the existing circumstances she had to strengthen her army. Her neighbours had long ago reached the strength he was now proposing for Germany. The speech included the famous sentence: 'We Germans fear God and nothing else in the world, and it is the fear of God which makes us love and cherish peace'. But, he went on, whoever broke the peace would learn that the martial patriotism of 1813 was now a common possession of the whole German nation and every soldier firmly believed that God was on the side of his fatherland. The army bill was passed, not only with the votes of the *Cartel* parties but also those of the Centre and the *Deutsch-Freisinnigen*.

In December 1887 the two *Cartel* parties moved that the life of the *Reichstag* should be increased from three to five years, although the Centre, the *Freisinnige Partei* and the Social Democrats were sharply opposed to this. The measure was passed, and, in addition, the anti-socialist law was prolonged for two years.

25

BISMARCK'S FALL

TWO CHANGES OF EMPEROR

On 9 March 1888 William I died in his ninety-first year and was succeeded by his son Frederick William, who as Emperor and King of Prussia took the title of Frederick III. As Crown Prince he had often shown a markedly liberal outlook and had many dealings with leaders of the *Freisinnige Partei* and other opposition politicians. He was very pro-British and far more progressive than his father. Although Bismarck by no means shared Frederick's views, he was prepared to continue as *Reichskanzler* under him and to confine himself to foreign policy. The Crown Prince had for a considerable time suffered from a hoarseness which was not at first diagnosed but which finally proved to be a symptom of cancer of the larynx. When he came to the throne he could no longer speak and was very near his end, which came three months later. His only significant action, and one which was prompted by his liberal views, was to dismiss the Prussian minister von Puttkamer, who was notorious for his electoral manipulations.

WILLIAM II AND BISMARCK

With the accession of William II a new epoch began, but his personality was not fully revealed until a year and three-quarters later, after Bismarck's dismissal. The young emperor thirsted for personal rule. Before he came to the throne he was firmly under Bismarck's spell, but this hold soon weakened. Bismarck had many enemies, open and secret, among the generals, senior officials and princes, and so there were many influences which joined in inducing William to dismiss his Chancellor. Numerous observers were struck by William's immaturity and impulsiveness and his tendency to overrate himself. He had a habit of blurting out any ideas which happened to occupy his mind at the time and naturally enough his remarks quickly gained currency. General

Count Waldersee, who fancied himself in the role of Chancellor and whom William appointed Chief of the General Staff, had great influence on the Emperor. Waldersee tried to win his support for a war against Russia and in this he was backed by other generals. To bolster his case he strove to convince William that Russia was planning a war of aggression and that Germany must strike first. This was the very opposite of Bismarck's policy; he sought to dissuade William from this idea. Some time before Waldersee had also drawn William's attention to the activities of Stöcker, the court chaplain who was trying to launch a political movement among the workers with a programme combining social reform with anti-Semitism. Bismarck warned William against Stöcker, and in other matters too tried to curb his headstrong master. This only strengthened William's wish to silence the warning voice. Waldersee aided the process with calculated remarks, one of which was that with a minister like Bismarck at his side Frederick the Great would never have achieved the fame he did. It was to prove William's undoing that he took Frederick as his military model, which none of his four predecessors on the throne of Prussia had done, and which, moreover, he did in the clumsiest way imaginable.

In the circumstances Bismarck took very good care not to give the diplomatic representatives of Austria-Hungary any assurances of unconditional military support from the *Reich*. He had Waldersee's warmongering attacked in newspaper articles; this was met by a declaration from Waldersee that he never meddled in foreign policy. On 22 November 1889 the Left Liberal leader Eugen Richter put a formal question to the Secretary of State for Foreign Affairs (Count Herbert Bismarck, the Chancellor's son) on whether there were any grounds for supposing that the Chief of the General Staff was seeking to frustrate the Government's efforts to keep the peace. Before Herbert could reply, the Prussian War Minister was on his feet, protesting violently against such an insult to the army. In May the Emperor said to the German diplomat Joseph von Radowitz: 'If Bismarck will not march with me against the Russians, then our ways must part. I have requested Herbert to tell him that my patience with the Russians is exhausted.' In August the German and Austro–Hungarian Chiefs of Staff agreed on an interpretation of the treaty of alliance which was totally at variance with Bismarck's. William declared to Beck, the Austro-Hungarian Chief of Staff, in the presence of Francis Joseph: 'For whatever cause you mobilise – whether because of Bulgaria or for some other reason – the day of your mobilisation is also the day of my army's mobilisation, and the Chancellors can say what they like about it'.

In the same year the big Berlin banks led by Bleichröder, Bismarck's banker, planned a conversion of Russian State Bonds, which would have helped Russia in her financial difficulties and reduced political tension. Waldersee said in conversation with the Emperor that Bismarck was the protector of rich Jews who wanted to give the Russians money, which they would then use for war against Germany. This remark made a deep impression on William. Waldersee notes in his journal that he was firmly convinced that this was a moment of decision for the Emperor and that in his heart he had now broken with Bismarck. William gave Herbert Bismarck instructions to campaign against the new Russian loan in the press. Herbert protested, but William was not to be moved. The difficulties put in the way of the Russians when they sought credit – and it had, incidentally, been Otto Bismarck who had started to provide facilities in 1887 – caused them to raise funds in Paris.

There were more clashes between Chancellor and Emperor in the field of social policy. William wanted to win popularity by social legislation and to make a solemn declaration of this intention at the outset. In 1889 Otto Bismarck had completed his scheme of workers' insurance by introducing old age and sickness benefits but, as has been mentioned, he set his face against shorter hours, measures for the welfare of women and children and Sunday rest-days. All this he considered dangerous, not only economically but also politically, because it represented a furtherance of socialist aims. He tried, unsuccessfully, to dissuade the Emperor, and then took measures to prevent William's plans from maturing. The *Reichstag's* refusal to prolong the anti-socialist law helped to aggravate the difference, and in February 1890 Bismarck told the Emperor that he feared he was in his way. The Emperor's silence clearly assented to the proposition. Bismarck therefore thought that he could perhaps resign his Prussian offices but retain control of foreign policy, and the Emperor seemed to agree in principle In the Prussian cabinet Bismarck indicated his intention of resigning his Prussian ministerial posts, to the relief of his colleagues. In his memoirs he had some bitter remarks to make about several senior officials who supported the Emperor against him – a consequence, no doubt, of his often cavalier treatment of ministers and officials in the past.

In the general election of February 1890 the *Cartel* suffered a heavy defeat and the opposition parties found themselves in a majority. After such a swing of the pendulum it was very difficult to assemble a parliamentary majority for the Government. Bismarck now debated the possibility of a coup, drew up a plan of campaign against the *Reichstag* and enlisted the Emperor's support. He also informed the Prussian ministers how he thought such a manoeuvre might be executed. A sharper anti-socialist measure was to be introduced, and in the almost certain event of its rejection the *Reichstag* was to be repeatedly dissolved. Its activity could also be paralysed by the recall of the plenipotentiaries in the *Bundesrat*. Bismarck even considered dissolving the *Reich* and setting it up afresh on a basis which eliminated universal franchise. Here he overlooked the fact that the *Reich* constitution had been created with the agreement of all the *Landtage*. All these possibilities came to nothing when the Emperor refused to play his part. William did not wish to subject his Government at the outset to grave internecine wrangles, and he also feared that if he did he would make himself dependent on Bismarck.

Now, as so often before, Bismarck toyed with several contrary courses of action. Perhaps a majority could be created after all, since the massive increase in the socialist vote had at the most merely given the other parties a shock. The strongest party was the Centre, and it suited Bismarck's book very well that its leader Windthorst, through Bleich-röder's intermediary, should call on him to discuss the situation, though the *Cartel* parties, whom Windthorst used to call 'Jesuits in disguise' could scarcely have been won over for any lasting collaboration with him. It was probably from sources in the *Cartel* that the Emperor was prompted to use Bismarck's interview with Windthorst as a pretext for dismissing his Chancellor. When he was received by William on the following day and reported that Windthorst had been to see him, William exclaimed: 'Well, no doubt you had him thrown out?'. The Chancellor replied that he was accustomed to see any deputy whose manners did not make him impossible, whereupon William retorted that Bismarck should first have sought his permission. Bismarck firmly rejected this unreasonable demand but the Emperor stuck to his guns. He knew, he said, that the visit had been arranged by Bleichröder and that 'Jews and Jesuits' always worked together. Broadening his attack, William complained that on the basis of a cabinet order of 1852 Bismarck had forbidden his ministers to have direct relations with the Emperor without his permission, and he demanded that this order be withdrawn. Bismarck refused on the grounds that the regulation was indispensable for the unified conduct of affairs by a Prime Minister. This view was undoubtedly correct, for to accept the Emperor's demand would have meant a relapse into autocracy. Bismarck brought the conversation round to William's intention to pay the Tsar a further visit. He had advised him against this and he now repeated the advice based on secret reports from St Petersburg which the German Ambassador in London had furnished; these, he said, contained remarks made by Alexander about William and his last visit quoted by alleged witnesses and now in his (Bismarck's) possession. William demanded that he should read them out; Bismarck refused on the grounds that they were insulting to the Emperor. At this the Emperor took the document from Bismarck's hand, read it and was obviously deeply offended. According to this document the Tsar was supposed to have said: 'C'est un fou, un garçon mal élevé et de mauvaise foi'. (He is a fool and an ill-bred boy who cannot be trusted.) The Emperor made no comment on the remarks but continued to insist on the withdrawal of the cabinet order.

Soon afterwards Bismarck received from the Emperor a demand that he should ask to be allowed to resign immediately. William also returned to him a number of reports, including some from a German consul in Russia, to which was attached an open note in William's own hand which had made its way through the various offices in the Chancellery and been read there. In this letter William declared that the reports revealed beyond any doubt that the Russians were making the fullest strategic dispositions for war. He much regretted that Bismarck had not drawn his attention to the terrible and imminent danger long ago. It was high time to warn Austria and take counter-measures. On this Bismarck comments in his memoirs that the consul's reports had been promptly communicated at the time to the Emperor and the supreme military authorities. They were far from containing any news of a threatening character. The criticism levelled at him by the Emperor, he wrote, included the charge of high treason. It was one of the whims of chance – history would perhaps call it the finger of fate – that just at this moment Shuvalov, newly arrived from St Petersburg, should call to see him to resume negotiations for the renewal of the Reinsurance Treaty, a striking proof that Russia was far from thinking about war at that time.

Bismarck now offered his resignation. Shuvalov declared to Herbert Bismarck that he was authorised to deal only with him and his father. If they both resigned, no negotiations could take place. The Emperor now revealed his egregious naïveté by expecting Herbert Bismarck to remain in office and assuring him of his unlimited confidence. Herbert, not unnaturally, refused. Although his father, already Prince Bismarck, had declined any further title or reward, William bestowed on him, when he resigned in March 1890 the title of Duke, which he never used. On the other hand, he relates in his memoirs that a part of his official residence was immediately taken away from him – a brutal act, in view of his age and length of service. At this juncture he found himself deserted by almost all who had any influence in political affairs. He himself remarks that an official and social boycott had obviously been imposed on him. It was put about that he had resigned voluntarily for reasons of health, but when the truth became known it was apparent that he still had numerous enthusiastic admirers in many spheres of life. A storm of indignation broke out among them; he was elected to the *Reichstag* and often fêted. For a long time he and his following waged a journalistic battle against the Emperor and his entourage. True, there was later an official 'reconciliation'; the Emperor visited Bismarck but avoided any serious conversation. In fact, nothing in their relations had changed.

The demonstrations by Bismarck's admirers lose much of their significance when one considers the results of the last general election before his fall. These show clearly that the great majority of the people were far from satisfied with his policy. The electorate amounted to 10·14 millions, of which 7·23 millions cast valid votes. The *Cartel*, Bismarck's supporters, gained 2·56 million votes, of which the two conservative parties polled rather more than the National Liberals. In comparison with the 1887 election, all three lost between a quarter and a third of their votes, one million in all. For the Opposition, on the other hand, 4·67 million votes were cast, which brought them close to a two-thirds majority. The 2·91 million men who did not vote probably also belonged for the greater part to the dissatisfied. In votes the Social Democrats were the strongest party; they were able almost to double their poll from 0·76 to 1·43 million. The Left Liberals and Democrats raised their total votes considerably. The Centre receded from 1·52 to 1·34 million. Of the small parties, the Alsace-Lorrainers lost more than half their votes; this figure remained fairly constant at the next elections and could therefore be put down to assimilation. An anti-Semitic party also appeared, but secured only 47,500 votes.

The distribution of seats did not match the aggregate votes, and for this the electoral system could be held responsible. Although the Social Democrats were top of the poll, they had only 35 seats, compared with the Centre's 107. Together with the small groups which usually voted with it, the Centre could count on 144 members. The Conservatives had 92 seats, the National Liberals, despite only a slightly smaller poll, a mere 42, the liberal-democratic parties 76 and the anti-Semites 4. In all, the Government parties numbered 134 members, to which the 4 anti-Semites could probably be added, while the Opposition mustered 255. Thus, even in seats there was an opposition majority of almost two-thirds.

26

THE RE-SHAPING OF AUSTRIA

UP TO THE HUNGARIAN COMPROMISE

This study seeks to describe the evolution of political thought among the German-speaking peoples, who did not, it is true, develop in national unity but in a historical union of destinies, from which were excluded those territories which left this community early, for the most part dissociated themselves from it linguistically and went their own political way. The Austrian Germans had belonged to the old *Reich* and its successor, the *Bund*, and when Austria left the *Bund* certain sentimental ties of political importance were preserved. While the *Reich* Germans and Austrian Germans did not form one political state, they were none the less two groups of peoples who were intimately related, rather like the North Americans and the British.

The re-shaping and preservation of the Danubian empire was of prime importance both for the eleven different peoples within its borders and for Europe as a whole. Its collapse after the First World War gave irrefutable proof of this, for its peoples mostly fell victim poverty and social disruption, the rise of Hitler was made possible and a world role was opened up to Communist Russia. Although all the experts were once convinced of the need to preserve the Austrian Empire,[2] many modern historians do not seem to realise this because they have been blinded by a mass of unscrupulous propaganda.[3] Today, especially, there are people, often highly cultivated, who are convinced that the national state is the only possible community and that any disgraceful action is justified when committed in the sacred name of the idol called 'the nation'. In the old Austria, the efforts of those with the greatest insight were directed at meeting justified national aspirations as well as preserving the supra-national principle of the rights of man.

[1] Cf. my book *The Economic Problem of the Danubian States*, 1947.
[2] Cf. my book *Nationality in History and Politics*, pp. 202 ff.
[3] A typical example is A. J. P. Taylor's book *The Habsburg Monarchy*, 1941, which created a great impression in England.

In the western half of the Empire considerable progress was made in this field. Francis Joseph upheld this policy to the best of his ability. He came to the throne at eighteen, heir to a long period of fateful stagnation, and, advised by generals and ministers who were not attuned to the spirit of the age, he had to grapple with bloody revolutions, civil wars, ill-starred campaigns and convulsive changes. Bitter experience gradually weakened his absolutism; he came to discharge his office with conscientiousness and was always ready to put his own personal feelings aside in order to try out any new policy which the times appeared to demand, though he never disregarded his sworn obligations or the prevailing code of justice. He often appointed ministers who had sharply attacked him or his dynasty, or who had indulged in the fiercest opposition, and repeatedly tried to promote understanding between the wrangling nations. It must be admitted that he often lacked toughness in pursuing a policy whenever it provoked dangerous resistance. But one can hardly criticise him for not being a Bismarck, whose guile, lack of scruple and insight into human weaknesses overcame formidable obstacles. Francis Joseph's main aim was to preserve his empire and this required, in addition to a strong army and prudent diplomacy, harmony and unanimity among the peoples which composed it.

The tensions between the peoples were rooted in the fact that the leaders of the most important nationalities laid claim to predominance rather than equality in certain areas which they regarded as their historic heritage but in which the minorities disputed this view. In some instances, more than one nationality laid claim to the same country. In the Austrian Empire, outside the Kingdom of Hungary, the Germans were by far the most numerous people, followed by the Czechs, Poles and Ruthenians. In the period with which we are concerned the Germans were far more advanced than the rest: they possessed a prosperous bourgeoisie, and wherever trade, industry, mines and banks were to be found in non-German territories, they had been set up and were owned by Germans or German Jews. All the towns had at one time been founded by Germans; many of them later took on a Slav character but even about the middle of the nineteenth century the capitals of Bohemia, Hungary and Croatia were mainly inhabited by Germans. The Czechs were largely a people of peasants and petty bourgeois, whereas in Hungary and Galicia the nobility had already acquired a fund of political experience. In earlier times the nobility and the Church had, as a general rule, shown more sympathy than the German liberal bourgeoisie for the national aspirations of backward peoples.

The 1848 revolution and its sequel ended with the constitution decreed by the Emperor in March 1849 which was, however, annulled after only two years and replaced by a completely absolutist system. Even the liberal institutions created in these two years, such as the *Gemeindegesetz* (parish ordinance), the code of criminal procedure and the separation of the judiciary from the executive, were abolished, though the redemption of feudal land obligations was carried through. Hungary was regarded as a conquered country which had forfeited its constitution. The system was based on the police and the military and, through the Concordat with the Pope, gave the Catholic Church extraordinary powers over education and marriage. The increase in the size of the civil service and the army considerably weakened national finances. In ruling circles warring interests and personalities struggled for influence on the young Emperor and the course of policy fluctuated. In the Crimean War the line taken by Austria irritated both Russia and the Western powers and in the Italian question her diplomacy proved utterly ineffective in the face of France. Discontent was widespread and Hungary was in a revolutionary ferment. Austria's reverses in the war of 1859, the dislocation of her finances and the threat of a fresh revolution led to the abandonment of despotism.

The first step was taken in 1860, when, on the basis of a resolution adopted by a gathering of notables, an imperial declaration was issued that in future legislation would be enacted only in consultation with the new diets due for election in Austria and Hungary along with a *Reichsrat* to which they would send delegates. This council was to deal with certain matters of common concern and, in questions concerning both parts of the Empire, was to include representatives of the Hungarian diet as well. A party of Hungarian magnates believed that they could induce their compatriots to take part in a joint Imperial council, but this caused a storm of indignation in Hungary and put paid to the plan. Although the Emperor had also restored Hungarian self-government, refusal to pay taxes ensued there. Even the German liberal bourgeoisie in Austria reacted sharply against this constitution, which seemed to them to favour Slavs and clericals. In an effort to win them over, Francis Joseph appointed Schmerling Prime Minister; he had played a great part as a minister in Frankfurt in 1848 and had the reputation of being a liberal. He worked out a new constitution which came into force in 1861. The *Reichsrat* was re-shaped into a proper parliament with extensive powers. It consisted of an upper house (*Herrenhaus*) and a lower house, the latter to be elected by the diets, including that of Hungary. For the diets themselves an electoral system was introduced which favoured the prosperous bourgeoisie, and this suited the interests of the Germans. Once again the Hungarians would have nothing to do with the scheme and most of the Slavs protested and held aloof.

In the Hungarian Diet there were two almost equally powerful parties, one representing the radicalism of Kossuth, now living in exile, while the other looked to Franz Déak as its leader. Déak, a statesman of unusual distinction and wisdom, supported an understanding with Austria, and as early as 1864 Francis Joseph had secret negotiations conducted with him which soon bore fruit. In Austria, too, the Emperor turned towards federalism; Schmerling resigned and Count Belcredi became Prime Minister. He suspended the Schmerling constitution, to which most of the peoples within the empire had expressed opposition. But soon afterwards the war of 1866 against Prussia and Italy broke out and led, among other things, to Austria's exit from the German Bund. Francis Joseph, however, never really grew reconciled to this and he appointed a new Prime Minister, Baron von Beust, who had formerly occupied the same post in Saxony; the Emperor probably wished by this to preserve the connection with those German states which were pro-Austrian.

Negotiations with the Hungarians were soon carried to success. In 1867 Francis Joseph restored the Hungarian constitution, accepted the agreed bases for a compromise and appointed Count Julius Andrássy, one of Déak's chief collaborators, Prime Minister of Hungary. On 8 June 1867 Francis Joseph's coronation as King of Hungary followed, and it was Andrássy who, condemned to death as a rebel after the 1848 revolution and pardoned in 1857, placed the crown on his head. The empire was now called 'the Austro–Hungarian monarchy' and Francis Joseph was Emperor in Austria only. Austria was, moreover, not an official name; the official style of the countries thus loosely designated was 'the kingdoms and lands represented in the imperial council', which underlined the federalistic character of the State.

By the compromise, Hungary's complete independence was guaranteed by Austria and only foreign policy and the army, as well as the finances necessary to meet their costs, were declared matters of joint interest subject to the control of both parliaments. The economic interests of the two countries were to be regulated by an agreement every ten years, there was a common customs area and a common currency – economically a signal advantage. Alongside the joint army, in which the administrative language was German, there was a Hungarian *Landwehr* in which Hungarian was the official language and an Austrian *Landwehr* which used German. The officers were required to understand the national language of their regiments. The compromise was also accepted by the Austrian *Reichsrat* which, furthermore, adapted the Austrian constitution in many respects to the Hungarian and extended it in a liberal sense by some important measures.

In 1868 there followed a compromise between Hungary and Croatia.

In certain matters of common interest the Croats sat in the Hungarian Parliament, while other affairs were dealt with in their own Croatian *Landtag*. The Croatian language was also used in the law-courts, the administration and the schools, and a Croatian *Landwehr* existed which was commanded in the national language and flew the Croatian flag. The head of the Croatian administration was a *Statthalter* (Governor), appointed by the King on the recommendation of the Hungarian cabinet and responsible to the Croatian *Landtag*. In the same year Transylvania was united with Hungary, and even before this the military frontier, which was mainly inhabited by Serbs and Croats, was recognised as belonging to Hungary.

In 1868 a nationality law was promulgated which regulated in a liberal sense the linguistic rights of the national minorities. Hungarian was proclaimed the national language and was used within the ministries and between them, but in their dealings with parties the authorities, under the nationality law, had to use the language prevailing in the district concerned. Although the spiritual fathers of the measure, Eötvös and Deák, were opposed to any forcible Magyarisation, a nationalistic trend soon appeared in Hungary and as a result some important provisions of the nationality law – particularly those affecting education – were not implemented. The Magyar nationalists tried as far as possible to force the official language on the minority, and this evoked strong opposition. Similarly a violent nationalism, directed against the Magyars, developed among the minorities.

OTHER NATIONALITIES

The relationship of the Poles to Austria was also laid down by legislation. In 1848 most Polish patriots were hostile to the State, and there was a movement among them which desired, first, wide autonomy for Galicia and hoped that Austria would later create an independent Polish state under a Habsburg ruler. The defeat of 1859 swung government policy into line with Polish aspirations. One result of the Austro-Hungarian compromise was that the Poles, just like the Hungarians, coveted an assured position. Hohenwart's federalistic ministry was prepared to grant this wish but in the end a different solution was found. In 1868, and later, the demands of the Galician Poles were met. Polish became the official language, both within the country and in its foreign transactions, and in Eastern Galicia, where the majority of the population was Ruthenian, this latter tongue also gained recognition and German vanished from the scene. The Poles were masters in their own country and in addition had great influence on the policy of both Austria and Austria-Hungary as a whole. Thus Poles provided Austria with Prime

Ministers, a Finance Minister, a Minister for Foreign Affairs, a Governor of Bosnia and a number of prominent diplomats. So the Poles enjoyed not only full self-government but also an important share in the running of a great empire. Their parliamentary representatives often proclaimed their allegiance to Austria in glowing terms; in debate they sought to mediate where there was controversy and were for the most part staunch in their support of the Government. They were often called 'the only Austrian patriots'. Such an attitude was of the greatest value to the Poles themselves. Taxes and capital from economically advanced countries within the empire helped underdeveloped Galicia, for example. There was a drawback in the position of power they had won in Austria: the Tsars, like Bismarck, were made uneasy by it. Moreover, the Poles exploited their position in Ruthenia to put the natives at a disadvantage in education and other respects. None the less, the great majority of Ruthenians remained loyal to Austria, since their fellow-countrymen in Russia suffered severe oppression. When, after the collapse of Austria, an independent Polish state emerged, the Ruthenians there also tasted persecution. It is deserving of mention that Francis Joseph advocated an understanding between Poland and Ruthenia and shortly before the outbreak of the First World War this was achieved, but it had come too late.

The most difficult task proved to be meeting the Czechs' national demands. The concessions won by the Hungarians and Poles confirmed the Czechs in their striving for a similar independent status. They designated this aim as *böhmisches Staatsrecht*, which meant an approximation to the independence enjoyed in former times by the Bohemian lands. The Emperor and many Austrian statesmen were far from unsympathetic to this demand and repeatedly indicated their willingness to have the Emperor crowned King of Bohemia, an act which would have symbolised Bohemian independence, since most of the Emperor's predecessors had had themselves crowned in Prague. But there were now reasons of domestic and foreign policy which militated against such a step and made its acceptance impossible. A decisive factor in thwarting the wishes of the Czechs was the vigorous opposition put up by the Germans, who occupied a much more powerful position in Bohemia than the minorities with which the Poles and Hungarians had to contend in their own countries. They formed about 38% of the population, controlled the economy and enjoyed strong support from the other Germans in Austria and the *Reich* as well as from the Hungarians. The Germans feared that the recognition of an independent Bohemian state would give the Czechs control they would use to oppress the German minority. There were certainly some Czech nationalists who cherished these hopes, although sensible politicians rejected any such policy. At the very moment when the position of the nations within the Empire was being re-shaped, the Germans were given a significant object lesson when the Hungarians used their newly-regained power against the German minority.

The Germans' fear that concessions to the Czechs would only encourage them to press more strongly for predominance in Bohemia was not completely groundless but it was exaggerated. The German side also evinced a considerable nationalism, based on the argument that Germans had founded the monarchy and pioneered economic and cultural progress and that without them the Empire would fall to pieces. At that time German was the language predominantly used in higher education; industry, the wholesale trade and banking were in German hands and German was in practice, if not officially, the language of the State, even though the courts and authorities dealt with the Czechs in their own language, which was taught in their schools, for even in the period of absolutism no Austrian could be forced to learn a language not his own or to accept judgements or official decisions formulated in it. All the same the German language enjoyed certain privileges. The Germans pointed to the fact that in Britain English was the official tongue, and in France, French, although both states contained minorities with a language of their own. This was the age of liberalism in which it was an established principle that the educated and propertied classes were alone called to represent the people in parliament. Now in Austria these classes were predominantly German, and in consequence the franchise was so organised that the Germans preponderated in the popular assemblies. In 1873 they had almost a two-thirds majority in the Austrian *Reichsrat*, and in the Bohemian *Landtag* they held a very strong position. On the other hand, it was precisely the rise of liberalism in the sixties and seventies which brought important progress along the path to national equality of rights, although the German liberals were centralists. The measures which they passed, however, safeguarded the freedom of speech and the press and a thorough education in the vernacular, and this naturally promoted political activity for equality of rights.

On 31 December 1867 Austria was given a responsible ministry whose members were mostly middle-class and which was consequently called the *Bürgerministerium*. It adopted several measures at variance with the provisions of the Concordat concluded with the Pope during the period of absolutism, notably ones concerning marriage and education. The predominance of the German liberals was, however, threatened by growing opposition from the Slavs and the clericals. The Czechs and other Slavs stayed away from the *Reichstag* and demanded far-reaching changes in the constitution which would give them a position similar to that of the Hungarians. The Czechs were at that time represented by the conservative 'Old Czechs', who joined forces with the conservative nobility and the clerical Germans to bring about a federalisation of Austria.

It was now urgently necessary to reach an agreement with the Czechs on their national demands. At the beginning of 1871, the Emperor appointed Count Karl Hohenwart, a Catholic Conservative, Prime Minister. His ministry contained Germans, Czechs and, later, Poles, and in it the political economist Professor Albert Schäffle, who had shortly before been summoned from his native Württemberg to Vienna, played an important part. The ministry declared itself non-party. Its appointment coincided with the great German victories in France which led to the proclamation of the German *Reich*. The liberals and German nationalists among the Austrian Germans arranged a number of demonstrations in which – only a few years after Königgratz – the German victories were acclaimed. Although a few Czechs had turned in the direction of Pan-Slavism, the Government pursued the sensible policy of trying to meet Slav demands for equality of rights. The Hohenwart ministry embarked on a whole series of important measures favouring the Czechs, Slovenes and Poles, to the intense irritation of the Germans. The *Reichsrat* was dissolved and a fresh election yielded a great majority for the Government – always assuming, of course, that all the *Landtage* would send delegates to the *Reichsrat*.

Draft measures intended to serve the policy of federalism were sent to most of the *Landtage*. A 'royal rescript' was put before the Bohemian *Landtag*, in which the historic rights of the kingdom were recognised. The *Landtag* was called upon to deliberate the constitutional position in a moderate and conciliatory spirit and to afford the Crown the chance of ending the constitutional dispute without detriment to the rights of the other countries or the basic law of the State. A nationality law under which every official was to speak both the national languages was also put before the *Landtag*. The franchise was altered in favour of the Czechs. The *Landtag* thereupon demanded a compromise such as the Government had earlier agreed on with the Czech leaders. These demands, known as the 'fundamental articles', were largely modelled on the Austro-Hungarian compromise. But whereas the latter set its face against any joint Austro-Hungarian parliament, the Czechs were prepared to accept such a body for all matters of common concern to all Austrian countries. Moreover, the scope of such matters was more widely conceived than in the compromise with Hungary. The law on nationalities, which had been settled between the Government and the Czech leaders, further provided that decisions on matters of national concern could be taken in the *Landtag* only if both Czechs and Germans agreed. Thus any 'violation' of either nationality by the other was quite out of the question. The re-shaping of the constitution was to be concluded by the crowning of Francis Joseph as King of Bohemia.

The liberal Germans vehemently resisted these plans, which, they declared, would reduce them to helots. They were particularly opposed to the provision that Bohemian officials should be bilingual. Schäffle countered this with the argument that every official must in any case have attended a secondary school, and hence learned Latin and Greek, and, if he wished to study theology, Hebrew as well. Why then should an official who wanted a position in Bohemia not learn both the languages of the country? The Germans' opposition was powerfully supported by the Imperial Chancellor, Beust, who voiced some misgivings on the score of foreign policy, and by Andrássy, the Hungarian Prime Minister. The Hungarians did not want a compromise with the Austrian Slavs, because they feared that they would then have to make bigger concessions to their own Slavs. Francis Joseph was favourably disposed towards the idea of compromise and ready to agree to it, but the opponents of the reform contrived to influence him in such a way that he finally faltered, and the whole scheme came to nothing.

After Hohenwart's resignation in October 1871, a new government under Adolf, Prince of Auersperg, was formed which put through an electoral reform in the *Reichsrat* whereby the delegates were no longer appointed by the *Landtage* but were to be directly elected by the people in four groups: big landowners, the towns, the chambers of commerce and the rural communities. Again the German liberals were the ruling party, but the Czechs boycotted the *Reichsrat*. The Concordat was now formally terminated. The years which followed were marked by great complications in foreign relations. In 1877 Russia went to war with Turkey, after first allowing Austria to occupy Bosnia and Herzegovina and recognising that Serbia came within Austria's sphere of interest. In the *Reichsrat* the German liberals spoke out firmly against the occupation of Bosnia. In 1878, at the Congress of Berlin, the Peace of San Stefano, which had been imposed on the Turks by Russia, was revised. The occupation of Bosnia required a campaign in which Austrian troops first had to conquer the country. Both the Austrian Germans and the Hungarians were unwilling that the number of Slavs in their domains should be increased, and so Bosnia was only occupied, her sovereignty remaining with the Sultan. All these events brought about a great growth of Pan-Slavism in Russia. In 1879, a defensive treaty against a Russian attack was concluded between Austria-Hungary and the German *Reich*.

A new attempt at a comprehensive national compromise was made in 1879. With brief interruptions the liberals had now controlled the

Reichsrat for eighteen years but for the last twelve the Czechs had stayed away from it. The *Verfassungspartei* (Constitutional Party), as the liberals called themselves, had won great credit for numerous progressive measures but it never succeeded in winning over the great Slav population within the state to parliamentary co-operation. This was not entirely the liberals' fault; in fact, there were great obstacles on the Czech side. It is worth noting that the liberals, although they consisted mainly of Germans, did not regard themselves as representing a nation but admitted non-German deputies to their ranks. They declared to the Emperor that the formation of parties on the basis of nationality was by no means desirable in Austria. All the same, some liberal members did represent a distinct nationalism and from time to time broke up into separate groups. The Slav members for the most part formed national groups in parliament, though they went their own way according to their political and social views. Among the German liberals, too, there was sometimes an especially strong tendency to split up, often through personal rivalries. One of the experts on the subject, Joseph Redlich,[1] says:

From the spring of 1878 the Auersperg ministry was already in a latent state of dissolution. Its most prominent members, the cream of Austria's political talent, were urging the Emperor to accept their requests to resign; they positively fled from the small-minded, petty bourgeois provincial tyrants and the well-meaning but politically inept doctrinaires who made up the majority of the leaders of the Constitutional Party. All the Emperor's personal exertions to form a fresh Government which would enjoy the support of at least the larger part of the Constitutional Party, and would be prepared to tread new paths in Austrian domestic policy, foundered, mainly on the personal spite with which the various factions and their leaders wrangled.

But important political considerations also played a part. The authoritarian foreign policy, which led to the occupation of Bosnia, armed intervention and huge new military expenditure, was utterly unacceptable to the liberal leader Eduard Herbst and other prominent members of his party, and the measures were finally passed only because a section of the liberals voted for them.

THE TAAFFE MINISTRY

For some time now Count Eduard Taaffe had been prominent as a statesman and had served in various liberal administrations. Taaffe,

[1] Cf. Joseph Redlich, *Kaiser Franz Joseph*, 1928, p. 336.

who came from a family which had emigrated from Ireland in the seventeenth century, was a friend of Francis Joseph's in the Emperor's youth and was said to enjoy his particular confidence. In 1879 he entrusted Taaffe with the formation of a fresh administration, principally in order to induce the Czechs to enter the *Reichsrat*. Taaffe declared it his task to reconcile the various nationalities and, if possible, to induce all parties to join the Government. But his overtures were decisively rejected by the liberals, who suffered a setback at the next election, so the Taaffe administration relied on the Czechs, Poles and conservative Germans, who were all represented in the Government. At the outset a few non-party liberals also belonged to it. Since the Constitutional Party had a majority in the upper house, Taaffe caused the Emperor to appoint a larger number of Slavs and Conservatives to this house.

The administration pursued a policy which went a long way to meet the Czechs and other Slavs. Especially notable was a decree that in all parts of Bohemia the courts should use the language requested by the plaintiffs to an action. Later on, other concessions were made to the Czechs over the use of their language in internal administrative affairs. Various changes in their favour were made in the franchise and the number of voters was considerably increased. Prague University was made into two – one German and one Czech, and numerous Czech *Mittelschulen* (secondary schools) were founded in Bohemia. As far as primary schools were concerned, the Slovenes and clericals also gained advantages. Further, by bringing influence to bear on the big landowners, Taaffe also caused the Germans in the Bohemian *Landtag* to lose their majority to the Czechs.

Taaffe's policy aroused great bitterness among the German liberals; they demanded, but in vain, a division of Bohemia into German and Czech districts. The Germans now decided to have nothing more to do with the Bohemian *Landtag*. Moreover, a radical movement sprang up among the German members which preached fierce nationalism and anti-Semitism. The fieriest spirit was the deputy Georg Schönerer, who had begun his career as a democrat but later became the representative of a fanatical nationalism and racialism and attracted many followers among university students. The liberals, who took a moderate line in national questions, lost more and more ground.

Not only national but also social differences intensified at this time. With the march of industrialisation came the rise of workers' movements. Socialist currents from Germany, checked at the outset by disunity, swept on, and in 1888 the Social Democrat party was formed. The leading spirit in its organisation was Viktor Adler. The party took its stand on the Marxist position and proclaimed itself supra-national.

A Christian Socialist movement, headed by Dr Karl Lueger, was also formed. It aimed at social reform in the interest of the workers and the lower middle class, but also developed clerical and anti-Semitic tendencies.

The Taaffe administration followed the German model by enacting an anti-socialist law in 1886 and combating Social Democracy, though it also pursued a wide-ranging social policy which on the one hand protected the workers from harmful working conditions and on the other aimed at improving their lot by sickness and accident insurance. As Adler declared, Austrian social legislation at that time was surpassed only in Germany and Switzerland.

In 1889 the Emperor again urged a compromise between Germans and Czechs, and Taaffe arranged and presided over conferences between representatives of both nationalities. And in fact a compromise on all controversial issues was reached and accepted by the representatives of both sides. The major national feud now seemed safely dead and buried. But once again hopes were dashed. Until now a moderate party, the so-called 'Old Czechs', had been at the head of affairs but another faction, nationalist and radical and styling itself the 'Young Czechs', rose up in opposition. This party had not been invited to the conferences and so it attacked the compromise with every demagogic means to hand. At the next election the Young Czechs gained a majority and the compromise was a dead letter.

Taaffe now sought to enlist the moderate liberals; he also conceived a bold plan for electoral reform, so that the spread of pernicious nationalism might be checked by full discussion of social issues. The principal backer of the plan was the Finance Minister, Emil Steinbach, a man of Jewish extraction who had campaigned energetically for social reform. The bill proposed a wide extension of the franchise which would have given a large section of the workers and other socially oppressed classes a voice in electing members. But the great majority of the House of Deputies felt this to be highly dangerous and threw out the measure. Taaffe, exhausted by work and ill-health, had to resign at the end of 1892 after fourteen years as Prime Minister. After his fall national radicalism increased more and more and many attempts were made to check it, until finally, fourteen years later, the Emperor once again put universal suffrage on the agenda and employed his whole influence to pilot the measure through parliament – this time successfully.

BIBLIOGRAPHY

ALBRECHT, CURT, 'Die Triaspolitik des Freiherrn K. von Wangenheim,' in *Darstellungen aus der Württembergischen Geschichte*, Stuttgart, 1914.

ANTONI, CARLO, *La Lotta contro la Ragione*, Florence, 1942.

ANON, *Die preussische Verfassung und die Stimme der Öffentlichkeit*, Leipzig, 1847.

ARNDT, ERNST MORITZ, *Versuch in vergleichender Völkergeschichte*, Leipzig, 1843; *Erinnerungen aus dem äusseren Leben*, Leipzig, 1842; *Geist der Zeit*, Berlin, 1807–18.

ASPINALL, ARTHUR, *Politics and the Press* 1780–1850, London, 1949.

ANTONOWYTSCH, MICHAEL, *Friedrich Ludwig Jahn, Ein Beitrag zur Geschichte der Anfänge des Deutschnationalismus*, Berlin, 1933.

AYME, F., *Wilhelm II. und seine Erziehung*, Leipzig, 1898.

BAASCH, ERNST, *Die Geschichte des Hamburger Zeitungswesens von den Anfängen bis 1914*, Hamburg, 1915.

BACHEM, CARL, *Vorgeschichte, Geschichte und Politik der Zentrumspartei*, Cologne, 2 vols, 1926–32.

BAHRS, CURT, *Friedrich Buchholz 1768-1843*, Berlin, 1907.

BALFOUR, M., *The Kaiser and His Times*, London, 1963.

BAMBERGER, LUDWIG, *Bismarcks Grosses Spiel*, 'Die geheimen Tagebücher L. Bambergers' (edited by E. Feder), Frankfurt/M, 1932.

BARANT, *Constitutionelle Fragen*, Berlin, 1849.

BASCH, VICTOR, *Les doctrines politiques des Philosophes Classiques de l'Allemagne Leibnitz, Kant, Fichte, Hegel*, Paris, 1927.

BAUER, EDGAR, und BAUER, BRUNO, *Die Geschichte der konstitutionellen und revolutionären Bewegungen im südlichen Deutschland 1831-4*, Leipzig, 1845.

BECK, CARL, *Lieder vom armen Mann*, Leipzig, 1846.

BELL, HERBERT, *Lord Palmerston*, London, 1936.

BELOW-FINCKE-MEINECKE, *Abhandlungen zur mittleren und neueren Geschichte aus dem Frankfurter Parlament*, Berlin, 1909.

BENSON, E. F., *The Kaiser and His English Relations*, London, 1936.

BENNIGSEN, L. A. G. VON (COUNT), *Mémoires des General E. Cazales*, Paris, 1907–8.

BERENHORST, GEORG HEINRICH VON, *Betrachtungen über die Kriegskunst* (über ihre Fortschritte, ihre Widersprüche, ihre Zuverlässlichkeit), Leipzig, 1827.

BERGHAUS, HEINRICH CARL WILHELM, *Deutschland vor 100 Jahren*, Leipzig, 1859.

N

BERGSTRÄSSER, L., *Geschichte der politischen Parteien in Deutschland*, Mannheim, 1928.

BERNARDI, M., *Die politische Weisheit des Fürsten von Bismarck und des Grafen Camillo von Cavour*, 2 vols, Hamburg, 1888.

BERNHARDI, FELIX T. VON, *Aus dem Leben Theodor v. Bernhardi*, 8 vols, Leipzig, 1893–1906.

BETZ, LOUIS P., *Studien zur vergleichenden Literaturgeschichte der neueren Zeit*, Frankfurt/M, 1902.

BIEDER, THEOBOALD, 'Beiträge zur Geschichte der Rassenforschung und der Theorie der Germanen-Heimat' (in *Beiträge zur Rassenkunde* No. 7 and 11), Hildburghausen, 1909.

BIEDERMANN, CARL, *Deutschland im 18. Jahrhundert*, Leipzig, 1854.

BIGELOW, POULTNEY, *History of the German Struggle for Liberty*, London, 1896.

BISMARCK, OTTO FÜRST, *Briefe an seine Braut und Gattin* (edited by Fürst Herbert Bismarck), Stuttgart, 1900; *Gedanken und Erinnerungen*, Stuttgart and Berlin, 1898-1919.

BITTERAUF, TH., *Die Gründung des Rheinbundes und der Untergang des alten Reiches*, Munich, 1905.

BLANC, JEAN JOSEPH LOUIS, *Lettres sur l'Angleterre*, (translated by J. Hutton, *Letters on England*), Paris, 1865.

BLUM, HANS, *Das deutsche Reich zur Zeit Bismarcks*, Leipzig–Wien, 1893.

BLUM, ROBERT, *Die Fortschrittsmänner der Gegenwart*, Leipzig, 1847.

BLUNTSCHLI, JOHANN CASPAR, *Allgemeines Staatsrecht*, Munich, 1852. *Lehre vom modernen Staat*, Stuttgart, 1875 (Translation: *The Theory of the State*, Oxford, 1885.
(with Karl Brater), Deutsches Staatswörterbuch, 11 vols, Leipzig, 1857–79.

BOEHM, WILHELM, *Bismarcks parlamentarische Reden*, 6 vols, Stuttgart–Berlin, 1890.

BORKENHAGEN, F., *Nationale und landespolitische Bestrebungen in Deutschland 1815–1822*.

BORNHAK, D., *Deutsche Verfassungsgeschichte*, Stuttgart, 1934.

BRAHN, MAX, *F. Nietzsches Meinung über Staaten & Kriege*, Leipzig, 1915.

BÜLOW, BERNHARD VON OFFENBACH (PRINCE), *Denkwürdigkeiten*, Berlin, 1930–1.

BULWER-LYTTON, EDWARD GEORGE (Earl Lytton), *Ernest Maltravers*, London, 1893.

BUSCH, MORITZ, *Tagebuchblätter von M. Busch*, Leipzig, 1899.

BUSSMAN, WALTER, *Treitschke – Sein Welt – und Geschichtsbild*, Göttingen, 1952.

CARDAUNS, HERMANN, *Der Werdegang eines Politikers, E. Lieber bis zu seinem Eintritt in das Parlament 1838–71*. Wiesbaden 1927. *Adolf Gröber*, München–Gladbach, 1921.

CARLYLE, THOMAS, *The French Revolution: A History*, London, 1837 (German Edition: *Die Grosse Revolution*, 1911); *The Moral Phenomena of Germany*, London, 1845.

CARROLL, EBER MALCOLM, *French Public Opinion and Foreign Affairs 1870–1914*, American Historical Association, 1931.

CAVOUR, CAMILLO BENSO DI, Count Cavour's unedited letters and British diplomacy in 1856, London, 1862.
Speech on 16.4.1858 on the proposed law relative to Conspiracy, etc., London, 1858.

CHALMERS, D. H. J., and ASQUITH, C., *Outlines of Constitutional Law*, London, 1930

CHAMBERLAIN, HOUSTON STEWART, *Die Grundlagen des 19. Jahrhunderts*, Munich, 1899.

CHARMATZ, RICHARD, *Dr Adolph Fischhof*, Stuttgart, 1910.

CONRADY, ALEXANDER, *Die Rheinlande in der Franzosenzeit 1750–1815*, Stuttgart, 1920.

CONRADY, W. v., *Aus stürmischer Zeit*, Berlin, 1907.

COBURG-GOTHA, ERNST VON (DUKE OF SAXE-COBURG AND GOTHA), *Aus meinem Leben und aus meiner Zeit*, 3 vols, Berlin, 1887–89.

DAHLMANN, FRIEDRICH CRISTOPH, *Die Politik, auf den Grund und das Mass der gegebenen Zustände zurückgeführt*, Leipzig–Bonn, 1847.

DIETERICI, CARL FRIEDRICH WILHELM, 'Verkehr und Verbrauch im preussischen Staat 1831–53', in *den Festschriften zum 100-jährigen Jubiläum der Korp. der Kaufmannschaft*, 6 vols, Berlin, 1838–57.

DIEST-DABER, OTTO VON, 'Berichtigungen von Unwahrheiten', etc., in *Erinnerungen des Fürsten Bismarck und deutsches Rechtsbewusstsein*, Zürich, 1899.

DROYSDEN, JOHANN GUSTAV, *Vorlesungen über die Freiheitskriege*, Kiel, 1846.

DUDONNE, FRANZ, *Die Kölnische Zeitung und ihre Wandlungen im Wandel der Zeit*, 1903.

EHRENREICH, H., *Heinrich Luden und sein Einfluss auf die Burschenschaft*, Heidelberg, 1913.

EICHSTÄDT, VOLKMAR, *Die deutsche Publizistik von 1830 an*, Berlin, 1933.

EISENMANN, *Aufruf zur Herstellung des Königreichs Polen*, Erlangen, 1848.

ENGELS, FRIEDRICH, *Die Lage der arbeitenden Klasse in England* (nach eigener Anschauung und authentischen Quellen), Leipzig, 1845; *Das Elend der Philosophie* (with preface and notes by F. Engels), Leipzig, 1885.

EPPSTEIN, G. VON und ROËLL, P. VON, *Bismarcks Staatsrecht*, Berlin, 1903.

ERNEST II, Duke of Saxe-Coburg and Gotha, *Aus meinem Leben und aus meiner Zeit*, 3 vols, Berlin, 1887–89 (English translation, London, 1888).

EULENBURG, BOTHO WEND AUGUST (GRAF ZU), *10 Jahre Innerer Politik 1862–72*, Berlin, 1872.

EULENBURG-HERTEFELD, PHILIPP ZU, *Aus 50 Jahren Erinnerungen Tagebücher und Briefe*, Berlin, 1923.

EYCK, ERICH, *Bismarck, Leben und Werk*, 3 vols, Erlenbach–Zürich, 1941-4. Abridged English version: *Bismarck and the German Empire*, London, 1950.

EYCK, FRANK, *The Prince Consort*, London, 1959.

FALLERSLEBEN, AUGUST HEINRICH VON (Pseudonym: HOFFMANN VON), *Unpolitische Lieder*, Hamburg, 1842.

FEJTO, F., (ed.) *The Opening of an Era 1848*, London, 1948.

FELDMANN, WILHELM, *Geschichte der politischen Ideen in Polen seit dessen Teilung 1795–1914*, Munich–Berlin, 1917.

FERRIER, L. AUGUSTE, *Du Gouvernement Considéré dans ses Rapports avec le Commerce*, Paris, 1822.

FEUERBACH, LUDWIG, *Das Wesen des Christentums* (edited by K. Quenzel), Leipzig, 1904.

FICHTE, JOHANN GOTTLIEB, *Der geschlossene Handelsstaat*, Tübingen, 1800; *Reden an die deutsche Nation*, Berlin, 1808.

FOLLEN, ELIZA LEE, *The Life of Charles Follen*, Boston (U.S.A.), 1844.

FOURNIER, AUGUSTE, *Napoleon I.: Eine Biographie*, Leipzig, 1886–9 (French translation by E. Jaegle, Paris, 1891–92).

FRAENKEL, HANS, *Politische Gedanken und Strömungen in den Burschenschaften* (Quellen und Darstellungen zur Geschichte der Burschenschaft, Vol. B), 1821–4.

FREILIGRATH, FERDINAND, *Ein Glaubensbekenntnis*, Stuttgart, 2 vols, 1844.

FRIEDJUNG, HEINRICH, *Österreich von 1848–60*, Stuttgart–Berlin, 1908. *Das Zeitalter des Imperialismus 1884–1914*, Berlin, 3 vols, 1919; *Der Kampf um die Vorherrschaft in Deutschland 1859–66*, Stuttgart, 2 vols, 1897.

FRIES, FRIEDRICH JAKOB, *Vom Deutschen Bund und der Deutschen Verfassung*, Heidelberg, 1816.

FREYTAG-LORINGHOVEN, H. VON, *Menschen und Dinge*, Berlin, 1923.

GAGERN, HANS CHRISTIAN ERNST REICHSFREIHERR VON, *Mein Anteil an der Politik*, Stuttgart–Tübingen, 1823-45.

GEBHARDT, BRUNO, *Handbuch der deutschen Geschichte*, vol. III, Stuttgart, 1960.

GEISMAR, MARTIN VON, *Deutschland im 18. Jahrhundert*, Leipzig, 1851.

GENTZ, FRIEDRICH VON, *Tagebücher 1800–28 aus dem Nachlass von K. A. Varnhagen von Ense*, Leipzig, 1861; *Österreichs Teilnahme an den Befreiungskriegen*, Vienna, 1887.

GERLACH, ERNST LUDWIG VON, *Aufzeichnungen aus seinem Leben und Wirken 1795–1877* (edited by Joseph von Gerlach), Schwerin, 1903.

GERVINUS, GEORG GOTTFRIED, *Hinterlassene Schriften*, Vienna–Leipzig, 1872; *F. C. Schlossers Briefe über den Nekrolog*, Leipzig, 1862.
Einleitung in die Geschichte des 19. Jahrhunderts, Leipzig 1853 (Translated, London, 1853).

GNEIST, HEINRICH RUDOLF VON, *Budget & Gesetz nach dem konstitutionellen Staatsrecht Englands mit Rücksicht auf die deutsche Reichsverfassung*, Berlin, 1867.
Das heutige englische Verfassungs- und Verwaltungsrecht, Berlin, 1857.

GOBINEAU, JOSEPH ARTHUR DE (COUNT), *Essai sur l'Inégalité des Races Humaines*, Paris, 1853–5.

GOTTSCHALL, RUDOLF VON, *Unsere Zeit. Lieder der Gegenwart*, Leipzig, 1842.

GOOCH, GEORGE PEABODY, *The Study of Bismarck* in *Studies in German History*, London–New York–Toronto, 1948.

GRAUERT, HERRMANN VON, *Graf Josef de Maistre und Josef Görres vor 100 Jahren*, Bonn, 1922.

GRÜN, ANASTASIUS (pseudonym for ANTON ALEXANDER GRAF VON AUERSPERG), *Spaziergänge eines Wiener Poeten*, Hamburg, 1832; *Eine Jahresfeier (Über Polen)*, 1844 (banned 1848).

GRÜNING, I., *Die russische öffentliche Meinung und ihre Stellung zu den Grossmächten 1878–1914*, Berlin–Königsberg, 1929.

GRUBE, AUGUST WILHELM, *Der Stuttgarter Landtag 1457–1957*, Stuttgart, 1957.

GSCHLIESSER, OSWALD VON, *10 Briefe des Erzherzogs Johann an Franz Lutterotti aus den Jahren 1842–52*.

GUGGISBERG, CURT, Carl Ludwig von Haller, Leipzig, 1938.

GUGLIA, EUGEN, *Friedrich von Gentz*, Vienna, 1901.

GUIZOT, FRANÇOIS PIERRE GUILLAUME, *Essais sur l'histoire de France*, 6 vols, lectures Sorbonne, Paris, 1833.

GUTZKOW, CARL FERDINAND, *Mitarbeiter an Cotta's Kulturzeitung*, Frankfurt/M, 1845–52.

GUTZKOW, KARL, *Rückblicke auf mein Leben*, Berlin, 1875.

HAFFNER, PAUL LEOPOLD, *Konstitution*, 1848; *Hardenbergs neuere Reformen*, 1870.

HAGEN, CARL, *Geschichte der neuesten Zeit*, Braunschweig, 1850–1.

HALLER, CARL LUDWIG VON, *Restauration der Staatswissenschaft oder Theorie des natürlich geselligen Zustandes*, 6 vols, Winterthur, 1816–34.

HALLER, M. J., *Manuskript aus Süddeutschland* (von einem Hamburger), Bremen, 1821.

HOLSTEIN, FRITZ VON, *Lebensbekenntnis in Briefen*, Berlin, 1932.

HANSEN, JOSEPH, *Quellen zur Geschichte des Rheinlandes*, Bonn, 1931–3; *Gustav von Mevissen: Ein Rheinisches Lebensbild 1815–99*, 2 vols, Berlin, 1906.

HANSEMANN, DAVID, *Preussen und Frankreich 1833*, Leipzig, 1834.

HARDEN, MAX, *Köpfe*, Vols, I & IV, Berlin, 1910–24.

HARTMANN, MORITZ, *Lieder aus der Heimat*, 1852; *Völkerstimmen.*

HAUPT, HERMANN (ed.), *Quellen und Darstellungen zur Geschichte der Burschenschaft und der deutschen Einheitsbewegung*, Heidelberg, 1910–39.

Die alte Würzburger Burschenschaft 1817–33: Ein Beitrag zur Universitätsgeschichte in der Reaktionszeit, Würzburg, 1898.

HAUSER, ERNST, and FREUND, CAJETAN, *Die Münchner-Augsburger Abendzeitung.*

HAWKINS, FRANCIS BISSET, *Germany – The Spirit of her History, Literature, Social Condition and National Economy*, London, 1838.

HAYM, R., *Reden und Redner des 1. vereinigten preussischen Landtages 1847 Aus meinem Leben*, 1902.

HAYMANN, FRANZ, *Jean Jacques Rousseau's Sozial Philosophie*, Leipzig, 1898.

HEGEL, GEORG WILHELM FRIEDRICH, *Complete Works*, Vol. I, Berlin, 1931.

HERMANN, J., 'Zur Kritik der Nachrichten über Attentate von 1819', in *Forschungen zur deutschen Geschichte*, XXIII, 1883.

HERREN, ARNOLD NERMANN LUDWIG, *Deutscher Bund und europäisches Staatssystem 1816*, Berlin, 1879.

HERWEGH, GEORG, *Gedichte eines Lebendigen 1841*, Zürich-Winterthur, 1842.

HERZBERG, WILHELM, 'Das Hambacher Fest', *Geschichte der revolutionären Strebungen in Rhein-Bayern um das Jahr 1832*, Ludwigshafen/R, 1908.

HERTZ, FREDERICK, 'Reden von Jakobinern', in *Nationalgeist und Politik*, Zürich, 1937.

Nationality in History & Politics, London, 1944.

HESS, MENDEL, *Heilige Geschichte der Menschheit, Rom & Jerusalem*, Leipzig–Breslau, 1862.

HEYDEBRAND, VON, 'Beiträge zur Geschichte der konservativen Partei', in *Konservat. Monatsschrift*, 1920.

HILLEBRAND, CARL, *Frankreich und die Franzosen*, London, 1881.

HOFMANN, HERMANN, *Fürst Bismarck 1890–8*, Stuttgart–Berlin–Leipzig, 1914.

HOHENLOHE-SCHILLINGSFÜRST, CHLODWIG FÜRST ZU, *Denkwürdigkeiten des Fürsten Chlodwig zu Hohenlohe-Schillingsfürst* (edited by F. Curtius), Vol. 3, Stuttgart–Leipzig, 1906–7.

HUBER, ERNST RUDOLF, *Deutsche Verfassungsgeschichte seit 1789*, Stuttgart, 1957.

HUMBOLDT, WILHELM FREIHERR VON, *Politische Denkschriften 1802–1834*, 3 vols (edited by B. Gebhardt), Berlin, 1903–36.

IPPEL, EDUARD VON, *Briefwechsel zwischen J. & W. Grimm, Gervinus, Dahlmann*, 2 vols, Berlin, 1885–6.

JAGEMANN, *75 Jahre des Erlebens und Erfahrens*, 1925.

JAHN, FRIEDRICH LUDWIG, *Deutsches Volkstum*, Leipzig–Dessau, 1817.
JUST, G., *Als die Völker erwachten*, Vienna-Leipzig, 1907; *Literarische Bewegung und Zeitstimmung vor Beginn des Feldzuges*, 1809.

KALTENBORN, CARL VON, *Die Vorläufer des Hugo Grotius*, Leipzig, 1848.
KAUTSKY, CARL J., *Elsass-Lothringen, eine historische Studie*, Stuttgart, 1917.
KEIM, AUGUST, *Erlebtes und Erstrebtes*, 1925.
KINDT, *Görres, Rheinischer Merkur und die deutsche Presse seiner Zeit*, Braunschweig, 1936.
KLACZKO, JULIAN VON, *The two Chancellors, Prince Gortchakof and Prince Bismarck*, London, 1876.
KLEIN, ROBERT, *Napoleon und die Presse*, 1918.
KLEIN, TIM (ed.), *Der Vorkampf deutscher Einheit und Freiheit, Urkunden, Berichte und Briefe*, Munich–Leipzig, 1914.
KLEMM, GUSTAV FRIEDRICH, *Allgemeine Culturgeschichte der Menschheit*, 10 vols, Leipzig, 1843–52.
KLÜBER, JOHANN LUDWIG, *Akten des Wiener Kongresses in den Jahren 1814–15*, Erlangen, 1819.
KOHN, HANS, *The Mind of Germany*, London, 1960.
KOTZEBUE, AUGUST FRIEDRICH FERDINAND VON, *Geschichte des deutschen Reiches, von dessen Ursprunge bis zu dessen Untergange*, Leipzig, 1814–32.
KRÄGELIN, P., *Heinrich Leo* in Beiträge zur Kultur und Universalgeschichte, Leipzig, 1908.
KRAUSE, HANS, *Die demokratische Partei von 1848 & die soziale Frage*, Breslau, 1921.
KREYSSIG, FRIEDRICH ALEXANDER THEODOR, *Literarische Studien und Charakteristiken*, Berlin, 1882.
KÜBECK, MAX FREIHERR VON, *Metternich und Kübeck, ein Briefwechsel*, Vienna, 1910.
KÜGELGEN, ALEXANDER GEORG WILHELM VON, *Jugenderinnerungen eines alten Mannes*, in letters to his brother Gerhard, (edited by P. Nathusius), Berlin, 1870 (English translation, London, 1871).
KULENKAMPF, L., 'Der erste vereinigte preussische Landtag 1847 und die öffentliche Meinung Südwestdeutschlands', in *Abhandlungen zur mittleren und neueren Geschichte*, No. 41, Berlin–Leipzig, 1907.

LANG, WILHELM, 'Die Tübinger Feuerreiter 1828–33', in *Quellen und Darstellungen zur Geschichte der Burschenschaft*, Vol. 3, 1912.
LANGSAM, W., *The Napoleonic Wars and German Nationalism in Austria*, New York, 1930.
LASKER, EDUARD, *Briefwechsel 1870–71 D.R.17*, Leipzig, 1893; *15 Jahre parlamentarische Geschichte*, 1866–80.
LEHMANN, JOHANN FRIEDRICH WILHELM, *G. Gervinus, Versuch einer Charakteristik*, Hamburg–Leipzig, 1871 (English translation, London, 1872).

LENAU, NIKOLAUS FRANZ (NIEMBSCH, EDLER VON STREHLENAU). *Collected Works* – N. L.'s dichterischer Nachlass (edited by Anastasius Grün), Stuttgart–Tübingen, 1851.

LEHMANN, MAX, *Scharnhorst*, Leipzig, 1886.

LENZ, MAX, *Geschichte der königlichen Friedrich Wilhelm Universität zu Berlin*, Halle, 1910.

LEO, HEINRICH, *Aus meiner Jugendzeit*, Gotha, 1880; *Geschichte der italienischen Staaten*, 5 vols, Hamburg, 1829–32.

LEVY, J. (afterwards JULIUS RODENBERG), *Fichte und die Juden* (undated).

LIMAN, PAUL, *Der Kaiser*, Berlin, 1904.

LORENSEN, UWE JENS, *Briefe an F. H. Hegewisch*, Schleswig, 1925.

LÜDERS, GUSTAVUS FRIDERICUS LUDOVICUS, *Die demokratische Bewegung in Berlin im Oktober 1848*, Berlin, 1909.

MANN, GOLO, *Friedrich v. Gentz*, *Geschichte eines europäischen Staatsmannes*, Zürich–Vienna, 1946.

MARCKS, ERICH, Bismarck Vol. I, *Bismarcks Jugend I 6th edition*, Stuttgart–Berlin, 1909.

MARTIN, KINGSLEY, *The Triumph of Lord Palmerston*, London, 1924.

MARX, KARL, *Das Kommunistische Manifest* (*with Engels*) *1848*, Berlin, 1891; *Das Elend der Philosophie* (*with Engels*), Stuttgart, 1885.

MAYER, SIGMUND, *Die Wiener Juden 1700–1900*, Vienna and Berlin, 1918. *Die Aufhebung der Gewerbefreiheit*, Vienna, 1883.

MEIER, EBERHARD, *Die aussenpolitischen Ideen der 48er Jahre*, Berlin, 1938.

MEINECKE, FRIEDRICH, *Radowitz und die deutsche Revolution*, Berlin, 1913; *Festschrift*, Tübingen, 1952.
Weltbürgerthum und Nationalstaat, Berlin, 1908 (Translation, Princeton N.J., 1970).

MEISNER, ALFRED, *Revolutionäre Studien aus Paris 1849*, Frankfurt/M, 1849.

MEISNER, H. O. VON (ed.), *Kaiser Friedrich III: Das Kriegstagebuch, 1870–71*, Berlin, 1926.

MENZEL, CARL ADOLPH, *Über die Undeutschheit des neuen Deutschtums 1818*, Breslau, 1818.

MENZEL, WOLFGANG, *Menzels Denkwürdigkeiten* (edited by his son K. Menzel), Leipzig–Bielefeld, 1877.

MEYER, A. G. VON, *Die Grundgesetze des deutschen Bundes*, 1845.

MEYER, ARNOLD OSKAR, *Bismarck: Der Mensch und Staatsmann*, Leipzig, 1944.

MICHELS, R., *Zur Soziologie des Parteiwesens in der modernen Demokratie*, Leipzig, 1925.

MIGUEL, J. VON, *Einige Mitteilungen aus meinen Erinnerungen* (edited by F. Thimme, Stauffenberg, 1915.

MITTELSTAEDT, ANNIE, *Der Krieg von 1859, Bismarck und die öffentliche Meinung in Deutschland* Stuttgart, Berlin, 1904.

MOHL, ROBERT VON, *Die Geschichte und Literatur der Staatswissenschaften*, 2 vols, Erlangen, 1855–8; *Lebenserinnerungen*, Stuttgart–Leipzig, 1902.

MOMMSEN, WILHELM, *J. Miquel*, 1928; *Bismarck – ein politisches Lebensbild*, Munich, 1959; *Bismarcks Sturz und die Parteien*, 1923; *Deutsche Parteiprogramme*, Munich, 1952.

MONOD, GABRIEL, *Allemands et Français* (Souvenirs de campagne Metz-Sedan), Paris, 1872–3.

MÜLLER, ADAM HEINRICH VON, *Vom Geiste der Gemeinschaft, Elemente der Staatskunst*, Berlin, 1809; *Theorie des Geldes* (collected and prefaced by F. Bülow), Leipzig, 1816.

MÜLLER, EGBART, *Bismarck im Urteil seiner Zeitgenossen*, Berlin, 1898.

MÜNCH, ERNST, *Karl von Rotteck*, 1831.

MÜNCH, FRIEDRICH, *Erinnerungen aus Deutschlands trübster Zeit*, St Louis, Mo., – Neustadt a.d. Haardt, 1873.

NAGEL, H., *Die Stellung der Sozialdemokratie zu Bismarcks auswärtiger Politik 1871–90*, 1930.

NAMIER, SIR LEWIS, '1848 – The Revolution of the Intellectuals, in the *Proceedings of the British Academy*, London, 30 (1944).

NAUMANN, F., *Demokratie und Kaisertum: ein Handbuch für innere Politik*, Berlin, 1905.

NIEBUHR, BARTHOLD GEORG, *Über geheime Verbindungen im preussischen Staat*, Berlin, 1815; *Historiker und die Politik; Geschichte der Zeitschrift der Revolution*, Hamburg, 1845.

NOVALIS (pseudonym for BARON FRIEDRICH FREIHERR VON HARDENBERG), *Novalis' Schriften* (edited by L. Tieck & F. Schlegel), 2 vols, Berlin 1802.

ONCKEN, WILHELM, *Das Zeitalter der Revolution des Kaiserreiches und der Befreiungskriege*, Berlin, 1884–7; *Österreich und Preussen in den Befreiungskriegen*, 2 vols, Berlin, 1876–9.

ONCKEN, HERMANN, *Rudolf von Bennigsen*, 2 vols, Stuttgart, 1910. *Napoleon II and the Rhine*, New York, 1928.

OPPENHEIM, HEINRICH BERNHARD, *B. F. L. Waldeck, der Führer der preussischen Demokratie 1878–80*, Berlin, 1873.

PALACKÝ, FRANTISEK, *Gedenkblätter: Auswahl von Denkschriften, Aufsätzen und Briefen aus den letzten 50 Jahren*, Prague, 1874.

PASTOR, LUDWIG, *Johannes Janssen 1829–91, Ein Lebensbild*, Freiburg im Breisgau, 1892.

PERTHES, CLEMENS THEODOR, *Friedrich Perthes' Leben*, Hamburg–Gotha, 3 vols, 1848–55; *Lebensnachrichten über G. B. Niebuhr*, 3 vols, 1838 (translated and abridged by S. S. Laurie, Edinburgh, 1858).

PFEIFFER, EDUARD, *Die Konsumvereine, ihr Wesen und Wirken*, Stuttgart, 1865.

o

Vergleichende Zusammenstellung der Europäischen Staatsausgaben, Leipzig, 1865.

Württemberg und sein Verhältniss zum Zollparlament und zum Nordbund, Ulm, 1868.

PFIZER, P. A., *Briefwechsel zweier Deutscher,* Stuttgart–Tübingen, 1832; *Über die Entwicklung des öffentlichen Rechts in Deutschland durch die Verfassung des Bundes,* Stuttgart, 1835.

PFLUGK-HARTUNG, JULIUS VON, *Das Befreiungsjahr 1813; Aus den Akten des geheimen Staatsarchivs,* Berlin, 1913.

PHILLIPSON, M., *Max von Forckenbeck,* in *Diercks, Männer der Zeit,* Vol. 6, 1897.

PINSON, KOPPEL, S. *Pietism as a Factor in the Rise of German Nationalism,* 1934.

PONTEIL, F., 'La situation économique, le Bas-Rhin au lendemain de la révolution française', *La crise alimentaire dans le Bas-Rhin en 1847,* Paris, 1927.

PONTEIL, FELIX, *L'Éveil des Nationalités et le mouvement Liberal 1815–1848,* Paris, 1930.

1848, An account of the events of the year in the various countries of Europe, Paris, 1937.

PORTER, GEORGE RICHARDSON, *The Progress of the Nation,* London, 1847.

PRECHT, H., *Englands Stellung zur deutschen Einheit 1848–50,* Munich, 1925.

PROKESCH-OSTEN, ANTON (GRAF VON), *Denkwürdigkeiten aus dem Leben des Feldmarschalls Fürsten Carl zu Schwarzenberg,* Vienna, 1823 and 1861; *Briefwechsel mit Herrn von Gentz und Fürsten Metternich,* 2 vols, Vienna, 1881.

PROUDHON, PIERRE JOSEPH, *Qu'est-ce que la Propriété?,* Paris, 1848.

PRUTZ, HANS GEORG, *Preussische Geschichte,* 4 vols, Stuttgart, 1900–02.

RACHFAHL, FELIX, *Deutschland und die Weltpolitik 1871–1914,* Vol. 1: *Die Bismarck'sche Ära,* Stuttgart, 1923; 'Eugen Richter', in *Zeitschrift für Politik,* 1912.

RAIF, A. F., 'Die Urteile der Deutschen über die französische Nationalität im Zeitalter der Revolution und der deutschen Erhebung', in *Abhandlungen zur mittleren und neueren Geschichte,* Vol. 25, Berlin, 1907.

RAMBAUD, ALFRED NICOLAS, *La Domination Française en Allemagne,* Paris, 1873–4.

RANKE, LEOPOLD VON, *Hardenberg und die Geschichte des preussischen Staates* (Complete Works) Vols 46–48, 1793–1813, Leipzig, 1879–81; *Hardenbergs Neuere Reformen 1870,* Vol. 3, Leipzig, 1881; *Genesis des preussischen Staates,* Leipzig, 1874; *Preussische Geschichte,* Leipzig, 1934.

RATKOWSKY, MATHIAS GEORG, *Das Recht und die Pflicht die Czechen und Slovenen zu germanisieren,* Iglau, 1892.

RAUMER, FRIEDRICH LUDWIG GEORG VON (ed.), *Historisches Taschenbuch*, Leipzig, 1830.

RAUMER, FRIEDRICH LUDWIG GEORG VON, *Briefe aus Frankfurt und Paris 1848–9*, Leipzig, 1849.

Geschichte der Hohenstauffen und Ihre Zeit, 6 vols, Leipzig, 1823–5.

REE, ANTON, *Über Gewissens Freiheit zur Verständigung über unser Streben*, Hamburg, 1859.

REDLICH, JOSEF, *Emperor Francis Joseph of Austria*, London, 1929.

REHBERG, AUGUST WILHELM, *Die Erwartungen der Deutschen vom Bunde ihrer Fürsten*, Hanover, 1834.

REIBERG, CARL, *Die deutschen Blätter von Brockhaus 1813–16*, Cologne, 1937.

REICHENSPERGER, PETER FRANZ, *Deutschlands Nächste Aufgaben*, Paderborn, 1860.

REINHARD, E., C. L. von Haller, 2. *Vereinsschrift, Görres Gesellschaft*, Bonn, 1915.

RENAN, JOSEPH ERNEST, *De la part des peuples Sémitique dans l'Histoire de la Civilisation*, Paris, 1862.

La Réforme intellectuelle et morale, Paris, 1871.

Vie de Jésus, Paris, 1863.

RICHTER, EUGEN, *Im alten Reichstag-Erinnerungen*, Berlin, 1894.

RODBERTUS, CARL, *Die Forderungen der arbeitenden Klassen 1857* (newly edited and introduced by M. Quarck), Vienna, 1885.

ROËLL, PAUL VON und EPSTEIN D. G. VON, *Bismarcks Staatsrecht*, Berlin, 1903.

ROSENBAUM, LOUIS, *Beruf und Herkunft der Abgeordneten zu den deutschen und preussischen Parlamenten 1847–1919*, in series 'Die Paulskirche', Frankfurt. M.

ROSSEL, VIRGILE, *Histoire des Relations Litéraires entre la France et l'Allemagne*, Paris, 1897.

RÖSSLER, HELMUT, *Österreichs Kampf um Deutschlands Befreiung 1805–15*, Munich, 1940; *Napoleons Griff nach der Karlskrone*, Munich, 1957.

ROTHFELS, HANS, *Carl von Clausewitz, Politik und Krieg, eine ideengeschichtliche Studie*, Berlin, 1920.

ROTTECK, CARL WENZESLAUS VON, *Sammlung kleiner Schriften*, 3 vols, Stuttgart, 1829–37. *Lehrbuch des Vernunftsrechts* (Staatslexikon with Welker & List), Altona, 1843.

Allgemeine Geschichte. Freiburg/B. 1834 (Translation: General History of the World, Philadelphia, 1840).

ROTTECK, C. W. VON and WELCKER, C. T. STAATSLEXICON, 15 vols, Altona, 1856–66.

ROTTECK, HERMANN, *Dr Carl von Rottecks Leben*, Pforzheim, 1841–3.

RUETE, HANS VON, *Herzog Ernst II von Sachsen-Coburg-Gotha*, Gotha, 1892.

RUSSELL, BERTRAND, *A History of Western Philosophy*, London, 1961.

SCHAUMANN, ADOLF FRIEDRICH HEINRICH, *Geschichten des 2. Pariser Friedens für Deutschland*, Göttingen, 1844.

SCHELLING, FRIEDRICH WILHELM JOSEPH VON, *Complete Works*, 14 vols. Stuttgart–Augsburg, 1856–61; *Münchner Vorlesungen zur Geschichte der neuen Philosophie*, 2 vols, Leipzig, 1797.

SCHLOSSER, FRIEDRICH CHRISTOPH, *Weltgeschichte für das deutsche Volk* Frankfurt/M, 1844–57; *Geschichte des 18 und 19. Jahrhunderts bis zum Sturz des französischen Kaiserreichs*, 7 vols, Heidelberg, 1836–49.

SCHMIDT, HANS, *Die polnische Revolution des Jahres 1848 im Grossherzogtum Posen*, Weimar, 1912.

SCHMIDT, HERBERT, *Friedrich Julius Stahl und die deutsche Nationalstaatsidee*, Breslau, 1913–14.

SCHMIDT, WILHELM ADOLF, *Elsass und Lothringen*, Leipzig, 1859. *Geschichte der deutschen Verfassungsfrage*, Stuttgart, 1890.

SCHNABEL, FRANZ, 'Der Zusammenschluss des politischen Katholizismus in Deutschland im Jahre 1848', in *Heidelberger Abhandlungen zur mittleren und neueren Geschichte*; 4 vols, *Deutsche Geschichte im 19. Jahrhundert*, 4 vols, Freiburg, 1929–37.

SCHNEIDER, WALTER, *Wirtschafts-u. Sozialpolitik im Frankfurter Parlament 1848–9*, Frankfurt/M, 1923.

SCHUBERT, EDUARD, 'Der Ideengehalt von Görres' Schriften'. *Deutschland und die Revolution*; 'Europa und die Revolution', in *Erste Vereinsschrift Görres Gesellschaft*, Cologne, 1922.

SCHULTHESS, HEINRICH (ed.), *Europäischer Geschichtskalender*, Nördlingen, 1861.

SCHULTHEISS, FRANZ GUNTRAM, *Friedrich Ludwig Jahn, sein Leben und seine Bedeutung*, Munich–Leipzig, 1894.

SCHULZE, F., *Die Franzosenzeit in deutschen Landen 1806–1815 in Wort und Bild der Mitlebenden*, 2 vols, Leipzig, 1908.

SCHULZE-GÄVERNITZ, GERHART VON, *Zum sozialen Frieden*, Leipzig, 1890 (English translation *Social Peace*, by C. M. Wickstead, edited by G. Wallis, London, 1893).

SCHÜSSLER, W., 'Die Nationale Politik der österreichischen Abgeordneten im Frankfurter Parlament, in *Abhandlungen zur mittleren und neueren Geschichte*, No. 51 (edited by V. Below), Berlin, 1907.

SEIFERT, HANS, *Die Deutsche Frage 1848–9*, Stuttgart (no date).

SEPP, JOHANN NEPOMUK, *Ernst Görres*, Berlin, 1896.

SERVIERES, GEORGES, *L'Allemagne française sous Napoleon I.*, Paris, 1904.

SOREL, ALBERT, *L'Europe et la Révolution Française*, Vol. 8, Paris, 1885.

SPAHN, MARTIN, *E. Lieber als Parlamentarier*, Gotha, 1906.

SPINDLER, GEORGE WASHINGTON, *Karl Follen*, Chicago, 1917.

SPRINGER, ANTON, *Friedrich Christoph Dahlmann*, 2 vols, Leipzig, 1870–72.

SRBIK, H. VON, *Metternich, der Staatsmann & der Mensch*, 3 vols, Munich, 1925–54; *Geist & Geschichte: Vom Deutschen Humanismus zur Gegenwart*, 2 vols, Munich, 1950–1; *Über Gottfried Gervinus, Geschichte der poetischen Nationalliteratur der Deutschen*, Leipzig, 1848.

STAËL, MADAME DE (ANNE LOUISE GERMAINE NECKER DE STAËL-HOLSTEIN), *De L'Allemagne*, London, 1813.

STAHL, FRIEDRICH JULIUS, *Die Philosophie des Rechtes nach geschichtlicher Ansicht*, Heidelberg, 1st part 1830, 2nd part 1837.

STEIN, AUGUST, *Es war ganz anders*, Frankfurt/M, 1922.

STEIN, LORENZ VON, *Der Sozialismus und Kommunismus des heutigen Frankreichs*, 2 vols, Leipzig, 1842; *Geschichte der sozialen Bewegung in Frankreich 1789 bis auf unsere Tage*, 3 vols, Hildesheim, 1959.

STEINMANN, FRIEDRICH, WALDECK, *Lebensbild für das Volk*, Berlin, 1849.

STENZEL, GUSTAV ADOLF HARALD, *Geschichte Preussens*, 5 vols, Leipzig, 1829-37.

STERN, ALFRED, *Geschichte Europas 1815-71*, Vol. I and II, Berlin, 1894-1924.

STILES, W. H., *Austria in 1842-49*, 2 vols, New York, 1852.

STILLICH, O., *Die politischen Parteien in Deutschland*, 2 vols, Leipzig, 1908-11.

STIRNER, MAX (pseudonym KASPAR SCHMIDT), *Der Einzige und sein Eigentum*, Leipzig, 1845.

STRAUSS, DAVID FRIEDRICH, *Das Leben Jesu*, Tübingen, 1837; *The Life of Jesus Critically Examined*, London, 1841.

STURM, KARL CHRISTOPH GOTTLIEB, *Über den Verfall des Bauernstandes in den meisten deutschen Staaten & über die Mittel, ihm wieder aufzuhelfen*, Jena, 1816.

SUTTER, O. E., *Die Linke in der Paulskirche*, Frankfurt/M, 1924.

SWEET, PAUL ROBINSON, *Friedrich von Gentz, Defender of the Old Order*, Madison, 1941.

SYBEL, HEINRICH CARL LUDOLF VON, *Die Begründung des deutschen Reiches durch Wilhelm I.*, 7 vols, Munich-Berlin, 1889-94.

TAINE, HIPPOLYTE ADOLPHE, *Les origines de la France contemporaine*, Vols V and VI, Paris, 1891-4.

TAYLOR, A. J. P., *The Habsburg Monarchy 1815-1918*, London, 1941.

'TEUT', *Jahrbuch der Jung-Germanischen Gesellschaft*, Nürnberg, 1860.

THEUNE, B., 'Volk & Nation bei Jahn, Rotteck, Welcker & Dahlmann' (*Historische Studien*, 319), 1937.

TIRPITZ, (ADMIRAL) A. VON, *Erinnerungen*, Leipzig, 1919.

THIERS, ADOLPHE, *Histoire de la révolution*, 10 vols, Paris, 1823-7; (Translated *History of the French Revolution*, London, 1838).

TREITSCHKE, GOTTHARD HEINRICH VON, *Deutsche Geschichte im 19. Jahrhundert*, 5 vols, Leipzig, 1879-94; *Treitschkes Aufsätze*, 4 vols, Leipzig, 1865-97.

TRÖGER, PAUL, *Stuttgarter Neues Tageblatt*, in Vol. 37, Zeitung und Leben, Munich, 1937.

TSCHIRCH, OTTO RICHARD SIGISMUND, *Geschichte der öffentlichen Meinung in Preussen*, 1795-1806, 2 vols, Weimar, 1933-4.

VALENTIN, VEIT (the younger), *Geschichte der deutschen Revolution 1848-9*, 2 vols, Berlin, 1930-1.

VALJAVEC, FRITZ, *Die Entstehung der politischen Strömungen in Deutschland 1770–1815*, Munich, 1951.

VENEDEY, JAKOB, *Die deutschen Republikaner unter der französischen Republik* (mit Benützung der Aufzeichnungen seines Vaters Michel Venedey), Leipzig, 1870.

VOGEL, WALTER, *Bismarcks Arbeiterversicherung*, Brunswick, 1951.

VOIGT, NIKLAS, *Vom deutschen Nationalsinn*, Leipzig, 1816.

VOSS, CHRISTIAN DANIEL, *Die Zeiten oder Archive für die neueste Staatengeschichte und Politik*, 64 Vols, Weimar-Halle, 1805–20; *Handbuch der allgemeinen Staatswissenschaft*, 6 vols, Leipzig, *1796–1802*; *Das Jahrhundert Napoleon I.*, Amsterdam–Leipzig, 1811.

WALDERSEE, ALFRED, GENERAL FELDMARSCHALL GRAF, *Denkwürdigkeiten*, 3 vols, Stuttgart and Berlin, 1922–3.

WAWRZINEK, *Die Entstehung der deutschen Antisemitenparteien 1837–90*, Berlin, 1927.

WEILL, GEORGES, *L'Europe du XIXè Siècle et l'idee de nationalité*, Paris, 1938.

WEITLING, WILHELM, *Garantien der Harmonie und Freiheit*, Vivis, 1842; *Evangelium eines armen Sünders*, Bern, 1845.

WENCK, M., 'Die Geschichte und Ziele der deutschen Sozialpolitik', in *Die Politik des deutschen Reiches in Einzeldarstellung*, Vol. 2, Leipzig, 1908.

WENTZKE, PAUL and KLÖTZER, WOLFGANG, *Deutscher Liberalismus im Vormärz, Heinrich von Gagern: Briefe und Reden 1815–48*, Göttingen, 1959.

WICHERN, JOHANN HINRICH, *Briefe, Tagebücher und ausgewählte Schriften*, 2 vols (edited by Martin Gerard), Hamburg, 1925.

WIEGLER, PAUL, *Wilhelm I.*, Hellerau-Dresden, 1928.

WHITE, A. D., *Sieben grosse Staatsmänner*, Munich, 1913.

WINDTHORST, L. E., *Lebenserfahrungen eines Idealisten*, Bonn, 1913.

WILLISEN, W. VON (GENERAL), *Meine Sendung nach dem Grossherzogtum Posen im Frühjahr 1848*, Kiel, 1850.

WILTBERGER, OTTO, *Deutsche Politische Flüchtlinge* in *Strassburg, 1830–49*, Berlin, 1910.

WURM, CHRISTIAN FRIEDRICH, 'Kritische Versuche über die öffentlichen Rechtsverhältnisse', in *Deutschland seit der Mitte des Jahres 1832*, Leipzig, 1835.

WUTTKE, HEINRICH, *Die deutschen Zeitschriften und die Entstehung der öffentlichen Meinung*, 2nd ed., Leipzig, 1875.

ZEHNTER, H., *Zur Geschichte des Frühliberalismus*, 1929; Das Staatslexikon von Rotteck & Welcker, Altona, 1843.

ZIEKURSCH, JOHANNES, *Politische Geschichte des neuen deutschen Kaiserreiches*, Frankfurt, 1930.

ZYCHA, A., *Deutsche Rechtsgeschichte der Neuzeit*, Weimar, 1937.

PRINCIPAL WRITINGS OF FREDERICK HERTZ

Die agrarischen Fragen im Verhältnis zum Sozialismus, Vienna, 1898.

Recht und Unrecht im Burenkrieg, Berlin, 1902.

Die österreichisch-ungarische Bank und der Ausgleich, Vienna, 1903.

Die Diskont-und Devisenpolitik der Österr. Ungarischen Bank, Vienna, 1903.

Moderne Rassentheorien, Vienna, 1904.

Rasse und Kultur, Vienna, 1915 & 1925.

Race and Civilization, London, 1928.

Die Reform des Wasserrechts vom industriellen Standpunkt, Vienna, 1909.

Öffentliche und private Feuerversicherung in der Schweiz, Zürich, 1914.

Die Produktionsgrundlagen der Österr. Industrie. Vienna and Berlin, 1918.

Deutschland and England, Vienna, 1918.

Ist Österreich lebensfähig?, Vienna, 1921.

Die Theorien über den Volkscharakter bei den Hellenen, Cologne, 1923.

Die Wanderung, ihre Typen und ihre geschichtliche Bedeutung, Cologne, 1927.

'Die allgemeinen Theorien vom Nationalcharakter', in *Archiv für Sozialwissenschaften*, 1926.

'Der Menschheitsgedanke bei den griechischen Tragikern', in *Ethos*, 1927.

Hans Günther als Rassenforscher, Berlin, 1930.

'Rasse und Geschichte', in *Propyläen Weltgeschichte I*, 1931.

'Zur Soziologie der Nation und des Nationalbewusstseins', in *Archiv für Sozialwissenschaft*, 1931.

'Rasse', in *Handwörterbuch Soziologie*, 1932.

'National Spirit and National Peculiarity' in *Sociological Review*, 1934.

Nationalgeist und Politik, Zürich, 1937.

Nationality in History and Politics, London, 1944.

The Economic Problems of the Danubian States, London, 1947.

The Development of the German Public Mind, Vol. 1, London, 1951.

Die Nationalitäten im alten Österreich, Munich, 1958.

'Die Rechtsprechung der höchsten Reichsgerichte im römisch-deutschen Reich und ihre politische Bedeutung', in *Mitteilungen des Instituts für Österr. Geschichtsforschung*, 1961.

The Development of the German Public Mind, Vol. 2, London, 1962.

'Nation, Nationale Ideologie und Nationalismus', in *Grundbegriffe der Geschichte*, Leyden, 1964.

I. INDEX OF SUBJECTS
II. RULERS AND THEIR FAMILIES
III. INDEX OF NAMES

Index prepared under the supervision of Notar Hans W. Hertz (Hamburg) and Mr John G. Hurst (London)

I

INDEX OF SUBJECTS

II

RULERS AND THEIR FAMILIES

AUSTRIA – Empire (1804), in union with the Kingdom of Hungary. Habsburg-Lothringen dynasty

Francis I, b. 1768, Holy Roman Emperor 1792–1806, Emperor of Austria 1804–35 17, 57, 73, 109-10, 113-14, 116-17, 121, 160, 224

Ferdinand I, 1793–1875, Emperor 1835–48 160, 239, 255, 257, 259-60

Francis Joseph, b. 1830, Emperor 1848–1916 260, 281-2, 295, 299, 306, 367, 373-5, 377, 379-83

Karl, Archduke, 1771–1847, Field Marshal 17

Johann, Archduke, 1782–59, German Vicar of the Empire 17, 239, 250, 252, 272

Marie Louise, Archduchess, 1791–1841, daughter of Francis I, consort of Napoleon I 18

Sophie, Archduchess, 1805–72, daughter of Maximilian I of Bavaria, mother of Emperor Francis Joseph 239

BADEN – Grand-Duchy (1806), formerly Margraviate. Zähringen dynasty – from 1830 Hochberg line

Charles, b. 1786, Grand Duke 1811–1818 132

Louis, b. 1763, Grand Duke 1818–30 132

Leopold I, b. 1790, Grand Duke 1830–52 153-4, 273

Frederick I, b. 1826, Regent 1852–6, Grand Duke 1856–1907 329

BAVARIA – Kingdom (1806), formerly Electorate. Wittelsbach dynasty

Maximilian I. Joseph, b. 1756, Elector 1799, King 1806–25 128

Louis I, 1786–1868, King 1825–48 128, 145-7, 149-51, 181, 237, 337

Maximilian II, b. 1811, King 1848–64 282, 296, 298

Louis II, b. 1845, King 1864–86, under Regency 1886–1912 292, 337

BRUNSWICK – Duchy. Guelph dynasty.

Charles II, 1804–1873, Duke 1815–1830 134, 136

William, b. 1806, Duke 1830–84 136

BULGARIA –

Alexander I, Prince of Battenberg, 1857–93, reigning Prince 1879–86 343

Ferdinand I, Prince of Saxe-Coburg-Kohary, 1861–1948, reigning Prince 1887–1908, Tsar 1908–18 343

DENMARK – Kingdom, 1460–1864, in personal union with the Duchies of Schleswig and Holstein. Oldenburg dynasty.

Frederick VI, b. 1768, Regent 1784–1808, King 1808–39 234

Christian VIII, b. 1786, King 1839–1848 236

Frederick VII, b. 1808, King 1848–63 236, 308

Christian IX, b. 1818, Prince of Schleswig - Holstein - Sonderburg - Glücksburg, King 1863–1906 308-309

FRANCE – Empire – Kingdom – Republic – Empire

Napoleon I, Bonaparte, 1769–1821, Emperor 1804–14, 1815 13-38, 46-60, 65, 73, 81, 92, 109, 191, 197, 204, 235, 277, 332

Marie-Louise, (see Austria)

Napoleon II, 1811–32, Duke of Reichstadt, King of Rome 59, 66

Louis XVIII, de Bourbon, Count of Provence, b. 1755, King 1814–24 61, 66

Charles X, de Bourbon, Count of Artois, 1757–1836, King 1824–30 135

Louis Phillippe, Duke of Orléans, 1773–1850, King 1830–48 135, 148, 158, 237

Napoleon III, formerly Prince Louis Napoleon, 1808–73, President

III

INDEX OF NAMES

All persons named are German unless otherwise stated. MFP denotes Member of the Frankfurt Parliament.

(Rulers and their families are listed in Index II)